Demystifying
Social Statistics

edited by John Irvine,
Ian Miles and Jeff Evans

Pluto  Press

First published 1979 by
Pluto Press Limited
Unit 10, Spencer Court, 7 Chalcot Road, London NW1 8LH

ISBN paperback 0 86104 068 6
ISBN hardback 0 86104 069 4

Text designed by Tom Sullivan
Tables and diagrams designed by John Finn
Cover designed by Terry Seago

Photoset by Bristol Typesetting Company Limited
Barton Manor, St Philips, Bristol
Printed in Great Britain by Fakenham Press Limited
Fakenham, Norfolk

Contents

Acknowledgements

Perhaps more so than most multi-authored volumes, this book is the product of a collaborative effort. It has involved many more people than are listed in the table of contents. Each chapter was circulated in draft form to a number of readers and revised in the light of their comments. The editors also contributed a great deal to the structure and content of the essays, most of which have been through at least three major drafts.

We are thus indebted to many people for assistance in discussing individual chapters and the overall orientation of the book. Many of the contributors played an active and vital role—while it is invidious to single out individuals, Dot Griffiths deserves special mention for her suggestions concerning every chapter produced in the later stages of this work. We should also express our indebtedness to the particularly helpful members of the British Society for Social Responsibility in Science, the Conference of Socialist Economists, and the Radical Statistics Group, and of course to the staff of Pluto Press, especially Anne Benewick, Karen Margolis, Brian Slocock and the ever-incisive and ever-encouraging Mike Kidron.

For their comments on one or more chapters, we would like to thank: Tony Agathangelou, Liliana Acero, Dave Albury, Pat Atkinson, Paul Atkinson, Rod Bond, Chris Brook, Irene Bruegel, Martin Bulmer, John Bynner, Judith Calder, Mohamed Cherkaoui, Sam Cole, Peter Corbyshin, Peter Coxhead, Sandra Dawson, Brian Easlea, Diane Elson, Raul Espejo, David Evans, Frank Field, Jack Field, Aryé Finkle, Mike Fitzgerald, Arthur Francis, Joel Gladstone, Harvey Goldstein, Fred Gray, Adrian Ham, Martyn Hammersley, Chris Hamnett, Laurence Harris, Roger Harris, Christine Hayward, Sue Himmelweit, Dougal Hutchison, David Hutton, Marie Jahoda, Pauline Jones, Krishan Kumar, Richard Kuper, Johan Kusch, Denise Lievesley, Ruth Lister, Bill Luckin, Madeleine Macdonald, Glen MacDougall, Alison Macfarlane, Maureen Mackintosh, Roy MacLeod, Pauline Marstrand,

David Matthews, Marjorie Mayo, John Mepham, Val Miles, Jim Mott, Roger Murray, Bernard Norton, Bill Page, Celia Phillips, Hilary Rose, Stephen Rose, Esther Saraga, Nat Saunders, Gulrez Shaheen, Tim Shallice, Chris Sinha, Keith Smith, Barbara Stocking, Ray Thomas, Grahame Thompson, Viv Walsh, David Webster, Dorothy Wedderburn, Tom Wengraf, Gary Werskey, Geoff Whitty, Michael Wilson, Eileen Yeo, Jock Young, Michael Young, and the many necessarily anonymous government statisticians.

A special debt is owing to the following people who made extensive written contributions at one stage or another. John Bibby, Stephen Bodington, Roy Carr-Hill, Paul Chalmers-Dixon, Len Doyal, Tony Fielding, Brian Klug, Gordon MacKerron, Bob Peacock, Andrew Sayer, David Triesman and Paul Walton.

Finally, for secretarial assistance and forbearance, our gratitude to the hard-labouring: Hazel Robards, Milena MacKay and Melanie Hempleman at the Science Policy Research Unit, and Marilyn Jenner, all at the University of Sussex; Liz Joseph and Margaret Stickland at the Open University; Angela Schroeter, Pauline Hunt and Wendy Gray at Middlesex Polytechnic at Enfield; Jenny Boyce, Ethel Noel and Joan Wright at Imperial College, London; and Penny Gardiner.

List of Contributors

LIZ ATKINS is a statistician working for the Medical Research Council Unit on Environmental Factors in Mental and Physical Illness. She is active in the Radical Statistics Group, which she helped set up.

LESLEY DOYAL is Senior Lecturer in Sociology at the Polytechnic of North London. She is active in the women's health movement, and is author of a forthcoming book: *The Political Economy of Health* (Pluto, 1979).

JEFF EVANS is Senior Lecturer in Social Statistics at Middlesex Polytechnic. His research interests centre on learning in groups and the teaching of statistics. He is an active member of both the Radical Statistics Group and the Chile Solidarity campaign. He worked on this book while seconded to the Research Methods course team in the Faculty of Social Sciences. at the Open University.

DOT GRIFFITHS is Lecturer in Sociology in the Industrial Sociology Unit at Imperial College. She is active in both the women's movement and the British Society for Social Responsibility in Science. She is co-author with Esther Saraga of a forthcoming book on *Women, Ideology and Biology* (Pluto).

CHRISTOPHER HIRD is a financial journalist currently working for the *New Statesman*. He is author of *Your Employer's Profits* (Pluto, 1975).

RICHARD HYMAN is Senior Lecturer in Industrial Relations at the University of Warwick, and has written a number of books including *Strikes* (Fontana, 1972), *Marxism and the Sociology of Trade Unionism* (Pluto, 1971) and *Industrial Relations: a Marxist Introduction* (Macmillan, 1975). A member of the International Socialists for fourteen years, until 1976. He is now in the International Socialists Alliance.

JOHN IRVINE is a Fellow of the Science Policy Research Unit, University of Sussex. He has been an active member of both the Radical Statistics Group and the British Society for Social Responsibility in Science. He worked on this book while teaching in the area of science and society at the Industrial Sociology Unit, Imperial College.

DAVID JARRETT teaches statistics at Middlesex Polytechnic. He is a member of the Radical Statistics Group.

RUSSELL KEAT is Lecturer in Philosophy at the University of Lancaster. He is co-author with John Urry of *Social Theory as Science* (Routledge & Kegan Paul, 1975) and is a member of the editorial collective of *Radical Philosophy*. He is an active member of the ASTMS Academic Group at Lancaster University.

JIM KINCAID is a member of the Socialist Workers' Party. He is Senior Lecturer in Social Policy at Bradford and author of *Poverty and Equality in Britain* (Penguin, 1975).

JOHN KRIGE teaches History and Social Studies of Science at the University of Sussex. With a background of science and philosophy, he is active in *Radical Philosophy*.

CATHERINE MARSH is a Fellow of Newnham College, Cambridge University, where she teaches Research Methods. Previously she worked for the SSRC Survey Unit where she developed an interest in survey methodology. She is a member of the Radical Statistics Group.

DONALD MACKENZIE is Lecturer in Sociology at the University of Edinburgh and has written several articles on the development of statistical theory in Britain. He is a member of both the Radical Statistics Group and the Trade Union Socialist Group.

MICK McLEAN edits *Electronic Times*, having previously worked at the Science Policy Research Unit, Sussex University, on computer simulation studies and changes in computing and electronics technology. His book *Demystifying Mathematical Models* is to be published in 1979.

IAN MILES is a Fellow of the Science Policy Research Unit, University of Sussex, where he works on forecasting and issues in world development. He is author of *The Poverty of Prediction* (Saxon House, 1975). His main preoccupation during the two years prior to publication has been *Demystifying Social Statistics* but has managed to retain his commitment to working on demolishing personal/political boundaries.

THEO NICHOLS teaches Sociology at Bristol University. He is author of *Ownership, Control and Ideology* (Allen & Unwin, 1969), and joint author of *Workers Divided* (Fontana, 1976) and *Living with Capitalism* (Routledge & Kegan Paul, 1977).

ANN OAKLEY is Research Officer in the Department of Sociology at Bedford College, University of London, and is currently carrying out research on first childbirth. Her publications include *Sex, Gender and Society* (Temple Smith, 1972); *Housewife* (Allen Lane, 1974); *The Sociology of Housework* (Martin Robertson, 1974); *The Rights and Wrongs of Women* (edited with Juliet Mitchell, Penguin, 1976)—and articles in various collections on medical sociology.

ROBIN OAKLEY is Lecturer in Sociology at Bedford College, University of London. He is editor of *New Backgrounds: The Immigrant Child at Home and at School*, and author of various articles in the field of race and ethnicity. He is currently working on a study of Cypriots in Britain and on problems of comparative sociology.

BOB PRICE is Lecturer in Industrial Relations at the University of Warwick. He has written widely in the area of trade unionism.

BILL RIDGERS works as an investigative journalist for Counter Information Services, London, which he helped set up. He also teaches sociology at Chelsea College, London University.

JONATHAN ROSENHEAD is a Lecturer in Operational Research at the London School of Economics. Previously he practised as an operational researcher in industry and consultancy. An active member of the British Society for Social Responsibility in Science since its foundation, he was joint author of the BSSRS pamphlet *The New Technology of Repression: Lessons from Ireland* and of *The Technology of Political Control* (Penguin, 1977).

MARTIN SHAW teaches sociology at the University of Hull, and is author of *Marxism versus Sociology* (1974) and *Marxism and Social Science* (1975), both published by Pluto. His main research interests include marxist urban studies and theories of the state and politics. He is involved in working towards socialist unity through his membership of the International Socialist Alliance.

COLIN THUNHURST is Senior Lecturer in Mathematics for Social Sciences at Sheffield City Polytechnic. He has been an active member of the British Society for Social Responsibility in Science for several years, and a member of the editorial collective of its journal, *Science for People* to which he has been a frequent contributor.

ROBERT YOUNG is a libertarian marxist and a member of the *Radical Science Journal* Collective. He writes on various aspects of science, the labour process and everyday life. His published work has hitherto mainly consisted of historical, conceptual and ideological studies in the biological and human sciences.

1.

John Irvine, Ian Miles, and Jeff Evans

Introduction: Demystifying Social Statistics

The extensive role social statistics play in the everyday workings of modern society goes hand-in-hand with the portrayal of statistical practice as a purely *technical* matter. Linked to this is the widely-held view of statistical data as a form of knowledge untainted by social values or ideology. *The Pocket Oxford Dictionary*, for example, defines statistics as 'numerical facts systematically collected on a subject', where facts are taken to be 'things known to be true'. This gives the statistician the seemingly enviable status of being an expert in numerical things known to be true, systematically collected on a subject.

Other common terms closely associated with statistical usage further reinforce its status as factual and objective. Thus, the term 'data'—often used to denote statistical material—derives from the Latin word which literally translates as 'given things'. Furthermore, the statistical products of quantitative research are often termed 'findings'; nature apparently yields up its true gifts only to those trained to search for them in an objective and dispassionate manner. Statistical data are portrayed, then, as asocial products practically untouched by human hand: the role of the statistician is simply to clinically collect and preserve *the* facts.

The umbrella term 'social statistics' also refers to the methods used to produce these 'numerical facts', and they too are presented as unusually free from the ideological contamination generally held to be so pervasive in other modes of social science and political analysis. Usually included in this wider definition is the whole range of technical and conceptual instruments used to 'collect', process, assess and present data: the theory of probability and the various associated models of frequency distributions, methods of ensuring rigorous 'collection' of data like sampling techniques; analytical methods for processing data such as regression techniques, tests of significance and factor analysis; and ways of presenting data such as pie-charts, histograms and cross-tabulations. Together these are depicted as constituting a 'science' which can be invoked to test and guarantee the authenticity of numerical knowledge as objective fact, and thus as providing a powerful way of demarcating ideology or metaphysics from scientific truth.

Quantitative knowledge is in this way set apart from all other forms of social knowledge: statistical data are held to be objective, whereas qualitative data are much more likely to be ideological; and statistical techniques said to provide a rather more scientific approach to collecting and assessing data than the essentially 'subjective' nature of alternative methods. Starting from a given set of social facts, the application of statistical technique is thus supposedly able to sift out those that are important, translate them into precise numbers free of any intrinsic political content, and process them to reveal whatever significant relationships they may contain. Or so it would seem.

It is this open-and-shut account of social statistics with which this book takes issue. Our point of departure, however, has little in common with the currently fashionable school of thought in social science which regards statistics as *inherently* suspect (a tradition reinforced in popular lore by the tendency to dismiss statistics as merely a way of putting one over on people by bewildering them with complicated numbers and mathematics). Our analysis is in no way intended to support this school of thought, which has often been of particular appeal to radical critics disillusioned with attempting to counteract and overcome the barrage of 'numerical facts' purporting to give an unquestionably objective picture of society. In a context where to take issue with such 'facts' is practically to deny the truth, wholesale rejection of statistics has for many would-be critics of society often seemed the only reasonable response.

While it is easy to understand how the orthodox view of statistics can evoke this reaction, it is nevertheless important to recognise that statistical data and techniques can be valuable resources, despite their very real limitations and their utter failure as a means of attaining objective knowledge. The total rejection of statistics is as one-sided as an uncritical acceptance of all that statistics orthodoxy tells us—both discourage critical scrutiny of the important part played by statistics and the social context in which they have developed. Rather than outright acceptance or rejection, a wide-ranging critique of statistics is called for—in order, first, to expose the political positions embedded in supposedly factual and technical arguments; and, second, to assess the possibilities for using statistics in developing radical social theory and practice. To undertake such an analysis is to begin to demystify social statistics.

This book is intended to contribute to this analysis. While the following chapters certainly differ in their orientation, and in the vantage points from which they make their analyses, a common thread runs through them all. Statistical data are treated neither as mere givens, nor as numerical smokescreens that serve to obscure social reality rather than illuminate it. Statistical techniques are similarly viewed neither as supra-social methods of producing self-evident knowledge, nor as no more than complicated cover-ups for theoretical ignorance or political manipulation. Like other scientific practices statistics needs to be situated squarely in its social and historical context: statistical practices are social in nature and their conceptual and technical instruments, orientation and uses all need to be seen in social terms.

In the analyses presented below, data are therefore conceived of as social products: statistics are not *collected*, but *produced*; research results are not *findings*, but *creations*. But just because data are not 'given' facts does not imply that they are meaningless artefacts. Their production is a social process which is carried out for specific reasons, and in specific ways. The particular concepts and techniques used in each piece of research are chosen and developed within a structure of interests encompassing those of both the funding agency and the institution in which the work is carried out—to say nothing of the individual commitments of the researcher. The complex statistical end-product is therefore no arbitrary creation: it is rather more in need of being explained than either being taken for granted or dismissed.

In the same fashion, statistical technique is most usefully seen as neither the mathematical handmaiden of pure logic, nor as metaphysical mystification dressed up in scientific garb. The techniques used to produce and to process data are, like the data themselves, social products: statistical techniques are developed, and are continually transformed, under particular historical circumstances. Like other bodies of scientific knowledge and technique, statistics can undergo revolutions in both thought and practice. There is no such thing as a universally applicable and acceptable method of going about doing science or statistics. (Indeed, even the basic assumptions of the dominant school of mathematical statistics are currently the subject of profound disagreement, with Bayesian statisticians arguing for an enormously different approach to the topic.) Furthermore, as a social practice, it is not necessarily the case that quantitative analysis makes social research any more 'scientific', let alone more 'objective'. The use of statistical techniques poses its own problems, in the same way as do other ways of presenting and assessing knowledge of society; it is inherently no more theory-free or value-neutral than other approaches.

There are five sections to this book, each of which covers a particular area of statistics. Together they span the many facets of statistical practice: the historical development of statistics; the philosophy of quantification; the use of statistics by the state and problems in re-using the official statistics it produces; the ways in which statistical data and technique are often used in society; and the opportunities and possibilities for using statistics in critical social science and political practice.

This is not to suggest that we are trying to separate rigidly some areas of statistical practice from others. Clearly, these areas overlap, and each section presents perspectives and arguments which inform, and are developed in, other sections.

This is certainly the case regarding the first section, which is concerned with exploring *Historical Perspectives on Statistics*. The three chapters here are not intended to segregate history from other modes of analysis, but serve to set the scene both by demonstrating that statistics is not a collection of timeless truths, and by introducing some of the general concepts and approaches needed to understand fully the arguments made in later chapters. These are provided by examining important aspects of the development of statistical science and usage, thereby demonstrating that such developments need to be situated in the context of the human activities, choices and conflicts that constitute the emergence and changing nature of modern society. Behind every great statistician there is a constraining institutional and cultural framework; behind every technique and textbook on its use there are implicit ideological structures.

By revealing the historically specific nature of statistics—that it is a set of concepts, techniques and practices which are developed at particular times for particular reasons—these chapters open up the possibility of a radically reconstructed statistics, for it becomes clear that statistics is by no means the finalised science it may often appear to be. Futhermore, these chapters indicate the *need* for such a reconstruction, in that statistics are not only shown to have played, but indeed *still* to play, an important role in maintaining and reproducing the social fabric of an exploitative and oppressive society.

The second section takes up some of the questions important to an assessment *Of Knowledge and Numbers*. Social scientists are often directed to statistics as the royal road which they should take if they are to scale the heights of rigour and utility supposedly reached by natural scientists. The four chapters in this section examine how it is that this road has come to be so well-travelled, and how the eagerly awaited milestones on this journey have so often turned out to be millstones instead.

While accepting that statistics can play an important part in producing and evaluating knowledge, these chapters criticise the epistemological foundations of the claims that are commonly made for the place of quantitative analysis and statistics in social research. Both *empiricist* and *positivist* philosophies form the basis on which statistics is accorded its privileged role in social science. This section therefore challenges the empiricist view that knowledge can be assembled and tested by the use of data, and in particular statistical data, that are somehow, through rigorous observation and measurement, themselves free of theoretical assumptions. It also outlines and exposes the dilemmas inherent in the positivist attempt to explain the social world in terms of the operation of laws, with statistical techniques often being called into play as automatic detectors of law-like regularities as well as providing the neutral language through which these regularities are expressed.

Besides being portrayed as the royal road for social scientists, statistics is also taken as a short cut by ideologists anxious to put a scientific gloss on conservative political convictions. The empirically determined 'laws' with which we are often presented—that, for example, the people who achieve dominance and power in modern societies are the most able; or that wage demands by workers inexorably lead to inflation—are rather the numerically codified expressions of bourgeois ideology. This section exposes the shoddy construction and dead-end nature of these all-too-popular thoroughfares.

It is not enough, however, merely to make the case that statistical data cannot be interpreted without reference to their underlying theoretical assumptions. All data, whether produced in the course of academic research or by state bureaucracies, are structured by the conceptual framework that is applied as well as by the technical instruments used in their production. It is the precise nature of these practical and theoretical commitments that needs investigating for each set of data.

Statistics and the State, the third section, illustrates the complexity of these commitments through a series of detailed investigations of British official statistics. Social scientists have often used these statistics as though they were the product of a neutral state, posing only technical problems in interpretation and use. By contrast, the chapters in this section demonstrate that the nature of the modern capitalist state and the significance of official data for its operation determine the range, volume and orientation of the official data produced—as well as the profoundly ideological framework within which they are presented.

It is because official statistics form such a uniquely valuable data resource for social scientists that it is especially important to recognise the particular problems posed in their use. Yet their official status has tended to discourage critical analysis of the concepts and techniques involved in their production—not to mention the practices of government statisticians. This section attempts to redress the balance by providing general analyses, as well as case-studies, that together constitute a guide to the critical study and use of British official statistics—a guide that could readily and valuably be applied to other countries too.

The *applications* of quantitative data and techniques in contemporary society also deserve rather closer scrutiny than they usually receive—a task taken up in the fourth section, *Statistics in Action*. Trading on the 'scientific' status of quantitative analysis, attempts have increasingly been made to provide decision-making with a supposedly more rational basis by basing it on the use of ever more sophisticated forms of statistical data and technique. Focusing in detail on several of the ways in which statistics are commonly used, this section provides a critique of such practices.

While it is common enough to find resentment of the manner in which power and control in society seem to be concentrated in the hands of experts, these chapters argue that these experts, and their statistical techniques, do not act in an arbitrary manner. They serve to channel the power exercised over the mass of people in a more efficient, and less visibly political fashion, while this power is used largely in the interests of the dominant class in our society.

The critique of social statistics developed in this book clearly has significant implications for political practice, and these are addressed more fully in the concluding chapter. *Social Statistics: Towards a Radical Science* attempts to link together the arguments made in the earlier sections of the book within an overall political framework. In so doing, it develops guide-lines for the contributions which statisticians and social scientists might most effectively make in putting statistics to work within a radical political practice. The strategies and perspectives advanced by critical scientists and the radical science movement provide the starting point for this analysis. As with other scientific practices in our society it is important that we be able both to understand and criticise the formation and use of social statistics, and also to determine when and how it may be developed and applied for purposes of facilitating radical social change.

The contents of this book are thus intended to reveal the basis of social statistics orthodoxy, and in so doing to help undermine it. This often daunting edifice of objectivity, this false monument to precision and truth, must be toppled if we are to begin to reconstruct statistics as a critical practice of use in the creation of a new society. All of the contributors would agree that the analyses presented are in many ways incomplete—for there really is very little to draw upon in the way of a critical tradition in quantitative social science—but their contributions certainly show that the foundations of orthodox claims are precarious indeed.

While setting out to topple a shibboleth, these chapters do not attempt to erect a monolith in its place. What unites the authors is their belief that there is no methodological monopoly of 'truth'. What unites them further is their commitment to the creation of a radical social theory and practice within which critical use can be made of quantitative approaches. Social statistics should gain, not lose, from the demolition of the mystifications which make it appear as a set of timeless, logical truths, and which obscure the possibilities for its reconstruction as part of the struggle to build a socialist society. This task of demolition and reconstruction is long overdue; this book is a preliminary and provisional attempt to do just that.

Section One:
Historical Perspectives on Social Statistics

Each of the three chapters in this section attempts to show that the historical development of social statistics should be understood in terms of broad societal factors; that statistics is more than an accumulation of ideas and techniques developed through the creativity of individual scientists.

The first chapter, by John Irvine and Ian Miles, examines the ways in which statistics teaching has been shaped by the changing intellectual commitments and institutional structures in education in Britain. By showing how the contemporary patterns of statistics teaching for social scientists have developed, this historical account should enable students to understand better the sources of the problems they may be experiencing with social statistics, and how they may set about overcoming them.

Martin Shaw and Ian Miles then provide a brief panoramic sketch of the main directions in which social statistics have been developed, indicating that the establishment and growth of statistics has been intimately related to the rise and development of capitalist society. They argue that although the increasing importance of money was a momentous stimulus to quantitative analysis (cf. also Robert Young, this volume), the historically recent expansion in the production of statistical data derived largely from the growing role of the state.

Finally, Donald MacKenzie discusses the influence of social interests—especially the eugenics movement—on the development of some of the most widely used techniques of mathematical statistics. This chapter is particularly relevant to assessing the statistical basis of contemporary racist and hereditarian approaches to IQ testing, which continue to rely upon essentially similar techniques.

Together these chapters indicate the value of an historical analysis of statistical techniques and practices. Historical analysis is not just the concern of this section of the book, however; chapters in every section raise issues relating to the origins and developments of the statistics they consider. These three chapters are intended to provide a framework which will be of use in reading such studies.

2.

John Irvine and Ian Miles

Statistics Teaching in Social Science: A Problem with a History

Most social science students in Britain take an elementary statistics course as part of their undergraduate degree training. Yet despite the central position occupied by social statistics teaching (SST) in most courses, it has faced intense and continuing difficulties. According to one professor of statistics:

> Students are often disillusioned with our introductory courses . . . They are 'turned off by statistics' and 'less numerate at the end of the course than at the beginning' . . . a particular complaint is that 'most of the course seems irrelevant to what we're doing'. . . . The students are right. Statistics courses *are* largely irrelevant—not just boring or technically difficult, but irrelevant. (Ehrenberg, 1976, p.1).

Further evidence of the problematic nature of SST is provided by an in-depth study of statistics teaching carried out at a university in the south of England. In this, the author cites a letter written by a first-year undergraduate student to his Dean in order to explain why the elementary statistics exam was being boycotted:

> It is accepted that several of the subjects involved (social psychology, economics, geography) find the statistics introduction essential to their major course . . . [but] several subjects at present involved in the course have no apparent justifiable need to do it. Students find it most disquieting to be distracted from their first term's work on their major by an *irrelevant* and in some cases *incomprehensible* course . . . (Hill, 1974, appendix, our emphasis).

Exam boycotts are, of course, carried out by students only as a last resort. More commonly, their response is to treat SST as a necessary hurdle to be stumbled over—no matter how boring, technically difficult or irrelevant it appears to be. Where SST is not compulsory, students have in large part voted with their feet, as they also tend to do with the quantitative and statistical options offered later in their courses.

In our view, these persistent problems with SST are related to a particular approach to statistics in the social sciences. This approach was built into both the institutional structure and the content of SST early in the development of social science in British universities. Despite a considerable number of attempts to explain and to provide solutions for SST's problems, this approach itself has not been adequately assessed with the result that little progress has been made in working out what might be suitable and relevant forms of SST for social science undergraduates.

At the same time, there has been a growing polarisation among faculty over the role of SST in social science courses. Many faculty champion a traditional form of SST—attributing any problems to the laziness or lack of numeracy of students. Others at the opposite end of the spectrum—particularly sociologists—cast doubt on whether statistics is of any real use to their students, and have concluded that such courses should be abolished. Typical student responses to SST reflect this polarity, and range between uncritical acceptance of statistical data and technique, and an equally uncritical rejection of all statistics as mystification.

Either way, students are turned off statistics—which poses problems for any attempt to develop the use of statistics within a critical social science. An analysis of the historical and intellectual origins of, and responses to, the present problems in SST is therefore essential if alternative forms of SST are to be developed.

The orthodoxy of statistics teaching

Although the problems of SST have often been the subject of heated debate both among and between social scientists and statisticians, there has been little attempt to evaluate critically the place of statistics in social science courses. What evaluation there has been has normally followed the position taken by the British social science establishment—which began to recognise SST as a serious problem in the late 1960s. In particular, the Social Science Research Council (SSRC) saw British social science as lagging far behind its American counterpart in quantitative sophistication, explaining this in terms of poor undergraduate training in SST. Thus, the *SSRC Newsletter* of December 1969 reported that:

> The Council has for some time been worried about three points: its inadequate knowledge of the extent and scope of research and taught courses in this field (social statistics) . . .; the need for a higher level of numeracy; and the small number of applications for research grants in social statistics . . . (p. 18).

As part of what was to become a continuing statistical crusade, the SSRC commissioned a wide-ranging study on the use of statistics in the social sciences. Carried out in conjunction with the Royal Statistical Society (RSS), this resulted in the *Report on the Use of Statistics in Social Science Research* (the Rosenbaum Report, 1971). Much of this report was devoted to the problems of SST which were seen as primarily responsible for the unsatisfactory nature of quantitative social science research.

Rosenbaum, significantly, was a statistician—in fact, an ex-President of the RSS. He admits in the report to a strong commitment to a particular role for statistics in social science—describing himself as engaging in 'missionary work':

> There seemed to be no merit in preserving a strict impartiality with the aim of producing a report on the current position, when some immediate good could be done through the machinery of the visits themselves. Hence, in addition to advocating closer ties between statisticians and social scientists, I did not conceal a conviction that financial support for projects involving statistics, including methodological and mathematical developments, should be forthcoming. If this has influenced competent people to apply to the SSRC for research grants, one of the objectives will have been achieved. (Rosenbaum, 1971, p. 585).

The expression of such views in this way is hardly in accord with the conventional notion of statisticians making 'unbiased collections' of 'the facts'. The way Rosenbaum presented the results of his survey of 40 institutions was also rather untypical. Despite the scope of these visits, and the expense of the report, the survey analysis he presented—particularly relating to course content—was little more than a set of general impressions.

Rosenbaum did, however, present a characterisation of the typical social statistics course which may sound familiar to many readers:

> . . . the emphasis is on data, their definition, collection, reliability, classification and interpretation (the latter sounds ambitious but without it the subject is arid). The students are taught about frequency distributions and descriptive statistics, such as means and standard deviations. They go on to elementary time series analysis and correlation. In some universities all the social science students get this much in a basic course in their first year. They may then go on to probability, the mathematical form of distribution functions (e.g. normal, binomial), significance tests and regression . . . many students consider that the statistics teaching is too mathematical, although the emphasis is on methods rather than theory. Special

topics are brought in as appropriate, for instance design of experiments for psychologists and life tables for demographers, whilst surveys and sampling method are widely taught. (Rosenbaum, 1971, p. 542).

The general impression given is of statistical technique being taught in isolation from theory, and of a tendency towards a common pattern of introductory SST, with a strongly mathematical tinge, for all social science students. These features reflect the positivist notion that the social sciences can emulate the achievements of the physical sciences only if 'methodology' is taken seriously. Statistics and quantitative methods are treated, and presented to students, as providing the foundations of an 'exact', more objective social science: that is, as the universal and unifying discipline, as the technical cement needed to erect an edifice of scientific social theory (see Keat, and Young, this volume). Since he shared this view, Rosenbaum's conclusions were entirely predictable: the problems of SST were due in large part to a lack of numeracy and inadequate motivation among students, coupled with an insufficient number of trained statisticians working within the social sciences. Such diagnoses have been standard fare among statisticians and empiricist social scientists attempting to come to terms with these problems.

The SSRC initiative continued: in 1972 they sponsored a conference at Sussex University on 'The Teaching of Statistics in the Social Sciences'. Despite the presence of a few critics of orthodox SST, the conference reports by and large reiterate Rosenbaum's perspectives. The focus was firmly placed on how to cope with the diversity and failings of students, rather than the diversity and requirements of the social sciences. As reported in the *SSRC Newsletter*, the origins of the problems with SST were again held to lie in 'the difficulties encountered in evolving appropriate curricula and teaching methods in statistics, particularly in view of the diverse characteristics of social science students when tested in such dimensions as mathematical attainment' (Hill, 1972, p.17). The issues selected for treatment at the conference reflected this focus, and included such items as 'The Curriculum for a General Course', and 'Teaching of Students of Different Mathematical Backgrounds, Interests and Experiences'. And the panel on 'The Teaching of Statistics in the Social Sciences' took as a main topic 'The concept of a general course—why should it exist and how its aims can be realised' (Hill, 1973, p. 85). The conference papers were published as a special issue of the *International Journal of Mathematical Education in Science and Technology* (vol. 4, 1973). The decision to publish in this journal, rather than in one with a circulation among social scientists, underlines that the audience for such work is composed primarily of statisticians.

A crisis in sociology

While the SSRC has fostered the orthodoxy outlined above, and while many statisticians and social scientists may continually reiterate it, the persistent problems of SST have led to other approaches gaining ground, especially in sociology.

Many of the sociological critics of SST accept that, in large part, student complaints are justified, although their criticisms have varied in range and nature. At one extreme, it has been argued that the contribution of quantitative methods to sociology does no more than give the 'appearance of solidity to pure wind' (Phillips, 1973, p. 179). This, and less extreme versions of such views, were popularised in the early 1970s through the spawning of a huge anti-quantitative literature constituting the 'interpretative critique' of positivist social science—which has been particularly attractive to many of the people disenchanted with mainstream social science. Other critics, rather than pressing for abolition, have argued for major reforms in SST, proposing that it be made less technical, be taught by social scientists rather than by statisticians, and that its study be focused rather more on data sources (like official statistics) and rather less on mathematical statistics.

In sociology, especially, these differences of opinion have been intense, as is shown by the immense variability in the nature and extent of statistics courses. Although there have been several general surveys of sociology degree courses in Britain (e.g. Clarke, 1976), none have taken up SST in detail (Rosenbaum's sketchy survey not excepted). However, it is possible to get an idea of its range and orientation from the various editions of *Which University*. The earliest reliable edition of this (1969) indicates that statistics was then an integral part of almost all sociology courses. More recent editions indicate a change in orientation towards SST: in the 1978 edition, of 42 universities in Britain offering sociology as a degree course, or at least as a major component, twelve universities do not insist on compulsory statistics training—and, of these, six do not even offer an option.

Thus the situation has changed a great deal over time and is, of course, still changing. Whilst most sociology undergraduates are still offered introductory statistics, increasingly it is optional. Some departments (e.g. Hull) have abolished such teaching altogether, whereas, at the opposite extreme, others (e.g. Newcastle) insist upon the study of quantitative methods to a relatively high degree of sophistication in all three years of the course.

In sociology, then, the problems of SST have reached crisis proportions. Yet neither of the polarised responses to these problems provides an adequate basis for radical social science. Much of the critique of existing SST can be accepted without dismissing statistics as irrelevant to social analysis and action. And, similarly, the potential usefulness of statistics can be recognised, without agreeing that it forms an especially privileged way of acquiring knowledge. Ideally SST should enable students both to undertake radical critiques of the dominant uses of statistics in social affairs as well as social science, and to recognise and develop applications of statistics to critical social analysis. However, in order to explore how far this ideal is possible and to move beyond inadequate responses to the SST problem, we need to examine the roots and development of the problem itself.

The development of SST

In Britain, significant growth of academic social science began to take place only after the second world war. In the academic year 1938/39, for example, only 33 honours degrees in total were awarded in sociology, social administration and social anthropology—with another 15 in psychology. This compared markedly with the 51 awarded in politics, 216 in economics, 258 in geography and 374 in law. (Heyworth Report, 1965, p. 9).

That social science had not developed in the pre-war period, as it had in America, was to have implications for the nature and content of new degree courses. The immediate post-war era was a period which witnessed an enormous expansion of state activities in all areas of social life. The trauma of the Great Depression and the experience of wartime planning had left many politicians convinced that only major state intervention into economic and social affairs could avert the political instability that might accompany any future economic crisis. The 'welfare state' and Keynesian economic management were thus established, and social science—quantitative social science—was seen as having an important role to play.

These developments underlay *The Report on the Provision for Social and Economic Research* (the Clapham Report, 1946), which argued strongly for the creation of a substantial social science research effort in Britain. As Clapham saw it:

> The prospects of return in national welfare are at least as great as in the natural sciences. With the national income running at its present

rate, for instance, the discovery of knowledge which made possible the reduction of the average of unemployment by as little as a half of one per cent would mean a gain of at least £40,000,000 per annum (p. 4).

Clapham placed great emphasis on the role of social statistics in this task:

an adequate supply of statistical competence is quite fundamental to the advancement of knowledge of social and economic questions . . . during the war, statisticians were probably the scarcest of scarce commodities . . . there are few more urgent needs today than the increase of the supply of first-class statisticians (pp. 8–9).

Most of Clapham's recommendations for greatly increased funding for the social sciences were soon put into effect. Different social

Table 1: **New university teaching posts set up 1947–52***

	Teaching posts	
	Professorial	*Others*
Economics	4	41
Statistics (incl. economic statistics)	1	11
Politics	1	9
Social Studies	2	8
Economic History	1	4
Social Anthropology	1	4
Social Psychology		5
Sociology		5
Industrial Relations		5
Philosophy		1

*This table is incomplete due to classificatory problems (referred to by Heyworth). These relate mainly to joint appointments. Because of this, for example, the resources allocated to Liverpool, Southampton and the LSE have not been included.

Source: Adapted from *Report of the Committee on Social Studies* (Heyworth Report), 1965, Appendix 2, pp. 80–85.

sciences, however, received different treatment. The more quantitative and 'policy-relevant' areas, such as economics (*Table 1*) were expanded most, and enjoyed a correspondingly rapid growth in student numbers (*Table 2*).

Table 2: **Students receiving honours degrees in different social sciences (absolute numbers)**

	1938–39	*1947–48*	*1951–52*	*1955–56*	*1959–60*
Sociology, Social Administration and Anthropology	33	90	120	122	252
Economics	216	529	520	691	885
Politics	51	141	200	107	179
Psychology	15	62	138	88	153

Source: Adapted from Heyworth Report, 1965, p. 9

These years, furthermore, were not just the golden years of quantitative social science: they also saw a particular structure of SST established. And it is this structure which remains at the heart of many of today's problems.

As with social science itself, the future course of SST was charted in another early report: the *Report on the Teaching of Statistics in Universities and University Colleges (1947)*—organised by the RSS and chaired by E. S. Pearson. Echoing many of Clapham's arguments, it recommended supplying the quantitative inputs to the expanding social sciences through the establishment and support of autonomous statistics departments which would, whenever possible, operate in close conjunction with economics departments. They were seen as providing SST on a 'service' basis, since:

> the main principles of statistical theory . . . are . . . basically common to all subjects of application . . . each university should establish a recognised centre for statistical methodology. In it could be given all the elementary courses . . . in addition, the separate faculties could have their own statisticians and do some teaching, particularly of special applications (p. 56).

Pearson also had strong views about the role and content of his proposed service courses; they should be:

> general courses designed to familiarise students with statistical ideas and the most commonly used elementary methods . . . should be part of the ordinary undergraduate course of at least all students in the social and natural sciences (p. 54).

And moreover:

> courses of a somewhat more advanced type . . . to enable students to utilise properly statistical methods as developed for application to their chosen science . . . should be taken by most students of the social and biological sciences in all universities as part of the normal curriculum for a first degree (p. 54).

These proposals, based largely on the experience of practising statisticians and economists, were widely taken up. In particular, general introductory courses in statistics for social scientists became standard practice. And with it the view of statistics as universally relevant to all the social sciences was built into the institutional structure of SST, as was a form of SST closely aligned to the needs of economists. This practice had become so firmly established by the early 1970s that Rosenbaum was able to report that:

> There is generally a compulsory course in elementary statistics in the first year of a social studies course . . . After the introductory course more advanced courses are widely offered which are not necessarily taken up, or sometimes only by a few . . . Opinions differed as to whether social statistics should be taught to social scientists by suitably trained persons brought up in the subject field, or by mathematicians . . . Certainly the practice varied: a course might be taught in some places by the mathematics department and in others by the social science department. (Rosenbaum, 1971, pp. 7–8).

While problems had been noted with SST from the outset, the institutional form of SST, and the conception of statistics linked to it, were rarely questioned. It was only with the transformation of higher education in the 1960s that the problems of SST were to be placed in a new and more troubled context.

The expansion of social science and the critique of statistics

In the wake of the report of the *Committee on Higher Education* (Robbins, 1963), and the subsequent major restructuring of educational policy, the 1960s saw a dramatic expansion of higher education (see Layard, King and Moser, 1969, and the critical remarks of Adelstein, 1969). This was particularly marked in the social sciences, where student numbers increased from 10,554 in 1961 to 24,675 in 1967 (University Grants Committee, 1968, p. 19). Given this burgeoning expenditure on social science, questions began to be raised about its direction.

The *Report of the Committee on Social Studies* (Heyworth Report, 1965) assessed the worth of social science research and advised on what co-ordination, supervision and support was needed. This report led to the creation of the SSRC—which now controls the funding and orientation of most academic social science research in Britain.

The import of Heyworth's recommendations was that the content of both teaching and research should be oriented more directly to the needs of the state and industry. To achieve success in this, it had to be 'scientific', and it hardly needs saying that the role of statistics was seen as paramount:

> Without mathematics and statistics the social sciences as a whole cannot flourish . . . [But] many (students) opt for the social sciences whose weakness in mathematics deters them from courses in the natural sciences. Some are paralysed by fear of the subject . . . others have given up the study of mathematics too soon.

This results, argued Heyworth, in the lack of numerate and statistically competent research staff, and thus:

> new approaches to the teaching of mathematics and statistics . . . [must be] developed in universities and colleges so that no student will in future graduate in the social sciences without a good working knowledge of statistics. (Heyworth, p. 32).

The infant SSRC likewise stressed the need to improve quantitative research and SST, identifying as the main obstacle the lack of numeracy of students. Even before the *Rosenbaum Report* of 1971, the *SSRC Newsletter* was able to report such items as the following:

> Michael Young, as chairman of the SSRC, has written to heads of all secondary schools, asking them to encourage would-be social scientists to continue with mathematics up to A-level . . . (*SSRC Newsletter*, May 1968, p. 11).

The expansion of higher education had, of course, results other than the establishment of the SSRC: of particular consequence to SST were institutional changes in social science departments. With the large increase in faculty numbers, many sociology groups were able to become rather more autonomous within their social science faculties. As departments in their own right, they gained a new measure of organisational power. No longer was it necessary for sociology departments to continue their participation in the traditional common first year course taken by sociologists, economists, political scientists and others. As a result, the position of SST within the sociology curriculum gradually came under scrutiny in many departments, especially as the composition of sociology teachers in higher education changed.

The sociology teachers appointed in the immediate wake of Robbins had been recruited from a variety of social science backgrounds. Relatively few 'pure' sociologists had been available for appointment, because Britain had been remarkably late, in comparison with other industrial countries, in developing sociology on any scale.[1] An eclectic borrowing of both personnel and theory was therefore occasioned by the postwar growth of academic sociology, and this practice was largely continued in the immediate wake of Robbins.

Empirical social research had remained at a fairly primitive level over most of this period, as the concern of the Heyworth Report and the SSRC demonstrates. Sociologists still relied to a great extent on statisticians for data and methodology. This situation began to change in the late 1960s, as increasing numbers of graduate sociologists became available for appointment. This new breed played a crucial role in the development of SST. Virden (1977) relates much of the turmoil in academic sociology in the early 1970s and the associated critiques of statistical and quantitative research emphases, to these institutional developments, talking of the resentment by junior, 'pure' sociologists of their senior, 'unsociological' colleagues. This was compounded by the involvement of junior faculty and students in the political conflicts (and associated intellectual questioning) in higher education associated with the rise of 'student politics' and the New Left.

Criticism of SST was thus expressed with increasing vigour by sociologists at the same time as the institutional autonomy of sociology made it possible to opt out of the common course provided by economics or statistics departments. The resultant conflicts were not confined just to sociologists; departments often came in conflict too. Statistics departments saw their existence threatened—after Pearson's report, increases in their faculty size were often dependent upon rising service teaching commitments—and existing courses were thrown into chaos. Depending on the balance of forces within particular departments and faculties, different solutions were developed. Sometimes SST remained unchanged; sometimes its technical content was watered down or it became non-examinable; sometimes control over teaching passed to sociology departments with the result that statistics was often taught as part of a more general methodology course; and, at other times, SST was dropped altogether.

Thus, the efforts to promote statistics as the means of

producing 'mature' social science in Britain have foundered. Certainly many university departments retain the model of SST propounded by Pearson, with its mandatory interfaculty courses based largely upon the particular technical needs of economists. But although this structure has been increasingly challenged, even where it has been modified or abandoned, problems with SST remain.

SST: a problem with a future?

With undiminished confidence the social science establishment has declaimed its various solutions to the problems of SST—from improving mathematics teaching in schools to using more sophisticated teaching aids in universities, from attracting statistically-trained staff into social science faculties to restricting entrance to social science courses to numerate candidates. These solutions have met with meagre success, for they are prescribed and implemented in terms of the view of statistics as a set of asocial methods for producing and analysing data, which are founded upon the timeless truths of probability theory that can be universally applied without involving social values and hypotheses. It is hardly likely that these solutions could overcome problems which spring directly from such mystifications.

The common reaction to this view of statistics on the part of many dissatisfied students and faculty, to reject statistics altogether, is superficially appealing. But it has tended to result in the adoption of 'interpretative' or 'phenomenological' approaches in social science, and to a neglect of questions of social structure in the effort to assign central importance to individuals' experiences and social meanings. A critical social science, however, needs both to analyse social structures and to accept the importance of social analysis at the level of meanings and experience. Meanings are integral to, but not exhaustive of, social processes. Experiential descriptions of exploitation and oppression, for example, while important, will not suffice for developing a theory of revolutionary social change: and statistics can play a useful role in developing such a theory and practice, and in assessing and depicting the social structures within which these experiences are produced (see Griffiths, Irvine and Miles, this volume).

To develop a radical approach to SST, then, must mean moving beyond such propositions as 'social science students are by nature innumerate', or that 'statistics is in essence irrelevant to social science'. But the lack of a recognised critical quantitative tradition means that few guidelines are provided for this task. The beginnings of such an alternative approach are provided by various chapters of this book (and in the bibliographic material they present). This is only a beginning, and further material will be required according to the specific character of each field of study. (Here critical analyses of the 'discipline' in question—in radical articles, books, and journals —are invaluable, but it is also worth exploring the 'technical' controversies and debates that are usually published in the mainstream literature.)

Such an approach to SST involves establishing courses which provide a framework for an understanding of the social roles of statistics, as well as communicating knowledge of the skills required to employ statistical data and techniques critically. Most import- antly, the mystique of scientific and technical issues in statistics would be overcome by presenting them as grounded in social practices, rather than as mechanical methods for ensuring objective social research. Students would be able to grapple with the conventions of statistics, while simultaneously analysing and criti- cising the dominant philosophies and applications involved.

To go further than this, and present a detailed outline of a general 'radical statistics' course, would be antithetical to an underlying theme of our historical analysis: that the failure to structure SST around the requirements of particular groups of students is a prime contributor to its problems. While there are many underlying continuities in the contemporary social sciences, there is little point in expounding upon these abstractly or in isolation from the substantive issues with which students are dealing. Nevertheless, it is clear that the non-positivist and non- empiricist nature of such courses, whatever their detailed form, would make them radically different from traditional SST.

Beyond these issues of course content, an appraisal of alternative SST needs to take into account some of the institutional factors we have mentioned—strategies for effecting change are, after all, likely to be opposed from many quarters. The strongest overt opposition will probably come from statisticians committed to the traditional type of service course who, in any case, have been fighting rearguard actions to defend their courses from attack by anti-quantitative faculty. Statisticians may well be supported in their opposition by empiricist social science faculty, and this alliance may be further strengthened by the social science professor who, as head of department, is generally in a strong position to influence such matters. Many of today's professors, recruited in the post-Robbins expansion, are likely to be strongly committed to traditional SST; and even those who are critical of it will probably regard a traditional quantitative course as giving a stamp of scientific authenticity to their degree courses—which is not without its advantages in the world of university politics.

While most sympathy and support for changing SST is likely to come from anti-quantitative faculty, they will, more often than not, be inclined towards the abolition of SST. Strongest support for radically changing, rather than abolishing, SST is most likely to come from those faculty whose unease with existing social statistics has not been elevated into an anti-quantitative epistemology. Most marxists, for example, whilst opposed to traditional SST would not be against the use of statistics as such. That they use statistics infrequently again reflects the lack of a critical quantitative tradition rather than a conscious rejection of statistics per se. Hopefully, the renaissance of marxist analysis throughout the social sciences may mean that an increasing proportion of faculty members will be prepared to support a more radical approach.

Important though the support of teachers may be in helping to effect changes in SST, there are limits upon their actions. Given the positions of faculty and students in the institutional framework, critical initiatives to change SST will generally require at least the stimulus of student action. The way forward to challenging SST and establishing radical alternatives depends crucially upon students moving from passive dissatisfaction to active course criticism. This is often the only way of prodding faculty into taking the problems of SST seriously.

The issues taken up by students in this way have tended to revolve around questions of course content—such as questioning whether the technical level of a particular course is too sophisticated. But they have also involved other aspects of teaching which can be even more threatening to faculty and administrative interests. For example, there may be a need in some circumstances to ensure that SST is carried out by experienced social scientists rather than by empiricist statisticians with little or no knowledge of social science. Or teaching methods may be questioned: it may be appropriate to argue for student-generated practical work to replace long stints with blackboard-based calculator exercises, or for changing assessment from tedious and irrelevant sit-down exams to methods based on collective project work.

While criticism of course content and structure generally takes the form of complaints and demands about problems in existing SST, such a defensive strategy is best complemented by an offensive approach. Here the strategy of developing a 'counter-course' (see Pateman, 1972) may be useful. Counter-courses, by demonstrating that alternatives are practicable and useful, have in some cases stimulated major changes in formal curricula, as well as involving their participants in actively developing new methods of studying and learning. A working alternative can pre-empt criticisms that student radicals are only attempting destructive dismissal of their courses.

Finally, just as there can be no universal alternative statistics course, there can be no universal prescriptions for bringing about change other than those couched in highly general terms. Any strategy has associated pitfalls as well as advantages, and these need to be appraised in terms of the specific circumstances involved. By informing this appraisal, and the actions which are undertaken, with an awareness of the historical roots of the SST problem, we are in a better position to take up the task of demystifying social statistics teaching.

Notes

1. This makes a story in its own right. Two factors in particular were relevant to the lack of a strong sociological tradition in Britain. First was Britain's nineteenth century imperial dominance. The needs of colonial administration led to social anthropology being the major influence in those fields of academic social science that were not subsumed under 'economics' and 'politics', and would-be sociologists had to fight against this dominant tradition—with so little success that only at the London School of Economics was there any significant development of sociology. (See the article on the 'Institutional Development of Sociology' in Sills, 1968). Second, and again related to British imperialism and Britain's uniquely early capitalist development, was the relative lack of political turbulence (other than in Ireland). As Anderson (1969) argued in a seminal and devastating analysis of British culture, there was little incentive to develop sociology in the absence of the sorts of intellectual challenges thrown up by revolutionary movements (bourgeois or working class). (Complementing the two sources cited here, Abrams (1968) provides a useful survey of the early development of British sociology).

Bibliography

Abrams, P., 1968, *The Origins of British Sociology*, Chicago, University of Chicago Press.

Adelstein, D., 1969, 'Roots of the British crisis', in Cockburn and Blackburn, 1969, below.

Anderson, P., 1969, 'Components of the national culture', in Cockburn and Blackburn, 1969, below (first published in *New Left Review*, no. 56).

Clarke, M., 1976, 'First year sociology courses: a report of a survey', *Sociology*, vol. 10, no. 1, pp. 83–100.

Cockburn, A., and Blackburn, R. (eds.), 1969, *Student Power*, Harmondsworth, Penguin.

Committee on Higher Education: Report of the Committee appointed by the Prime Minister under the Chairmanship of Lord Robbins, 1961–63, Cmnd. 2154, London, HMSO.

Ehrenberg, A. S. C., 1976, 'We must preach what is practised: a radical review of statistical teaching', *The Statistician*, vol. 25, no. 2, pp. 1–7.

Hill, B., 1972, 'Teaching of statistics in the social sciences', *SSRC Newsletter*, no. 17, pp.17–18.

Hill, B., 1973, 'Report of Panel on the teaching of statistics in the social sciences', *International Journal of Mathematical Education in Science and Technology*, vol. 4, pp. 85–86.

Hill, B., 1974, 'A working paper in the teaching of statistics: part of the higher education work within a southern university' (mimeo).

Layard, R., King, J., and Moser, C., 1969, *The Impact of Robbins*, Harmondsworth, Penguin.

Pateman, T. (ed.), 1972, *Counter-Course*, Harmondsworth, Penguin.

Phillips, D. L., 1973, *Abandoning Method*, San Francisco, Jossey Bass.

Report of the Committee on Social Studies, 1965, (Chairman, Lord Heyworth), Cmnd. 2660, London, HMSO.

Report of the Committee on the Provision for Social and Economic Research, 1946, (Chairman, Sir J. Clapham), Cmnd. 6868, London, HMSO.

Rosenbaum, S., 1971, 'A report on the use of statistics in social science research', *Journal of the Royal Statistical Society*, A, vol. 134, pp. 534–610.

Royal Statistical Society, 1947, *Report on the Teaching of Statistics in Universities and University Colleges* (Chairman, E. S. Pearson), *Journal of the Royal Statistical Society*, A, vol. 110, pp. 51–57.

Sills, D. (ed.), 1968, *International Encyclopedia of Social Science*, New York, Collier-Macmillan.

University Grants Committee, 1968, *University Development 1962–67*, London, HMSO.

Virden, P., 1977, *Words (inc) . . . .: Social Science and the Knowledge Machine*, York, Tiger Papers Publications (available through Publications Distribution Co-operative, 27 Clerkenwell Close, London EC1R 0AT).

3.

Martin Shaw and Ian Miles

The Social Roots of Statistical Knowledge

Why do we use statistics? A textbook will give us one sort of answer to this question: the advantages of exact information, quick calculations and easy comparisons. Popular lore will supply us with another: lies and damned lies are not good enough! However that may be, people have not always used statistics. In the scale of human history, they are a recent development. And although histories of statistics have been written, few of them have tried to answer the question, 'What has the rise of statistics to do with the kind of economic and social order which has emerged in modern times?' But it is a question whose answer throws a lot of light on what statistics are about.

We had better state at the outset that our attempt to link statistics to the history of modern capitalist society is not made in order to 'dismiss' statistics. Some radical critics , in rejecting the cult of facts and figures, have expressed a yearning for the altogether more simple life of days gone by. We can acknowledge the attractions of such an ideal, but we must insist that things are not really so simple. In the first place, the complexity of modern society reflects the richness and diversity of life within it as well as the extent to which people are reduced to being 'cogs in the machine'. In our view, a better society would be one which retained this complexity, and would therefore still need complex ways of quantifying itself. Second, the counting and measuring of things is something which has been developed over a very long historical period. It is only certain ways of quantifying human activities which are really specific to the present, capitalist form of industrial society.

In order, then, to work out how useful statistics are, to those who want to change society as well as those who run it now, it is valuable to look not just at the present uses of statistics—which is done in later sections of this book—but also to examine how they have developed historically out of earlier forms of quantification.

The early quantification of economic life

Quantity is an essential aspect of expressing quality, so even the most simple forms of human society have developed concepts of numbers. As people acquired some control over their environment, they developed concepts for different species of life and categories of objects. They also needed ways of distinguishing the members of these species and categories. The first use of numbers may actually have been qualitative: to distinguish, for example, between 'a man' and 'some men' (Struik, 1956).[1]

People in early human societies, who grew food, herded animals, and made pottery and clothing, largely for their own use, must have needed to count and compare goods, to find out how far their production was sufficient for their needs. Once a class of chiefs, priests and kings arose, they will have needed to quantify production to establish how much tribute was to be paid to them.[2] But as long as goods are largely produced for use, whether by the producers themselves or by those who receive them in tribute, quantification will be limited in kind. Each of the different sorts of product will be counted or measured separately.

When, however, communities are able to produce in excess of their immediate needs, it becomes possible to produce commodities —goods which are exchanged for other goods. For such exchange, some means of comparing commodities is needed, and money was developed to express the exchange-value of commodities in a convenient way. The use of money relieves the producers of the burden of finding someone to accept their commodity in exchange for exactly the goods they require for their own use. It enables a general process of exchange of commodities to take place. It also means that all commodities can be quantified in common terms— and this is a big leap in the process of quantifying economic life.

Such general exchange, based on money, reveals what is implicit in the exchange of commodities for each other—that a quantitative comparison is being made between qualitatively different goods, whose common element is that they are all products of human labour. The value of, say, a certain quantity of grain, as compared to a certain amount of cloth, or a given amount of money (their common 'exchange value'), is based upon the amounts of labour needed to produce these commodities in a particular society.[3]

With the increase of trade in the ancient world, the calculation and recording of exchange values provided powerful stimuli to quantification and numeracy, but they were by no means the only ones. Sciences such as astronomy and geometry, which were needed for navigation and building, also made a major contribution. Rulers, too, were sometimes driven to make surveys of population and wealth, so as to know the resources they could draw upon. A census is said to have been carried out in Egypt around 3000 BC, before the building of the pyramids, and the Bible mentions David's 'numbering his people', as well as Herod's census.

In feudal times, the Domesday Book is a similar example, and it is worth noting the limited nature of the quantification it involved. William was seeking to establish his precise entitlements from the defeated English. Accordingly, the inventory was unique rather than part of a series. William was not concerned with determining the gross national product, the total revenue of the state, or even the sum of his own entitlements. These were recorded, rather, as specific payments, which could be made over to particular applications as they became due; they were not all monetary, many concerned food and services of various kinds (Clark, 1948).

Thus, although quantification is involved in such inventories, they cannot reasonably be regarded as statistical analyses. Nor did record-keeping and monetary comparisons, in themselves, necessitate the development of statistics. This was because people in both ancient and feudal societies were still mainly involved in producing goods for their own use. Although commodity production grew, it was still limited in scope: it had not become the typical form of production. The full dynamism of a money economy, in which more and more things are quantified, had not yet developed.

The seventeenth century: mortality statistics and customs duties

Recognisably 'statistical' enquiries can be dated back to seventeenth-century England (Kendall, 1970), when trade, and manufacture for the market, were becoming the foundation of the more advanced national economies.

However, the 'crisis of the seventeenth century' was a many-sided affair (Aston, 1965), and the impetus it gave to early statistical developments came as much from the social consequences of economic change, and the new financial needs of the state, as it did from the expansion of commerce itself.

The rise of 'merchant capital'[4] involved major social changes: markets and towns sprang up, international communications improved. One important consequence was that insanitary town dwellings, combined with maritime trade, provided ideal conditions for epidemic disease to spread. It was these epidemics which, in sixteenth century London, occasioned some of the first mortality statistics; the data were published intermittently at first, then from 1603, during another severe bout of the plague, in a weekly series (Cartwright, 1977; Howe, 1972).

These were possibly the first regular statistics of any kind, and they remained of considerable significance for the development of statistics in the next century. In 1662, the merchant John Graunt, in his *Observations on the London Bills of Mortality*, constructed the first table displaying the life expectancies of people in different age-groups. He showed that death itself was orderly: a structure underlay mortality rates, so that there were seasonal variations, urban rates exceeded those of rural areas, and the like. And in the 1690s, the astronomer Edmund Halley pointed out that life-tables could have a number of uses: in estimating, for example, the military force that could be drawn from a population; or in calculating the values of annuities (lifelong pensions paid in exchange for the donation of a sum of money to the state). The latter was important, precisely because of the new military and commercial context of the period.

At the time Halley was preparing and publishing his own, more accurate life-tables, annuities were a significant means of raising state finance (Marchal, 1948; Parker, 1974). William and Mary's government was raising loans for the conduct of the war against France, paying for these with life annuities, which could be raised more rapidly than taxation. Life-tables were also useful to capitalists: they provided the basis on which life insurance could be run more profitably (the first such 'scientific' company, the 'Equitable', was set up in 1762; see Raynes, 1964). The success of such companies reinforced belief in the statistical method, and interest in health and insurance encouraged the development of the calculus of probabilities.[5]

Most important for state finance, and hence for the development of statistics, were trade and commerce. Their expansion was a striking feature of this period and was stressed by economic writers of the 'mercantilist' school, who saw trade rather than production as the source of wealth. Certainly for the state, commerce rather than production was the source of expanding revenues, and so statistics on commodity prices and trade were prepared long before those on production and employment. Customs duties, income from which doubled in England between 1650 and 1688, were centralised in 1671; in 1695 the first official statistical department was set up, involving the Inspector General of Imports and Exports, who was placed in charge of data concerning the quantities and money values of trade. Previously, only occasional calculations of the volume of trade had been made; now continuous statistical series were set up (Clark, 1938).

'Political arithmetic' and 'state-istics'

The setting up of this statistical department reflected a growing interest in the use of numerical information to monitor and control the complex economic and social situation. One major champion of the use of quantitative data, and advocate of a state statistical department, was Sir William Petty who used the term 'Political Arithmetic' as the title of a book published in 1690. He was most concerned with data which would now be classified as demographic and economic statistics. Taking population as the source of all wealth, Petty argued in his *Treatise of Taxes and Contributions* (1662) for the use of demographic data in policy-making: thus one could calculate the levels of expenditure required for poor relief, and devise an efficient taxation system. In 1695, Davenant attempted to calculate the population size in order to work out the likely taxation yield.

Petty and his colleagues also applied their methods to political affairs, Petty using statistics to argue, for example, that England was potentially a stronger sea power than France, and that London was wealthier than Paris. More generally, the purpose of political arithmetic, as its name suggests, was to provide a science of society, founded on numerical data which would be as free from the influence of sectional interests as mathematics was believed to be.[6]

Thus 'political arithmetic' did not become known as 'statistics' until the late eighteenth century, when the word was borrowed from the German *Statistik*, or 'state-istics'. 'State-istics' had begun in the mid-seventeenth century as straightforward compilations of the population, trade, finance, armed forces and administration of the many statelets which existed in Germany. Over time, scholars had concentrated on presenting numerical information in tabular form for ease of comparison (Lazarsfeld, 1961; Westergaard, 1968).

'State-istics' differed radically from England's political arith-metic. The German work was a systematisation of knowledge, for static and comparative analysis of states, presenting 'snapshots' of their power and capabilities. Political arithmetic, in contrast, was more concerned with past and present changes, with dynamic processes and causal regularities.

Statistics and the rise of industrial capitalism

It was only with the rise of industrial capitalism, however, that statistical knowledge of society was widely developed. The eighteenth century, the heyday of agricultural capitalism in England, saw a decline of political arithmetic which Buck (1977) argues was directly related to the political stability of the times. After the 'Glorious Revolution' of 1688, the monarchy was finally placed under the control of the large landowners; the manufacturing capitalists were too weak to challenge the landed interest, while the industrial working class was still in its embryonic stage.[7] There was no generally felt need among the propertied classes for statistical knowledge to control social conditions; Bills proposing a census (in 1753) and the registration of births, deaths and marriages (in 1758) were rejected by Parliament.

By the beginning of the nineteenth century, circumstances had changed decisively. The first of what were to become ten-yearly censuses of population was eventually held in 1801, by which point industry was growing fast and new centres of population with it. Britain was involved in the Napoleonic wars, a bad harvest had led to soaring food prices, and poverty was widespread. A new and rebellious working class was in the making (Thompson, 1963). Population statistics had many uses to England's rulers: they helped to improve military recruitment policies, to establish the levels of food production and imports that were needed to feed the population, and to estimate the costs of relief for the poor and the dependents of servicemen.

As industry and trade expanded, the state grew in importance. Even in the new age of *laissez faire*, the state had the indispensable and difficult role of securing many of the general conditions in which private industry and trade could thrive. One such condition was the organisation of knowledge about the new, more complex and fast-changing economy and society. The statistical apparatus of the state was expanded and centralised: in 1832 the Statistical Department of the Board of Trade was charged with collating material concerning British 'wealth, commerce and industry'; in 1836 the General Register Office was organised to deal with vital statistics; in 1854 the first official *Statistical Abstract* appeared.

Here the state was often systematising what private individuals had already attempted to provide; but while it developed its statistical apparatus, there were still many areas in which the state did not 'intervene'. The disease and destitution in the big cities were becoming apparent to the middle classes, whose concern with working class conditions was heightened by the new upsurge of workers' activity after 1830 (the previous wave of revolt at the end of the Napoleonic wars had been repressed). During the 1830s, statistical societies were formed by professional men in many British cities, in what Cullen (1975) calls *The Statistical Movement in Early Victorian Britain*.[8]

The gentlemen researchers who belonged to these societies sought knowledge that would establish the kinds of reform necessary to secure a stable hierarchical society, and would be evidence in favour of them. They stressed the virtues of education, which would train the working class in discipline, frugality and self-help, and impart the essentials of political economy as seen by the middle classes (the benefits of *laissez faire*, etc.). While topical issues such as the poor law and public health were followed up, education was probably the most investigated topic: for example, over half the twenty-three original surveys organised by the Manchester Statistical Society in the late 1830s directly concerned schools and schooling. Door-to-door surveys of working people inquired into children's education and the presence of books in the home—but not into family income or hours of work.

The statistical societies' heyday was brief: by the mid-'forties they had abandoned all original empirical research. Their members were interested in building a case for reform, rather than in charting social change. The cost of continuing research must hardly have seemed worthwhile, since the statistics produced hardly constituted adequate material for social control. There were too many divisions among the ruling and middle classes for that, and it was the different interests involved which determined matters, not the exact state of knowledge. Besides, from the middle of the nineteenth century there were several decades of economic expansion and political stability in which reform seemed to proceed at a steady rate. The state began to produce more information on reform issues such as education and public health, but the wave of private statistical studies subsided.

Privately-sponsored research had a later, very major, revival. Towards the end of the nineteenth century, economic depression and the emergence of the new socialist and trade union movements prompted a new wave of poverty studies. The socialist leader H. M. Hyndman documented poverty in London in 1885, provoking Charles Booth into his own studies which were originally intended to show up Hyndman's work as sensationalist. Booth, however, encountered such squalor that he began to argue that only major reforms could stave off the threat of full-blooded socialism. Booth was followed by others such as Bowley and Rowntree, whose work proved significant for subsequent social research—Bowley, for example, developed the sample survey in his work. Other successors included some of the early Fabians who argued for a state-socialist system based on the scientific expertise of trained administrators (Shaw, 1975).

These pioneer efforts finally reached fruition in the twentieth century with the development of the 'welfare' state. The need for a more highly educated, trained and well-maintained workforce in advanced capitalism—particularly in times of war, and during the long boom after the second world war—has been one major reason for this development. The pressure of working-class demands for better education, health and welfare, together with higher and more secure living standards, has been the other main factor. The result is that the state provision desired by the late nineteenth-century reformers has been made on a large scale; with it, their statistical work has been taken over by the various departments of the state, together with the related 'applied' disciplines in academic institutions.

Statistics and modern bureaucracy: explanations and alternatives

In our time, statistical control has become a major activity in the main institutions which dominate society—the large corporations and the state—as well as in virtually every other sort of organisation. Almost all areas of life are subject to one or other sort of bureaucratic control, largely on the basis of statistical knowledge. Such statistics are reviewed in the later sections of this book; what we want to do here is to look at general explanations of the pervasiveness of statistical activity and what conclusions we can draw from our historical survey.

One very influential perspective is offered by the classical sociologist, Max Weber, who saw modern society as based on 'rational capital accounting' in the production of commodities for the market (Weber, 1964). He argued that the ability to make an exact mathematical calculation of all aspects of the situation in a money economy was essential to all 'social actors', for only in this way could they maximise their advantages. Weber saw bureaucracy, which he defined as formally rational organisation based on the principle of recorded information (files), as the inevitable outcome of this sort of society (Weber, 1948). Statistical knowledge is obviously ideally suited to bureaucracy, so defined, since it produces information in standardised, comparable forms which facilitate exact calculation.

Marxists would agree with Weber's argument, but argue further that an economy in which everything is ruled by money arises only when the social relations of production are set in a particular way. When labour, which produces goods, is itself bought and sold on the market like any other good, then all goods are measured in terms of the quantities of labour which are expressed in them. It is the relationship between wage-labour and capital—apparently a market relation although in fact a social relation of exploitation— which makes possible a universal money economy, in which everything can be expressed in comparable quantities and hence can be statistically rationalised. We saw above that it was when commodity production became widespread that recognisably statistical activity emerged; but it is with the domination of industrial capital that statistics become universal.

Second, we would argue that bureaucracy is also the result of these relations in economic life, and the system which is built on them. It is competition between different capitalists to accumulate profits from the labour power of their workers which has led to the concentration of capital in large bureaucratic corporations. In order to compete with their national and international rivals, firms are forced to see workers simply in terms of their contribution to costs, output and consumption. They must seek to 'rationalise' these contributions if they are to survive. For this they need statistical monitoring and control. Similarly, we have seen how the state's development of its statistical apparatus has responded to the social contradictions arising from the industrial capitalist system.

Weber argued that while capital accounting had led to this sort of rationalisation in the first place, and 'the capitalist system has undeniably played a major role in the development of bureaucracy', these processes were no longer peculiar to capitalism. Socialism, he said, would be even more bureaucratic, since this was the most formally rational kind of organisation conceivable. Many people now believe that what has happened in Russia proved Weber only too correct. Russian society is certainly run by large bureaucratic organisations, all under the aegis of one centralised state machine. Planning and decision-making are carried out by relatively few people at the tops of the hierarchies; ordinary working people 'figure' only in the statistics, precisely as the producers and consumers of certain quantities of goods, which others have decided should be produced.

If it were true that Russia (and other countries with similar economic and political systems) were genuinely socialist, the Weberian argument would be valid. But most marxists, apart from the apologists for these states, would argue that the social relation-ships of production have not been fully transformed in these countries. Workers have no more control over the state, and hence over production, than they do in the West. The state, and those who run industry, appear as alien forces controlling them (for a very readable account by a writer who worked in a Hungarian factory, see Haraszti, 1977). Given such social relations, it is not surprising that the statistical rationalisation of society by the state bureaucracy resembles the use of statistics in the West.

We would argue that a socialist alternative to the present uses of statistics can still be created. Socialism in Marx's sense, rather than that of James Callaghan or Leonid Brezhnev, would involve genuinely different social relationships, in production and in all areas of life. We would replace accountancy in terms of money and profit by accountancy in terms of social needs. We would replace the definition of social goals by those at the tops of the bureaucratic pyramids, by democratic self-control over all collective activities. We would then require new ways of measuring our needs and goals, which expressed their great variety rather than reduced them to money values or standards imposed from above.

Notes

1. Struik's *A Concise History of Mathematics* does a remarkable job of relating the development of mathematical concepts to the development of human societies. In it, mathematics is revealed as a set of concepts and techniques that were originated by men and women seeking to solve problems in their world. On modern mathematics, see Hodgkin (1976).
2. In an interesting sidelight on the relationship of quality and quantity, the origins of writing have been traced to early means of record-keeping in ancient Mesopotamia. Around 8,500 B.C. members of a relatively stable economic system began to record shipments of goods by keeping geometric clay pieces indicating the number and type of goods involved. Over the course of several thousand years this led to the inscribing of records on clay tablets—symbols were developed to indicate different goods, numbers, weights and measures (Schmandt-Basserat, 1977).
3. We have outlined here the basic argument of Marx's 'labour theory of value', developed in Volume 1 of *Capital*. Two recent concise accounts of the theory may be found in Mandel (1970) and Fine (1975). Mandel (1975) provides a more detailed outline of economic history.
4. I.e. the accumulation of monetary wealth on the basis of commerce. 'Merchant capital' developed in the later middle ages in Europe, and merchants formed the basis of a new class—the bourgeoisie. 'Merchant capital' is, however, to be distinguished from 'capital' in the modern sense, which is based on capitalist relations of production, and which is sometimes called 'industrial capital'. The period of 'merchant capitalism' is similarly to be distinguished from that of modern ('industrial') capitalism.
5. Probability theory had been developed over the previous two centuries, notably from the analysis of dice games. In 1713, Bernoulli's *Ars Coniectandi* argued for the application of mathematical statistics to social and economic issues.

Accounts of the development of mathematical statistics can be found in the short article by Dudycha and Dudycha (1972), and parts of the books by Walker (1929) and Westergaard (1968). All of these are, however, presented more in terms of the history of ideas than in relation to the interplay with social and economic conditions. On the history of quantification in the social sciences, see Woolf (1961).
6. A valuable study of political arithmeticians by Buck (1977) relates their social goals to the political crises of seventeenth century England and considers their relations with social philosophers such as Robert Boyle and Thomas Hobbes. Strauss's (1954) life of Petty provides insights into his career and milieu, and Westergaard (1968) describes the statistical contributions of political arithmetic. Letwin (1963) focuses on Petty's use of Baconian philosophy, and points out that Jonathan Swift's *Modest Proposal* (1729) is a brilliant satire on the 'value-free', technocratic designs of political arithmetic, particularly Petty's writings on Ireland; it may be read with profit today.
7. The fact that England's 'bourgeois revolution' took place before the emergence of a class of manufacturing capitalists, resulting in the domination of the landed interests, has been much discussed. An influential school of analysts traces many of the peculiarities of British history to this 'premature' birth of the capitalist state. See, e.g., Nairn (1977), and the bibliography of relevant literature in Pateman (1972).
8. Several sociological analyses of these societies have been written: as well as Cullen (1975), see Abrams (1968), Cole (1972) and Ebesh (1972). This wave of social research is by no means the only example of reformers turning to statistics in the hope of heading off social unrest: Le Play and Quetelet, whose contributions to quantitative sociology are assessed by Lazarsfeld (1961) are further examples. It is not difficult to draw analogies between the Victorian statistical movement and the 'social indicators movement' that surfaced in the United States during the social unrest of the 1960s.

Bibliography

Abrams, P., 1968, *The Origins of British Sociology*, Chicago, University of Chicago Press.

Aston, T. (ed.), 1965, *Crisis in Europe, 1560–1600*, London, Routledge & Kegan Paul.

Buck, P., 1977, 'Seventeenth century political arithmetic: civil strife and vital statistics', *Isis*, vol. 68, pp. 67–84.

Cartwright, F. F., 1977, *A Social History of Medicine*, London, Longmans.

Clark, G. N., 1938, *Guide to English Commercial Statistics, 1696–1782*, London, Royal Historical Society.

Clark, G. N., 1948, *Science and Social Welfare in the Age of Newton*, London, Oxford University Press.

Cole, S., 1972, 'Continuity and institutionalisation in science: a case study of failure', in Oberschall (ed.), 1972, below.

Cullen, M. J., 1975, *The Statistical Movement in Early Victorian Britain*, Hassocks, Harvester Press.

Dudycha, A. L., and Dudycha, L. W., 1972, 'Behavioural Statistics: a historical perspective', in Roger E. Kirk (ed.) *Statistical Issues*, Monterey, California, Brooks-Cole.

Ebesh, D., 1972, 'The Manchester Statistical Society', in A. Oberschall (ed.), 1972, below.

Fine, B., 1975, *Marx's Capital*, London, Macmillan.

Glass, D. V., 1973, *Numbering the People*, Farnborough, Hants., Saxon House.

Haraszti, M., 1977, *A Worker in a Worker's State*, Harmondsworth, Penguin.

Howe, G. M., 1972, *Man, Environment and Disease in Britain*, London, David and Charles.

Hodgkin, L., 1976, 'Politics and physical sciences', *Radical Science Journal*, no.4.

Kendall, M. G., 1970, 'Where shall the history of statistics begin?', in E. S. Pearson and M. G. Kendall (eds.), 1970, below.

Kendall, M. G., and Plackett, R. L. (eds.), 1975, *Studies in the History of Probability and Statistics*, vol. 2, London, Griffin.

Lazarsfield, P. F., 1961, 'Notes on the history of quantification in sociology – trends, sources and problems', in H. Woolf (ed.), 1961, below.

Letwin, W., 1963, *The Origins of Scientific Economics*, London, Methuen.

Mandel, E., 1970, *An Introduction to Marxist Economic Theory*, New York, Pathfinder Press.

Mandel, E., 1975, *Marxist Economic Theory* (in one volume), London, Merlin Press.

Marchal, J., 1948, 'The state and the budget', *Public Finance*, vol. 3, no. 1.

Marx, K., *Capital* (in 3 volumes) London, Lawrence and Wishart; vol. 1 paperback, Harmondsworth, Penguin/New Left Review.

Nairn, T., 1977, *The Break-up of Britain*, London, New Left Books.

Oberschall, A. (ed.), 1972, *The Establishment of Empirical Sociology*, New York, Harper and Row.

Parker, G., 1974, 'The emergence of modern finance in Europe 1500–1730', in Carlo M. Cippola (ed.), *The Fontana Economic History of Europe*, vol. 2, London, Fontana.

Pateman, T. (ed.), 1972, *Counter-Course*, Harmondsworth, Penguin.

Pearson, E. S., and Kendall, M. G. (eds.), 1970, *Studies in the History of Probability and Statistics*, London, Griffin.

Raynes, H. E., 1964, *A History of British Insurance*, London, Pitman.

Schmandt-Basserat, D., 1977, reported in 'From reckoning to writing', *Scientific American*, vol. 237, no. 2.

Shaw, M., 1975, *Marxism and Social Science*, London, Pluto Press.

Strauss, E., 1954, *Sir William Petty*, London, Bodley Head.

Struik, D., 1956, *A Concise History of Mathematics*, London, G. Bell.

Swift, J., 1729, 'A modest proposal . . .', in *Gulliver's Travels and Other Writings*, ed. M. K. Starkman, 1962, New York, Bantam.

Thompson, E. P., 1963, *The Making of the English Working Class*, Harmondsworth, Penguin.

Walker, H. M., 1929, *Studies in the History of Statistical Method*, Baltimore, Williams and Wilkins.

Weber, M., 1948, 'Bureaucracy', in H. H. Gerth and C. Wright Mills (eds.), *From Max Weber*, London, Routledge & Kegan Paul.

Weber, M., 1964, *The Theory of Economic and Social Organisation*, New York, Free Press.

Westergaard, H., 1968, *Contributions to the History of Statistics*, New York, Agathon (reprint of 1932 edition).

Woolf, H. (ed.), 1961, *Quantification*, Indianapolis, Bobbs-Merrill.

4.

Donald MacKenzie

Eugenics and the Rise of Mathematical Statistics in Britain

Many people who are prepared to admit that the *use* of statistical techniques in particular instances may be ideological, hold firmly that the techniques in themselves are always neutral. This chapter will cast doubt on this assumption, examining a crucial episode in the development of modern mathematical statistics, the rise of a 'British school' of statistical theory between the 1870s and the 1920s. I shall argue that the rise of this school, which was led by Francis Galton, Karl Pearson and, at the end of this period, R. A. Fisher, and the type of statistical theory they developed, in part reflected features of the culture and ideology of British society in this period. The point is not that the techniques developed by this school necessarily continue to reflect, in their contemporary use, the conditions of their origin. To argue this would be to commit the 'genetic fallacy' of assuming that the present function of an activity is necessarily the same as its original function. I want to establish, from this one instance, that there is nothing in statistical theory that makes it immune from this kind of analysis. Mathematical techniques are not necessarily neutral.

Some readers of the following account will immediately recognise many of the themes: class differences, intelligence, heredity. This is not surprising, because in the period discussed lie the historical origins of the debate about race, class and intelligence. Francis Galton (1869) suggested that there was an individual, definable, inherited and measurable entity called 'mental ability'. Karl Pearson (1903) designed the first major attempt to *prove* it to be inherited. R. A. Fisher (1918) provided the first estimate of 'heritability' (though of height, not intelligence).

This work should be seen not as neutral psychological and genetic investigation, but as the work of people with clear social and political goals which were largely *prior* to their scientific researches. For example, Galton was quite convinced that 'intelligence' was inherited and followed a normal distribution, and that the way to improve society was to increase the fertility of the 'able' and decrease that of the 'unfit', long before any method of measuring 'intelligence' was suggested (Galton, 1865, 1869).

The social and political programme embraced by these three leading statisticians was eugenics. All three believed that the class structure of Britain reflected in large part a hierarchy of innate ability, at the top of which were the élite of the professional middle class and at the bottom of which were the poor, unemployed and 'criminal'. All three believed that the professional middle class should be encouraged to have more children, and that the 'unfit' should be discouraged (and perhaps ultimately prevented) from propagating. In this they were not alone. The eugenics movement, especially after 1900, was a prominent part of British intellectual life.

The eugenics movement was composed almost exclusively of members of the professional middle class, and its ideology reflected certain crucial aspects of the situation of this group (Farrall, 1970; Searle, 1976; MacKenzie, 1976). It owed its social standing not to its ownership of capital or land, but to its possession of educational qualifications and supposedly uniquely valuable knowledge and mental skills. Its situation of privilege as compared with manual workers was justified in terms of the assumed superiority of 'mental' over 'manual' labour. The eugenists' focus on individual mental ability as the determinant of social standing, and their assumption that this was unequally distributed and to be found in greatest quantity amongst the children of the successful of the previous generation, can be seen as an attempt (even if largely unconscious) to legitimate the social situation of the professional middle class. The social division between 'mental' and 'manual' labour was, according to the eugenists, the reflection of natural, genetic, differences between types of people (see, e.g., Pearson, 1902).

At the same time, the eugenists had a solution (which might be described as a biological version of a technological 'fix') for one of the major problems faced by the British establishment. At the end of the nineteenth century and the beginning of the twentieth, the focus of establishment fears was not the working class as a whole, but the unemployed and semi-employed in the large urban centres, especially London (see Jones, 1971). Unlike the bulk of 'respectable' workers who were seen as largely integrated into the system, this group was seen as politically volatile, liable to outbursts of rioting, mentally inferior, and physically degenerate (e.g., Pearson, 1881). Britain's failures in international competition, difficulties in army recruitment, and even British military defeats in the Boer War were attributed to this 'residuum', as it was called (e.g., White, 1901;

Gilbert, 1966, pp. 85 ff.). Early attempts by the social workers of the Charity Organisation Society to control this group had failed; more drastic solutions such as moving the poor out of the slums into labour colonies were proposed even by 'humanitarians' such as Charles Booth (Jones, 1971, pp. 305–8). The eugenists' proposals to restrict the mentally defective, the alcoholic and the chronic poor to institutions so as to prevent them breeding did not, in such a climate, seem extreme. Eugenists argued that the 'residuum' was a distinct hereditary group (see, e.g., Galton's (1909) analysis of Booth's data on the London poor): by preventing them from breeding, it could be ensured that the next generation of workers would be fit and loyal. The Fabian, Sidney Ball, could argue for

> a process of conscious social selection by which the industrial residuum is naturally sifted and made manageable for some kind of restorative, disciplinary, or, it may be 'surgical treatment'. (Quoted in Jones, 1971, p. 333).

The eugenists proposed to bring the science of the biologist, statistician and doctor to bear on this process of 'sifting': to replace the vagaries of 'natural selection' by a 'scientific' artificial selection.

Francis Galton (1822–1911) coined the term 'eugenics'. His work in statistics, genetics and the psychology of individual differences derived largely from his central passionate concern for racial improvement (Cowan, 1972 a and b, 1977). His key statistical innovations, the concepts of regression and correlation, arose from his eugenic research—directly in the case of regression, indirectly in the case of correlation. As a eugenist, he was interested in predicting the characteristics (say, the height) of offspring from those of their parents. The technique of regression enabled him to do this[1] (Galton, 1877, 1886). Work on a scheme for the personal identification of criminals took him from the concept of regression to that of correlation (Galton, 1888).

Karl Pearson (1857–1936) developed Galton's notions of regression and correlation into a systematic theory. Galton had evaluated his coefficients graphically: Pearson derived formulae for doing so. Galton had worked with only 2 variables: Pearson generalised the theory to any number of variables (thus making it theoretically possible to take account of the entire ancestry of an individual in predicting her or his characteristics). He established an institutional base for British statistics at University College, London, where he was a professor, recruited and taught many students who were to become important statisticians, and for 35 years edited *Biometrika*, building it into the world's leading journal of statistical theory (E. S. Pearson, 1938). This work was motivated by a set of political and intellectual beliefs which he had held prior to becoming a statistician (and, indeed, which largely led him to become one) (Norton, 1978).

Pearson developed and championed perhaps the most coherent form of eugenic ideology, integrating it into a framework of social Darwinism, Fabianism and positivism. As a social Darwinist, he believed that the theory of evolution by natural selection applied to human societies, though he claimed that what were selected were not primarily individuals, but nations. Trading rivalry and war were seen as the struggle for survival between nations (Pearson, 1901); to achieve national fitness called for planning. As a Fabian (though never in fact a member of the Fabian Society), Pearson believed in gradual advance towards socialism by the use and extension of the existing state apparatus and the replacement of the bourgeoisie by technical experts and administrators (Pearson, 1888, Chs. 11 and 12; Pearson, 1902). As a positivist, he believed that only science was worthy of the name knowledge, and that science should seek only to describe appearances, 'the routine of perceptions', not using theoretical concepts unless these can be shown to be reducible to sets of observational data (Pearson, 1892). Pearson sought to construct a theory of evolution which would serve as the key social and political science (Pearson, 1900 a, p. 468). He hoped to provide a scientific basis for planned social intervention: for example, for a eugenic programme. This basis had to be properly scientific in his terms, which meant positivist and quantitative. Hence he wanted to give Darwin's rather loose concepts an exact mathematical form. Most of his statistical theory was developed in this attempt and is to be found in a long series of papers entitled 'Mathematical Contributions to the Theory of Evolution' (e.g. Pearson, 1896).

Although R. A. Fisher (1890–1962) belongs to a later generation, eugenics played an important part in his earlier work. His interest in statistics and genetics developed largely as a result of his extra-curricular undergraduate involvement with the Cambridge University Eugenics Society. A folder of that Society's records, found in the library of the Eugenics Society in London, reveals Fisher to have been one of the driving forces behind it. He quickly read, mastered and went beyond Pearson's work. Thus a paper read to the Society in 1911 ('Heredity: Comparing the Methods of Biometry and Mendelism') already pointed in the direction that took him to heritability estimates and the statistical technique of the analysis of variance. His eugenic interests remained in his later work on population genetics: thus his classic *Genetical*

Theory of Natural Selection (1930) concluded with several chapters on eugenics.

Not all British statisticians of this period were motivated by an interest in eugenics. Yule (of Yule's Q) and Gosset ('Student' of the t-test), for instance, were not. I shall discuss below some of the differences between the ways in which statisticians who were and were not eugenists developed the theory of statistics. There were also differences in terms of their organisational importance between men like Galton and Pearson, on the one hand, and Yule and Gosset on the other. Galton and Pearson were organisational leaders. Pearson in particular played the key role of 'intellectual entrepreneur' and builder of the discipline (teaching Yule and Gosset, for example). He was able to do this in large part because of the connection between statistics and eugenics. Though the department he founded in 1911 was called the Department of Applied Statistics, his chair had been established and funded as a chair of Eugenics. An appeal for funds for a building for his department was supported by a leader in *The Times* of 7 October 1911 on the following grounds:

> The state of morals and of intelligence disclosed by the recent strikes, the state of health of the rising industrial populations as disclosed by the medical inspections of schools are alike in showing the need for the study and application of Eugenics. (quoted by E. S. Pearson, 1938).

Up to this point my analysis has been in terms of individual motivation and institutional development. This, however, can only provide a background to the central question of the effect of social and cultural factors such as eugenics on the technical content of statistical theory. Might statistical theory not have developed in the way it did anyway, even had the eugenics movement not existed? Perhaps it was only incidental that some British statisticians happened to be eugenists, and they left this behind when they took up their pencils to write down formulae.

Hilts (1973) implicitly asks this question when he considers Galton's statistical work. He argues that Galton's concepts were a revolutionary breakthrough from the approach of such earlier statisticians as Quetelet and the mathematicians interested in the treatment of observational errors. There is no reason to suppose that workers in this earlier tradition would eventually have developed the concepts of regression and correlation. Some 'error theorists' did produce similar mathematical formalisms (Bravais, 1846; Schols, 1886): but they handled and interpreted these quite differently. For the error theorists, statistical variation was error: it was to be eliminated. For Galton, the eugenist, it was the source of racial progress. For Bravais and Schols statistical dependence (the value of one variable depending on that of another) was a nuisance. Good experimental technique should provide independent observations. For Galton, statistical dependence (son's height depending on father's height) was what made eugenics possible. Thus Galton, because he was a eugenist, worked in a different framework of meanings and assumptions from his predecessors: he developed the theory of statistics in ways that would have seemed pointless to them.

Differences of opinion *within* the British statistical community are of particular interest in throwing light on the relations between statistics and eugenics, for here we have an instance of people with similar technical backgrounds disputing how best to develop statistical theory. By far the most bitter dispute (at least before 1914) was a controversy between Pearson and Yule over how best to measure the association between nominal variables (i.e. those variables for which no scale of measurement is available, which can at best be classified into different categories)[2]. The ordinary coefficient of correlation as developed by Galton and Pearson applies only to interval variables such as height, where a scale of measurement exists. Thus British statisticians needed a new approach to deal with problems such as, for example, that of measuring the relationship between being vaccinated and one's chances of surviving an epidemic. Here we have two variables, both nominal. Individuals are either vaccinated (X_1) or unvaccinated (X_2); and either survive an epidemic (Y_1) or die in it (Y_2). We arrange our data in the form of a four-fold table:

	X_1	X_2	
Y_1	a	b	a + b
Y_2	c	d	c + d
	a + c	b + d	N

Thus a individuals are vaccinated and survive, b are un-vaccinated but still survive, c are vaccinated but die, d are unvaccinated and die. How does one measure the association between vaccination (X) and survival (Y)? The problem was not simply to produce an *ad hoc* measure for a particular problem such as this, but to develop a general 'coefficient of association' which could be used in all such four-fold tables, whatever they referred to.

Yule (1900) approached the problem by laying down three criteria that a coefficient of association must meet. First, it should be zero if the table indicates no association between X and Y. Second, it should be +1 if there is perfect positive association between X and Y (if, for example, c=0 and all the vaccinated survive). Third, it should be −1 if there is perfect negative association between X and Y (if, for example, a=0, and all the vaccinated die). He put forward his coefficient

$$Q = \frac{ad - bc}{ad+bc}$$

and showed that it fulfilled these three conditions. But he was aware that Q was by no means the only coefficient that would do this (e.g., Q^3, Q^5, etc., also do so). Indeed Yule (1912) later put forward other coefficients of a similar type to measure association; he was able to advance only loose pragmatic arguments as to which to use for a given table.

Pearson (1900b) argued differently. He proceeded not empirically, but theoretically. He proceeded *as if*, for example, X were height and Y were weight—both of which are normally distributed interval variables (i.e. variables which can be measured on a scale of some sort). X_1 might be 'tall', and X_2 'short', with a cut-off point at, say, 72 inches. Y might be 'heavy' (weighing more than 160 lb), Y_2 'light' (less than 160 lb). Height and weight, being interval variables, have an ordinary coefficient of correlation. Pearson showed that it was possible, mathematically, to estimate the value of that coefficient knowing only a, b, c, d (the numbers of 'tall' and 'heavy' individuals, and so on). The procedure for doing this is long and complicated and does not give rise to a simple formula, such as that for Yule's Q. Now, if Pearson really had been dealing with interval variables like height and weight, the process would have been uncontentious.[3] His suggestion, however, was that this procedure should be used for *nominal* variables (such as vaccination and survival) by *assuming* that the given four-fold table had in fact arisen (as in the height and weight example) by applying a cut-off to more basic interval variables. In the majority of cases this could only be a theoretical assumption, and could not be proven. Yule argued that individuals were either dead or alive, and it was difficult to imagine a continuous variable of which these are subdivisions in the same way as tall and short are subdivisions of height. Pearson could reply that 'dead' and 'alive' corresponded to divisions of an underlying continuous variable 'severity of attack'. He had not, however, any way of proving that such underlying variables as severity of attack were normally distributed (and this was necessary for his coefficient to be valid)[4]. How did he (as a positivist, and opposed in general terms to theoretical assumptions of this kind) come to be in this situation?

His approach (which he called the tetrachoric method) makes sense if we look at it in the overall context of his work, in particular in terms of the relationship between statistics and eugenics. For interval characteristics such as height, Pearson had a measure of what he called 'the strength of heredity'. He would take a group of families, measure the heights of parents and those of offspring (or the heights of pairs of brothers or sisters) and work out the ordinary coefficient of correlation. The correlation of parental and offspring heights was, for him, the strength of heredity for height. It is interesting to note that this definition (Pearson, 1896, p. 259) assumes implicitly that resemblances between parental and offspring heights are entirely genetic and that, for example, similar nutrition does not play a part. But Pearson was already a convinced hereditarian and confident that the value of this coefficient of correlation reflected the genetic connection of parent and child, and not any similarities in environment. He had, however, a technical problem. Many characteristics of eugenic importance were not measurable in the way height is. The Binet scale of intelligence had yet to be invented; the best he had to go on was teachers' classifications of pupils into broad categories ('intelligent', 'slow', and so on). Similarly eye colour (which was of theoretical importance because even environmentalists would agree that it was not influenced by environment) was not measurable, even though eyes could be classed into 'brown', 'blue', and so on. Pearson wanted to measure the 'strength of heredity' for such characteristics, and compare it with the values he had already obtained for characteristics such as height; to do this he developed the tetrachoric method.

A coefficient such as Yule's Q would not have served his purposes, because there is no way a value of Q can be validly compared to that of an ordinary coefficient of correlation, not even if we produce a four-fold table from the height data by dividing into 'tall', 'short', etc., because the value of Q varies considerably according to where we take the arbitrary cut-off point. A coefficient obtained by the tetrachoric method *can*, however, be compared with an ordinary coefficient, if one grants the assumption that the observed nominal data were in fact generated from underlying interval variables for which the ordinary coefficient of correlation was meaningful.

Pearson was thus able to use the tetrachoric method in the following way (Pearson, 1903). He had found the ordinary correlation of the height of pairs of brothers (say) to be about 0.5. Using teachers' judgements he would class each of a pair of brothers as either 'bright' or 'dull', and work out the tetrachoric coefficient of correlation for sets of brothers. Doing this for a wide range of mental and physical characteristics, measuring correlation by the ordinary method when the characteristics were interval and by the tetrachoric method when they were nominal, he found values of the coefficients closely clustering round 0.5. Thus he concluded that the 'strength of heredity' of all these characteristics was equal, and as the list included eye-colour (on which presumably heredity was the only influence), he felt the eugenic argument to be proven. The way to improve the British race for survival in international competition was by eugenic measures, not environmental reform (Pearson, 1903, p. 207).

I would argue, then, that it was the needs of Pearson's research programme in heredity and eugenics that led him to choose to measure association in this way (and not, say, in the way developed by Yule, who was not a eugenist). Of course this was only one aspect of the development of statistical theory in this period (though it was the single statistical topic that occupied most of Pearson's energy in the period from 1900 to 1914). But this instance, together with such others as Galton's work on regression, demonstrates the influence of eugenics on the development of statistical theory as a system of knowledge.

Eugenics was not, however, to remain for long the dominant influence on British statistical theory. The needs of industrial and agricultural production came, from the 1900s onward, to play an increasing role, as seen for example in Fisher's work in the 1920s at the Rothamsted agricultural research station and the establishment by E. S. Pearson and others of an 'Industrial and Agricultural Research Section' of the Royal Statistical Society in 1933. These new needs led to new theoretical developments. Thus E. S. Pearson (1939) showed how the demands of W. S. Gosset's work as an industrial scientist for Guinness Brewers led him to focus on small sample statistics (as distinct from the large samples of humans, plants and animals dealt with by Karl Pearson) and thus to develop new concepts and techniques (notably the t-distribution). To follow through these new developments would however take us far beyond the period considered here and the scope of this chapter.

The general conclusion to be drawn is, I think, that it is mistaken to see statistical theory as a field of knowledge developing simply by its own internal logic and giving rise to necessarily value-free techniques. Rather, statistical theory has evolved in historical interaction with conceptual change in other sciences, with the needs of production and with theological (Hacking, 1975), political (Baker, 1975) and ideological developments. It is a social, historical and ideological product and not merely a collection of neutral techniques.

Notes

1. Thus he could say that if a father had a height x inches above the average, then his son would have a height bx inches above the average, where b is a constant that can be evaluated from empirical data (the 'coefficient of regression').

2. This controversy is discussed in more detail in MacKenzie, 1978.

3. Even though it would have been redundant, as much better ways of estimating the ordinary coefficient of correlation were known.

4. In fact an even stronger assumption, that the two underlying variables jointly follow a bi-variate normal distribution, is necessary.

Further Reading

The most accessible sources of information on the history of statistical theory are two large but expensive collections of articles (Pearson and Kendall, 1970; Kendall and Plackett, 1977). Karl Pearson's mammoth biography of Galton (1914–30) remains a valuable resource and the more recent Forest (1974) should also be consulted. Egon Pearson (1938) and C. Eisenhart (1974) are the best sources on Karl Pearson. The collected papers of R. A. Fisher (1971–74) contain many of his eugenic as well as statistical writings. There is also a huge bulk of unpublished material that can be consulted (letters, etc.), much of it collected in the Galton and Pearson archives at University College, London.

Bibliography

Baker, R. M., 1975, *Condorcet: from Natural Philosophy to Social Mathematics*, Chicago, University of Chicago Press.

Bravais, A., 1846, 'Analyse mathématique sur les probabilités des erreurs de situation d'un point', *Mémoire présentés par Divers Savants a l'Académie Royale des Sciences de l'Institut de France*, vol. 9, pp. 255–332.

Cowan, R. S., 1972a, 'Francis Galton's statistical ideas: the influence of eugenics', *Isis*, vol. 63, pp. 509–28.

Cowan, R. S., 1972b, 'Francis Galton's contribution to genetics.' *Journal of the History of Biology*, vol. 5, pp. 389–412.

Cowan, R. S., 1977, 'Nature and nurture: the interplay of biology and politics in the work of Francis Galton', *'Studies in History of Biology*, vol. 1, pp. 133–208.

Eisenhart, C., 1974, 'Pearson, Karl', in C. C. Gillispie (ed.), *Dictionary of Scientific Biography*, vol. 10. New York, Scribner's.

Farrall, L. A., 1970, *The Origins and Growth of the English Eugenics Movement, 1865-1925*, Ph.D. thesis, Indiana University, Bloomington.

Fisher, R. A., 1918, 'The correlation between relatives on the supposition of Mendelian inheritance', *Transactions of the Royal Society of Edinburgh*, vol. 52, pp. 399-433.

Fisher, R. A., 1930, *The Genetical Theory of Natural Selection*, Oxford, Clarendon.

Fisher, R. A., 1971-74, *Collected Papers* (ed. J. H. Bennett), Adelaide, University of Adelaide.

Forest, D. W., 1974, *Francis Galton: The Life and Work of a Victorian Genius*, London, Elek.

Galton, F., 1865, 'Hereditary talent and character'. *Macmillan's Magazine*, vol. 12, pp. 157-66 and pp. 318-27.

Galton, F., 1869, *Hereditary Genius*, London, Macmillan.

Galton, F., 1877, 'Typical laws of heredity', *Proceedings of the Royal Institution*, vol. 8, pp. 282-301.

Galton, F., 1886, 'Family likeness in stature'. *Proceedings of the Royal Society of London*, vol. 40, pp. 42-73.

Galton, F., 1888, 'Correlations and their measurement, chiefly from anthropometric data'. *Proceedings of the Royal Society of London*, vol. 45, pp. 135-45.

Galton, F., 1909, 'The possible improvement of the human breed, under the existing conditions of law and sentiment', in his *Essays in Eugenics*, pp. 1-34, London, Eugenics Education Society.

Gilbert, B., 1966, *The Evolution of National Insurance in Great Britain*, London, Michael Joseph.

Hacking, I., 1975, *The Emergence of Probability*, Cambridge, Cambridge University Press.

Hilts, V., 1973, 'Statistics and social science', in R. N. Giere and R. S. Westfall (eds.), *Foundations of the Scientific Method: the Nineteenth Century*, pp. 206-33, Bloomington, University of Indiana.

Jones, G. Stedman-, 1971, *Outcast London*, Oxford, Clarendon Press.

Kendall, M. G. and Plackett, R. L. (eds.), 1977, *Studies in the History of Statistics, and Probability*, vol. 2, London, Griffin.

MacKenzie, D., 1976, 'Eugenics in Britain', *Social Studies of Science*, vol. 6, pp. 499-532.

MacKenzie, D., 1978, 'Statistical theory and social interests: a case study', *Social Studies of Science*, vol. 8, pp. 35-83.

Norton, B., 1978, 'Karl Pearson and statistics: the social origins of scientific innovation', *Social Studies of Science*, vol. 8, pp. 3-34.

Pearson, E. S., 1938, *Karl Pearson: an Appreciation of some Aspects of his Life and Work*, Cambridge, Cambridge University Press.

Pearson, E. S., 1939, ' "Student" as a statistician', *Biometrika*, vol. 30; reprinted in E. S. Pearson and M. G. Kendall (eds.), 1970, below.

Pearson, E. S. and Kendall, M. G. (eds.), 1970, *Studies in the History of Statistics and Probability*, London, Griffin.

Pearson, K., 1881, 'Anarchy', *The Cambridge Review*, vol. 2, pp. 268-70.

Pearson, K., 1888, *The Ethic of Freethought*, London, Unwin.

Pearson, K., 1892, *The Grammar of Science*, London, Scott.

Pearson, K., 1896, 'Mathematical contributions to the theory of evolution, III: regression, heredity and panmixia', *Philosophical Transactions of the Royal Society of London*, A, vol. 187, pp. 253-318.

Pearson, K., 1900a, *The Grammar of Science*, 2nd edn., London, Black.

Pearson, K., 1900b, 'Mathematical contributions to the theory of evolution. VII: on the correlation of characters not quantitatively measurable'. *Philosophical Transactions of the Royal Society of London*, A, vol. 195, pp. 1–47.

Pearson, K., 1901, *National Life from the Standpoint of Science*, London, Black.

Pearson, K., 1902, 'Prefatory Essay. The function of science in the modern state.' *Encyclopedia Britannica*, 10th ed., vol. 32, pp. vii–xxxvii. Volume 8 of new volumes.

Pearson, K., 1903, 'On the inheritance of the mental and moral characters in man, and its comparison with the inheritance of the physical characters. The Huxley Lecture for 1903'. *Journal of the Anthropological Institute of Great Britain and Ireland*, vol. 33, pp. 179–237.

Pearson, K., 1914–30, *The Life, Letters and Labours of Francis Galton*, Cambridge, Cambridge University Press.

Schols, C. M., 1886, 'Théorie des erreurs dans le plan et dans l'espace'. *Annales de l'Ecole Polytechnique de Delft*, vol. 2, pp. 123–78 (first published in Dutch in 1875).

Searle, G., 1976, *Eugenics and Politics in Britain 1900–1914*, Leyden, Noordhoff.

White, A., 1901, *Efficiency and Empire*, London, Methuen.

Yule, G. U., 1900, 'On the association of attributes in statistics', reprinted in Stuart and Kendall (eds.), *The Statistical Papers of George Udny Yule*, pp. 7–69. London, Griffin.

Yule, G. U., 1912, 'On the methods of measuring association between two attributes.' Reprinted in Stuart and Kendall (eds.), *The Statistical Papers of George Udny Yule*, pp. 107–70, London, Griffin.

Section Two:
Of Knowledge and Numbers

Science and its technological products provide both a material and ideological framework for contemporary capitalist society. As a powerful way of developing knowledge about the world, science has been elevated to the central role once held by religion. The application of the methods of the natural sciences to human affairs provide, it is often argued, a means of resolving many of the problems facing society. Indeed, these problems are sometimes seen as a consequence of people not being sufficiently scientific, and letting emotional and political factors interfere with reason. Statistics is often presented as a way to make social analysis more scientific.

In the first chapter in this section, John Krige takes issue with the equation of statistical data with 'objective facts'. He argues that all too often such data derive from the same conceptual framework as that which informs 'commonsense' views of the world. Given that commonsense is generally little more than a rationalisation of the ideology of the *status quo*—bourgeois ideology—then statistical data can (and often do) serve to reinforce such uncritically accepted tenets of everyday life. He uses the example of sexism to illustrate how social theory is integral to attempts to change or preserve social practices and to suggest therefore that critical scientific knowledge needs to be more than commonsense or passive contemplation. Although radicals invariably face problems when confronted with statistical data produced within the society they seek to criticise and change, there are, as Krige shows, important ways in which they may use such data in their theory and practice.

Bob Young's chapter focusses on the role of quantification in science. He provides a convincing demonstration that the firm distinctions often drawn between fact and value, and science and non-science, in the dominant conception of knowledge, are themselves historically relative notions. He points out furthermore, that these distinctions reflect and support an exploitative capitalist social system. Therefore, the supposed non-neutrality of scientific and statistical practices must be challenged by radicals. Young, thus, simultaneously challenges the status typically accorded to quantitative data and raises the possibility of developing radically different forms of science.

Russell Keat then provides an introduction to, and critique of, positivism in the social sciences. As Keat points out, the positivist approach often supports the empiricist use of statistics, and is often oriented towards the prediction and control, rather than the explanation, of social processes. The treatment of human social activity as basically analogous to the motion of objects deterministically obeying physical laws which often accompanies this must be challenged and rejected if we are to develop a radical social science.

The concluding chapter of this section carries the discussion of these issues in the philosophy of science to the analysis and critique of the techniques of mathematical statistics. Liz Atkins and David Jarrett show that significance testing is often used as if it were a mechanical guarantor of scientific objectivity, an automatic detector of lawlike regularities in social statistics. They demonstrate that not only are these tests applied both with technical ineptitude and to trivial issues in much social science research, but also that they are often used to attach a spurious certainty to inadequate theories and accounts of social processes.

Together, these four chapters point to ways in which we must develop our criticism of the uses of empirical data. By demonstrating that knowledge is fundamentally a social and historical product, they help us appraise the social relations involved in the production and use of statistical data and techniques. This is essential if we are to assess the usefulness and limitations of social statistics.

5.

John Krige

What's so Great about Facts?

In a study of the attitudes of nine- to eleven-year-olds in our culture towards toys, 97% of the boys and 100% of the girls thought that a doll was an exclusively feminine toy (Oakley, 1976, pp. 190–1)[1]. One could hardly hope for a less controversial or more seemingly obvious fact. Empirical research informed by statistical methods has here produced evidence on children's attitudes to toys —evidence which can be used with confidence by those who want to analyse the forces which steer boys and girls into different social roles.

One way in which a fact such as this is used is to confirm the view that women are biologically or naturally equipped to play the role of mother. In her attachment and concern for the doll, it may be argued, we have one of the earliest manifestations of a girl's maternal instinct. Child-rearing is a basic biological necessity for the female; it is satisfied only when she has children of her own to care for. Playing with dolls anticipates the future in which the child, then adult, will minister to her own offspring. Furthermore, the argument continues, the attention which her future offspring will need as children and which she will need to give them as a mother requires that she be both wife and domesticated. Only in the security of a home and provided for by a husband, will she have the time and opportunity to fulfil herself as a woman, and that by devoting herself to her family.

The stated numerical facts appear not only to be evidence *for* the view that motherhood is a biological necessity for women, and that it is a role most satisfactorily played out in the nuclear family. They can also be taken as evidence *against* the feminist argument which contends that not all women need to be mothers, and that those who are not are not necessarily frustrated, emotionally disturbed or unfulfilled in some way because a basic biological instinct has been thwarted. Women, so this argument runs, do not need to have children to lead satisfying lives; nor do children need mothers, as such, if they are to grow into well-rounded people.

Rather, a caring and supportive environment is what counts during childhood, and this can readily be provided by mothers or fathers, or by structures and institutions other than the nuclear family unit.

Facts as self-evident as that a doll is a 'feminine' toy in our culture play an important role in the struggle between these two theories. The data in Table 1, which are extracted from a more extensive table given by Oakley (1975, p. 53), extend the earlier example, and are as unsurprising. The table lists the estimates made by a group of young psychology students as to the desirability of

Table 1: **Desirability of particular toys for boys and girls**

Toy	*Rating*
Football	1.5
Construction set	2.7
Sports car	3.6
Banjo	4.5
Roller skates	5.3
Blackboard	5.3
Teddy bear	5.8
Skipping rope	7.0
Sewing machine	8.2
Doll wardrobe	8.7

particular toys for girls and boys. The ratings run from 1 (strongly masculine) through 5 (appropriate for both sexes) to 9 (strongly feminine), and were found to be highly predictive of the choices actually made by the children of each sex. The toys preferred by boys link them to the exciting and adventurous world outside the home, with an emphasis on physical and mechanical activity. The toys preferred by girls, on the other hand, confine their world to the relatively safe and mundane domestic interior, with an associated emphasis on domesticity and caring for others. These choices reflect temperamental differences between the sexes, themselves allegedly biologically based, to which the sexual division of labour is a 'natural' response. As Oakley notes,

> Only the *everyday observation* of men and women in society is needed to 'prove' that differences of personality follow the biological differences of sex. Men are more aggressive and independent than women; they are braver, more outgoing and extroverted, confident in their own ability to control and manipulate the external environment. Women are more sensitive and perceptive in their relationships with other people; they are more dependent on these relationships. They are introverted and domesticated and emotionally labile. (1975, p. 49, my emphasis).

So much for the facts.

Facts and values

The weight of evidence in favour of the view that motherhood and domesticity are natural and inescapable female roles is thus substantial. Rooted in everyday observation, built into contemporary common-sense about women in our culture, and confirmed by statistical procedures, the facts appear to provide incontrovertible *support* for the notion that these roles are biologically determined— that they are part of what it is to be female. Correlatively, they *undermine* the feminist view that the roles of housewife and mother are socially constructed, not biologically ordained. In so doing they buttress a theory which reflects and reinforces the existing social order. Feminist theory, critical of that order, seems to run counter to everyday observation, to common-sense, and to the statistical results of research such as that reported above.

A general and crucially important feature of facts thus immediately comes to light: that *facts have evaluative implications*. They comprise, or are wielded as, *reasons* for or against particular points of view, which they accordingly buttress or discredit. It is thus quite wrong to think that statisticians, whose business includes establishing facts and their degree of reliability, are engaged in a value-neutral activity. In common with all sciences, statistical results, while not morally evaluative, evaluate theories, and the acceptance of those theories (as well as the associated practices) from what may be called a rational point of view. For example, in the argument under consideration, observations that girls and not boys play with dolls or sewing machines are advanced as reasons for thinking that females are endowed with a maternal instinct. Those who resist this inference are accordingly dismissed as irrational and 'emotive'—just what you'd expect of a woman! The statistical evidence for these preferences, far from being value-neutral then, as some would like to think, legitimates (by allegedly confirming) those beliefs, and the associated social order, which take it for granted that a woman's place is in the home and that it is natural for her to be a wife and a mother. What's more it discredits as irrational those who are struggling to liberate women from the narrow and constraining roles traditionally preserved for them in our culture.

Confronted by this seemingly indubitable observational base against which her views are being tested, and found defective, the feminist is in some difficulty. If she adopts the approach advocated by a presently well-entrenched empiricist philosophy of science, she will take well-confirmed observational experiences and statements more or less for granted. Accepting that her theory is in trouble, the only logical thing for her to do then is to jettison, or at least modify, it and her associated political practice. One kind of alternative to doing so is for her to claim that her political commitment, if not irrational, is non-rational or ideological, and predominantly informed by values, not by facts. Feminism, she may argue, is an ideology which she and others oppose to the prevailing sexist ideology rampant in our advanced capitalist society. But in making this move she, and other politically committed activists, are accepting the terms of the debate laid down by their adversaries. In particular, they are colluding in the maintenance of a fact-value distinction which, as I have already suggested, is fundamentally misconceived. To escape these consequences a different strategy is called for.

The lessons of history

The predicament faced by contemporary feminists is not without historical precedent. On the contrary, doctrines sanctified by the establishment at the dawn of the Scientific Revolution also derived much of their plausibility from appeals to common-sense and everyday observation. More specifically, the general belief that the earth was stationary at the centre of the universe, and that the sun literally rose in the east and set in the west, circling the earth once a day along with all the heavens, was not based simply on superstition or on obedience to religious authority. For to the ancients it was self-evident that the sun moved daily through the heavens; sense experience confirmed it. And when, in 1543, Copernicus argued that the earth rotates daily on its own axis, and moves annually around a stationary sun, he was assailed on two fronts. On the one hand, Luther poured scorn on this 'upstart astrologer' who put forward views so plainly at variance with divinely revealed truths, as embodied in the writings of the prophets. On the other hand, one of Luther's close associates, Melanchthon, pointed out that not only did Copernicus' sun-centred system contradict divine truths; in addition 'The eyes are witnesses that the heavens revolve in the space of twenty-four hours'. Publicly to assert the contrary reveals a 'want of honesty and decency'! (quoted by Kuhn, 1957, p. 191)[2]

The commonsensical belief that the earth was stationary was particularly difficult to dislodge—because it was based on everyday observations of this kind. In fact, in the struggle to establish Copernicanism over and against its rivals, an assortment of ingenious arguments based on sense experience were used to support the orthodox alternative, namely the complex earth-centred system of astronomy developed by Ptolemy in about 150 AD. For Ptolemy, whose theory was virtually unchallenged among mathematical astronomers for 1,400 years, the movement of the earth was contradicted by seemingly uncontroversial observations. If the earth rotated daily from west to east, he argued, flying birds and clouds should be seen to move westwards at great speed—but they are not. What is more, a stone thrown vertically into the air should fall to the earth some distance away from the person who propels it. The fact that it falls at that person's feet plainly refutes the idea that the earth is moving. To these arguments, others were added in Copernicus' day. For example, it was pointed out that a cannon ball dropped from a tower on a moving earth should strike its surface at some distance from the tower's base—a conclusion easily refuted by experience. In short, in the sixteenth century the weight of sense evidence adduced in favour of an Aristotelian cosmos, which placed a stationary earth at the centre of the universe, was overwhelming.

And yet, inspired to search for a more harmonious astronomical system, Copernicus disdainfully brushed aside, or ignored, contradictory sense experience, and postulated that the earth moved. The Pythagoreans had done so some 2,000 years earlier; Aristarchus of Samos had been condemned for making the same suggestion in the third century BC. But it was Copernicus who developed a full-blown mathematical theory which could be used to predict planetary positions about as accurately as its Ptolemaic rival. The Polish astronomer did not even bother to develop a dynamical theory which could be used to refute the arguments against terrestrial motion given above. This was the task to which Galileo addressed himself, filled as he was with admiration for those who had blazed the sun-centred trail before him:

> Nor can I ever sufficiently admire the outstanding acumen of those who have taken hold of this opinion and accepted it as true; they have through sheer force of intellect done such violence to their own senses as to prefer what reason told them over that which sensible experience plainly showed them to the contrary . . . I repeat, there is no limit to my astonishment when I reflect that Aristarchus and Copernicus were able to make reason so conquer sense that the former became mistress of their belief. (Galileo, 1967 edn., p. 328).

To conquer disconfirming sensory evidence through sheer force of intellect, to tear oneself free from the obviousness of everyday observation—this achievement marked the Scientific Revolution, initiated by Copernicus and Galileo. Now, with the wisdom of hindsight, it is generally conceded that the *weakness* of Ptolemaic astronomy, and of Aristotelian cosmology in general, lay in their over-reliance on sense evidence. Thus Ptolemy has been chastised for placing 'too great a reliance upon naïve observation . . . The difficulty was that Ptolemy was too empirical' (Kattsoff, 1947, p. 22). And the Aristotelians have been condemned for lacking 'a healthy distrust of the testimony of their own and others' senses' (Dijksterhuis, 1969, p. 70).

Philosophers and historians are gradually appreciating that a strategy of this kind, in which apparently recalcitrant facts are *bracketed*, has played a crucial role in the growth of scientific knowledge. Detailed analyses of Galileo's procedure suggest that, confronted with doctrines which relied on appeals to apparently well-entrenched everyday observations, he proceeded 'counter-inductively'. (See Feyerabend, 1975, section 2 onwards; see also Feyerabend, 1970). Sticking to his theory in the face of recalcitrant evidence, he used it to produce new facts which were inconsistent with the reigning dogma. These facts, while corroborating his point of view, discredited the alternative. Thus evidential support for a novel theory was accumulated until ultimately it was able to compete on an equal footing with its established rival. To have capitulated too readily to the 'facts' which were wielded against it would have been fatal to the Galilean program—and science as we know it may never have been produced.

Other times, other places

The strategy followed by Galileo also underpins contemporary feminist struggles. However, to implement it in defence of their argument against the biological determinism of women's roles as housewife and mother it has to be further enriched. In particular, our culture as it is presently constituted is an unpromising source for facts which can undermine the prevailing orthodoxy. This is because, as Oakley has noted, 'only the everyday observation of men and women in society is needed to "prove" that differences of personality follow biological differences of sex'. And indeed this is not surprising. For, as she also points out, 'In Western societies today, sex *is* an organising principle of social structure' (Oakley, 1975, p. 150), and it *does* play an important part in shaping one's temperament and determining social roles. If we are to get the case against biological determinism off the ground other sources are essential. It is here that historical and cross-cultural studies come into their own. For if we can show that in other times and in other places women did not, and do not, in fact, play the roles allotted to them now in our culture, the feminist case is substantially strengthened.

With the development of the women's movement in the last decade, an increasing amount of historical evidence has been produced which discredits the view that women are biologically suited to perform domestic tasks which, so it is alleged, do not require the physical strength and stamina of 'productive' male-dominated roles. Attention is being drawn to the exhausting manual labour which women in Britain were called upon to perform in armaments factories during the two wars. Furthermore it is being pointed out that heavy agricultural labour was done by women in Britain until technological change reduced the need for work of this kind. Such work is, of course, often done by women in pre-industrial cultures. Thus, in a cross-cultural study of over 200 cultures, it was found that the building of dwellings was an exclusively feminine task in about 17 per cent of the recorded instances, and that it was shared by both women and men in about 52 per cent of them (see Oakley, 1976, p. 163 onwards). In our culture, as we know, building work is male-dominated. The hostility to the recent attempts by a woman to work on a building site in London as reported in the daily press bore witness to the extent to which a sexual division of labour is taken for granted in this area of employment. It is all too easy to justify such discrimination by appealing to biological characteristics like the male's (allegedly) superior strength and stature. In the face of evidence from other times and places such justifications crumble to dust.

The similarities between the strategy pursued by Galileo and the procedures adopted by contemporary feminists are striking. Both are prepared to bracket incontrovertible evidence, rooted in everyday observation, which seemingly undermines their theories while providing substantial support for rival views. Furthermore, having initially done so, they are then able to assimilate this evidence into their alternatives, turning an apparent defeat into a victory. Thus Galileo can agree that a cannon ball dropped from a tower will strike the earth near its base; but, he argues, this is not because the earth is stationary, but because earth, ball and tower share the same translational and rotational motion. Similarly, feminists can agree that most women in our culture are, and feel the need to be, housewives and mothers. But, they argue, this is not because these roles are biologically necessary, but because from infancy girls are socialised into them. Those facts which were originally considered to be reasons for the established views, and to be reasons against their novel and radical rivals, now support the latter! At the same time, empirical support for the old theory is removed. What had formerly seemed like reasons now emerge as rationalisations. What had looked like science turns out to be ideology.[3]

Dialectics and social science

The similarities between Galileo's strategy and that pursued by contemporary feminists locates them in a tradition of militant opposition to establishment dogma. However, those similarities should not blind us to a crucial difference between the role of facts and, more generally, of criticism in the natural and in the social sciences.

I pointed out above that as (putative) reasons, facts have evaluative implications, lending support to, or discrediting, theories and beliefs about the world. However, what needs to be recognised is that there is an essential difference between the objects of the natural and of the social sciences. For, in contrast to the natural world, social reality is constructed in and by people's more or less conscious beliefs and practices. Criticism of a natural scientific theory in the light of facts or a rival theory, while directed at the beliefs of those who hold it, leaves the object of the theory (the natural world) as it is. On the other hand, the object of the social sciences is the same as that which is being criticised, namely, people's beliefs and practices. Thus in criticising those beliefs and practices one aims to change both them and the social order which they reflect and reproduce.

As such, the relationship between social scientific theories and their objects, we might say, is dialectical.[4] This has profound consequences. In advanced capitalist societies, for example, sexist views are enmeshed into every level of the social order: sex is an organising principle of social structure, as Oakley put it. More specifically,

A system of institutional sexism dominates work and social relationships both at jobs and at home. In fact, in order to understand this institutionalised system we must see the mutually reinforcing relationship of home and job, and the special position of women in the paid labour force. Much of the paid work that women do is an extension of their family work: serving, cleaning, supporting, restoring, caring. One third of all women work in seven job categories: clerical, domestic, retail sales, waitressing, bookkeeping, nursing, teaching. Throughout the labour force women are 'sexegated' into a separate labor market with different, less desirable jobs and lower pay. (Baxandall et al., 1976).

The procedures outlined above revealed that statistically backed common-sense theories which 'reflect' these structures of domination deal with a social order which is historically and culturally relative, not a product of biology. By developing their alternative, feminists therefore do not merely aim to describe, explain and predict the reality of which they speak. Through criticism, including revolutionary practice, they aim to change it.

Notes

1. Throughout this essay Oakley's work is used almost exclusively to defend the feminist position. This is not to say, of course, that she is the only important feminist writer but merely that she is one particularly perceptive member of the movement.
2. The standard work on the Copernican Revolution is Kuhn (1957). Easlea (1973) provides a very helpful introduction to the topic, particularly in Chapter 2.
3. The idea that the development of science as a cognitive system involves a 'rupture' with everyday observation and commonsense has been argued for by Bachelard (see Lecourt, 1976). This view has inspired Althusser's interpretation of Marx's work (particularly in Althusser and Balibar, 1970), and also underpins a recent analysis of Marx's concept of ideology (Mepham, 1972, but see also McCarney, 1976).
4. This section owes a great deal to Edgley (1976). But see also Dews (1977). I am indebted to Roy Edgley for invaluable comments on earlier drafts of this paper.

Bibliography

Althusser, L. and E. Balibar, 1970, *Reading Capital*, London, New Left Books.
Baxandall, R., E. Ewen and L. Gordon, 1976, 'The working class has two sexes', *Monthly Review*, July–August, pp. 1–9.
Dews, P., 1977, 'Misadventures of the dialectic', *Radical Philosophy*, no. 18, pp. 10–15.
Dijksterhuis, E. J., 1969, *The Mechanisation of the World Picture*, New York, Oxford University Press.
Easlea, B., 1973, *Liberation and the Aims of Science*, London, Chatto and Windus.
Edgley, R., 1976, 'Science, social science and socialist science—reason as dialectic', *Radical Philosophy*, no. 15, pp. 2–7.

Feyerabend, P. K., 1970, 'Against Method', in M. Radner and S. Winokur (eds.), *Minnesota Studies in the Philosophy of Science*, vol. 4, pp. 17–130.

Feyerabend, P. K., 1975, *Against Method*, London, New Left Books.

Galileo, 1967, *Dialogue Concerning the Two Chief World Systems* (trans. by Stillman Drake), Berkeley, University of California Press.

Kattsoff, L. O., 1947, 'Ptolemy and scientific method,' *Isis*, vol. 38, pp. 18–22.

Kuhn, T. S., 1957, *The Copernican Revolution*, Cambridge, Mass., Harvard University Press.

Lecourt, D., 1976, *Marxism and Epistemology*, London, New Left Books.

McCarney, J., 1976, 'The theory of ideology', *Radical Philosophy*, no. 13, pp. 28–31.

Mepham, J., 1972, 'The theory of ideology in *Capital*', *Radical Philosophy*, no. 2, pp. 12–19.

Oakley, A., 1975, *Sex, Gender and Society*, London, Temple Smith.

Oakley, A., 1976, *Housewife*, Harmondsworth, Penguin.

6.

Robert M. Young

Why are Figures so Significant? The Role and the Critique of Quantification

Some attitudes and assumptions are so basic to how we think about and experience the world that it is difficult to consider them critically. For anyone educated in an 'advanced' technological society it is practically impossible to imagine that our ideas of *objectivity* and *factual accuracy*, and the basic place of *numbering* or *quantification* in our world-view, are historical products rather than eternal principles of analysis. However, stress has been placed on these as part of an experimental, investigative methodology only since the late sixteenth and seventeenth centuries. It was in that period that modern capitalism and its way of knowing nature— modern science—were developing as a new and unified socio- economic order with a new way of defining reality and knowledge.

Earlier definitions of what counted as knowledge and truth were cast in very different terms—terms which did not sharply separate facts from values or the realm of the objective from that of the subjective, or place much emphasis on quantification. This is not to say that those distinctions were not made, or that counting and sophisticated mathematical reasoning did not take place. Indeed, great mystical significance was attached to certain forms of geometrical reasoning, to certain proportions and to numerology. Neo-Platonists, astrologers and alchemists considered that numeri- cal relationships represented the quintessence of order, while certain numbers had mystical qualities. However, these roles for numbers must be distinguished from the modern concept and significance of quantification.

Before the changes associated with the so-called Scientific Revolution took place in Western Europe, the issue of quantifi- cation was therefore not at the centre of the problem of what is fundamentally real (ontology), the nature and limits of knowledge (epistemology), and how we should pursue our enquiries about the world (methodology). Instead, events were interpreted qualita- tively as a part of their evaluative relations; that is, they were seen in terms of purposes, utilities, natural places and affinities, forms of motion, growth and development. Objects and natural processes were analysed and classified as being in a more organic relationship with the cosmos. Their origins, motions, material aspects, formal or structural features, and purposes and uses were thus seen in terms of a single framework of 'coming to be' or causation. Quantification was peripheral to this form of explanation, which had developed within the tradition inspired by the work of Aristotle (Dijksterhuis, 1961). Bodies fell because it was their 'nature' to attain their natural places. The coming to be of, for example, a chair would be explained in terms of the carpenter's actions, the wood, the plan, essence, or ideal of 'chairness', and the purpose of providing seating.

If this way of thinking about things seems vague and perhaps woolly, it is because we have been brought up within a philosophy of nature and society which is very different from the Aristotelian and pre-capitalist world-view. Our characteristic way of thinking about phenomena is a capitalist, mechanistic one which makes certain sharp separations for the purpose of manipulating, dominating and exploiting both natural processes and social relationships (Leiss, 1972). The separation of events into, on the one hand, things and, on the other, their contexts and evaluative relations, lies at the heart of the modern world-view. That separation is what is meant by 'positivism' (see Keat, this volume, and Kolakowski, 1972). It treats the world as a set of interacting facts.

To revert to the above examples, falling bodies are now explained by Newton's 'inverse square law' of gravitation. As for the chair, scientists and technologists simply don't think of chairs— or other objects—in such terms: a physicist's analysis would not give us back an everyday object like a chair at the end of the argument, while in the history of technology each aspect of a chair eventually became an area for specialists in, e.g. design, draughtsmanship, ergonomics, materials science, the technologies of furniture machinofacture, quality control, consumer research, and the labour processes of factory production, wholesaling, retailing and advertising—all of which are overseen by management and accountancy. So, from explaining bodies and chairs we come to the related separations in the labour process at work, where the capitalist mode of production treats workers as things, i.e. they are reified (from the Latin word for thing: *res*; see Lukács, 1923). They are interchangeable, and hired for their labour power alone; they are paid money so that they can get their human satisfactions from the commodities they buy and consume elsewhere than in the workplace.

It was in the late sixteenth and seventeenth centuries that the model of explanation—the definition of what counts as knowledge —shifted decisively; it did so as part and parcel of a system of production based on a single, abstract measure. The myriad qualities and the individual natures of the everyday experiences and activities of laypeople came to be seen as less important than their quantifiable aspects according to the single standard of exchange value as commodities (see Shaw and Miles, this volume). In manufacture and commerce, the particular usefulness of the product being made became increasingly incidental to the owners of the means of production, whose main preoccupation became the circulation and expansion of capital. The development of this economic system coincided, moreover, with a changing conception of knowledge (Marcuse, 1964). The resultant link between objectification and commodity exchange has been put succinctly: 'Only objects can be measured, which is why exchange reifies' (Vaneigem, 1972, p. 79). In science, particular sensuous attributes or qualities of events came to be considered secondary to others which were defined as objective and primary. The 'primary qualities'—extension and motion—could be readily treated mathematically. Colour, odour, taste and all other subjectively experienced qualities were, in turn, to be explained in terms of the primary qualities which were (a) less vulnerable to variations arising from subjective judgements and social evaluations, (b) amenable to mathematical treatment, and (c) suited to the investigation and control of certain phenomena, e.g. physical bodies. Qualitative and semi-quantitative measures in terms of more and less, were replaced by precise measurement and quantification (Hirst, 1967; Jackson, 1929).

These developments in the capitalist mode of production, and in science, were mutually constitutive; for example, in trade, exploration, ballistics, navigation and astronomy the commercial and scientific changes were part and parcel of one another. In the subsequent history of the mode of production, there has been an ever-increasing role for scientific and technological quantification, and the mechanisation and control of nature and people (Marx, 1867, Ch. 15). This history came to define the idea of *progress* in industrial civilisation. 'Progress' and 'science' were increasingly seen as synonyms in the late eighteenth and nineteenth centuries, while our own generation has become ambivalent about 'progress' in such fields as nuclear energy and high-technology medicine.

Matter, motion and number

In the philosophy of nature elaborated by those who laid the metaphysical foundations of modern science—first in astronomy and physics and then in physiology and biology—a set of key distinctions was elaborated:

subject - object
purpose - mechanism
value - fact
internal - external
secondary - primary (qualities)
thought - extension
mind - body
culture - nature
society - science

The history of thought and practice based on these distinctions contains two contradictory interpretations. One requires a demarcation of the two realms, while the other seeks to explain one in terms of the other. Most scientists and commentators on science pursue these two interpretations in different spheres of their activities and for different purposes. For example, Newton was involved in both the mathematical principles of natural philosophy, and hermetical and alchemical studies and Biblical exegetics. In our own period, Sir John Eccles and Sir Karl Popper are, respectively, an eminent neurophysiologist and a famous philosopher of scientific method. One might expect them to be committed to explaining mind in terms of body, yet they have recently joined forces to mount a strong defence of mind-body dualism (Popper and Eccles, 1977).

'Reductionism' is the explanation of the concepts and phenomena of the first column by those in the second. In the reductionist programme, the nearer an explanation comes to the fundamental concepts of matter, motion and number, the more basic it is said to be: Galileo said that the book of nature is written in the language of mathematics (Burtt, 1932, p. 64), and Newton argued that the whole business of science was to explain all the other phenomena in terms of matter and motion, treated mathematically (Burtt, p. 204). The revolution in thought associated with Copernicus, Kepler, Galileo, Descartes, Newton and Locke led to treating this new fundamental framework of concepts and explanations as the basis for all knowledge of nature, including living nature and the human body (the history of attempts to treat mental phenomena in these terms is one of analogies and of mental parallels to physical processes; quantitative methods for investigating sensory and ideational phenomena began to be developed in the late nineteenth century (Young, 1967, 1973)). The reductionist programme became the overall research project for modern science.

Quantifying other phenomena

Quantification has undoubtedly been a powerful tool in the reductionist programme but need not itself imply a reductionist approach. Mathematical reasoning can apparently be applied to any phenomenon. So, when it rapidly became clear that all phenomena would not easily yield to explanations in terms of the most fundamental qualities, other—intermediate—concepts were employed as relatively acceptable way-stations between subjective and social conceptions, on the one hand, and the fundamental explanations of physics, on the other. Two examples can illustrate this process: (1) Physiologists in the eighteenth century worked on *biological properties*—'irritability', 'contractility', 'sensibility', 'muscular motion'. Various branches of experimental biology have continued to use and test these intermediate concepts in parallel with the slow development of the more basic physico-chemical explanations, which have only recently been producing dramatic results in biochemistry, biophysics and molecular biology (Young, 1971). Yet both sorts of work are seen as reputably 'scientific'. (2) Chemistry can also be seen as an intermediate discipline. Until the very recent development of particle physics and physical chemistry, chemical explanations in terms of fundamental particles, e.g. neutrons, protons, electrons and a growing list of others, were a will-o'-the wisp. The physical, chemical and biochemical properties which we associate with the elements and compounds of chemistry, and with the molecules and microstructures of biochemistry and cell physiology, were defined experimentally and quantitatively, e.g. 'malleability', 'ductility', 'solubility', 'valency', 'dextro-' and 'levo-rotary', 'hygroscopic', 'respiratory', 'photoperiodic'.

The above examples have been drawn from well-established natural sciences (and have included esoteric concepts) to help emphasise that there is plenty of precedent for developing *any* concepts which look promising, and doing some experimental and/or quantitative work to see if the phenomena show regularities which can be seen as part of science. Therefore, the history of quantification cannot be equated with the history of the reductionist programme. The history of science is often described as 'the advancing edge of objectivity', from planetary motion to terrestrial motion to chemistry to physiology to the earth, life, mind, behaviour and society—bringing all of nature and society under the scientific explanations of regularities which are themselves expressed in quantitative terms (Gillispie, 1960). But it is clear that it is a history of a *growing* list of conceptions rather than one which is reducing everything to matter and motion. (The complement of this 'advance' is an ambivalence about whether subjectivity is thereby retreating and declared merely 'irrational' or only demarcated as another way of knowing.)

Quantitative approaches to social phenomena were not the last station on the travels of the advancing edge of objectivity: they were among the first (see Shaw and Miles, this volume). The statistical study of mortality came early in the scientific revolution —for political and actuarial purposes. Insurance, annuities, raising revenues, population and disease all provided early applications of quantitative approaches to society. The *Political Arithmetic* of William Petty appeared in 1690, the same year as John Locke's *Essay on Human Understanding*, which treated the study of epistemology as a labour subordinate to science. Petty characterised his method in terms of 'number, weight and measure' (Buck, 1977, p. 74). But it was in the nineteenth and twentieth centuries that the social sciences developed most dramatically, beginning with distinct programmes of research on the political economy of 'labour' and welfare studies of 'the poor'. These were treated as separate topics, although they concerned the same people. The investigators had perfectly opposed approaches—one group sought to minimise production costs and the other to relieve the consequent destitution (Berg, 1976, pp. 256–270). The list of social sciences in our own period is a long one and covers all aspects of social data, including demography, sociology, consumer research, psephology (the study of voting behaviour), scientific management, operational research, general systems theory, epidemiology, public health, and games theory. Quantitative methods now seem to 'cover', as they say, every aspect of society.

Critique: the diverted gaze

The foregoing panoramic sketch should indicate just how fundamental and how pervasive is the quantitative study of matter, motion, physico-chemical and biological properties and—ultimately—any phenomenon. No wonder it is difficult for us to appreciate the full extent to which this world-view prevents or diverts us from asking certain kinds of questions. By representing variations in numerical forms, the quantitative approach tends to direct our attention away from the evaluation of the concepts and variables themselves—whether they be quantitative analyses in chemistry, 'standard of living' studies in economics and economic history, 'affluent worker' and 'upward social mobility' studies in sociology, or IQ research in educational psychology and pupil placement. We can thereby be drawn unwittingly into an uncritical acceptance of the overall framework of theories and approaches to nature and society (and the structure of forces and relations of production and reproduction) within which such studies occur. Thus, this pervasive set of metaphysical assumptions and methodologies plays an important role in muting social criticism.

Quantitative and statistical approaches can be made to any phenomenon, and in that sense it is often argued that they are neutral tools. But the role characteristically assigned to them in scientific arguments makes the debate about the appropriateness of a given concept or variable *extrinsic* to the enquiry itself (Marcuse, 1968). The investigator becomes concerned with the quantitative presence, absence and variations of phenomena—at the expense of qualitative and evaluative debates about different ways of seeing and engaging in events (not 'things'). This is very obvious when one begins to scrutinise statistically based enquiries into affluent workers' aspirations, willingness to work overtime, or consumption behaviour in a study of 'upward social mobility'. It is blatant when one reflects on the games theorists' studies of 'megadeaths' in various 'scenarios' and 'postures', and plans for 'pre-emptive strikes' and 'second strike capability'—when the game in question is thermonuclear warfare. It is less obvious with respect to the educational psychologists' measurement of Intelligence Quotient. But who could possibly want to sort people according to an ordinal scale of abstract ability and why, other than for serving the requirement for gradations of 'general talent'—a hierarchy from top management to abstract labour power, separating mental, clerical and manual tasks for a reified labour process specific to a commodity society with its graded rewards for work and responsibility (Debord, 1970)? It is even less obvious when one seeks to re-examine the fundamental categories of explanation defined as 'primary' and 'secondary' in the Scientific Revolution— matter and motion *versus* colour, odour, taste; materiality *versus* beauty; and mechanism *versus* purpose—one set of categories supposedly objective and scientific, the other subjective and relative.

Even though certain philosophers have made eloquent critiques of the metaphysical assumptions of this world-view, they have not connected their arguments with an explicit analysis of how the history of scientific and mathematical reification is central to the alienation—of nature, work and its products, and one's relations with other people and indeed oneself—which characterises the labour process in the capitalist mode of production.

Burtt says of the distinction between primary and secondary qualities:

> The features of the world now classed as secondary, unreal, ignoble, and regarded as dependent on the deceitfulness of sense, are just those features which are most intense to man [sic] in all but his purely theoretic activity, and even in that, except where he confines himself strictly to the mathematical method. It was inevitable that in these circumstances man should now appear to be outside of the real world; man is hardly more than a bundle of secondary qualities. Observe that the stage is fully set for the Cartesian dualism—on the one side the primary, the mathematical realm; on the other the realm of man. And the premium of importance and value as well as of independent existence all goes with the former. Man begins to appear for the first time in the history of thought as an irrelevant spectator and insignificant effect of the great mathematical system which is the substance of reality. (Burtt, 1932, p. 80).

And Whitehead completes the philosophical aspect of the critique:

> The seventeenth century had finally produced a scheme of scientific thought framed by mathematicians, for the use of mathematicians. The great characteristic of the mathematical mind is its capacity for dealing with abstractions; and for eliciting from them clear-cut demonstrative trains of reasoning, entirely satisfactory so long as it is those abstractions which you want to think about. The enormous success of the scientific abstractions, yielding on the one hand *matter* with its *simple location* in space and time, on the other hand *mind*, perceiving, suffering, reasoning, but not interfering, has foisted onto philosophy the task of accepting them as the most concrete rendering of fact.
>
> Thereby, modern philosophy has been ruined. It has oscillated in a complex manner between three extremes. There are the dualists, who accept matter and mind as on an equal basis, and the two varieties of monists, those who put mind inside matter, and those who put matter inside mind. But this juggling with abstractions can never overcome the inherent confusion introduced by the ascription of *misplaced concreteness* to the scientific scheme of the seventeenth century. (Whitehead, 1925, pp. 81-2).

The return of the reified

If we connect the philosophic critique of the metaphysical foundations of modern science with the political and ideological critique of the mode of production, they make up *one* analysis. In the *Grundrisse* and in *Capital* (especially the sections on commodity fetishism and the labour process), Marx provides the critique of political economy which makes sense of the constitutive role of the objectifications and abstractions which Burtt and Whitehead criticise. Their laments about the impoverishment of the philosophy of nature can be integrated with the understanding of key concepts in the critique of capitalism: alienation, objectification, exploitation, machinofacture, scientific management and automation. Science and technology, scientific and technological rationality, and scientific and technological experts, are also integrated into the system and subject to the same unified critique. Think, for example, of how the reification of people and labour processes occurs in the management sciences, say, operational research into 'chemical process design' or the reorganisation of the National Health Service by management consultants. Any attempt to separate these two domains—philosophy from political economy or world-view from the mode of production—is itself part of capital's preferred way of representing the world. According to that argument, chemical process designers and management consultants are to be seen as solely concerned with increasing efficiency, rather than with the elimination of opportunities for class struggle or with refining the hierarchical division of labour. It is also part of the same problem that many of the above terms in marxist political-economic analysis may be unfamiliar to many social scientists, as well as to scientists and statisticians. Their unfamilarity is an index of capital's success in representing the world in terms which separate science and technology from political economy.

The status of scientific abstraction and quantification has been gained largely at the expense of open debate about the competing values and value systems which underlie alternative forms of social relations. Once again, quantification is not the same as reductionism. In principle, it leaves as rich a list of phenomena as you like and makes no claim to explain the more complex in terms of the simpler, the more mechanical or material. But it can be impoverishing, even when not in tandem with reductionism, though the impoverishment is of a different sort: closure of qualitative debate. In effect, it depoliticises whenever qualitative and evaluative aspects are made less prominent than the numerical representation.

But in science the evaluative relations, though taken as extrinsic to the scientific activity, are at the same time implicitly propagated by the science. They are not, consequently, amenable to scrutiny and challenge. The critique of positivism argues that facts are inseparable from interpretations, which are in turn determined by values. Events are only meaningful in terms of the structures which establish them as such (e.g. Jones, 1972, p. 113).

This is as true of the history of quantification as it is of any set of events. And the structures which have placed a premium on quantification are the most basic ones in our socio-economic order: the capitalist mode of production, in which labour is conducted socially but the product is appropriated privately, with the circulation and expansion of capital as its goal. The history of the sequestering of controversial qualities, their banishment to the private, subjective realm and the emphasis on the measurement of quantities is at the centre of the development and maintenance of that structure. It is so basic to our world-view and social order that it is very hard indeed to recover a critical perspective on it.

The principle of total calculability—the quantitative measurability of the elements of the production process, of machinery and human labour power, and of the rest of nature and society in the service of exploitation—has made possible the ascendancy of capitalism (Schneider, 1975, pp. 135, 144; c.f. Rosenhead and Thunhurst, this volume). But there is a fundamental contradiction in the dominant scientific, positivistic world-view. Science is represented as the objective sphere, separate from the vicissitudes of subjectivity and clashes of values and interests—the servant of policies which are supposed to be determined elsewhere. Yet, at the same time, science is supposed to be the basis, the model, and the guide for society—eliminating uncertainties, achieving the 'correct' solutions, and reconciling conflicts and priorities by neutral means. Not only do scientists and other experts elicit deference on this argument, but certain supposedly neutral meta-disciplines are specifically devoted to this role—cybernetics and general systems theory (Emery, 1969; Kaplan, 1971). In trying to have it both ways, the proponents and practitioners of these approaches and roles vacillate between innocence of any evaluative, political and ideological influence and the false consciousness of claiming that science provides the only sure basis for social policy (Huxley, 1977; Young 1977b). They thereby collude with the propagation of values constituted by the production and reproduction of social relations in the capitalist mode of production, while believing themselves to be humble seekers after truth and progress—models of disinterestedness, fully deserving their mandarin role, status and perks. Neither of these rationalisations will do, because the claimed separation of fact and value, of science and society, is itself a mystification, while the absorption of values inside a claimed objective science of society is a powerful ideological weapon.

The critique of total calculability and quantitative measurability—and of the role of the experts who practise and defend those activities and perspectives—is central to the de-alienation of experience and the development of solidarity. To overthrow this requires the development of different perspectives on nature, people, work, and the ownership of the means of production and the distribution of the fruits of human labour (Young, 1977a). Of course, there are significant numerical dimensions to all these, but their place is likely to be much more modest than of late, and conflicts over social priorities and strategies will loom larger. The work will involve different people doing different activities in different ways for different reasons, creating a different world—one whose book is written in the language, not of mathematics, but of socialist social relations.

Bibliography

Berg, M., 1976, 'Political economy and scientific philanthropy: the Statistical Movement', in her *The Machinery Question: Conceptions of Technical Change in Political Economy during the Industrial Revolution c. 1820 to 1840*, Ph.D. Dissertation, University of Oxford, pp. 256–70.

Buck, P., 1977, 'Seventeenth-century political arithmetic: civil strife and vital statistics', *Isis*, vol. 68, pp. 67–84.

Burtt, E. A., 1932, *The Metaphysical Foundations of Modern Physical Science: A Historical and Critical Essay*, revised ed., London, Routledge & Kegan Paul; New York, Doubleday Anchor pb., 1955.

Debord, G., 1970, *Society of the Spectacle*, Detroit, Black & Red.

Dijksterhuis, E. J., 1961, *The Mechanization of the World Picture*, Oxford, Oxford University Press, esp. pp. 431–44.

Emery, F. E., (ed.), 1969, *Systems Thinking: Selected Readings*, Harmondsworth, Penguin.

Gillispie, C., 1960, *The Edge of Objectivity: An Essay in the History of Scientific Ideas*, Oxford, Oxford University Press; also Princeton pb.

Hirst, R. J., 1967, 'Primary and secondary qualities', in P. Edwards (ed.), *The Encyclopedia of Philosophy*, New York, Macmillan, vol. 6, pp. 455–57.

Huxley, Sir A., 1977, 'Evidence, clues and motives in science' (Presidential Address to the British Association), *Times Higher Education Supplement*, 2 September 1977, pp. 4–6; (see also 7 October 1977, p. 21).

Jackson, R., 1929, 'Locke's distinction between primary and secondary qualities', *Mind*, vol. 38, pp. 56–76.

Jones, G. Stedman-, 1972, 'History: the poverty of empiricism', in R. Blackburn (ed.), *Ideology in Social Science: Readings in Critical Social Theory*, London, Fontana, pp. 96–115.

Kaplan, M., 1971, 'Science and social values' in W. Fuller (ed.), *The Social Impact of Modern Biology*, London, Routledge & Kegan Paul, pp. 192–98.

Kolakowski, L., 1972, *Positivist Philosophy from Hume to the Vienna Circle*, Harmondsworth, Penguin.

Leiss, W., 1972, *The Domination of Nature*, New York, Braziller; Boston, Beacon pb.

Lukacs, G., 1923, 'Reification and the consciousness of the proletariat', in his *History and Class Consciousness*, London, Merlin Press, 1971, pp. 83–222.

Marcuse, H., 1964, *One Dimensional Man: The Ideology of Industrial Society*, London, Routledge & Kegan Paul: also Abacus pb.

Marcuse, H., 1968, 'Industrialization and capitalism in the work of Max Weber', in his *Negations: Essays in Critical Theory*, Boston, Beacon; Harmondsworth, Penguin; pp. 201–226.

Marx, K., 1857–8, *Grundrisse: Foundations of the Critique of Political Economy (Rough Draft)*, Harmondsworth, Penguin 1973.

Marx, K., 1867, *Capital: A Critique of Political Economy*, vol. 1., Harmondsworth, Penguin/New Left Review 1976.

Popper, Sir K., and Sir J. C. Eccles, 1977, *The Self and Its Brain: An Argument for Interactionism*, London, Springer-Verlag.

Schneider, M., 1975, 'On the pathology of the capitalist commodity society'; 'On the pathology of the capitalist organization of work'; and 'On the pathology of the capitalist "consumer society" '; in his *Neurosis and Civilization: a Marxist/Freudian Synthesis*, New York, Seabury Press, pp. 125–253.

Vaneigem, R., 1972, *The Revolution of Everyday Life*, London, Practical Paradise.

Whitehead, A. N., 1925, *Science and the Modern World*, Cambridge, Cambridge University Press.

Young, R. M., 1967, 'Animal soul', in P. Edwards (ed.), *The Encyclopedia of Philosophy*, New York, Macmillan, vol. 1, pp. 122–27.

Young, R. M., 1971, 'Evolutionary biology and ideology: then and now', *Science Studies*, vol. 1, pp: 177–206.

Young, R. M., 1973, 'Association of ideas', in P. Wiener (ed.), *Dictionary of the History of Ideas*, New York, Scribner's, vol. 1, pp. 111–18.

Young, R. M., 1977a, 'Science *is* social relations', *Radical Science Journal*, no. 5, pp. 65–129.

Young, R. M., 1977b, 'Can we really distinguish fact from value in science?', *Times Higher Education Supplement*, 23 September 1977, p. 6 (see also 4 November 1977, p. 27).

See also two novels which are greatly concerned with the relationship between the quantitative-scientific rendering of experience and the qualitative-lived aspect.

Alther, L., *Kinflicks*, Harmondsworth, Penguin 1977 (although there is much which is unacceptable in her sexual politics).

Pirsig, R., *Zen and the Art of Motorcycle Maintenance*, London, Bodley Head 1974; also in paperback (however there is much which is politically unattractive about Pirsig's approach).

7.

Russell Keat

Positivism and Statistics in Social Science

Introduction

Debates about 'positivism' in the social sciences have become fairly frequent in the last ten years or so (Giddens, 1974; Adey and Frisby, 1976), but the term itself gets used in many rather different senses. There is some danger of its becoming a vague and over-general term of epistemological and political abuse; or, alternatively, of too much discussion taking place about its 'correct' definition, what it 'really' means. What matters most are the merits, defects, and consequences of the actual claims and practices that get called 'positivist', since these raise issues that are central to the possibility of a *science* of the social, and to what *kind* of science it could be.

The 'positivist' position in the social sciences, in the sense of the term I will be using, has two main elements. First, there is the belief that in their basic features the social sciences can and should be modelled upon the natural sciences, especially physics and chemistry. This is the 'thesis of methodological naturalism'—a demand for the use of similar methods and approaches in the social and natural sciences, with the latter providing the model for the former. Second, there is a *specific conception* of science itself, of the kind of knowledge it provides, and the ways in which claims to this knowledge are justified.

It is this positivist conception of science that was accepted in the late eighteenth and nineteenth centuries by the advocates of a science of society, such as Saint-Simon, Comte and Mill (see Kolakowski, 1972; Keat and Urry, 1975, Ch. 4; Benton, 1977, Ch. 2). And, as will be seen, it assigns an important, and specific, role in science to statistical data. Further, much of the statistical work done in the social sciences has been based upon this positivist view of science. Any evaluation of the possible uses of statistics must therefore take account of the more general issues involved in the debates about positivism and social science. My aim in what follows is to provide an informative, critical guide to these issues.

The positivist view of science

I will describe the positivist view of science—which, together with the thesis of methodological naturalism, constitutes 'positivist social science'—by outlining its view of the nature of scientific explanation and theories, of the function and character of empirical observation, and of the relations between scientific knowledge and political or moral values (see Lessnoff, 1974, Ch. 1; Keat and Urry, 1975, Ch. 1; Benton, 1977, Chs. 3 and 4).

Within a positivist approach, to explain something is to show that it conforms to well-established scientific laws, such as those relating the pressure, volume and temperature of gases (e.g. $PV=kT$ where k represents a constant), or the Newtonian laws of motion (e.g. that a body with no external forces operating on it continues either at rest or in rectilinear motion). Statements expressing these laws are descriptions of regular relationships that are taken to hold at all times and places, past, present and future; they are 'strictly universal'[1]. We can explain something by showing that the statement describing it follows as the conclusion of an argument whose premises include statements of such laws. Thus, 'the volume of this gas increased' could be deduced from a set of premises, which would include both the law, $PV=kT$, and a number of particular facts (often called 'initial conditions'); e.g. that its pressure had remained the same, and its temperature had increased.

In the social sciences, this view of explanation has been explicitly endorsed, for example, by Homans—who makes use of what he sees as the basic laws discovered by behavioural psychologists—to explain a wide range of social and historical phenomena. Examples of such 'laws' are: 'when a response is followed by a reward, the frequency or probability of its recurrence increases', and 'the higher the value a person sets on the reward, the more likely he is to take the action or repeat' (Homans, 1964).

This account of explanation reflects the significance assigned by positivists to the use of scientific knowledge for prediction and control (Fay, 1975, chapter 2). For the information used to explain something is such that, had it been known in advance, the phenomenon could have been successfully predicted. Indeed, many positivists have argued that explanation and prediction are essentially the same in their structure and content, differing only in whether they are performed retrospectively or prospectively (Hempel, 1965).

In addition to explaining particular *phenomena*, science also explains *laws*, by deriving them from higher-level ones. Ideally, positivists suggest we will discover a hierarchy of laws, so that at the top there is a small number of laws with a very wide range of application from which other, less general, laws can be deduced. It is this kind of hierarchical system that constitutes a scientific theory, and its higher-level components will typically make use of what are called 'theoretical' terms, i.e. terms which do not refer to any observable phenomena. 'Magnetic field', 'electron', or 'kinetic energy' are examples; as are 'class', 'social integration', or 'the unconscious', in the social sciences.

But the use of these theoretical terms poses a serious problem for positivists. They have always been centrally concerned with distinguishing genuine, scientific knowledge from various non-scientific or pre-scientific approaches, especially 'metaphysical' or 'religious' ones. And they have attempted to achieve this by tying down science to the realm of the observable.

This has been done by ascribing two forms of primacy to what can be observed. First, an *ontological* primacy: the only kinds of items that can properly be said to *exist* are those that are accessible to the senses. For positivists, it is typical of non-scientific approaches to populate the world with all sorts of mysterious, unobservable entities (e.g. God, vital spirits, Hegel's *Geist*, etc.) and to explain phenomena by reference to their activities. This practice is ruled out by the ontological restriction to the observable. But how, then, are the theoretical terms of a *genuine* science to be understood? The main positivist answer has been: by giving them (often highly complex) definitions in statements that make use of observational terms; these are often called 'operational definitions'. For instance, the theoretical term 'magnetic' might be partly defined by the statement 'something is magnetic if, whenever a small piece of iron is placed near it, the iron moves towards it'. Or, in the social sciences, the concept of social class may be defined in terms of apparently more readily observable data about income, wealth, and education.

The second form of primacy is *epistemological*. Positivists have insisted that the only relevant test for the acceptance or rejection of scientific claims is whether or not they are consistent with the empirical *data*, with the body of facts that is established via the senses. But what precisely are to count as 'data': how is 'observation' to be defined? There have been several, slightly different answers given by positivists, but in most, two characteristics of empirical data have been emphasised. First, data must be 'theory-neutral', in the sense of being described in an observation language which is devoid of theoretical assumptions or presuppositions. Second, they must be 'objective', in the sense that all competent, honest observers, whose senses operate in a normal, non-defective manner, can agree upon them. This requirement of what might be termed more precisely 'intersubjective agreement'[2] is taken to be met most effectively by data produced in quantitative form. Further, with this kind of data, it becomes possible to calculate the *degree* of support given to various, competing theories by the available evidence, and to make choices between them on this basis.

So the positivist conception of empirical data provides an important rationale for the role of statistics in positivist social science. Indeed, given the way positivists have invoked the primacy of the observable to distinguish science from non-science, it is easy to see how the use of statistical data and techniques in the social sciences could come to be seen as actually demonstrating their scientificity.

The use of statistics may also appear to show that another important requirement of scientificity for a positivist social science has been met, namely *value-freedom*. One element of this doctrine is basically a consequence of the epistemological primacy ascribed to observation: the political and moral values of scientists are seen as totally irrelevant to the truth or falsity of scientific theories. For scientists to allow their commitments to such values to influence their assessment of rival scientific theories—i.e. of the extent to which they are supported or undermined by the data—would be to allow bias or prejudice to distort objectively decidable issues. And there is a further element in this concept of value-freedom. No moral or political judgements can be established by purely scientific argument and evidence. Science can discover what is the case, and explain it, but it cannot show what should, or ought to, happen. (Weber, 1949; Lessnoff, 1974, chapter 6).

Since much of our everyday, qualitative language seems to have significant politically and morally evaluative connotations, there is a strong tendency for positivist social scientists to try to eliminate these, to avoid the dangers of not meeting the requirement of value-freedom. For instance, the use of the concept of *exploitation* in marxism has often been taken by positivists to show its lack of scientificity. So what is needed is a value-free, purely factual 'language'—such as that of statistics—to replace the 'unscientific' language of politics and morality.

Positivist social science: an example

To see how this account of science applies to the social sciences in more detail, consider the way positivists could (and indeed, often do) interpret, and make use of Durkheim's theory of suicide (Durkheim, 1952)[3]. Suppose one wants to explain why the rate of suicide in Denmark is higher than that in Spain. This can be done by deducing the statement of this fact from the following premisses: the suicide rate of Protestants is generally higher than that of Catholics; the population of Denmark is predominantly Protestant; and the population of Spain is predominantly Catholic. The first of these premisses (which expresses a lower-level law) can itself be explained by deducing it from a higher-level, theoretical law, that suicide rates vary inversely with the degree of social integration, together with the additional premiss that Catholics display a greater degree of social integration than Protestants. The same theoretical law can also be used to explain other lower-level regularities, such as the higher rate of suicide amongst the unmarried, as compared with the married.

Further, all these claims can be tested by reference to empirical data, such as the differences in rates of suicide between different countries, religious groups and so on. For instance, between 1960 and 1964, the suicide rates in Denmark and Spain averaged 18.8 and 5.1 per 100,000 population respectively (Giddens, 1971, p. 421). Durkheim, working in the 1890s (when suicide data do not appear to have been available for Spain), selected as part of his evidence for the general relations between suicide rates and religious affiliation, the figures in *Table 1* for Switzerland because 'as French and German populations exist there, the influence of the confession is observable separately in each case'. (Durkheim, 1952, p. 154).

Table 1: **Suicide rates (1876) for Swiss Cantons**
Classified according to religion and race

	Per million inhabitants	
	French Cantons	*German Cantons*
Catholics	83	87
Protestants	453	293

A problem for empirical testing might seem to arise for the claims about 'social integration', since this is clearly a theoretical, rather than an observational, concept. However, this difficulty is dealt with by defining and measuring social integration in terms of various empirical indicators such as: the number of individuals interacted with in a given time, the frequency of these interactions, the number of different types of social relations, and their degrees of intimacy—particularly in the area of familial relations (see Douglas, 1967, p. 39). These indicators are held to be 'objective' or reliable in the sense that all competent observers would report the same 'observations'.

Finally, in this positivist interpretation of Durkheim's theory, moral or political attitudes towards suicide and religion are to be seen as completely irrelevant in assessing the merits of the theory. Nor does anything follow from it about the rights or wrongs of suicide itself, though the theory could possibly be used to predict changes in suicide rates, and as a basis for social policies aimed to reduce these. Indeed, for positivists the study of suicide can be seen as an exemplary case of a phenomenon that, having for centuries been the subject of philosophical and religious debate, often involving moral evaluations of the victim's *motives*, eventually became, by the early nineteenth century, an object of properly scientific investigation, especially in the work of the 'moral statisticians', such as Quetelet (see Giddens, 1965; and Atkins and Jarrett, this volume). The value-neutrality of the scientific analysis is reflected in the way Durkheim carefully excluded any reference to the victims' motives from his definition of suicide, following his general methodological rule that 'science, to be objective, ought to borrow the material for its initial definitions directly from perceptual data' (Durkheim, 1964, p. 43).

Alternatives to positivist science

Before considering some criticisms of positivist *social* science, I want to emphasize that the positivist conception of science has been widely attacked as an account of the *natural* sciences. For instance, the idea of 'theory-neutral data' involved in its view of the relations between theory and observation has been rejected by many philosophers of science (see Hindess, 1973, Appendix; Benton, 1977, chapter 4; and Krige, this volume). Further, a number of alternative, non-positivist, conceptions of the natural sciences have been developed, both in the past, and more recently. I will briefly outline one of these, usually called *'realism'*. It can best be introduced via its argument that the positivist account of explanation fails to distinguish between predictive and explanatory knowledge.

The objection goes like this. By presenting explanation simply as an argument from statements of laws and conditions, positivists confuse providing information that would enable us to predict something, with describing how and why it came about. What is missing is any reference to the actual connections between phenomena, to the underlying structures and mechanisms that generate the regularities expressed in statements of scientific laws. To describe these connections, it is often necessary to postulate the existence of unobservable entities such as molecules, viruses, or magnetic fields.

For the realist, then, theories are primarily seen as attempts to characterise the nature and mode of operation of such entities. The chief virtue of theoretical laws is not, as it is for the positivists, that lower-level laws can be derived from them—thereby achieving economy and rigour in a deductive system. Rather, it is that they describe the fundamental processes that actually sustain the observable regularities represented in those lower-level laws. Thus, for example, Marx's account of modes of production, and Freud's of the unconscious, might be treated in this sense, as theories, by the realist[4].

Nonetheless, despite their rejection of the ontological primacy of the observable, realists retain the view that some form of empirical testing is an essential element in the assessment of scientific theories. In this respect, realism differs significantly from certain other, non-positivist conceptions of science, especially those influenced by the *rationalist* tradition in the history of science and philosophy. According to this, scientific knowledge is basically established by *a priori* forms of argument and analysis; and empirical data are seen primarily as *illustrations* of theories, rather than crucial tests of their truth or falsity.[5]

Since there are these alternatives to the positivist view of science, it is worth keeping the following question in mind, when considering criticisms of positivist social science. Do these criticisms result in all forms of methodological naturalism being rejected, or only that involving a specific, positivist conception of science? In other words, to what extent would the criticisms be met by a methodological naturalism based on a *non*-positivist view of science? These questions are relevant to issues raised in the next section.

Experience and meaning

A number of important objections can be made to positivist social science, and the suicide example can illustrate them. First, there is the claim that positivism systematically excludes any account of the experiences, perceptions, feelings and other 'subjective states' of the participants in social relationships. But without any grasp of these, it is impossible even to *describe* the so-called 'data', let alone *explain* anything. A strict positivism in the social sciences—especially psychology—results in *behaviourism*, in the attempt to describe social action in terms of observable behaviour. However, what counts as a particular action cannot be defined purely in terms of its overt, observable features. Indeed, the very same pattern of behaviour can constitute quite different actions, depending upon the intentions and rules involved (Lessnoff, 1974, chapter 2).

Thus, suicide statistics cannot be regarded merely as 'observational data'. A suicide is not simply a dead body. Although Durkheim tried to define suicide without reference to the person's *intention* to end his or her life, this not only departs from the ordinary meaning of the term, but from the meaning given to it by those upon whose decisions the official statistics of suicide are normally based, e.g. coroners. For to *describe* death as a 'suicide' is not simply a matter of observation, but also requires the attribution of intentions (Atkinson, 1968). And to *explain why* people kill themselves requires a grasp of the way they perceive their situation; references to religious affiliation, marital status, or the degree of social integration, mean little unless they can be spelled out in terms of the agent's viewpoint, experiences, etc. (Douglas, 1967). Yet positivism's doctrine of the ontological primacy of the observable rules this out.

One response to such objections would be to suggest that, although they are powerful arguments against positivism, they do not necessarily have force against a realist naturalism, i.e. a methodological naturalism based on a realist conception of science. For, with its rejection of the positivist restriction to observables, a realist social science might be able to incorporate 'subjective states' and meanings on the model of unobservable items in the natural sciences (Keat and Urry, 1975, chapter 7). But even if this could be done, there is a second objection to positivist social science that is more fundamental, and would seem to apply also to realism, since it is aimed at something their epistemologies share.

The basic claim of the objection is that whereas in the natural sciences the data consist of empirical observations, the 'data' in the social sciences consist of social meanings; and the interpretation and understanding of meanings cannot be assimilated or reduced to the discovery and validation of observational data. This can be brought out most directly by considering the process of reading a literary text. Although this clearly involves the visual perception of physical marks, to understand the text is not to observe or causally explain those marks: it is to grasp the sense or meaning that they are used to express, through various conventions and rules. Similarly, in listening to someone talking, one is trying to understand what is said, not to describe or explain the acoustic phenomena. In the social sciences, we are studying a subject-matter one of whose distinctive characteristics is its use of language, and, at a variety of different levels, the understanding of social action requires the understanding of language and related forms of meaning (Taylor, 1971; Apel, 1972; Connerton, 1976, Part II).

For instance, an important source of evidence for the study of suicide is suicide-notes. What sort of 'understanding' is involved in using these? Apart from grasping their literal meaning—which may sometimes be quite difficult, and is anyway a quite different process from scientific observation—we need to decide which of various possible overall meanings, such as 'revenge', 'repentance', or 'escape', is being expressed in a particular note (Douglas, 1966). Furthermore, we may want to show how these form parts of more general systems of shared meanings in a particular group or form of society—and to discover what are sometimes called the 'basic notions' presupposed by these systems, specific conceptions of human agency, authority, work, nature, masculinity and femininity, and so on (Fay, 1975, chapter 4).

This idea of 'interpreting meanings' has been a significant element in the rather vague and diffuse concept of *verstehen* that has been central to much of the opposition to positivist social science (Outhwaite, 1975). It has often been connected with doctrines of empathy, intuitive insight, or imaginative re-enactment, especially by its positivist critics (e.g. Nagel, 1961, ch. 13), but I think this is misleading, since the processes are quite different (Leat, 1972). And it is often presented, even by its proponents, as showing that the social sciences are essentially subjective, lacking in objective criteria of validity. But against this it can be argued that, whilst the criteria of validity for interpretive knowledge may be *different* from those for (empirical) scientific knowledge, this does not mean that they are inferior, much less non-existent. Further, it is important to see that this kind of interpretive understanding is necessarily involved in the production of knowledge in the natural sciences. For this is a *social* process, of which communicative interactions between scientists are an essential feature (Apel, 1972; Giddens, 1976).

Criticisms of value-freedom

The remaining two objections to be considered concern the claims of positivist social science to value-freedom. The first is this. The basic concepts of any theoretical framework in the social sciences can always be shown to express specific evaluative attitudes towards human existence, the organisation of society, the relationships between individuals or groups, and so on. To adopt one such framework rather than another is, amongst other things, to accept that evaluative position, to commit oneself to the political and moral values it reflects (Taylor, 1967; Israel, 1972). For instance, the concept of social integration, and the related concept of normative integration, which are involved in Durkheim's accounts of egoistic and anomic suicide, are bound up with a specific view of what are to be seen as normal, and pathological, conditions of society. Thus the concept of 'anomie' is essentially evaluative, just as that of 'alienation' is in Marx's earlier writings (Ollman, 1971), but the values are by no means identical (Lukes, 1967), and part of what is involved in choosing between Durkheimian and Marxist theories is the commitment to one set of values rather than another.

The second objection is this. The positivist conception of the natural sciences presupposes a view of the physical world as a possible object of prediction and human technological control. It is for this reason that a central role is given to the discovery of laws, and that prediction and explanation are so closely connected. But if this conception of science is used as the model for the social sciences, what will be produced is a technology of social control, which treats humans as objects to be manipulated, and the design and organization of societies as an engineering problem, to be solved by scientific expertise—and, of course, political power (Marcuse, 1964; Fay, 1975). Thus positivists are mistaken in claiming, as they often do, that the social sciences only provide information about the likely results of various actions and processes, without in any way determining for what political ends this information is used. For to see politics in terms of using the most 'effective' means to given ends is in itself to adopt a distinctive political position, a technocratic and elitist one.

These two objections operate at significantly different levels, and are largely independent of each other. The former is concerned with the different values presupposed by the specific contents of different theoretical frameworks, whereas the latter is aimed at the more general values presupposed by *any* such framework constructed from a positivist standpoint. And each objection can be used as a basis for quite different, and mutually incompatible, responses to positivism. For instance, the first can lead to a total scepticism about the possibility of producing scientific knowledge about social reality and withdrawal from any such attempt: or instead to the call for politically committed, explicitly 'partisan' social science, which makes its evaluative assumptions clear, and, while striving for technical competence does not try to fulfil the expectations of people who do not share them. The second can lead to the attempt to construct a conception of social science that does not involve positivism's technocratic values, such as the Frankfurt School's idea of 'critical theory' (Jay, 1973; Connerton, 1976); or to a total rejection of any kind of science of society, and the adoption instead of some form of romantic anti-scientism.

Notes

1. For simplicity, I have excluded the use of statistical laws here, which involve a slightly different form of explanatory argument; see Lessnoff (1974, Chs. 1 and 3) and Benton (1977, Ch. 3).

2. This requirement is closely related to the concept of reliability in measurement, introduced in most social science methods tests; for a brief critical discussion, see Sjoberg and Nett (1968, pp. 298-302).

3. The account that follows is in the spirit of the kind of positivist interpretation adopted by many American sociologists; e.g. Homans (1964) and Merton (1968, chapter 4). Recently, several writers have challenged this positivist 'appropriation' of Durkheim; see Hirst (1975) and Benton (1977, chapter 5). I discuss only one of Durkheim's three types of suicide, *egoistic*, and in outlining anti-positivist criticisms of the theory, in Section 5 below, I ignore the problem of relating explanations of *individual* suicides to explanations of *rates* of suicide: see Giddens (1965) on this.

4. Freudian theory could be considered as an attempt to explain human activity by means of a description of the instinctual sources of various desires and wishes, and the operation of unconscious mental processes to generate characteristic patterns of behaviour and experience. For a realist discussion of Marx, see for example, Keat and Urry (1975, chapter 5). In addition, Bhaskar (1975) and Benton (1977) are attempts to develop a generally realist view of the social sciences, and criticisms of the positivist conception of science. Whether realism is consistent with some versions of the attacks on theory-neutrality seems to me an unresolved issue.

5. The rationalist element in the 'Scientific Revolution' is emphasised in e.g. Koyré (1968). Losee (1972) provides useful information on some rationalist philosophers of science. Some critics consider that there are rationalist elements in Althusser's view of science, which is discussed, for example, in Benton (1977, chapter 9).

Bibliography

Adey, G., and Frisby, D. (eds.), 1976, *The Positivist Dispute in German Sociology*, (translation by the editors), London, Heinemann.

Apel, K. O., 1972, 'Communication and the foundations of the humanities', *Acta Sociologica*, vol. 15, pp. 7-27.

Atkinson, M., 1968, 'On the sociology of suicide', *Sociological Review*, vol. 16, pp. 83-92, reprinted in Giddens, 1971, below.

Benton, T., 1977, *Philosophical Foundations of the Three Sociologies*, London, Routledge & Kegan Paul.

Bhaskar, R., 1975, *A Realist Theory of Science*, Leeds, Alma Books.

Connerton, P. (ed.), 1976, *Critical Sociology*, Harmondsworth, Penguin.

Douglas, J., 1966, 'The sociological analysis of social meanings of suicide', *European Journal of Sociology*, vol. 7, pp. 249-75, reprinted in Giddens, 1971.

Douglas, J., 1967, *The Social Meanings of Suicide*, Princeton, Princeton University Press.

Durkheim, E., 1952, *Suicide: A Study in Sociology* (first published in 1897 as *Le Suicide*; translated by J. A. Spaulding and G. Simpson), London, Routledge & Kegan Paul.

Durkheim, E., 1964, *The Rules of Sociological Method*, New York, Free Press.

Fay, B., 1975, *Social Theory and Political Practice*, London, Allen and Unwin.

Giddens, A., 1965, 'The suicide problem in French sociology', *British Journal of Sociology*, vol. 16, pp. 3-15, reprinted in Giddens, 1971, below.

Giddens, A. (ed.), 1971, *The Sociology of Suicide*, London, Frank Cass.

Giddens, A. (ed.), 1974, *Positivism and Sociology*, London, Heinemann.

Giddens, A., 1976, *New Rules of Sociological Method*, London, Hutchinson.

Hempel, C., 1965, 'Aspects of scientific explanation', in his *Aspects of Scientific Explanation*, New York, Free Press.

Hindess, B., 1973, *The Use of Official Statistics in Sociology*, London, Macmillan.

Hirst, P., 1975, *Durkheim, Bernard and Epistemology*, London, Routledge & Kegan Paul.

Homans, G., 1964, 'Contemporary theory in sociology', in R. Faris (ed.), *Handbook of Modern Sociology*, Chicago, Rand McNally.

Israel, J., 1972, 'Is a non-normative social science possible?', *Acta Sociologica*, vol. 15, pp. 69-89.

Jay, M., 1973, *The Dialectical Imagination*, London, Heinemann.

Keat, R., and Urry, J., 1975, *Social Theory as Science*, London, Routledge & Kegan Paul.

Kolakowski, L., 1972, *Positivist Philosophy*, Harmondsworth, Penguin.

Koyré, A., 1968, *Metaphysics and Measurement*, London, Chapman and Hall.

Leat, D., 1972, 'Misunderstanding Verstehen', *Sociological Review*, vol. 20, 1972, pp. 29-37.

Lessnoff, M., 1974, *The Structure of Social Science*, London, Allen and Unwin.

Losee, J., 1972, *A Historical Introduction to the Philosophy of Science*, Oxford, Oxford University Press.

Lukes, S., 1967, 'Alienation and Anomie', in P. Laslett and W. Runciman (eds.), *Philosophy, Politics and Society*, Series III, Oxford, Blackwell.

Marcuse, H., 1964, *One-Dimensional Man*, London, Routledge & Kegan Paul.

Merton, R., 1968, *Social Theory and Social Structure*, New York, Free Press.

Nagel, E., 1961, *The Structure of Science*, London, Routledge & Kegan Paul.

Ollman, B., 1971, *Alienation*, Cambridge, Cambridge University Press.

Outhwaite, W., 1975, *Understanding Social Life*, London, Allen and Unwin.

Sjoberg, C., and Nett, R., 1968, *A Methodology for Social Research*, New York, Harper and Row.

Taylor, C., 1967, 'Neutrality in political science', in P. Laslett and W. Runciman (eds.), *Philosophy, Politics and Society*, Series III, Oxford, Blackwell.

Taylor, C., 1971, 'Interpretation and the sciences of man', *Review of Metaphysics*, vol. 25, pp. 3-51; partly reprinted in Connerton, 1976, above.

Weber, M., 1949, *The Methodology of the Social Sciences* (translated by E. A. Shils and H. A. Finch), New York, Free Press.

8.

Liz Atkins and David Jarrett

The Significance of 'Significance Tests'

Significance tests perform a vital function in the social sciences because they appear to supply an objective method of drawing conclusions from quantitative data. Sometimes they are used mechanically, with little comment, and with even less regard for whether or not the required assumptions are satisfied. Often, too, they are used in a way that distracts attention from consideration of the practical importance of the questions posed or that disguises the inadequacy of the theoretical basis for the investigation conducted.

We shall show how these tests developed historically from methodological ideas imported from the natural sciences and from ideological commitments inherent in nineteenth century social thought. We shall use the results of a recent investigation to present and criticise tests of significance. And in describing alternative approaches to evaluating research we shall argue that the central status of these tests in social science is by no means based on a consensus, even amongst statisticians, as to their appropriateness.

1. The meaning and appeal of significance tests

Significance tests are the most widely used technique of *statistical inference*, the branch of statistics which aims to draw general conclusions from small amounts ('samples') of data.[1] In this century, the problem of inference has been formalised through the use of probability theory, and eventually a set of rules was developed for deciding when such generalisations should be made.

The setting up of formal rules has led to the impression that generalisations based on tests of significance are objective, in the sense that any bias on the part of the person reporting the results is eliminated. The pursuit of objectivity through the adoption of quantification and statistical methods would, it was hoped, lead to value-free social science. Advocates of this approach asserted that it was 'not the business of the social scientist in arriving at laws of group behaviour to permit himself to be influenced by considerations of how his conclusions will coincide with existing notions, or what the effect of his findings on the social order will be . . . Students of the class struggle in economics and sociology have much to learn from this attitude.' (Lundberg, 1929, pp. 404-5). It was at the turn of the century that the newly emerging social sciences were attempting to establish their credibility as respectable academic disciplines in the universities and as valuable aids to understanding the social and political problems faced by governments. An obvious way of doing this seemed to be the adoption of as many as possible of the methods which appeared to be so successful in the natural sciences. In pursuit of this aim, precise measurement and the search for social laws—often taking the form of crude analogies of laws from the physical sciences—were seen as the way to achieve a science of the social world. Methods of statistical analysis, and tests of significance in particular, gave these disciplines just what they were looking for—an automatic method of producing general-isations which, by its objectivity, conferred scientific status. The sociologist C. C. Taylor, advocating that social science pursue quantitative approaches, exemplifies this view: 'Any fact is simple that can be measured. Any body of facts that can be measured can be tabulated. From any body of facts that can be tabulated laws can be formulated.' (Taylor, 1920, p. 731).

Within the framework of this commonsense empiricist ap-proach to the production of knowledge, he explicitly pointed to the importance of gaining legitimacy for social science through its incorporation of scientific method.

> It is imperative that the social sciences win for themselves the acceptance of their generalisations as trustworthy. A faith in such trustworthiness has almost as great a part to play in converting a body of knowledge into 'science' as has the established method of analysing phenomena or an adequate set of working tools. (Taylor, 1920, pp. 731-2).

The encouragement of healthy scepticism towards social science 'findings' is often precluded by the seemingly unchallenge-able assertion that the results of an investigation have passed a statistical 'test of significance'. A typical example of the way such 'findings' are reported is: A higher proportion of middle-class than working-class women claim to have happy marriages, and the difference in proportions is statistically significant. But the word *significant* is ambiguous, and this ambiguity has resulted in a general confusion about what significance tests mean, and, what they do *not* mean. The term was coined to mean strictly only that the sample data 'signify', in the sense that they *indicate*, the existence of a difference in the population(s) sampled. However, a 'significant' result sounds as if it must be an important result scientifically or socially—such as the clarification of a socially important problem, the development of an explanation for some puzzling phenomenon, or the success of a new programme of action. Not only the general public, but social scientists, politicians and even statisticians are apt to confuse statistical significance with these other kinds of significance. Most standard textbooks on statistics do, admittedly, contain a paragraph warning the reader not to assume that statistical significance is the same thing as *substantive* significance (that is, theoretical or practical importance); but having delivered this warning they proceed to present the student with a tool-kit of tests to be applied in a variety of standard situations, leaving questions of substantive significance aside.

Not all social scientists, however, have adopted the use of tests of significance in trying to develop theories about the social world: some have argued that the ritual, uncritical use of such methods has held back the development of the social sciences (see, for example, Willer, 1967; Ford, 1975, esp. ch. 19; and MacKenzie, 1976); yet others reject them altogether along with the whole gamut of quantitative approaches to social science. Nor have social scientists been alone in criticising the conventional test of significance; quite soon after such tests were presented as a systematic way of making inferences from data, statisticians, aware of their limitations, attempted to put them on firmer theoretical foundations. As a result, there are now several rival schools of statistical inference.

This raises an interesting question. If tests of significance are seriously limited as a way of making scientific inferences (as will be argued below), and if superior methods are claimed to exist, why are they still the dominant technique used by social scientists and taught to students? This question prompts us to look not just at the theoretical claims made for significance tests, but also at why they are used in social science. We shall then see more clearly that, as well as their practical or theoretical functions, these methods have a particular ideological role different from that of other methods of statistical inference.

2. Historical development: from the study of stars to the study of people

Reviewing briefly the historical development of significance tests gives a number of insights into their present-day role.[2] It can be shown that they derive mainly from attempts in the late nineteenth century to provide a more rational and objective basis for the consideration of social and political questions (see Young, this volume).

An earlier stage in the development of statistics, however, was the application to the study of human characteristics of a model originally developed in the early nineteenth century for theorising the errors of observation in astronomy. This model, involving the so-called 'law of error', has come to be known as the Normal distribution; it is one of the most commonly assumed distributions in tests of significance. In astronomy, it was demonstrated that the probability of any observation differing from the 'true value' by a specified amount could be calculated using the Normal model; this was justified by assuming that the overall error is composed of a number of 'elemental' errors—small and random mistakes which accumulate to give an overall error which is *probably* small (i.e. close to zero, but which *may* be large.[3] This method was presented in popular (if garbled) form in the *Penny Encyclopaedia* of 1839, in which instructions were given for finding 'the probability that *truth* lies within a certain degree of nearness to the average' (cited in Walker, 1929, p. 61, our emphasis).

The Belgian Adolphe Quetelet, turning from astronomy to social analysis in his concern over the social upheavals of the 1830s in Europe (Lazarsfeld, 1961), imported this theory into the study of human characteristics. Making a direct analogy with the 'true value' of an astronomical observation, he assumed the existence of *L'Homme Moyen*, the typical or average man that Nature consistently aimed at. The variation of human characteristics would then be due to 'errors' in her aim. Analogous to the centre of gravity of a body in physics, the *homme moyen* would be 'the mean about which the social elements oscillate . . . a fictitious being for whom everything takes place in conformity with the mean results obtained for society. If one seeks to establish, in any way, the basis of a social physics, it is he whom one must consider' (Quetelet, 1835; quoted by Gillispie, 1963, p. 446; our translation). Thus a justification was provided for the reduction of the study of variety among human beings to the study of the average, which could typify a whole population or group of people.

The justification for making the analogy between human variation and errors of observation was put by Francis Galton, who developed its application to the study of human genetics:

> I need hardly remind the reader that the Law of Error upon which these Normal Values are based, was excogitated for the use of astronomers and others who are concerned with extreme accuracy of

measurement, and without the slightest idea until the time of Quetelet that they might be applicable to human measures. But Errors, Differences, Deviations, Divergencies, Dispersions, and individual Variations all spring from the same kind of causes . . . The Law of Error finds a footing wherever the individual peculiarities are wholly due to the combined influence of a multitude of 'accidents'. (Galton, 1889; cited by Walker, 1929, p. 47).

The appeal of this 'Law' to statisticians, particularly those working in genetics and eugenics (see MacKenzie, this volume) was so strong that it was *imposed* theoretically on the development of measurements for all human characteristics—the most notorious example being that of intelligence testing, where the measurements are constructed so that they follow a Normal distribution for the population of individuals on which the test is 'normed'. Although the logic of a test of significance can in principle be applied whatever distribution is assumed, this assumption about the 'normality' of human characteristics has dominated the theoretical development of tests and hence is implicit in many applications of significance tests.[4]

Galton was not alone in eulogising these new ideas of Quetelet's. The English astronomer Sir John Herschel saw statistics as a foundation for social science:

> Among those branches of knowledge which are most effectually advanced by consideration of mean or average results concluded from great masses of registered facts, to the exclusion of individual instances, statistics hold beyond all question the most important rank as regards the social well-being of man. . . it is the basis of social and political dynamics and affords the only secure ground on which truth or falsehood of the theories and hypotheses of that complicated science can be brought to the test . . . it is the business of sound theory so to analyse or to combine [statistical observations] as to educe from them those deeper-seated elements which enter into the expression of general laws. (Herschel, 1857, pp. 434–5, 436).

But Herschel was also aware that the causes of statistical regularities were not automatically evident. 'It must never be forgotten that tendencies only, not causes, emerge as the first product of statistical inquiry—and this consideration, moreover, ought to make us extremely reserved in applying to any of the crude results of such inquiries, the axioms or the language of direct unimpeded causation' (*ibid.*, pp. 439–40).

The possibility of discovering regularities and laws concerning the average or typical man brought the hope of a scientific approach to social problems. Combined with the methods of estimation of the 'probable error' of an average, the nineteenth century had, according to some of its leading thinkers, developed the means of measuring the political, social and economic world and of distinguishing differences and associations which were 'due to chance' from those which indicated the operation of some Law.

The first systematic presentation of a test of significance to the Royal Statistical Society was in 1885, when F. Y. Edgeworth described it as the method of 'elimination of chance'. As an illustration of its potential he used it 'to determine whether the observed differences between the mean stature of 2315 criminals and the mean stature of 8585 British adult males belonging to the general population is significant' (Edgeworth, 1885, p. 187) and found 'that the observed difference between the proposed means, namely about 2 inches, far exceeds thrice the modulus[5] of that curve, namely 0.2. The difference therefore "comes by cause"' (*ibid*, p. 188). Then, as so often happens today, the question of what the cause might be was ignored, or dealt with by off-the-cuff speculations—the significance test being seen as an end in itself.

The use of these methods for determining 'facts' about the characteristics of human beings was markedly extended in twentieth century social science, so that by the 1950s it was even necessary for researchers at the Columbia Bureau of Applied Research to make an extended defence of the omission of significance tests from their reports.[6] However, around this time, a number of other social scientists also began to criticise the ritual use of these tests and to suggest that they were in fact often inappropriate, misleading or inferior to other methods of inference.[7]

3. The conventional test of significance

To make the discussion more concrete we will begin by following the procedure of a typical test of significance taken from a recent article in social psychology (Iwawaki, Eysenck and Eysenck, 1977). Its authors use a 'personality inventory' to investigate what they claim is a widely held belief, that different nations are characterized by different 'personality traits' such as 'the stereotyped views of the extroverted Italian and the introverted Swede' cited in a parallel paper (Eysenck, Adelaja and Eysenck, 1977, p. 171).Through the application of such an apparently objective personality inventory in their research, they claim that their findings support the existence of these stereotypic popular views. The method chosen was to compare the responses of samples of Japanese and English people on scales for three characteristics the inventory was supposed to measure—neuroticism, extroversion and psychoticism. They concluded that 'it will be clear that the Japanese are much more introverted, much more neurotic, and much higher on [the psychoticism scale] than are the English.'

The authors are referring here to the average scores of their samples (see columns headed 'Mean' in *Table 1*) and describing, for example, the result that the *mean* score of the Japanese sample is higher than the *mean* score of the English sample on the neuroticism scale. (Note that this does not imply that *every* member of the Japanese sample is more neurotic than *every* member of the English sample.) These differences between the average scores thus seem to support their

Table 1: **Means and standard deviations on psychoticism (P) extroversion (E) and neuroticism (N) for Japanese and English university students**

		P Mean	P SD	E Mean	E SD	N Mean	N SD
Male	Japanese	5.9	3.2	10.9	4.3	12.6	3.9
	English	2.4	2.6	13.2	3.9	9.4	4.4
Female	Japanese	4.8	2.8	10.3	3.8	12.8	3.7
	English	1.7	1.8	12.7	3.4	10.5	3.7

Source: Iwawaki, Eysenck and Eysenck (1977) Table 1

hypotheses about national characteristics. Having carried out a number of significance tests the authors report: 'all the differences, for both sexes, are well beyond the .001 level of significance.'[8]

We shall reconstruct the steps involved in carrying out such a test of significance in order to see what this statement means. The problem they are attempting to solve in using this test is that of drawing a general conclusion about the populations of England and Japan when the information to hand is about samples selected from these populations. A test of significance lays down a set of rules for deciding when sample results are inconsistent with a hypothesis about the populations. The steps in this procedure are:[9]

a. Formulation of the null hypothesis

The purpose of the test is to decide whether the sample results support the *research hypothesis* that there is a difference between the Japanese and English population means. A *null hypothesis*,[10] stating that there is no difference, is set up in contradistinction to this, and tested against the data; if the null hypothesis is 'rejected', the research hypothesis is 'accepted'.

b. Specification of a probability model for the process assumed to have produced the sample data

A sampling procedure can generate different results depending on the 'luck of the draw' in selecting members of the sample(s) from the corresponding population(s). So, in this example, although the means of the *selected* samples are known, we are not sure how far they might differ. from the means of other possible samples, or—more to the point—from the respective population means. A probability model, given certain assumptions, can be used to represent this uncertainty, and to calculate the chance of each of the possible results we might observe using the sampling procedure (just as one can calculate the chance of each Bridge hand which a player might possibly get). Iwawaki et al. do not describe the probability model they use but the usual test[11] for the difference between two means involves assuming that

1. the variable of interest has a Normal distribution within each population;
2. the variance of the variable is the same in the two populations; and
3. members of the samples are selected at random, and independently of each other, from the two populations.

c. Calculation of a test-statistic and decision about rejecting the null hypothesis

As we mentioned above, tests of significance have been devised for many standard situations (the t-test and the X^2 (chi-squared) test are common examples). These provide 'test-statistic' formulae to be calculated from the sample observations. The more extreme the value of the test-statistic the more improbable the observations would be—if the null hypothesis were true. The most extreme values of the test-statistic are thus taken as evidence against the null hypothesis.[12]

Objectivity is supposed to be built into the procedure by deciding, *in advance* of calculating the particular samples' test statistic, what range of extreme values will constitute grounds for rejecting the null hypothesis. If the test statistic calculated from the sample value falls in this range we reject the null-hypothesis in favour of the research hypothesis. Thus the decision is not supposed to involve a post-hoc subjective judgement that the test statistic was 'big enough' to reject the null hypothesis.

The range of extreme values is chosen so that it is 'practically impossible' that such values will be observed *if* the null hypothesis is true. By 'practically impossible' is meant that they have a very small probability of being observed; this small probability is called the *significance level* of the test. In most uses of these tests one of three small probabilities is conventionally used: .05 (1 chance in 20), .01 (1 chance in 100) or .001 (1 chance in 1000). This convention appears to be linked with earlier attempts to give a numerical definition of 'moral certainty' by the Swiss mathematician Jacques Bernoulli at the beginning of the eighteenth century (see Walker, 1929; and Hacking, 1975). In connection with decisions about the guilt or innocence of an accused person he suggested that a probability of .99 or .999 would be 'practically' equivalent to 1 (certainty).[13] However, the choice of a value to be regarded as numerically 'close' to 1 (certainty), or 0 (impossibility), is usually arbitrary.[14]

While in theory the choice of significance level is supposed to be made before analysing the data, in practice researchers often state the smallest level at which their sample results are significant, or choose the level *after* carrying out the calculations. Iwawaki et al. state that their results were 'well beyond the .001 level of significance', which tells us that, if they had chosen in advance a range having a .001 probability, they would reject their null hypothesis and conclude that the population means were different. By stating that the differences were *well beyond* the .001 level they are saying that they could have rejected their null hypothesis at a significance level much smaller than .001. This is taken as even more conclusive evidence against the null hypothesis.

This use of probability to judge the plausibility of a hypothesis has an intuitive rationale. We are confronted with a set of data supposed to have been produced by a chance mechanism; the idea is to judge the plausibility of a hypothesis by the probability it gives to these observed data. For example, if you were at a bus stop where Number 7 and Number 15 buses are both supposed to run roughly every five minutes, you might at first hypothesise that each bus which appeared in the distance was equally likely to be a 7 or a 15. Having waited for an hour and seen nothing but 15s you might begin to cast doubt on this hypothesis and find some other hypothesis (for instance that there is a severe traffic jam on the Number 7 route or that their drivers have gone on strike) that gives a more plausible explanation of the data. But this simple idea requires elaboration to be developed into a formal theory of inference—hence the rival schools referred to above.

4. What's wrong with the conventional test?

We shall first discuss the problems associated with the testing procedure as such before going on to consider the wider context influencing the use of significance tests—such as those concerned with publishing opportunities, research funding and policy-making.

a. The nature of the null hypothesis under test

Consider again the paper by Iwawaki et al. discussed above. A significance test was used to try to answer the question: Is the hypothesis that there is no difference between the population mean scores true or false? The mathematics of statistical theory involves interpreting this question literally: Is the difference between the population means *exactly* zero? But this is not usually the question which a social scientist wishes to ask: a small difference between the population means is unlikely to be regarded as important—and only rarely could any credence be attached to the hypothesis that two population means were *exactly* equal. In fact by choosing large enough samples we can effectively *guarantee* that this null hypothesis will be rejected—for the conventional significance test becomes increasingly sensitive to any small difference between the population means as the size of sample is increased.[15] So if researchers have the resources to obtain large enough samples the null hypothesis is likely to be rejected.

b. The explanation given if the null hypothesis is rejected

The zero-difference hypothesis is often defended as being the first stage in research, and is typically expressed as a hypothesis that any difference observed between samples is 'due to chance'. If chance alone could have produced the results in question it is taken that no other explanation needs to be considered; if the hypothesis that 'chance' produced the results is rejected, the inference is drawn that some 'cause' is at work (as in the quotation from Edgeworth above). An early example of such reasoning was presented in John Arbuthnot's 'Argument for Divine Providence' (1710). On the basis of calculations that the probability of the observed excess of male over female births would be very small if it were due to chance alone (i.e. if male and female births were actually equally likely), he concluded that a divine hand was at work in ensuring the excess of male births. In Arbuthnot's time only these two explanations (chance and God) would have been considered. In contemporary social science vastly different sets of theories are available, each claiming to explain the social world.

Nowadays the theoretical choice is not between chance and the researcher's theory, but amongst chance and *all other* possible explanations of the data. The rejection of the null hypothesis of chance says nothing about the plausibility of these competing alternatives.

c. The assumption of a particular probability model

A probability model involves assuming that some random process is at work producing the data. Most commonly this is assumed to result from the random selection of the sample from the corresponding population. In the Iwawaki example we would assume that random samples should thus have been drawn independently from the Japanese and English populations. In addition, as we saw above, it is usually necessary to make assumptions about the distribution of the variable of interest in the population, and only with these assumptions can our probability calculations be made. These assumptions require justification, since different assumptions require different tests and possibly lead to different conclusions. It is clear that Iwawaki, Eysenck and Eysenck did not select their samples at random; in the social sciences, tests of significance are commonly applied to data from samples which have not been randomly selected from any real population. The use of statistical inference then rests merely on hopes that the data can be regarded *as if* they had been obtained from a random sample drawn from some defined population.

This hopeful assumption is often accepted without question, partly because evidence rarely exists about whether it is reasonable or not. But different disciplines vary in the emphasis they give to procedures which might make it plausible. Psychologists often use any samples which are available—typically university students who volunteer or are recruited as 'subjects' for experiments—and treat these, without any justification, as if they were a randomly selected sample of the whole population. Opinion pollsters similarly tend to take whoever will answer their questions, but try to ensure that they get a sample which contains representatives of all sections of the population (see the discussion of 'quota sampling' in Marsh, this volume). In the kinds of surveys used by social administrators, educationalists or sociologists there is often an elaborate attempt to select the members of the sample using a random device.

But there is one reason—often mentioned but rarely allowed for in statistical analyses—why samples of people often cannot be treated as if they were randomly selected from the population of interest. Almost all samples consist only of people who volunteer to cooperate with the investigation, and there are usually good reasons to think that these people differ from those who do not co-operate or who are missed by the investigation (often called 'non-respondents'). It is very difficult to deal with this problem technically using the basic probability model;[16] it can be dealt with fully only by theorising the social processes by which some people became 'non-respondents'.

d. The sampled population and the general population

The fundamental point is that according to its theoretical assumptions the test of significance can only be used to produce a conclusion about the population from which the sample is *actually* randomly drawn. Suppose samples are selected at random from the populations of this year's university students in England and Japan, and the sample difference is found to be significant—leading us to conclude that there is a difference between the population means. This conclusion concerns the populations of this year's university students, and not next year's students, nor the English and Japanese races. But clearly an inference about some more *general population* is usually desired, and any such inference rests on an *additional* assumption that the sampled population is representative of the more general population. This assumption would have to be justified by arguments outside the test of significance, on which the level of significance has no bearing. Iwawaki et al., like most users of tests of significance, make no attempt to state, let alone justify, the assumptions on which their inferences depend. The important point is not that a statement of these assumptions would improve the technical presentation of the test of significance, but that the machinery of the test disguises their absence. The 'significant' result and the apparently objective conclusions rest on implicit assumptions, all of which must be assessed *theoretically* before any meaningful conclusions can be drawn.

e. The significance level

We have seen that tests are often based on unrealistic null hypotheses and unrealistic probability models, but let us discuss the situation where these are considered satisfactory. Here, the significance level is being used as a decision rule—to decide whether the null hypothesis is true or false. Assuming that is what we want to decide, does the choice of an *a priori* significance level serve our purpose?

Although the choice of a significance level is supposed to be rational and objective, in much social research there are no purely technical criteria on which this choice could be based. This problem forces the choice straight back to 'subjective' criteria (though these need not be just the researcher's personal whims) or else to 'arbitrary' conventions. There is no objective reason for regarding a probability of 1 in 20 (.05) as 'practically impossible' rather than a probability of 1 in 10 (.1); however, researchers often take .05 as the largest probability which is 'respectable' as a significance level. Events with probability .05 sometimes happen—data can be expected to be significant at the .05 level once in twenty times even when the null hypothesis is true; conversely, data may fail to reach the conventional significance levels despite the null hypothesis being false. By its very nature statistical inference is *uncertain* inference, concerned with probability and not certainty. Instead of recognising this uncertainty, however, an arbitrary significance level is chosen to mark a rigid cut-off point beyond which data are regarded as inconsistent with the null hypothesis.

f. The obscuring of 'measurement' problems

The very question of what the measurements used in a study mean can be disguised by the uncritical acceptance of significance tests. In the Iwawaki study the use of significance tests provides no assurance that the results are not due to cultural differences in the way the inventory is perceived, rather than to 'racial personality' differences. Measurement problems such as these were admitted to exist in a parallel study of Nigerians (Eysenck, Adelaja and Eysenck, 1977)—where the measure of 'psychoticism', for example, included a number of questions about treatment of animals which embodied the English norms of sentimentality about pets. But to the Nigerians 'animals' meant domestic animals, with consequent effects on their psychoticism scores. The use of sophisticated forms of measurement such as these 'scales' involves many assumptions about their meaning, and the application of a test of significance can distract attention from alternative explanations of the social origins of the differences observed. The social, racial or class origins and orientation of a research tradition are often embodied in the methods and assumptions which are generally taken for granted and thus are difficult to detect from within. They are often easier to detect—and challenge—from outside the particular research tradition (or in retrospect), when the social and political context of the study and its methods of measurement are seen in a comparative framework.

5. Why are tests of significance used for inference in the social sciences?

Of course, it might be argued, it is not a fault of statistical theory as such if the lack of theoretical precision in social science leads to the shoddy use of statistical methods. Statisticians may claim that the use of significance tests in these circumstances results from social scientists failing to understand that alternative approaches to inference avoid the problems detailed above. But there may be powerful reasons, apart from misunderstanding, for the dominance of significance testing over other methods.

An empiricist social researcher might argue in this respect that social science does not yet exist as a coherent set of well-established theories and that the task of research is to build up generalisations based on reliable data, and then to develop these into theories. In order to build up these generalisations and to avoid the researchers' own biases and preconceptions interfering in the process, there is a requirement for objective practical rules for deciding when a generalisation is justified, or when the data are inadequate for this purpose. Significance tests are claimed to provide such rules.

This argument may appear crude, but quite a lot of survey research in the social sciences is carried out in this kind of atheoretical way. 'Let's look and see what's significant' is not too far from the approach of some researchers, and when the data involve perhaps several hundred variables the practical temptations to use a ready-made decision rule are enormous.[17]

Of course, this whole approach to social science—the accumulation of 'facts' without any explanation—has been largely discredited as a methodology (see, for instance, Willer and Willer, 1973). Yet, even for research which avoids a crudely empiricist approach, the pressure to *decide*, in situations where the very use of probability models admits the uncertainty of the inference, has certain consequences for the presentation of knowledge. The significance test appears to guarantee the objectivity of the researcher's conclusions, and may even be presented as providing crucial support for the whole theory in which the research hypothesis was put forward. As we have seen, tests of significance cannot do either of these things—but it is not in the interests of anyone involved to admit this too openly.

In practice, the pressures on researchers to produce 'findings' supporting their hypotheses means that a non-significant result is rarely regarded as a refutation of the research hypothesis—instead the usual conclusion reached is that the study failed to *establish* that the differences were there. There is consequently an understandable reluctance to report such non-significant results, further encouraged by many journals accepting for publication only those articles which report significant results (see Sterling, 1959). Now, we have already seen that, say, twenty tests of the same hypothesis done at the .05 level can be expected to produce one significant result—even if there is no difference (or no relationship) in the population. Thus, either through the persistence of an individual researcher—whether playing the odds intentionally or not—or simply as a result of a number of attempts by different researchers holding similar theories to find confirmation for them, a result not established by previous testing may eventually be 'found' significant in some investigation and be reported. Obviously the interpretation of a significant result is different if it comes from a single test rather than after a run of 'unsuccessful' tests; yet if non-significant results go unreported no one can tell which situation applies.[18] This means that the formal justification for tests of significance is undermined by the pressures on social scientists indicated above.

Add to this the formidable career pressures on social researchers to produce new results rather than replications of other people's work and the significant result can reign unchallenged. Finally, the common practice of reporting only the significance level of the test and not the data on which it was calculated (often justified on grounds of space) ensures that no conflict with other research can be detected.

Significance tests are not only important for their effects on academic social theory. Like other forms of social statistics, they may be used to present political ideology as scientific fact. In the early part of this century Karl Pearson, one of the founders of modern statistical theory, became involved in the Eugenics movement (see MacKenzie, this volume). His encyclopaedic paper on 'The Problem of Alien Immigration into Great Britain' was written to discuss 'whether it is desirable in an already crowded country like Britain, to permit indiscriminate immigration, or if the conclusion be that it is not, on what grounds discrimination should be based' (Pearson and Moul, 1925, p. 3). His eugenic principles led him to assume that immigrants with what he held to be low 'intelligence' and physical inferiority should not be admitted. But he saw the 'problem' as even more difficult: would the immigrant 'blend with our population?' (*ibid*, p. 6). (This is where the 'rational' eugenic argument begins to crack a little and to show an underlying hostility to racial mixing.) Further, would the continued inflow of immigrants lead 'not only to economic distress, but to a spread of doctrines incompatible with the stability of our social and political systems?' (*ibid*, p. 7). For Pearson, there was

'only one solution to a problem of this kind, and it lies in the cold light of statistical inquiry. . . . We firmly believe we have no political, no religious, and no social prejudices. . . . We rejoice in numbers and figures for their own sake and, subject to human fallibility, collect our data—as all scientists must do—to find out the truth that is in them. . . . We can safely say that while it is impossible to avoid errors, they are not biased errors.' (*ibid.* p. 8)

His paper presents an extremely detailed statistical analysis of Jewish children's physical characteristics, together with ratings of their intelligence and home circumstances—the significance of each statistic being carefully assessed. The picture presented is of a group with poor health, low intelligence, having dirty clothes and bodies and often with illiterate parents. Having assessed these 'facts' with the objective method of statistical inquiry the conclusion is expressed rather curiously: '*The law of patriotism* for a crowded country surely must be to admit not those who merely reach our own average—and a fortiori not those who fall below—but only those who can give us either physically or mentally what we do not possess or possess in inadequate quantity.' (Pearson and Moul, 1925 p. 127; our emphasis). This conclusion is not derived from the facts as presented; it is a simple appeal to nationalism based on eugenic ideas. The careful amassing of facts does not answer the problems he started from, but it does give the *appearance* of providing a scientific answer.

With hindsight we do not have to look far for technical problems and preconceptions. What is presented as a *random* sample of the Jewish immigrant population was in fact the pupils at one Jewish school conveniently placed for the measurements to be made. More importantly, Pearson appeared to view these measurements, even such assessments as the cleanliness of clothes and bodies, as fixed racial attributes, which were neither the result of the living conditions of immigrants nor likely to change with time. Given the technical weaknesses and the transparent ideological preconceptions in Pearson's work, the test of significance provides illusory support for his claims of objectivity. It is obvious here that statistical methods were being used to legitimate a policy recommendation to which Pearson was already committed, and which can be readily recognised as racist.

This does not imply, of course, that tests of significance are always used for such purposes. But the political context of the social sciences, especially their role in social policy decisions, is a much more powerful determinant of which methods are used and in what way, than are the technical strengths or weaknesses of the methods themselves.

The use made of social research by government and other administrators stems from the need both for control of productive processes and for social control, as well as for the legitimation of policies designed to achieve these ends.[19] In such situations, administrators require a certain amount of crude information about the scale of the 'problem' and a clear framework for making rapid decisions that will not unduly disturb the status quo; they also need to be able to persuade people, first, that something is being done, and, second, that because the problem is being investigated 'scientifically', the results will present objective solutions. Tests of significance are clearly admirably suited for such requirements in that they provide *definite* and *apparently objective* decisions, in a basically *superficial* way.

6. Alternatives to the test of significance

We shall consider briefly two alternative approaches to statistical inference which are available, to illustrate further why any explanation of the continued dominance of tests of significance needs to consider social and political factors, in addition to technical ones.

One method, which has been in existence for as long as tests of significance, is called 'estimation'.[20] This involves calculating from the data an estimate of the value we are interested in—the average earnings of men compared with women, for example—together with an estimate of how imprecise the sample estimate might be. Methods of estimation share many of the problems of significance tests—being likewise based on probability model assumptions and requiring 'arbitrary' limits of precision.[21] But at least they do not require irrelevant null hypotheses to be set up nor do they force a decision about 'significance' to be made—the estimates can be presented and evaluated by statistical *and other* criteria, by the researcher or the reader. In addition the estimates of one investigation can be compared with others. While it is often the case that different measurements or methods of investigation or theoretical approaches lead to 'different' results, this is not a disadvantage: these differences reflect important theoretical differences about the meaning of the research and the conclusions to be drawn from it. And it is precisely those differences which are obscured by simply reporting the significance level of the results.

Methods of statistical estimation can be used with tests of significance—a (population) value is estimated, then the estimate is assessed for significance—but too often the estimates get submerged in the emphasis on the results of the tests of significance, which in some research reports replace the estimates completely by 'a galaxy of stars' (Guttman, 1977, p. 87) indicating their level of significance.

Statistics has almost come full circle—from the study of people to the study of stars.

The emphasis of social researchers on tests rather than estimation results not merely from the more spectacular appearance of the former in reports of findings. Many of the commonly-used social science computer packages lack convenient procedures for estimation. While this is to *some* extent a result of theoretical difficulties with certain estimation procedures, it is nevertheless important to recognise that this itself results from considerably more research effort in statistics having been put into developing tests than into estimation methods. This can be attributed fairly directly to the statisticians' professional position—namely of providing a technology which can immediately be recognised as useful by their 'clients'. As one prominent statistician has put it: 'It is often easier to be "exact" about significance procedures than confidence procedures [i.e. estimation]. By considering only the most null "null hypothesis" many inconvenient possibilities can be avoided.' (Tukey, 1954, p. 710).

The problems of trying to use probability as a key to objective inference are explicitly recognised in the major alternative approach to statistical inference. Some statisticians (usually referred to as 'Bayesians' after Thomas Bayes (1702-1761) whose principle of inverse probability forms the basis of their approach) have attempted to construct a theory of inference starting from the acceptance of subjective assessments of the plausibilities of the competing alternative models of the data. Their idea is that these subjective weightings of the relative plausibility of different hypotheses can be quantified as probabilities, and may then be updated or revised as a result of examining the data, rather in the way that the odds on the result of a General Election change over time as information (such as the results of opinion polls) is weighed up by punters and bookmakers.

But there are dangers in the Bayesian approach. It has been suggested that this method could be applied to all political decision-making by extending the logic of subjective assessment of plausibility into general social and political 'utility' functions. It is claimed that this would produce some decision of maximal utility to the community and would rationalise political (and other decision-making) processes. Used as an approach to both science and politics this fails to recognise the realities of the *sources* of these subjective evaluations. They are not freely determined, but are related to the existing forms of social and political structure and the associated ideologies and behavioural norms. While advocates of this approach have argued that it makes evaluations *explicit* and thus leads to greater recognition of conflicting value structures, the suggestion that a consensus decision could be produced technically by a weighted aggregation of these different values would merely result in another way of disguising or defusing these conflicts.

The Bayesian approach is, not surprisingly, anathema to those statisticians who insist on the need for statistics to be objective. But there is very little evidence that it is gaining adherents even among social scientists or public policy-makers, despite occasional articles presenting and recommending its use. We suggest that this is primarily because the *explicit* introduction of subjectivity would undermine the credibility of social science and policy research.[22]

7. Conclusion

There are no grounds for assuming that significance tests can serve as guarantors of the validity of research results, or that they can automatically sift out underlying laws of society buried in statistical data.

It is hardly surprising that empiricist views of science, and the structure of careers and institutions in social science, provide fertile ground for the use of procedures which tend to disguise the inadequacy of measurements, and the lack of developed theoretical explanations—as well as discouraging debate about alternative procedures. Nevertheless, the conclusion is clear: the use of significance tests is no substitute for analysis and interpretation founded on critical theory capable of addressing both the subject matter of the social sciences, and the research process itself, as social products.

Notes

1. We should point out here that statistical inference includes both significance tests (also called 'tests of hypotheses') and methods of estimation, of which the most commonly used method is that of confidence intervals.

2. For the history of probability and statistics see Hacking (1975), Walker (1929), Pearson and Kendall (1970) and Kendall and Plackett (1977).

3. The assumptions specified determine the familiar 'bell-shaped' normal distribution which depicts the probability of different sizes of overall error for a particular measurement; see *Diagram 1* overleaf. For details of the normal distribution, see Blalock (1972). For a discussion of the work of Gauss and others working in astronomy, see Pearson and Kendall (1970).

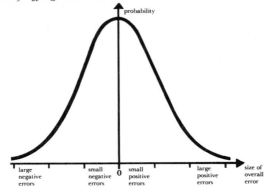

Diagram 1: The normal distribution of errors of measurement

4. Because of the Central Limit Theorem (see Blalock, 1972, pp. 220–222), normality assumptions may not be required for large enough samples.

So-called non-parametric or distribution-free tests (see Blalock, 1972, pp. 243–244) do not require strong assumptions about the distribution of the variables, though they still require randomly selected samples.

5. The *modulus* is a measure of the variation of possible sample values; it is slightly bigger than the standard error which is used today.

6. Members of the 'Columbia school' have explicitly shunned the use of significance tests in their work in favour of estimating the relative size of 'effects' of different variables; see the articles by Lipset, Trow and Coleman (1956) and P. Kendall (1957), and the criticism of Davis (1958), all reprinted in Henkel and Morrison (1970).

7. See, for example, many of the contributions in Henkel and Morrison (1970), and also Gould (1970).

8. This example was chosen as a typical test of significance for the difference between the mean (average) scores in two populations(Japan and England). This 'classical' test is very commonly used in social research to make comparisons between groups. Although our discussion is related to this test, the points apply equally to testing a correlation coefficient or any other measure of the association between variables (see the references mentioned in Note 9).

For the purpose of exposition we have presented only the data for university students from the article. We have done this to exemplify the very common use of samples of university students in psychological research, but in fairness to the authors we should point out that they also present data for other groups within the populations.

9. The steps given here are essentially those outlined in Blalock (1972). Kalton (1966) gives a clear and simplified introduction to these techniques.

10. There is some disagreement in the literature about whether the null hypothesis is so called because it states that there is no difference between the means (or no association between the variables, etc.), or because the researchers seek to nullify it (see Bakan, 1967); for this research, both interpretations would be appropriate. The research hypothesis is called the *alternative* hypothesis in some approaches.

11. This is the two-sample t-test, described in the references given in Note 9.

12. In tests of null hypotheses of zero difference or zero correlation, 'extreme' values are large numerical values, whether positive or negative. In general, the choice of 'extreme' values is guided by consideration of the research hypothesis as well as the null hypothesis. For a discussion of this see the references given in Note 9.

13. For a contemporary example of the use of probability in connection with legal decision-making see Lindley (1977) and the appended discussion by Carr-Hill.

14. For further development of this point, see the discussion of 'Type I' and 'Type II' errors of inference in Blalock (1972). Later developments of the theory of significance tests proposed that the choice of significance level should be made by considering the relative costs of wrong decisions when deciding whether to accept the null or any alternative hypothesis; these involve considerations of the 'power' of the test (see Blalock 1972, p. 244). In much social research, however, there is no clear basis for a balancing of 'costs'.

15. This property of tests is not quite as undesirable as it sounds because the larger the sample, the more accurately we can estimate the population mean, and thus the more reliably we can tell whether two means are the same or not—though we still have the problem of deciding whether a reliable small difference is of any theoretical interest.

16. For further discussion of 'non-response' and of techniques for dealing with it, see Moser and Kalton (1971), pp. 166–186.

17. But see also Oldman's (1973) claim that much survey research is fundamentally 'theory-guided', and that the sociologists concerned use significance tests as a secondary source of conviction that something is 'there' to be explained.

18. Similarly, the results of applying tests of significance to a number of hypotheses in one investigation can be quite misleading as far as the rationale of the procedures is concerned (see Selvin and Stuart, 1966).

19. For a discussion of the role of the state in these areas, see Miles and Irvine, Section 3 of this book. There appears to have been little analysis of the use of statistical methods in industrial processes, but see E. S. Pearson (1973) and Rosenhead and Thunhurst, this volume.

20. For a discussion of confidence intervals, see Blalock (1972) and Kalton (1966).

21. Typically, 95% and 99% confidence intervals are produced; these correspond directly to 5% and 1% significance levels, respectively. For further details, again see Blalock (1972) and Kalton (1966).

22. For an introduction to Bayesian methods see Phillips (1973). One area where Bayesian methods *do* appear to have made an impact is in business decision-making, especially in the U.S. Of course, the internal procedures of private organisations are generally not open to public scrutiny—nor do they have to be presented as objective to the same extent as research findings or policy decisions.

Bibliography

Arbuthnot, J., 1710, 'An Argument for Divine Providence, taken from the constant regularity observed in the birth of both sexes', *Philosophical Transactions of the Royal Society*, vol. 27, pp. 186–190; reprinted in Kendall and Plackett, 1977, below.

Bakan, D., 1967, 'The test of significance in psychological research', from D. Bakan, *On Method*, San Francisco, Jossey-Bass, pp. 1–29; reprinted in Henkel and Morrison, 1970, below.

Blalock, H. M., 1972, *Social Statistics* (2nd. edn.), New York, McGraw-Hill.

Davis, J. A., 1958, 'Review of Merton et al., *The Student Physician*', *American Journal of Sociology*, vol. 63, January, excerpted as ch. 8 in Henkel and Morrison, 1970, below.

Edgeworth, F. Y., 1885, 'Methods of statistics', *Royal Statistical Society Jubilee Volume*, pp. 181-217.

Eysenck, S. B. G., Adelaja, O., and Eysenck, H. J., 1977, 'A comparative study of personality in Nigerian and English subjects', *Journal of Social Psychology*, vol. 102, pp. 171-178.

Ford, J., 1975, *Paradigms and Fairy Tales* (two vols.), London, Routledge & Kegan Paul.

Galton, F., 1889, *Natural Inheritance*, London, Macmillan.

Gillispie, C. C., 1963, 'Intellectual factors in the background of analysis by probabilities', in A. C. Crombie (ed.) *Scientific Change*, London, Heinemann.

Gould, P., 1970, 'Is *statistix inferens* the geographical name for a wild goose?', *Economic Geography*, vol. 46, pp. 439-448.

Guttman, L., 1977, 'What is not what in statistics', *The Statistician*, vol. 26, pp. 81-107.

Hacking, I., 1975, *The Emergence of Probability*, Cambridge, Cambridge University Press.

Henkel, R. E., and Morrison, D. E. (eds.), 1970, *The Significance Test Controversy*, London, Butterworths.

Herschel, J. F. W., 1857, 'Quetelet on probabilities', in J. F. W. Herschel, *Essays*, London, Longman.

Iwawaki, S., Eysenck, S. D. G., and Eysenck, H. J., 1977, 'Differences in personality between Japanese and English', *Journal of Social Psychology*, vol. 102, pp. 27-33.

Kalton, G., 1966, *Introduction to Statistical Ideas for Social Scientists*, London, Chapman and Hall.

Kendall, M., and Plackett, R. L. (eds.), 1977, *Studies in the History of Statistics and Probability*, vol. II, London, Griffin.

Kendall, P., 1957, 'Note on significance tests', appendix C of R. K. Merton, G. G. Reader and P. Kendall, *The Student Physician: Introductory Studies in the Sociology of Medical Education*, Cambridge, Mass., Harvard University Press; reprinted as ch. 7 in Henkel and Morrison, 1970, above.

Lazarsfeld, P. F., 1961, 'Notes on the history of quantification in sociology—trends, sources and problems', *Isis*, vol. 52, pp. 277-333; reprinted in Kendall and Plackett, 1977, above.

Lindley, D. V., 1977, 'Probability and the law' (with discussion), *The Statistician*, vol. 26, pp.203-220.

Lipset, S. M., Trow, M. A., and Coleman, J. S., 1956, 'Statistical problems', Appendix to *Union Democracy*, Glencoe, Free Press; reprinted as chapter 6 in Henkel and Morrison, 1970, above.

Lundberg, G., 1929, 'The logic of sociology and social research', in G. Lundberg et al. (eds.), *Trends in American Sociology*, New York, Harper.

MacKenzie, B., 1976, 'Darwinism and positivism as methodological influences on the development of psychology', *Journal of the History of Behavioural Sciences*, vol. 12, pp. 330-337.

Moser, C. A., and Kalton, G., 1971, *Survey Methods in Social Investigation*, London, Heinemann.

Oldman, D., 1973, 'Sociologists, survey analysis and statistical testing', *International Journal of Mathematical Education in Science and Technology*, vol. 4, pp. 51-60.

Pearson, E. S., 1973, 'Some historical reflections on the introduction of statistical methods in industry', *The Statistician*, vol. 17, no. 3, September, pp. 165-179.

Pearson, E. S., and Kendall, M., 1970, *Studies in the History of Statistics and Probability*, vol. I, London, Griffin.

Pearson, K., and Moul, M., 1925, 'The problem of alien immigration into Britain I', *Annals of Eugenics*, vol. 1, pp. 5–127.

Phillips, L. D., 1973, *Bayesian Statistics for Social Scientists*, London, Nelson.

Quetelet, L. A. J., 1835, *Sur l'Homme et le Developpement de ses Facultés, ou Essai de Physique Sociale* (two vols.), Paris, Bachelier.

Selvin, H. C., and Stuart, A., 1966, 'Data-dredging procedures in survey analysis,' *American Statistician*, vol. 20, pp. 20–23.

Sterling, T. D., 1959, 'Publication decisions and their possible effects on inferences drawn from tests of significance—or vice versa', *Journal of the American Statistical Association*, vol. 54, pp. 30–40; reprinted in Henkel and Morrison, 1970, above.

Taylor, C. C., 1920, 'The social survey and the science of sociology', *American Journal of Sociology*, vol. 25, pp. 731–756.

Tukey, J. W., 1954, 'Unsolved problems of experimental statistics', *Journal of the American Statistical Association*, vol. 49, pp. 706–731.

Walker, H. M., 1929, *Studies in the History of Statistical Method*, Baltimore, Williams & Wilkins Company.

Willer, D., 1967, *Scientific Sociology*, Englewood Cliffs, N. J., Prentice-Hall.

Willer, D., and Willer J., 1973, *Systematic Empiricism: Critique of a Pseudoscience*, Englewood Cliffs, N. J., Prentice-Hall.

Section Three:
Statistics and the State

Having considered some of the central historical and philosophical aspects of social statistics, we now turn to a particularly important source of such data: official statistics. In the first chapter in this section, Ian Miles and John Irvine take up some general issues which must be confronted if official statistics are to be used critically. Beginning with a critique of the way in which the Government Statistical Service (GSS) presents official data as objective fact, they demonstrate that in order to assess official statistics it is necessary to take into account both the conceptual and the technical factors that structure their production. It is vital, but not enough, they argue, to accept that data are a social product: they need to be seen as *particular* products, which reflect the administrative and political practices of the state.

The second chapter gives a general outline of the system in which official statistics are produced. Informed by a unique inside-view of this system, this chapter, written collectively by a necessarily anonymous group of government statisticians, details the stages in the production of official statistics and shows how this labour process structures the form of the statistics produced. This article provides a useful contrast to the conventional image of statisticians as independent and neutral enumerators of the facts, as well as being extremely informative about the structure and operation of the GSS.

The following two chapters take up central issues in the ideological framework of official statistics—class and sex. Social critics have often made telling use of official data to illustrate the widespread existence of social inequalities. But these chapters, by Theo Nichols, and Ann Oakley and Robin Oakley, go further and address the ways in which class and sex divisions are reflected and reproduced in the statistical categories used by the GSS.

Moving onto a rather more detailed level of analysis, the next four chapters present case-studies of particular areas of official statistics. Christopher Hird and John Irvine take issue with the data on the ownership and control of wealth and Jim Kincaid with poverty statistics; Richard Hyman and Bob Price consider the official statistics on work and employment, while Lesley Doyal considers those concerning medical care and health. These articles do not adopt an identical approach, but each provides a critical outline of the origins, conceptual underpinnings, means of production, and uses of the data. They indicate both how and why particular statistics are produced in particular ways, and why official data on certain important social issues are just not available at all. Lack of space prevents us from presenting a comprehensive overview of all areas of official statistics, but these chapters, taken together, should provide a model that can be extended to the analysis and critique of other areas of official statistics.

9.

Ian Miles and John Irvine

The Critique of Official Statistics

In Britain, there has been a striking increase in the scope and volume of official statistics—especially over the last few decades. The Central Statistical Office (CSO), established in 1941, now publishes seventeen periodical statistical digests, in marked contrast with the solitary *Monthly Digest of Statistics* of 1946. The expanding scale of data production is matched by a broadening of its scope: almost every aspect of social life now has some statistic relating to it.[1]

The data that official publications provide can be obtained nowhere else, for the state is the only institution in modern society with both the economic resources and political mandate needed to generate it in large quantities on a national scale. The costs of large-scale data production are enormous—the decennial *Census of Population*, for example, costs many millions of pounds (the 1971 Census cost over twenty million pounds).[2] The state is also in a unique position of power, being able to *demand* information concerning the activities of individuals and organisations. The 1920 Census Act, for example, obliges the general public to answer fully its enquiries—a requirement backed up by penal sanctions.

Thus, the Government Statistical Service (GSS) produces data that can be made available in no other way in our society. This is, however, a mixed blessing: it means that the state possesses a near-monopoly of both the production and dissemination of many items of information. Moreover, this monopoly power is wielded according to a particular structure of political interests, although the GSS appears to believe otherwise. The results are, first, a stress on particular forms of data in official statistics—which reflects, we shall argue, the needs of the various state agencies for information to co-ordinate their activities and justify their programmes; and, second, related to this, a single ideological framework underpinning the concepts and categories used. To use official statistics critically, we need to be aware of the limitations which these factors impose on the data.

A numerical picture of society

Official statistics tend to be regarded as particularly authoritative and objective sources of data. This view is supported by the GSS, which portrays itself as a neutral fact-finding agency, as a kind of statistical 'camera' used by the government to provide information to help run social affairs more effectively. Thus in the introduction to the first (1970) edition of the now annual *Social Trends* it is stated that:

> Our aim is to be presenting a manageable selection of statistical material relating to social policies which provides a *picture* of some significant ways in which our society is changing. (our emphasis)

The very title of *Facts in Focus*, a compendium of statistics intended for the mass market, further promotes this view of official statistics as a numerical picture of British society. So too does its cover, which depicts the aperture of a camera perfectly encompassing a graph.

It is a powerful analogy. Not only is it claimed that putting social facts into numerical form brings them into better focus, but there is a strong implication that any imperfections in the statistics can be treated as a purely *technical* problem. What is needed is to take more snaps when part of the scene has been missed out, or to develop and print the film in a different way. As the director of the CSO put it in 1970, when introducing the first edition of *Social Trends*: 'the combination and confrontation of tables bearing on different aspects of social life may produce a more rounded picture of the social scene than now exists.' (Moser, 1970, p. 11). According to this line of argument, there is little wrong with official statistics that cannot be solved by purely technical means or more resources. With enough professionally trained photographers, taking enough snaps, *Social Trends* would be the complete photograph album of British society.

For radical critics of society to adopt this frame of reference towards official statistics would be to reduce debate about official social 'facts' to a purely technical level. Yet if taken a little further, the 'snapshot' analogy may itself be used to challenge this view. We may go on to ask whether the nature of the numerical picture produced is dependent in any way upon who takes the picture, the particular instruments they use, or the requirements of those who commission the picture in the first place. Posing these questions is to raise the whole issue of *whose* picture of society is reflected in these data. We shall argue that official statistics present not a neutral picture of British society, but one developed in support of the system of power and domination that is modern capitalism—a system in which the state plays a particularly important role.

The beginnings of such a critique can be made by asking just how objective a reflection of reality is captured in a typical photograph. To be sure, there are in camera work technical criteria for good and bad photographs (although even these depend upon the purposes for which the photograph is intended). But other criteria are fundamental to the decision to produce any particular picture or class of pictures. Portrait photographers, for example, are out to capture a certain pose or quality of their subject, rather than to give a 'well-rounded' view; newspaper and TV photographers are out to capture the 'newsworthy' details; police photographers at a demonstration hope to capture those personal features useful in identifying the participants, and so on. There are consequently no universally applicable guidelines dictating decisions about where to position the camera, what lighting to employ, the type of film to use, what instructions to give, whether the photographer's presence is to be known, and so on; and many of these decisions relate to the ways in which the act of photography actually influences the situation itself, both directly and through the photograph eventually produced. The 'social reality' captured in a photograph is thus perhaps more of a creation than a 'reflection': it is certainly mediated by all sorts of social and ideological factors.

Similarly, official statistics are not objective reflections of social reality, neutral pictures emerging from purely technical decisions. Their production involves a host of decisions about the objects, techniques and methods involved. Even when the task of the statistician is merely to pull together others' records, statistical data are not already existing and waiting in an 'outside world', to be plucked like ripe apples on a tree of knowledge.

This is a far cry from the empiricist approach to statistics which tends to see the open-minded *collection of data*, and the unbiased *discovery of findings*, as the key to knowledge about the social world. To the empiricist, the question of *whose* numerical picture official statistics portray may seem surprising, perhaps even offensive. Are we suggesting political 'bias' or conspiracies in the ranks of the GSS? Surely official statisticians do not deliberately distort their data or misapply their techniques? The empiricist may rest easy, at least on this point: we also find conspiracy theories of little use in accounting for the large majority of everyday official statistics—although, as we will show, this is not to say that such practices never take place. Certainly, conspiracy theories can become very contorted indeed as an explanation of the social reality captured in official statistics—they can't for example, explain why the state regularly publishes figures embarrassing to the government, like high unemployment rates. In arguing that official statistics are ideological it is far more important to look at the role of the state in modern capitalist society, and how this *structures* the production of data, than it is to point a finger at the occasional malpractice that surfaces to public light. But, as we will see, the empiricist notion of official statistics fits in well with a view of the state as a neutral technocracy; it is a picture that needs to be challenged.

Statistics as subjectivity

It was during the 1960s ferment in sociology that developing a critique of official statistics became a major issue of concern for social scientists (see Irvine and Miles, section one, this volume; for more extensive discussion of the crisis in sociology, see Gouldner, 1970; and Shaw, 1972). The critique, coming from the so-called 'pheno-menologists', has been the most sustained and influential alterna-tive to the official statisticians' and orthodox social scientists' view of numerical data as objective fact about social reality. In its place they have substituted a view of statistics as essentially subjective.

The leading edge of their critique has been concerned with statistics relating to crime and suicide. Here a number of researchers have made the point strongly that data on deviant behaviour reflect more than the existence of 'real' deviant acts being committed, if indeed such acts have taken place at all. They have argued that such statistics depend crucially upon the operation of the organis-ations which deal with such actions and on the activities of the individuals within these organisations.[3] The data are, in short, social constructions. Thus:

> *rates of deviant behaviour* are produced by *the actions taken by persons in the social system* which define, classify and record certain behaviours as deviant. (Kitsuse and Cicourel, 1963, p. 135, their emphasis).

and:

> Official data are social products. To understand and hence to explain them, we need to examine those factors which contribute to their formation and variation . . . With respect to the social construction of data on official criminal deviance . . . the end product is not a valid indicator of a country's 'real' extent or pattern of criminal activity. Its formation and variation is determined by organisational, legal and social pressures, rather than by a rigorous attempt to measure criminal activity accurately. (Box, 1971, pp. 208, 210).

These are certainly important points, and are well-illustrated in studies such as those cited. They show that the administrative guidelines and conceptual categories used to produce and process official data are by no means definitive or unambiguous when applied to specific cases. Thus, whether or not a death is classified as a case of suicide depends not just on the causes of death as revealed by an autopsy, but also on a whole set of judgements and attributions about the intentions and state of mind of the deceased (see Keat, this volume). Likewise, whether or not an activity is judged to be criminal depends upon a host of claims about 'what really happened': cases where police perjury results in wrongful convictions, for example, while being included in data claimed to indicate the existence of real crime, say more about the activities of the police than those of their victims—as may the absence of proceedings in other cases.

Such statistics are clearly produced in specific organisational contexts and involve in their production the active *interpretation* (and even creation) of events, as well as their simple recording in terms of officially defined categories. This is also argued to be the case for official data other than those on suicide or crime. Perhaps there is less appeal to the liberal conscience with other data, perhaps such a critique would be more difficult to develop; whatever the case, it has rarely been extended in this way.

The main limitation of the phenomenologists' analysis, however, involves rather more than this. For while the phenomenologists have demonstrated the social nature of official data, they often allow the flourishes with which they have pronounced their views to be the finale of their analysis. They have tended to replace the empiricist view of official statistics as objective facts by a perspective treating them solely as subjective judgements reflecting the social reality of individual and organisational decisions and definitions. But individual experience is constituted within social structures—structures that themselves make possible and delimit individual and organisational practices. To emphasise the subjectivity of statistical data fails to address the processes involved. Phenomenologists thus often seem to treat society as a given environment in which individuals are free to create their own social realities and practices; it would be easy to conclude that they have replaced the view of statistics as a neutral snapshot of reality with one that treats them as no more than a patchwork aggregation of the impressionistic sketches of individuals.

However, this would fail to capture the nuances in the phenomenological position. Phenomenologists have, to varying degrees, sought to take into account the structures within which these individuals are located and through which data are produced. For example, Cicourel has argued not that official statistics are the product of arbitrary individual judgements, but that they are indicators of organisational processes. Thus the judgements of individuals about how to classify and report events need to be related to the specific circumstances in which they work. An example here might involve explaining the police handling of minority groups in terms of the ideologies within, and pressures upon, the police force—thus recent claims that there has been a sharp increase in mugging in Britain have been said to reflect a shift in the official classification of personal theft crimes by blacks. Similarly, the promotion structure of the police force might result in more attention being paid to some allegedly criminal activities than to others—drug offences may achieve some of their statistical weight because of their potential for high clear-up and conviction rates.

One cannot deny that the phenomenologists' discussion of the ways in which the social context of statistical production may structure statistical data is in many respects illuminating (as Freund and Abrams, 1976, have argued). But even that is limited. The social context to which the more sophisticated phenomenologists sometimes refer—the 'common-sense' categories people use, and the wider structure of social and economic organisation—is itself taken as largely unproblematic. Thus, while in the case of data on mugging, for example, the existence of different 'interest groups' in the community might be used to explain the changed definitions employed by the police and the courts, the pervasiveness of racism is taken for granted. This feature of our society remains part of an unexamined wider social environment out of which the phenomenologists' subjects construct their meanings. The underlying structure of social interests in capitalist society, and the existence of 'interest groups' are a priori facts in these analyses. The reporting and arresting practices of the police may thus be described at length without raising questions about how it is that police organisation of a particular type has come into existence. To understand these practices as being more than simply the assignation of meanings to an organised social world it is necessary to raise such questions— and, for the police, as for other agencies producing statistics, this necessarily involves an analysis of the role of the state in contemporary society.

It is only through such an analysis that one can begin to appreciate how the structuring of individual 'subjective' experiences and group interests alike takes place through systems of meaning and social institutions which have been formed as part of a wider structure of power, that of class relationships. The phenomenological approach is hardly more forthcoming about these determinants of official statistics than are those of the GSS and orthodox social science. Like the GSS, one version of the phenomenological approach would consider the question, 'whose picture of society is reflected in official statistics?' to be a meaningless one: in this case, all state officials are seen as free to make an impression of their own on the data they produce. Other phenomenologists would argue that the picture expresses the outcome of a struggle between different interest groups: it is a pluralist photomontage of the elements each has managed to inject into it. But the state institutions in which official statistics are produced are neither a natural efflorescence of industrial society, nor an arbitrary environment resulting from an accidental confluence of individual practices or group interests. They are themselves social products, that have been formed through a definite historical process. The structures and social relations of these institutions, and the formal categories of statistics they produce, are just as much a product of human interests and conflicts as are the different interpretations of these formal categories by their officials. Official statistics are, therefore, not just a social product but a *particular* product whose form and content are structured by much more than individual and organisational practices.

The meanings of official statistics

The phenomenological sociologists forcefully make the point that official statistics are social products. But in itself this conclusion is not an adequate basis for a critical analysis of these data. The relativism towards which some phenomenologists tend, the view that knowledge of society is based on individual experience and meanings, gives no guide for differentiating one person's perceptions from another's, or for assessing what construction of social reality is most appropriate for changing that reality. At best, relativism can only inform an attitude of criticism to the claim that official statistics present privileged knowledge of the world; at worst it may support the search for a fuhrer-figure to impose a desired vision of reality.

Hindess (1973) and Triesman (1974) have strongly criticised this relativism. They have argued that the meanings imputed to events by the producers of official data are by no means arbitrary, but depend upon implicit theories of social processes; and that, furthermore, an analysis of these theories can make possible critical assessment of the categories used by the producers, thus enabling judgements to be made about the usefulness or otherwise of the data. The specific circumstances and attitudes of the individual statistician are not seen by them to be all that important—but the concepts and techniques used are.

Thus, Hindess argues that:

> Official statistics are in no way reducible to the subjective experiences of enumerators and other officials. On the contrary, all such statistics are the product of a determinate process of production of knowledge governed by a determinate system of concepts . . . (1973, p. 56).

Like the phenomenologists, Hindess sees statistics as a social product, but not as one governed by individuals' meanings. He directly challenges both the orthodox empiricist and the phenomenological approaches:

> official statistics are never mere givens to be taken as they are or else dismissed as inadequate. Like other productions they must be explained in terms of the conditions and instruments of their production. (p. 12).

Hindess then goes on to distinguish between two sets of instruments, 'the "technical" instruments of (e.g.) the social survey and the "conceptual" instruments—the system of concepts and categories governing the assignment of cases into classes.'

Cicourel was not slow to respond:

> A central feature of Hindess' critique is the curious notion that the foundation of knowledge is not derived from human experience . . . Hindess pretends that the key issues have to do with the system of categories and the conjunction of conceptual and technical instruments . . . Hindess would have us believe that official statistics are not dependent upon the experiences and situated decisions of census-workers or survey interviewers. (1976, pp. 16–17).

Let us relate this discussion to a concrete set of official statistics. Hindess makes the point that as well as the conditions of production, the instruments of production determine the statistics that are produced: that is, that the use of different concepts or technical instruments will result in different statistical products, even though these may appear equivalent by virtue of having the same label.

The data on unemployment are a currently salient case. Unemployment statistics are produced on a monthly basis by the Department of Employment (see Hyman and Price, this section) and are extensively reported in the media as one of the most important indicators of national economic performance. Yet the social basis of these data is rarely discussed; they are just accepted as a more-or-less objective picture of unemployment.[4] To identify this social basis involves analysing the process of production of the data.

Briefly, the monthly unemployment statistics are based on returns from all the unemployment exchanges in the country; that is, they are computed by totalling the number of people who are 'signing-on' for unemployment benefit and certain social security benefits. The category of 'unemployed' thus includes only those unemployed people said to be 'actively seeking a job' who are, at the same time, eligible for such benefits. Certain groups of people are not included in the figures—for example, many women with working husbands who themselves want to work: they are often not eligible for unemployment benefit, almost never for social security benefits, and so see little point in 'signing on' week after week when there is neither a financial reward nor much likelihood of finding a job.

Quite a stir ensued upon the publication of the 1971 Census, when it was revealed that 1,365,775 people claimed to be unemployed, contrasting with the 773,800 shown in the official Department of Employment figures for the week in question. While the *Economist* was able to dimiss this as a 'statistical quirk', the vast difference in figures signifies more than a freak problem. It reflects the use of what are in Hindess' terms, different conceptual and technical instruments. Two entirely different concepts of unemployment are implied in asking people about their status and in DE regulations concerning who can and cannot sign on for benefit. Similarly, the technical instruments of production of the data are entirely different: the Census is a 100 per cent survey, the DE figures, by-products of a state administrative system whose primary purpose is to service the so-called 'labour market' and administer welfare benefits.

This case illustrates that the techniques and concepts used are important determinants of the form of official statistics. Using the Hindess framework we can understand *how* it is that two entirely different pictures of the same social conditions are provided by the official unemployment statistics and by the unemployed themselves. But to understand fully the meaning of official employment statistics we need to go further than this and ask *why* they are produced in this way. This means examining some of the social factors governing the production of these statistics, as well as those which determine and have determined the development and choice of particular concepts and techniques—and here some of the phenomenologists' work is useful.

Most importantly, the concepts and techniques used by the DE need to be set in the context of its organisational development. Among the factors structuring the DE's administrative practice are workers' insistence on welfare benefits, state support for the search by business for the labour appropriate to its needs, and political pressures on the government to limit unemployment. The role of DE officials also needs to be assessed in the light of these factors. As phenomenologists would expect, there is some room for officials to decide whether an individual should be allowed to register as unemployed or not; and officials may well be encouraged, directly or indirectly, to apply more restrictive criteria at times of high unemployment. But the assignment of cases into categories is not, in the main, simply a matter of individual officials differing in the meanings they assign to events, nor of an existing group recognising that it has an interest in portraying events in one way rather than another. It is part of a social practice which is itself conditioned by a structure of power within which the ability and motivation of officials to decide how an individual is to be classified may reflect, for example, the particular relationships of authority existing between clients and officials, between officials and their superiors, etc.

Different state agencies vary considerably in the amount of latitude permitted relatively junior staff in classifying their 'clients', depending in large part upon the complexity and clarity of the discriminations sought by more senior officials (the police being extremely flexible in this respect). There may also be variations in practice in the offices of a particular agency in different parts of the country. In regions of high structural employment, with many older people without jobs, there are pressures for health claims to be more rigorously examined in assessing whether claimants are 'willing and able' to work. By transferring people from the unemployment to the social security register in this way, small but politically important reductions are made in the regional unemployment levels. Certainly, then, in any evaluation of official statistics, it is at least worth considering the representation and communication of material that goes on between senior civil servants (and their political bosses), the officials charged with producing data, and the individuals whose actions or status form the content of the statistics. Thus the legal formulations of the requirements to be satisfied for a case to be classified as employed, the implementation of these formulations by officials in the context of particular state employment exchanges, and the conditions and self conceptions of individuals in respect of their employment status, are all relevant to understanding the statistics on unemployment.

So while Hindess rightly stresses the determining role of concepts and techniques, and the need to assess data in these terms, the assignment of events and individuals into categories by officials is, nevertheless, much more than the mechanical operation of theoretical categories and technical instruments. Official statistics result from the application of concepts and techniques within a social practice—not solely from these instruments, nor from the unmediated (transcendental) subjective judgements of those who produce the data. The relationship is dialectical: concepts are interpreted and techniques modified in their concrete application, often in ways that are difficult for outsiders to be aware of (cf. the chapter by the Government Statisticians' Collective in this volume); and the form of the practice and nature of the data produced are determined by these instruments.

This leads to a rather more limiting feature of Hindess' approach: the lack of attention he pays to the social factors structuring the actual production, reproduction and development of these instruments themselves—most significantly in regard to the organisation of the state statistical apparatus, but also in regard to the practice of its individual officials. At the organisational level, development and modification of these instruments is, in fact, usually a matter for higher officials who are in a position to deliberately impose systematic changes—most obviously when 'political' manipulations of data or concepts are involved—but one cannot assume that the attitudes and interests of lower officials will always represent a minor or random influence on their practice. As is shown in the case of the remarkable divergence between official statisticians and members of the public concerning what is to count as 'unemployment', the development and modification of statistical instruments are in turn conditioned by wider political and social factors.

We are arguing, then, not only that data are social products, but that the concepts, techniques and practices involved in producing official statistics reflect particular histories (cf. Shaw and Miles, this volume). Moreover, as structured social products they can be critically assessed. Thus in evaluating the nature of unemployment statistics we are not attempting to argue that self-reports in Census questions are necessarily a more accurate or correct measure of 'real' employment, nor to deny the importance of the official figures by tying their production down to a set of totally arbitrary and subjective judgements. The meaning of official statistics is determined by practices with specific conditions of production, it is tied to the structured actions of a particular state agency operating within—and affecting—a particular historical instance. To use them intelligently, we need to realize this.

Indeed, later articles in this section show in rather more detail, in respect of particular areas of statistics, that the conceptual and technical instruments of official statistics are rooted in social practices (cf. Doyal; Hird and Irvine; Hyman and Price; Kincaid; Nichols; and Oakley and Oakley). But just assembling such examples does not, however, completely explain the rationale underlying them, nor does it explain why it is that the state invests considerable resources in the production of statistics. The state itself exists within a broader society; it is itself a historical product whose analysis has intimate relevance for the critique of official statistics.

Statistics and the state

As in the self-portrait of the GSS, itself just one of many state agencies, the state as a whole is typically presented by its officials as a set of neutral institutions. Governments may come and go, but the state is non-partisan; it may at times be used to further the interests of 'the peoples' elected representatives,' but it is an instrument that is in principle uncommitted and equally available to any expression of the public interest, a kind of referee that stands above society, mediating between contending interests. On this view the statistician, *par excellence*, stands outside and above social interests, the GSS's role being seen as accumulating the facts necessary to maintain effective government in an informed pluralistic society, facts which are supposedly of equal use to all sides in the political arena. For example: '*Social Trends* is thus designed to present a wide range of information which all sides in the political arena can accept as setting the factual context within which divergent political forces and pressure groups can argue about policy' (Editorial in *Social Trends*, no. 7, 1976).

But these divergent political forces, and the state, do not appear from nowhere: both exist and developed historically within the social totality constituted by the capitalist system. A critical analysis of the developing role of the state produces a rather different picture of its statistics.

Living in a capitalist society means living in a society in which class divisions are crucial determinants of social life, in which the class that controls the means of production, the means to produce and reproduce capital, needs to control the labour of the working class. Control is necessary because this labour is *alienated*: the producers of wealth do not themselves freely and consciously decide what they will produce, under what circumstances, and how the product will be used. They are also *exploited* in that only a proportion of the wealth they produce is returned to them as wages. The rest is allocated, first, to maintaining, replacing and expanding the means of production; and second, to non-productive workers, management, shareholders and financiers—with certain revenues going to the state as taxation. It is in relation to the creation, development and maintenance of this system of power that the role of the state has been formed.

The capitalist state plays both economic and political roles in society.[5] The first includes the provision and maintenance of the conditions necessary for economic activity—both production and distribution—to take place. This is not a technical, neutral, role. Capitalist production and the market system are directed towards ensuring profitability rather than to achieving social and economic goals determined by democratic planning processes, and this has profoundly structured the nature of both economic and social life (see Rosenhead and Thunhurst; and Griffiths, Irvine and Miles, this volume). Among the many responsibilities of the state that have developed are ensuring the existence of a fit, educated and disciplined workforce; providing infrastructures such as a transport system, energy and power services; maintaining external and internal security through the police, military and judiciary; and attempting to moderate the scale and consequence of economic crises through economic planning.

The more obviously political role of the state concerns the creation of the conditions, other than those apparently technical ones, necessary for capitalist production. It is important to maintain social cohesion within an alienated class society—by consent where possible, by force when necessary. The working class must be educated to accept its exploitation, and the grievances of the oppressed cannot be permitted to upset this situation, or otherwise endanger the role of the hegemonic social class.

The state thus defends and legitimates the capitalist social order. The portrayal of the state as neutral facilitates this non-neutral political role. It is at best only a neutral referee in the sense of maintaining the balance of forces *within* often conflicting fractions of a ruling class fighting for control of capital and markets.[6]

This brief discussion of the state is no digression. Its economic and political functions are embedded in the production of official statistics, structuring both what data are produced and how this is done. First, statistics are vital information inputs into administrative, policy-making and planning processes—for private industry as much as for the state itself. It is the role of the GSS to organise the production and dissemination of this data. Often, however, relevant data already exist as a by-product of administrative activities and need merely to be collected, processed and distributed—as we saw with the statistics on unemployment. Other information requirements have stimulated the production of new series of data. The use of official statistics in the operations and planning of private industry has grown particularly rapidly in recent years: for instance, official statistics on commodity prices, wage rates and much else are used in planning production and marketing strategies. The financial pages of most newspapers thus regularly present a wide range of statistics. The importance of this role of the state is such that, in the words of Claus Moser, at the time director of the CSO:

> Economic statistics are on the whole more advanced than social: largely because they were (with the exception of population statistics) developed first, they tend to be more regular, comprehensive and sophisticated. The pressure to improve economic statistics has come partly from industry but mainly from the modern interests of Governments to tune and steer their economies and to forecast future economic developments. (Moser, 1970, p. 7).

Second, while it is in general wrong to see statistics as being produced by the state (at least in liberal capitalist economies) as a deliberate attempt to create deception and mystification, this does not mean that official statistics do not have this effect. Because of the nature of the state's activities, its need only for certain forms of data, and its use of particular forms of statistical categories and techniques, a specific and limited view of society is presented in and through official statistics. Not only are official statistics profoundly ideological in nature (e.g. see Nichols; and Oakley and Oakley, this section), but the range of statistics available is such as to give a picture of society in which some features are remarkably out of focus. For example, there is a plethora of information on fire-damage to properties, but little on industrially-related diseases; the number of house-starts is well documented, but figures on homelessness are minuscule; and the measurement of social security scrounging is clearly given priority over tax evasion, the consumption of consumer durables over poverty, and so on.

Behind the veil of neutrality, official statistics thus form part of the process of maintaining and reproducing the dominant ideologies of capitalist society. While masquerading as neutral facts with which 'divergent political forces and pressure groups can argue about policy', official statistics are in fact a selection of data typically offering far less of use to the radical critic than to the reactionary. Sometimes, official statistics are clearly manipulated in attempts to adjust the terms of a political debate: for example, the categories of people regarded as unemployed have been subtly re-adjusted over time, so as to reduce the total (students on Christmas and Easter vacation being the latest casualty since they can now no longer sign on). At other times they are merely used in extremely devious ways: by, for example, taxes on items in the Retail Price Index being reduced or not levied so as to minimise the official figures on inflation. But even without such blatant interventions in the production of statistics, the concepts employed serve to reinforce the arguments advanced by the political and intellectual representatives of the ruling class. Only by understanding that statistics are produced as part of the administration and control of a society organised around exploitative class relations can we grasp their full meaning; and only with the aid of this understanding can we determine their uses, and usefulness, in critical social research.

Notes

1. Some idea of this scope can easily be gained by quickly flipping through one or two of the major digests. Of particular relevance to social scientists are the *Annual Abstract of Statistics*, *Economic Trends* and *Social Trends*. The full range of official statistics is, however, summarised in the *Guide to Official Statistics* (2nd edn., 1978). The index to this guide makes it clear that all government departments have statisticians from the Government Statistical Service attached to them.

2. Information obtained by letter from the Government Statistical Service. Thanks are due to the official statisticians who went to the trouble to provide us with this and other information for this chapter.

3. Important in this literature are: Douglas (1967); Box (1971); and Cicourel (2nd edn., 1976).

4. By mid-1978, this situation seemed to be changing: union leaders were publicly challenging the statistics as part of their attempts to mobilise opinion and action against the recent high levels of unemployment, hoping, by so doing, to reduce the likelihood of these levels continuing, if not worsening, during the next decade. This stemmed, perhaps, from the government insisting that those on short-term job creation schemes be classified as employed.

5. The role of the state in the Eastern bloc, China and certain Southeast Asian and African countries requires a separate analysis, which we cannot provide here. The journal *Critique* is a valuable source on Eastern Europe and the Soviet Union; see also Bahro (1978) and Therborn (1978).

6. Space constraints prevent our presenting here a fuller analysis of the state. In any case, the intention is only to provide sufficient background knowledge to make discussion of the rationale for the production of official statistics more meaningful. Most importantly, we need to recognise that, like the ruling class, the state is not a monolithic and totally co-ordinated social entity. As is the case with fractions of the ruling class, there are often conflicts between different elements of the state apparatus; funding agencies, for example, may often conflict with spending agencies. Conflict between them can break out into the open. Subsequent debates between the legislature (eg MPs) and state officials, may (fortunately for critical social scientists) sometimes lead to more data being made available—for example, in less than usually discreet answers to parliamentary questions. Even as a matter of routine, different state agencies may publish contradictory data on the same topics which provide opportunity for critical assessment—like that on unemployment by the DE and GSS, or on serious accidents at work by the DHSS and the Health and Safety Executive (HSE).

The analysis of the state has recently become a priority for radicals and analyses have proliferated as political struggles have become more closely linked to economic ones (with the end of the post-war boom). Useful contributions to the development of state theory include the books by Miliband (1969); Poulantzas (1973); Therborn (1978); O'Connor (1973); and for the ensuing debate between Miliband and Poulantzas, see Blackburn (1972). For influential shorter English-language treatments, see Warren (1972); Mandel (1975); Fine and Harris (1976); Gough (1975); and Holloway and Picciotto (1977). The journal *Kapitalistate* is devoted to radical analysis in this area; *Politics and Society* has presented interesting studies of the constitution of political forces; and *Capital and Class* has published valuable material concerning state economic policy.

Bibliography

Bahro, R., 1978, *The Alternative in Eastern Europe*, London, New Left Books.

Blackburn, R., (ed.), 1972, *Ideology in Social Science: Readings in Critical Social Theory*, London, Fontana.

Box, S., 1971, *Deviance, Reality and Society*, London, Holt, Rinehart and Winston.

Cicourel, A. V., 1976, *The Social Organisation of Juvenile Justice*, London, Heinemann.

Douglas, J. D., 1967, *The Social Meanings of Suicide*, Princeton, Princeton University Press.

Fine, B., and Harris, L., 1976, 'State expenditure and advanced capitalism: a critique', *New Left Review*, no. 98, pp. 97–112.

Freund, P. and Abrams, M., 1976, 'Ethnomethodology and marxism: their use for critical theorizing', *Theory and Society*, vol. 3, no. 3, pp. 372–393.

Gough, I., 1975, 'State expenditure in advanced capitalism', *New Left Review*, no. 92, pp. 53–92.

Gouldner, A., 1970, *The Coming Crisis of Western Sociology*, New York, Basic Books.

Hindess, B., 1973, *The Use of Official Statistics in Sociology*, London, Macmillan.

Holloway, J., and Picciotto, S., 1977, 'Capital crisis and the state', *Capital and Class*, no. 2, pp. 76–101.

Kitsuse, J. I., and Cicourel, A. V., 1963, 'A note on the uses of official statistics', *Social Problems*, vol. 11, pp. 131–39.

Mandel, E., 1975, *Late Capitalism*, London, New Left Books.

Miliband, R., 1969, *The State in Capitalist Society*, London, Weidenfeld and Nicolson.

Moser, C. A., 1970, 'Some general developments in social statistics', *Social Trends*, no. 1, London, HMSO, pp. 7–12.

O'Connor, J., 1973, *The Fiscal Crisis of the State*, London, St Martins Press.

Poulantzas, N., 1973, *Political Power and Social Classes*, London, New Left Books.

Shaw, M., 1972, 'The coming crisis of radical sociology', in Blackburn (ed.), 1972, above.

Therborn, G., 1978, *What Does the Ruling Class Do When it Rules?* London, New Left Books.

Triesman, D., 1974, 'The radical use of official data', in N. Armistead (ed.), *Reconstructing Social Psychology*, Harmondsworth, Penguin.

Warren, B., 1972, 'Capitalist planning and the state', *New Left Review*, no. 72, pp. 3–29.

10.

Government Statisticians' Collective

How Official Statistics are Produced: Views from the Inside

There is little awareness, except on the part of those directly involved, of the ways in which official statistics are produced. Reasons for this neglect include the legally enforced secrecy, except for literature officially published, in which all Government operations are shrouded; the conventions of academic writing which in all fields tends to obscure the muddled and makeshift nature of what really happens; and a general lack of interest in a matter usually assumed to be of trivial importance. Yet an awareness of this labour process, and of the state institutions in which it takes place, is crucial to understanding the meaning of official statistics. We provide here an account of this process and of its implications. We also hope to communicate a little of what statistical work feels like, as we and our colleagues experience and have experienced it.

The Government Statistical Service (GSS)

Official statistics are produced primarily to provide the information required by administrators, 'mandarins' (the very highest civil servants) and ministers in government departments. A secondary function of increasing importance is the provision of an information service to industry and commerce. On the first page of *Government Statistics: a Brief Guide to Sources* (Central Statistics Office (CSO), 1977), we read: "The GSS exists first to serve the needs of modern government. But much of the information it compiles is readily usable by business management, particularly in marketing, and indeed large parts of the system have been shaped with this in mind.' An even clearer indication of these priorities is provided in the booklet *Profit From Facts* (CSO, 1973), produced for and issued free to businesses (see also Stibbard, 1972). Academic researchers and other users of published data are, not surprisingly, assigned the lowest priority of all in GSS planning.

The GSS was created as a distinct section of the Civil Service in 1941. Wartime planning had necessitated more direct state control of the economy, and thus a firm quantitative base for government

decision making. Harold Wilson fondly recalled the heroic impro-
visations of those years in his 1973 Presidential Address to the Royal
Statistical Society (Wilson, 1973). After the war, extensive government activity continued with the mixed economy and the welfare
state: the GSS consequently expanded at a phenomenal rate,
doubling in size every seven or eight years.

This expansion continued through the 1960s, especially under
the enthusiastic patronage of Prime Minister Wilson, who had (as
did Heath) a close relationship with the head of the GSS, Claus
Moser. The GSS was to be part of the 'white heat of the
technological revolution', which the Labour government hoped
would modernise the British state and economy, and make British
capital more competitive against its overseas rivals. Certain
politicians and officials have seen statisticians as a new innovating
influence in the fusty, out-of-date atmosphere of Whitehall.

As with all government expenditure in the present colder
economic climate, so also for the GSS: the party is over. Its growth
has levelled off at about 550 professional staff, and 7,000 in all,
including all types of support staff (see Pite, 1975, on the allocation
of staff; Moser, 1973, is of interest though out-of-date). The end of
GSS expansion has been felt by statisticians in increasing work
pressures and declining promotion prospects.

Moser's good relations with Wilson and Heath not only
promoted the quantitative growth of the GSS, but also secured for it
greater prestige and influence than are enjoyed by the statistical
services of most countries. Whereas most countries and international organisations have giant central offices for statistics—
'statistics factories', such as 'Statistics Canada' and the 'Statistical
Office of the European Communities'—isolated from centres of
power[1], the GSS is relatively decentralised and less isolated.
Notwithstanding recent moves in the direction of more centralisation, it is likely to remain so.[2]

In large part, the GSS is constituted by the Statistics Divisions
(or, in some cases, combined Statistics and Economics Divisions) of
which there is one or more in most government departments.
Statisticians advise administrators—and, mainly through them,
ministers—and often work closely with administrators in the
formulation of policy. In addition, there are three statistical
agencies outside the departments: the Central Statistical Office, the
co-ordinating centre of the GSS whose Director also heads the GSS,
and which is directly under the Cabinet Office and thus the Prime
Minister; and, of lesser importance, the Business Statistics Office,
and the Office of Population Censuses and Surveys (OPCS), which

includes a semi-autonomous Social Survey Division. This division, not usually considered part of the GSS, is commissioned by government departments to conduct surveys for them (on, for example, family expenditure or alcoholism).

Thus decentralisation to the departments is combined with some central co-ordination—an attempt to enjoy the best of both worlds. Statisticians are regarded as having a 'dual loyalty': their lines of command run, via the heads of statistics branches, up the departmental hierarchies, while at the same time they have links (which, in practice, may be highly attenuated) with the rest of the GSS, and with the statistical profession as a whole.

In contrast to the many Civil Service specialists (scientists, architects, surveyors, meteorologists, etc.) concerned only with technical tasks, statisticians are often in positions which bridge the gap between technical problems (sample design, computing, etc.) and administration and policy making. They are closely integrated into the bureaucratic machine. They share the salary and promotion structure of the administrators—a more favourable one than most other specialists (including, to touch a sore point, the Research Officers of the OPCS Social Survey Division). For rank, or grade, is a pervasive and oppressive influence in the Civil Service, and, if statisticians are to be listened to, their rank must correspond with that of the administrators they work with. These circumstances they share only with economists.

Most members of the public who come into contact with the GSS do so through inclusion in the surveys and censuses carried out by OPCS. Apart from such special surveys, government statisticians work on a great variety of projects with specific purposes.

For example, they design and operate statistical computer models with purposes ranging from the projection of economic and population trends (Treasury, OPCS), the analysis of the supply of teachers (Department of Education and Science), the examination of energy policies (Department of Energy), the allocation of Rate Support Grant to local authorities (Department of the Environment), the planning of manpower systems (Civil Service Department) to the control of inventories of military equipment (Ministry of Defence). Unfortunately, even when details of such models are published in technical journals, there is often no public or academic discussion of them, in spite of the importance of their applications. We can cite the calculation, on a very dubious basis, of the 'needs element' of the Rate Support Grant, which determined the distribution of £3,700 million to local authorities in 1977-78.

However, the largest part of government statistical work is the

continuous routine data collection and processing in the departments. In several, this involves extensive use of computers.[3] It is to
some typical examples of such work that we now turn. Let the reader
judge whether these are appropriate examples of the 'varied
and interesting work' advertised in the Civil Service Commission
recruitment pamphlet, *Statisticians in Government Service* (1974, p. 15).

The process of production of statistics[4]

The most crucial documents in the whole process of producing statistics are the *forms*, or *returns*, sent out by the government
department (not necessarily by the statisticians) to the organisations
from which information is needed: for example, to the offices of
business firms, local tax offices, police stations, employment
exchanges and local authority social services departments. The
unfortunate people given the job of filling in these forms collect (or
sometimes invent) and record the requisite information with
varying degrees of accuracy and comprehensibility. While some
forms are specially designed for statistical purposes, others have a
completely different primary purpose—claims for grants, say, or
National Health Service records—and provide statistical information only as a by-product.

The completed forms are typically posted, or ferried by van,
to a data processing and computer centre in a provincial town.
Medical certificates, for example, end up in Newcastle, and
Population Census forms in Titchfield. This centre will form part of
the statistics branch (or division or organisation) of the department
concerned. The work of statisticians, usually located in London
offices, and that of technical staff at the computer centre, is co-
ordinated by telephone and travel between the centre and the
departmental office. It is the statisticians' job to order, analyse and
interpret computer output so as to meet the requirements of the
departmental administrators for information, and to compile
statistical volumes and reports.

It is useful at this point to consider in more detail the division
of labour between the different types of staff involved. Diagram 1
shows the hierarchical structure of a statistics branch (including a
computer centre) in a government department, and the main lines
of communication and command within it, and between it and the
administrative and policy-making sector of the department. The
size of statistics branches varies considerably: the example shown
here is of a large branch with a staff of 100. *Table 1* gives job
descriptions for different types of staff and the specific grades they
occupy in the Civil Service hierarchy.

Table 1: **Job descriptions of Government Statistical Service staff**

Position in hierarchy	Civil Service grades	Job description
'Mandarins'	Permanent Secretary Deputy Secretary	Development and administration of general policies; advising ministers; overall management of the department
Administrators	Under Secretary Assistant Secretary Principal Higher Education Officer (A) Administration trainee	Development and administration of policies in specific areas; advising superiors; management of sections of department; enquiries, correspondence, etc.
Administrators of Statistics Branch	Director of Statistics Chief Statistician	
Statisticians	Statistician (main grade)	Management of collection and processing of data on specific topics; production, analysis and interpretation of statistics

Assistant statisticians	Senior Assistant Statistician Assistant Statistician	Assistance to main-grade Statisticians (training grades)
Executive support staff	Senior Executive Officer (rarely) Higher Executive Officer Executive Officer	Organisation and supervision of clerical staff; skilled de-processing and preparation; enquiries, correspondence
Clerical support staff	Clerical Officer Clerical Assistant	Unskilled data processing and preparation, checking
Administrators of Computer Centre	Principal Senior Executive Officer	
Systems analysts, computer programmers etc.	Higher Executive Officer Executive Officer	Operation and maintenance of computer; design of computer systems and programs to process data
Card-punchers		Machine punching of computer cards

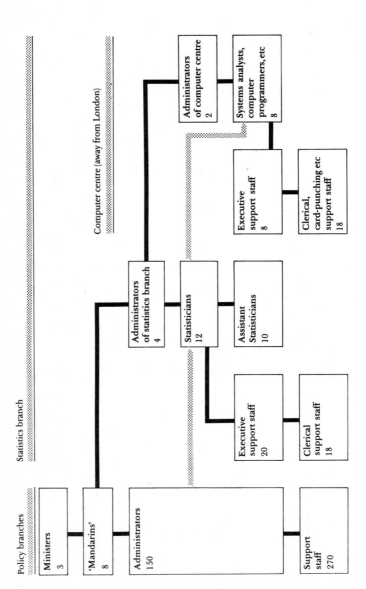

Diagram 1: Structure and relationships of a large statistics branch containing a computer centre in a government department

The cycle of statistical production

Within this structure, statistics are produced in a cyclical process. Under the influence of departmental policy, as formulated by its ministers, mandarins and administrators, and drawing on their own experience, the statisticians elaborate and revise the concepts and procedures for categorising and measuring the matters of concern to the department. These form the basis on which statisticians, computer specialists and supervisory staff design, adjust and maintain the entire statistical production system.

Such a system is often extensive and unwieldy. To change it, except very gradually, is often difficult and disruptive of work schedules. Thus, once a statistical system has been designed and is in operation, revision of its concepts and organisation in the light of experience and of changing requirements is likely to be slow. *Diagram 2* indicates the stages in which statistics are produced, which staff are responsible for each stage, and how the stages interconnect. The sequence shown by arrows is one of influence (in practice, often a two-way influence) rather than of time, or of workflow. All stages may occur simultaneously.

At the base of both the process and of the hierarchy, subordinate staff perform routine clerical and data processing tasks of many kinds, such as form-filling, coding and card-punching. The end-results of their work, in the form of computer output, are analysed and interpreted by statisticians, and used by administrators, mandarins and ministers in the department, and in other departments, to develop and justify policies.

The 'attitudes' of different layers of staff to their work, shown in *Diagram 2*, whilst being simplified representations, are nevertheless worth recording on this understanding. Administrators are not all cynical—some really believe in 'serving the state', or even 'reforming society'; while cynicism may be found among routine employees, as well as naive commitment or indifference to their work. Powerful influences, however, do tend to structure attitudes in the directions shown. For example, the higher placed people are in the hierarchy, the more information they have about the real rationale for policies (often so different from those publicised), and the more useful cynicism is in adapting to this information.

By 'professionalism' is meant the ethos by which professional workers try to maintain a certain independence, and standards of competence, accuracy and integrity, within their own narrow technical sphere, while carefully abstaining from questioning, or taking responsibility for, the ends to which their skills are used.

Statisticians, working in closer contact with administrators than most other professional staff, retain only an attenuated professional ethos, and partly come to share the attitudes of administrators.

In the rest of this article we consider in turn the stages of statistics production indicated in *Diagram 2*.

The 'elaboration of concepts' stage

There is no one set of methods and concepts which must be used to make sense of our social environment and to gather and assimilate information about it. The methods and concepts developed and used for official statistics are shaped by the sorts of policies powerful people in the state wish to consider and by the concerns which preoccupy them. These concerns determine, at least partly, which phenomena are to be investigated as 'social problems', and which neglected.

Later articles in this book criticise specific areas of statistics. Such isolated critiques of separated subject areas generally fail to expose the deeper influences of the social order on the range of issues considered in official statistics and the treatment of these issues. It is extremely difficult, if not impossible, to make a really radical criticism of society using available statistical sources, which imprison us in the concepts and concerns that dominate official political and economic life. Yet, unless we are prepared to abandon quantification altogether, we have no choice but to use government sources, as only the state has the power and resources to produce statistics on such a large scale.

We consider two examples of such difficulties. The first arises in the definition of geographical regions. The regions of England to which statistics relate are standardised—North-East, North-West, Midlands etc. This makes it difficult to compare regions constructed on different criteria, for example, coastal, lowland, mountain etc. And virtually all statistics relate to particular nation-states, while in developing a critique of the nation-state as an institution, we may well need to study regions whose boundaries do not coincide with national frontiers.

The second example concerns statistics of production and distribution. Overwhelmingly these are collected and presented in money terms, a consequence of production and distribution being determined by the imperatives of buying and selling on world markets, rather than by the direct assessment of human needs. This poses enormous problems if we seek to analyse the use for different economic purposes of given raw materials, productive capacities or labour time. How can we find out how many tonnes of aluminium,

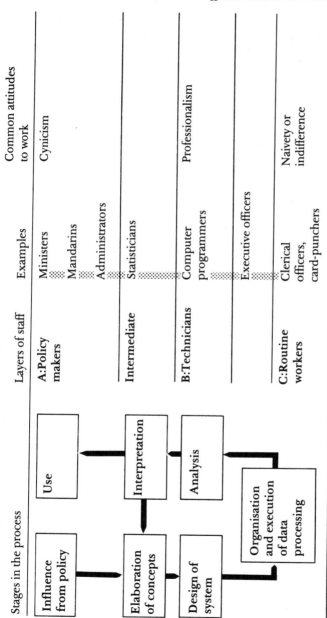

Diagram 2: The cycle of statistics production in a typical government department

millions of person-days, or items of electronic control equipment are squandered by British capitalism (as well as other capitalist and bureaucratic societies) on war preparations, protection of property and non-productive activities (advertising, banking, accounting, political and religious rituals, etc.), and thus develop alternative plans for these resources?[5] One is not able to 'profit from facts' in carrying out such forms of quantitative assessment.

Practical constraints reinforce the conservatism of statistical systems. Conventions on how to handle data, even when they are generally admitted to be inappropriate, are retained—from inertia, from the desire to maintain the consistency and comparability of statistics over different areas and over time, and in view of the costs and difficulties of change. For example, only extremely serious reasons could conceivably impel fundamental change in the vast and complex classification system of firms and industries which is the *Standard Industrial Classification*, given the great problems and costs of discontinuity in processing, analysis and interpretation. In fact, the revisions being undertaken in the late 1970s have no theoretical rationale, but are aimed at achieving consistency with the classification used by the EEC.

Even seemingly harmless conventions may have implications deserving some thought. What value judgements are hidden, for instance, in such routine decisions as those to treat a part-time worker as equal to one-half of a full-time worker, a child as one-half of a person, or a bathroom as one-half of a room? There are also less structural aspects of statistical conservatism. For example, some figures are not needed for action, but nevertheless continue to be collected, almost as a matter of tradition.

A further important problem arises when statistics are produced as by-products of administrative systems existing mainly for other purposes. Many regular official statistics are in fact produced in this way. Examples are Inland Revenue estate duty statistics being used to derive statistics on the distribution of wealth (see Hird and Irvine, this volume; and Atkinson, 1974); unemployment statistics being based on the records kept by employment exchanges (see Hyman and Price, this volume); and homelessness statistics being based on the records kept by local authorities on those who apply to them for help.

What such statistics tend to monitor is not so much the social conditions of wealth, unemployment or homelessness, but rather the operations of the state agencies responsible for dealing with the matter. Wealthy people who avoid estate duty through timely gifts to relatives, unemployed married women who do not register at the

employment exchange (because they are not eligible to claim benefits), and homeless people who do not apply to local authorities for
help (knowing that they do not fall into a category of people which
the authority is prepared to help) are ignored by the agencies and
thus structurally excluded from the statistics. The consequence,
often very convenient to the state, is a lack of reliable information on
social problems about which little or nothing is being done.

An excellent example of this phenomenon is provided by an
account in *Statistical News* of a new system of statistics on homelessness (Morrison, 1976). (It should be noted that the new system is
in fact a considerable improvement on the old one.) The statistics are
derived from computer analysis of forms sent in (sometimes) by
local authorities, recording applications for help made to them and
how such applications have been dealt with.[6] Morrison tells us:

> . . . Some homeless households, after the Authority has accepted
> responsibility, make no further contact or leave temporary accom-
> modation provided without contacting the Authority; if no further
> contact is made during the following six months, it is assumed that
> they are no longer homeless, and a 'permanent solution' is recorded.
> Although when contact is lost this is recorded as a 'permanent
> solution', this is partly a matter of statistical convenience; *it is
> permanent in the sense that the case is now closed.* If the household re-
> applies at a later date, this is treated as a new case; to do otherwise
> would make the statistical system too complex. (Our emphasis).

and:

> . . . The statistics reflect the practices of individual Local Authorities
> in their dealings with the problem of homelessness as manifested in
> the applications they receive and the actions they are able to take. It
> is recognised that there are some shortcomings in the new system (of
> statistics), particularly since this is an area where there are no clear
> and unequivocal definitions. For example, those households who
> approach the Local Authority and do not fall into one of the groups
> which it is the policy of that Local Authority to help often never
> reach the stage of making a formal application.[7] Local Authority
> officers are understandably reluctant to ask for detailed information
> from someone they know they will be unable to help. The collection
> of information on those without shelter who did not contact the Local
> Authority would be even more difficult; it is extremely doubtful
> whether a comprehensive set of statistics could be maintained on
> those people.

The 'design of system' stage

A vast clerical operation exists to distribute and collect forms,
to check and clarify information on incoming forms, to convert it

into a form which the computer can handle (that is, computer codes punched on computer cards), and to perform related tasks. This operation must be maintained and adjusted to changing circumstances and requirements. In these jobs—which include the design of forms, the specification of processing instructions, the supervision of processing staff, and the organisation of the channels through which paper flows—both statisticians and supervisory staff (in small operations the same person may well be both) play a part. The problem of organisation is more complicated for those systems where the documents used do not have solely statistical functions but are first used outside the statistics organisation for other purposes.

Also included in this stage are the organisation of the operations of the computer centre and the develoment by computer specialists of computer programs and systems to handle the computer processing of the data, and to produce tabulations and other output for analysis.

The 'data processing' stage

The data to be processed are usually taken from a set of forms completed in commercial or government offices, offices in which such form-filling tends to be the lowest priority. One indication of this prioritisation is the 'statistics strike', a mild kind of industrial action, in which forms are not completed. Such a strike paralysed the statistical organisation of the Department of Employment from August 1976 to January 1977, as many pages of the *Department of Employment Gazette* for those months made clear. Admittedly, the world did not come to an end as a result.

The annoying chore of form-filling tends to be shoved onto the least knowledgeable or least competent clerical staff, or simply onto whomever happens to be available at the time, although forms are often not designed with such people in mind. Thus forms are often not completed fully, accurately or even comprehensibly, and at busy times perhaps not dealt with at all. Sending incomplete data is especially tempting when there is no way for the collectors to tell whether the data are complete or not (as in the case of the local authority returns on homelessness).

Businesses are urged to co-operate by drawing their attention to the profit they may derive from the statistics to which they contribute. However, many types of data (for example, on industrial accidents) can be neglected or falsified without risk of discovery. Nor do guarantees of confidentiality necessarily prevent falsification of returns. One of our correspondents wrote of his experience in a large company: 'I was pressed time and again to use false figures for turnover, cost of raw materials etc., for fear of the taxman. They did not realise that the taxman would never see the forms—or so I hoped. I fought bitter battles, and once threatened to give notice to prevent the fraud. I know that others do not have the power to do this, or do not care.'

The data processing stage is marked above all by tedium. The DHSS computer centre handles millions of medical certificates per year, the Inland Revenue centre millions of forms from tax offices. Storeroom attendants spend their days keeping track of the bundles of paper taken to and from the long dusty shelves. Clerks sit in rows in large open-plan rooms (designed so that everyone is visible to the supervisor) and sort out the forms into categories, or put every nth form aside for processing of a sample. Others translate the scrawl on the forms into computing codes, written on coding sheets in accordance with prepared coding instructions. From these the 'card-punch girls'—it's 'women's work', of course—punch out computer cards on rows of machines hammering out like very loud typewriters, and the cards are fed, after checking, into the hungry jaws of the computer's card-readers. Supervisors make spot checks and try to keep to schedule. All to the sound of soft piped pop music, year after year. The computer, supposed to usher in an age of automated freedom from clerical toil, has so far merely raised the productivity of boredom, and added new varieties of routine work to the old ones.

These people are not only bored, it seems, but boring also. Paper-shuffling jobs seem to lack the mystique that attracts wide interest to the work of car-workers, managers or prostitutes. Where are the paperbacks on the experience of the coding room or the computer floor?

Even the overseers of this dull empire, the statisticians, are exposed to this public indifference (mingled with superstitious fear), though some of them may half-heartedly try to cultivate an exciting professional image. Yet to what avail, when the very word 'statistician' conjures up in most minds a picture of a frightening, soulless, mechanical robot? No wonder that a sample of sociology students, asked to list members of 15 occupations in order of preference for being locked up with alone in a room, put 'statistician' last![8]

While the work of the statisticians is admittedly less boring than that of their staff, particularly if they are lucky enough to be working in a field that interests them,[9] they are saddled with more worry and responsibility. They know that the consequences of slipping up on, or forgetting, any of a thousand and one details can be disaster in the form of confusion, error and missed deadlines.

From the time when figures are first entered on a form in a local Government or business office, until the statistics are published in statistical volumes and reports, data processing is highly sensitive to many mundane sources of error—misunderstood instructions on forms, misreading of hastily written figures, misplacing a decimal point, losing one's place in copying, accidental 'corruption' of data in computer files, or printing errors. It is quite possible for a mistake anywhere along the line to go undetected and work its way through into published figures. Once in a while such a case emerges into the glare of publicity, giving newspaper cartoonists a chance to re-use their civil servant caricatures.

One example was when, following the accidental omission of a zero by an Olivetti employee reporting the firm's exports, an underestimate of national exports (and thus an overestimate of the excess of imports over exports) generated a phoney balance of payments crisis. Another was when the trade figures went haywire over a period of many months because a clerk at one point copied two lines of figures onto a coding sheet in the wrong order. (The first assumption, as reported in the press, was that it was the fault of an excessively complex computer program for carrying out seasonal adjustments on the figures.) A major error in Home Office migration figures resulted from accidentally counting the same set of movements twice.

High-level post-mortem investigations are usually held when such large errors in politically important statistics come to light. (Less important errors may never come to light, since many statistics never come under critical scrutiny.) Statistics administrators respond by making pleas for simpler, less error-prone procedures, and for more effective checking arrangements. But such expedients have limited potential: everything cannot be checked and cross-checked, and the person doing the checking may well repeat the errors of the person being checked.

Serious errors would certainly occur less often if staff had the ability to recognise figures as implausible and the initiative then to get them sorted out. Yet the necessary knowledge of the subject matter is rarely available to clerical staff, while initiative is discouraged by the clearly defined roles of the hierarchical division of labour, in the interests of control and uniformity of processing.[10] Clerks are supposed to refer anomalies and ambiguities in the data to their supervisors, but it takes initiative and knowledge to realise that something needs questioning. Even the best writer of instructions cannot foresee all sources of confusion and misunderstanding, or be able to guard against them. For example, an empty box on a form (especially on a poorly designed form) may mean 'no', 'none', 'don't know', 'won't tell', 'does not apply' or 'forgot to fill in this box'. The differences between these meanings are crucial, and it would be very difficult to give precise advance instructions on how to resolve the ambiguity.

Automatic checks of the internal consistency and plausibility of data can often be programmed into the processing of computer data files, although it is impossible within the computer to check other aspects of data quality: to spot consistent errors or incorrect but plausible data. The computer can check whether values are in a given range, whether two figures add up to a third, and so on. For example, in a survey of household accommodation, the computer might be programmed to draw attention to, or reject, cases where the number of toilets was recorded as less than zero, more than six, or more than one-half of the total number of rooms.

But, even when a comprehensive series of such checks is built in, it cannot even detect *all* implausible, let alone plausible but invalid, data. To take the case mentioned of a tenfold under-recording of Olivetti exports, the recorded figure was within a plausible range of values for firms in general; it needed someone with a knowledge of the export activities of different firms to spot that it was an unlikely figure for Olivetti in particular. In the last resort, therefore, the crucial check must be that of use.

The extent of the inaccuracy introduced by these problems depends, among other things, on how 'close to the data' the statisticians are: that is, on how far they are able, or inclined, to involve themselves effectively in the details of data processing. To minimise such problems, they need to spend a day doing each of the processing jobs in the system—a rare practice!

A final key factor is the attitude of processing workers to their work. Statisticians are forced, by the responsibility imposed on them, to care about the reliability of data. But there is no good reason why a clerical officer should worry. Many staff are, nevertheless, painstakingly conscientious about such things. (Indeed, among the older generation of civil servants, there are those prepared to work unpaid overtime and take work home; this work ethic, though, seems to be on the decline.) But those who are indifferent—either sinking into tedium-induced stupor, or concentrating on conversation with others (where conditions allow this), or on daydreams—are engaged in passive resistance to their work situation, a work to rule.

Thus those who call, for whatever reason, for more timely, comprehensive, useful or reliable statistics should remember that, under present conditions, they thereby call for more stress on, and regimentation of, statistical workers.

The stages of 'analysis, interpretation and use'

Many computer tabulations are produced on a regular schedule for use in published statistical volumes, or for reference by statisticians as needed. Other output is ordered, or obtained through computer terminals, by statisticians for special purposes. They select what is needed, analyse it and interpret its meaning for administrators or enquirers.

If coordination between statisticians and computer staff has been inadequate, statisticians may at this stage find themselves unable to carry out desired analyses, for reasons such as the way the data are stored in the computer.

The best use possible has to be made of whatever data are available. As administrators are reluctant to accept that whatever information they require may not be available, 'guesstimates' are often provided where reliable estimates are impossible, however doubtful the assumptions made to derive them. The requirement for clear-cut conclusions, the pressure of work and the petrification of the original theoretical knowledge of the statistician, encourage such misleading practices as the automatic mechanical use of (perhaps inappropriate) significance tests at 95 per cent level of significance—without the proviso, however, that 1 in 20 of results so obtained is expected to be incorrect. (The easy availability of standard tests on computer programs and packages is a standing invitation to such procedures.)

Another problem which statisticians face in presenting statistics for the use of mandarins and administrators is the latter's preference for figures which are easy to remember, have straightforward meanings and are not subject to frequent revision. An apocryphal story relates that after the war Sir Godfrey Ince, then Permanent Secretary at the Ministry of Labour and National Service, complained about the changes in the figures of unemployed: once he had learnt to remember them, they should not be changed at such frequent intervals.

Under the pressure of schedules for the production of statistics, statisticians usually lack enough time also to analyse and interpret them thoroughly. However, in those places where different people are made responsible for production and for interpretation (for example, Department of Industry statisticians interpret statistics produced by the Business Statistics Office, and economists interpret statistics in several Departments—a smouldering demarcation dispute), misunderstandings and failures of communication, as well as friction and frustration, are much greater.

Much statistical material is published in official publications, and much more remains unpublished in order to keep down the bulk and cost of publications. It is often possible to obtain unpublished or not yet published data, and—for a price—even to obtain specially produced tabulations of unpublished data; for example, Census data for small areas. In general, the more acceptable are enquirers' political and academic credentials, and the more trustworthy they are regarded by a Department, the more cooperative the Department will be in releasing information to them. One of the constraints is that it should not be possible to identify from released data individual households or firms, though in practice it sometimes is.[11]

There is, however, a certain amount of unpublished data which is considered politically sensitive. Even trusted contacts of a Department will find it difficult to get hold of such material, meeting with evasion, claims of ignorance, and—as a last resort—outright refusal. 'When in doubt, say nowt' is the course often recommended to civil servants in such situations.

Although we have tried to correct the balance in the way official publications are usually uncritically accepted, by concentrating on difficulties and problems, the extent to which official statistics are unreliable should not be exaggerated. In many areas they are an important source of information, if examined critically, and, where possible, used in conjunction with other evidence. It is especially important that they should be interpreted in the context of the assumptions, definitions and methods of collection on which they are based, and GSS publications generally describe these, at least to some extent.

However, administrators, mandarins, politicians, social scientists and the mass media tend to disregard this small print. Misinterpretation of statistics, accidental or deliberate, in the form in which they reach a wide public, is common. As secrecy about what they learn in the course of official duty, and abstention from public controversy, are conditions of employment for civil servants, the former backed up by the all-encompassing provisions of the Official Secrets Act, Government statisticians are unable (except occasionally with special permission) to protest publicly at such misinterpretation.

Due to the enforced secrecy in which such practices take place, it is difficult to assess the extent of deliberate manipulation of statistics for political purposes.[12] Serious manipulation, however, seems to be rare except in a few sensitive areas (such as the concealment of staffs, budgets and even existence of the security services and of Government Communications Headquarters). Wages and prices statistics, because of their importance in justifying and implementing wages policies, are also susceptible to manipulation under pressure from the Treasury.[13]

Although statisticians are prevented from protesting publicly at such practices, it is open to them to protest internally, to seek the support of GSS superiors against administrators, and in the last resort to resign and look for a new job. People vary in how far they are prepared to stick their necks out in such circumstances. Collective protest is very unlikely for a host of reasons: the isolated situation of statisticians (in their work and even physically), the competitive structure of the hierarchy, and—perhaps most important of all—the fears, customs and attitudes of the milieu. The likelihood of success in internal individual protest will depend on the power of the opponent: it is easier to protest about the speech of a politician seeking party-political advantage than it is to protest about matters whose necessity is advocated by mandarins.

As the outright falsification of figures is risky, it is very rare. More common tactics include non-publication ('the truth, nothing but the truth, and as little of the truth as possible'), delay of publication (such as the six-month delay of 'race' statistics by Crossman, who feared the reaction to projections of the number of 'immigrants'), misleading or inadequate commentaries on published figures (for example, in order to be 'optimistic' about the economic situation), and 'massage'.

Massage is the manipulation of the way figures are derived or presented in order to create desired impressions. It covers a continuum of deception ranging from the choice of the most presentable of several equally accurate modes of presentation, to subterfuges which, in practice at least, amount to falsification. We mention four types of massage:

1. *Changing the definitions of terms* in order to create a desired effect. The unemployment figures reported over the years in the *Department of Employment Gazette* reflect a successive narrowing of the definition of unemployment, to keep figures down—with regard to the inclusion or exclusion of such groups as married

women, school-leavers, people out of work for short periods and part-time workers.

2. *Unjustifiable extrapolation of trends.* For example, Chancellor of the Exchequer Healey claimed in an election campaign that inflation was running at $8\frac{1}{2}$ per cent per year. He could claim to be right only by ignoring seasonal adjustment and extrapolating from a short untypical part of the year; the rate of inflation at the time, taken over any reasonable period, was much higher.

3. *Manipulation of adjustments.* Here advantage is taken of the practice of adjusting figures so as to reduce the impact on them of atypical circumstances at the time of collection. An example has been the selective application, under pressure from the Treasury, of adjustments to the Retail Prices Index, made with the purpose of reducing the impact on the Index of rapid fluctuations in the prices of eggs, fresh vegetables and other perishable foodstuffs, *when and only when such adjustments served to depress the Index.*

4. *Manipulation of categories.* The categories into which items (foods, people, or whatever) are divided may be chosen in order to clarify or in order to obfuscate. A relatively small group of items, which is nevertheless of interest, may be included in a larger category, or in a rag-bag category marked 'other' or 'miscellaneous' for the purpose of concealment. Thus are concealed, for example, the staffs and budgets of secret agencies, and the embarrassing survival in a handful of villages of all-age schools.

Conclusion

We have not in this article aimed at a comprehensive overview of the government statistical system. But we hope we have focused the mind of the reader on the fact that statistics do not, in some mysterious way, emanate directly from the social conditions they appear to describe, but that between the two lie the assumptions, conceptions and priorities of the state and the social order, a large, complex and imperfectly functioning bureaucracy, tonnes of paper and computing machinery, and—last but not least—millions of hours of human grind.

Notes

1. Policy Departments in fact try to overcome this situation by such subterfuges as employing their own statisticians disguised as 'economists' (as in Holland).
2. The question of centralisation is linked to the controversy over the possible linkage of data banks held in the computers of different departments (see *Financial Times* 18 October 1977: 'Society today—awesome model for government statistics: building in the safety devices', by Joe Rogaly).

3. For example, Business Statistics Office (computer centre at Swansea); Civil Service Department (Chessington, Surrey); Ministry of Defence (London); Department of Education and Science (Darlington); Department of Health and Social Security (Newcastle); Board of Inland Revenue (Worthing); OPCS (Titchfield, Hants.); Scottish Office (Edinburgh).

4. We pay no attention to technical problems of statistical work such as bias and sampling error. Though important, many texts on survey methods (Moser and Kalton, 1971) deal with them. Such texts also deal with the pitfalls of form design (see also the booklet *Ask a Silly Question*, issued by the CSO Survey Control Unit).

5. For contrasting monetary and material approaches in the field of input-output analysis, see Berman (1968), and Roberts (1976), respectively. In the wake of problems over the supply of natural resources, studies such as Roberts' have begun to attract attention.

6. For a useful attempt to interpret the meaning of homelessness statistics, see Bailey, 1977, chapter 2.

7. Single people are rarely helped.

8. This agonised report appeared in *News and Notes*, the informal journal of the Royal Statistical Society.

9. The level of boredom varies enormously from job to job, but has tended to increase as the GSS has grown and posts become more specialised. In the tiny GSS of the 1950s, main-grade statisticians, for example, had more frequent contact with, and influence on, ministers and mandarins.

10. In these and many other ways are the inefficiencies of hierarchy and the division of labour revealed. Many support staff lack the confidence to point out an error made by a superior, for example, or even underestimate their own intelligence.

11. The rights of privacy on the whole safeguarded by this and other rules of confidentiality are at least as much concerned with protecting the affairs of powerful companies from public scrutiny as they are with protecting ordinary citizens. The collection of statistics, in which the identity of individuals is of no interest, is a relatively minor threat to privacy. The publicity about it, culminating in the mild public hysteria of the Census period, contrasts intriguingly with the media's acceptance of the *real* power which employers, schools, credit agencies, security services etc. derive from detailed non-statistical information on millions of specific individuals (see Hewitt, 1977).

12. Secrecy extends even to refusal of permission to publish academic papers whose political implications are unwelcome. The suggestion by a government statistician (Nicholson, 1975) of a more 'democratic' prices index which, unlike existing ones, would give equal weight to the expenditure of each household in the sample on which the index was based, was published after an enforced delay of 20 years.

13. Those exerting pressure on statisticians do sometimes have valid points to make, which the statisticians have neglected.

Bibliography

Atkinson, A. B., 1974, *Unequal Shares: Wealth in Britain*, Harmondsworth, Penguin.

Bailey, R., 1977, *The Homeless and the Empty Houses*, Harmondsworth, Penguin.

Berman, L. S., 1968, 'Developments in input-output statistics', *Statistical News*, (CSO), no. 3, November.

Central Statistical Office, CO:CSO Section, 1977, *Government Statistics: A Brief Guide to Sources*.

Central Statistical Office, Survey Control Unit, 1976, *Ask a Silly Question!*

Central Statistical Office and Central Office of Information, 1973, *Profit From Facts*.

Civil Service Commission, 1974, *Statisticians in Government Service*.

Department of Employment, *Department of Employment Gazette* (monthly).

Hewitt, P., 1977, *Privacy: The Information Gatherers*, London, National Council for Civil Liberties.

Morrison, H., 1976, 'New system of statistics on homelessness', *Statistical News* (CSO). no. 35, November.

Moser, C. A., 1973, 'Staffing in the Government Statistical Service', *Journal of the Institute of Statisticians*, Part 1.

Moser, C. A., and Kalton, G., 1971, *Survey Methods in Social Investigation*, 2nd edn., London, Heinemann.

Nicholson, J. L., 1975, 'Whose cost of living?', *Journal of the Royal Statistical Society*, Series A., vol. 138, Part 4.

Pite, J. C., 1975, 'The deployment of staff in the Government Statistical Service', *Statistical News* (CSO), no. 30, August.

Roberts, N., 1976, 'Energy balances', *Statistical News* (CSO), no. 35, November.

Royal Statistical Society, *News and Notes* (monthly).

Stibbard, P. J., 1972, 'Use of official statistics in firms and *Profit From Facts*', *Statistical News* (CSO), no. 17, May.

Wilson, J. H., 1973, 'Statistics and decision-making in government—Bradshaw revisited: The Address of the President (with Proceedings)', *Journal of the Royal Statistical Society*, Series A, vol. 136, part 1.

11.

Theo Nichols

Social Class: Official, Sociological and Marxist

This chapter considers how official statistics relate to 'social class' — both in terms of what their content implies about our society, and in terms of the issues they raise about different concepts of 'class' itself.

It would be possible to simply outline and summarise here the various statistics which the state provides that are related to social class. However, some headway has been made already in detailing the statistics that are available (Reid, 1977; *Social Trends* 1975) and a critique which merely pointed to the absence of data concerning certain distributions might easily give the impression that what was required was a simple matter of 'more facts'. Obviously, if we are to understand how societies work we do need facts. But we have to be careful not to put the cart before the horse. For there is a good case to be made that the 'coverage' of statistics relating to social class (whether, for example, state statistics tabulate 'social class' by this or that 'variable') is of secondary importance, and the same may be said of questions of a 'technical' kind (Hindess, 1973, p. 12). Indeed, the present chapter has been constructed in the way it has in the hope that this will underline that the problems involved in the analysis of class cannot be reduced to purely technical statistical ones. It is in order that the primary importance of *theory* will become evident that it deals not only with social class in official statistics but also with different concepts of social class, in sociology and marxism. And, since theory can have political implications, this is also why, by way of conclusion, some tentative remarks are made about the possible correlates for political practice of certain concepts of the working class; in particular about those which define it in a broad or narrow way.

The Registrar General's 'social classes' are introduced in the first section. These are much used in social research, sometimes with only slight modification. But they are essentially descriptive categories that relate to *status*, and, as we see in the second section, they have something in common with some concepts of social class in sociology. These sociological concepts of class often stress the importance of different *dimensions* of social *stratification* (and the possible non-correspondence between different dimensions). But, like the Registrar General's 'social class', they invite criticism from marxists on the grounds that they do not *explain* the generation of inequalities in the structural dynamics of society, and only describe its results.

Yet in hard reality, this business about different concepts of social class in official statistics, sociology and marxism is by no means as simple as it might seem so far. First, and this point has to be made as soon as one touches upon marxist concepts of class relations (which are discussed in a third section), some marxism looks remarkably like some sociology. Second, even those marxists who claim that their concepts are of explanatory value, still of course at some point take into account descriptive material, for example concerning what sociologists call 'work' and 'market situations'. This, it will be argued, raises a key issue in the analysis of class relations (restricted here to contemporary capitalist societies). The issue is not, to make this plain, whether reference to such matters should be included, but whether they should be included to the *exclusion* of a further, and different, level of analysis.

In this article, I introduce the term *'condition'* to refer to the level of analysis that tends to be the only level in official and sociological treatments (and in some marxist ones). The other level which, as a simple exposition shows, figures prominently in the analysis of Poulantzas, is termed, following its author, that of *'place'* (a term that refers, as we shall see, to place within the social division of labour as a whole).

The analysis which Poulantzas himself conducts at the level of 'place' has been criticised, among other things, for its functionalism (Clarke, 1977). However, the present article is not concerned with the adequacy of this particular analysis. Rather, it is concerned to draw attention to the general possibility that class relations can be analysed at this level; to suggest that this level is a different one to the more familiar one which is here called 'condition'; and to suggest also that the object and purpose of such an analysis means that the statistics appropriate to it (for instance those that relate to categories of productive and unproductive labour) necessarily differ from those likely to be relevant to official concepts of social class (which rest on assumptions about status) and from those likely to be considered pertinent to many studies of social class in sociology (which often have as their main object the investigation and description of differences in work, status and market situations).

Table 1: **Social class composition of people aged 15 and over in Great Britain in 1971, for various groups**
In percentages and thousands

	Men only			Women only			Men and women aged 15 and over		
				Married		Single, widowed and divorced			
	Economically active	Retired	Economically active and retired	Own[1] class	Husband's[2] class	Own[3] class	Own occupation of economically active and retired	Head of family	Chief economic supporter
	(1)	(2)	(3)	(4)	(5)	(6)	(7)	(8)	(9)
Percentage in each social class:									
I	5.2	3.0	5.0	0.9	5.3	1.2	3.6	5.1	4.9
II	17.8	19.1	18.0	16.2	19.8	19.2	17.8	20.0	19.8
III Non-manual	11.9	12.1	11.9	35.4	11.3	41.2	21.1	11.9	14.2
III Manual	39.0	34.2	38.5	10.0	39.0	10.8	28.4	37.9	34.8
IV	17.8	20.3	18.1	28.2	17.5	22.7	20.9	18.0	18.6

V	8.3	11.2	8.6	9.4	7.1	4.9	8.2	7.3	7.7
Total classified (=100%)	15,368	1,911	17,279	5,697	12,365	3,834	26,809	13,150	15,907
Total unclassified[4]	516	323	909	1,101	471	1,549	3,488	694	1,374
Total in Great Britain	15,884	2,304	18,188	6,797	12,835	5,383	30,367	13,844	17,281

Source: *Social Trends* 1975, No. 6, p. 11. (Arithmetic errors in the original) Data from 1971 Census.

[1] Economically active and retired married women by own social class.

[2] Married women enumerated with their husband by the social class of husband including both the economically active and retired, and those economically active.

[3] Economically active and retired single, widowed, and divorced women.

[4] Unclassified persons: those for whom no occupation or inadequate information was reported in the Census. A large proportion of this group were out of work, retired, or inactive at Census date.

The status of social class in the census

In 1801, in the first of the ten-yearly censuses, enumerators were required to answer the question: 'what number of persons in your parish, township or place are directly employed in agriculture, how many in trade manufactures or handicraft, and how many are not comprised in any of the preceding classes?' The question was deemed to be a failure and revisions were made, and continued to be made, until a predominantly industrial classification of 17 classes, and sub-classes, was introduced in 1851. This classification included categories such as persons engaged in Imperial or local government; in religion, law, medicine; and in agriculture. With some amendment and addition it continued to be used throughout the century, leading Charles Booth (1886, p. 318) to comment that 'generally there is such a want of fixity of principle or method, that even competent authorities have been seriously misled concerning the apparent results'. Certainly this is a verdict from which no social historian would dissent[1]. In 1911, though, the practice was instituted of summing birth and infant deaths into a number of groups 'designed to represent as far as possible different social grades'. These 'social grades' were very similar to the five 'social classes' used by the Registrar General today: I. Professional Occupations; II. Intermediate Occupations; III. Skilled Occupations (split in 1971 into Non-Manual and Manual); IV. Partly Skilled Occupations; V. Unskilled Occupations. *Table 1* shows the distribution of the population across these categories at the *1971 Census*. (It also serves to draw attention to some of the different possible social bases to which this classification may be applied; husband's class or 'own class' for married women, etc.).

Apart from these 'social class' categories the Registrar General provides a classification of 'socio-economic groups' (SEGs). Introduced in 1951, and modified in 1961, these constitute seventeen groupings of occupations, but in contrast to the Registrar General's 'social classes' there is no pretension that the SEGs are ranked one to another in terms of social standing. The groupings distinguish manual and non-manual occupations, and separate out the Armed Forces and those in Agriculture. Employment status (whether employed or self-employed) is used as a further differentiating factor. Although of relatively recent origin, the SEGs are particularly useful for plotting occupational shifts (as can be seen from the case of Agriculture in *Table 2*). A source of confusion here is that a collapsed version of the SEG groupings (see *Table 3*) is used by the General Household Survey. These collapsed groupings are

Table 2: **Socio-economic groups of males, 1961 and 1971 in Great Britain**

	1961	*1971*
	in thousands	
Employers and managers: large establishments	640	642
Employers and managers: small establishments	1,051	1,444
Professional: self-employed	144	155
Professional: employees	500	703
Intermediate non-manual	685	965
Junior non-manual	2,252	2,158
Personal service	162	174
Foreman: manual	595	647
Skilled manual	5,549	5,286
Semi-skilled manual	2,657	2,299
Unskilled manual	1,568	1,432
Own account (non-professional)	621	773
Farmers: employers	195	156
Farmers: own account	191	157
Agricultural	444	286
Armed Forces	336	254
Inadequately described	489	654
Total	18,080	18,187

Classification: own occupation of economically active and retired
Source: *Census 1961* and *1971*

sometimes referred to as 'social classes'. But it is better to term them 'the GHS socio-economic groupings'. This is precisely what they are, and it leaves the way open to regard the Registrar General's I-V hierarchy as the nearest thing we have to an official definition of 'social class'[2].

To answer the question of what principle or method lies behind the Registrar General's summing and ranking of occupations into 'social classes' it is appropriate to go back to a paper which

Table 3: **Possession of consumer-durables, in Great Britain, 1972**

	Television	Telephone	Washing machine	Refrig- erator	1 car	2 or more cars
	in percentages					
Economically active heads of household* Socio-economic grouping						
Professional	94	85	77	94	65	25
Employers and managers	96	81	82	93	57	26
Intermediate	92	62	69	86	55	9
Junior non- manual	95	48	69	83	40	6
Skilled manual	97	37	76	81	49	7
Semi-skilled manual	95	25	67	69	28	3
Unskilled manual	94	14	60	56	16	2
All groupings	96	46	73	81	43	9

*All heads of household for cars

Classification: GHS socio-economic groupings of head of household
Source: *General Household Survey 1972*

Stevenson, Statistical Officer at the General Register Office, read to the Royal Statistical Society in 1928 (Stevenson, 1928). In this we find Stevenson arguing against classification by income, and, *more importantly*, asserting that 'any scheme of social classification should take account of culture'—'culture', as he construed it, being something that 'the occupational basis of social grading has a wholesome tendency to emphasise'. It is of course the very emphasis of this 'wholesome tendency' in the construction of the Registrar General's *social* classes—rather than of the relationship to the means of production, which is central to marxism—that continues to make these classes so many categories of *status* ('culture'). In fact, in the words of the Census, the basic criterion continues to be 'the general standing within the community of the occupations concerned'.

Now it is obviously possible to point to the lack of continuity in the Census, to query the internal homogeneity of any class (status) category, to point to omissions and so on. In *Classifications of Occupations 1951*, for instance, the 'capitalist', the 'business specu-lator', the 'fundholder' and the 'landowner' were lumped into the same residual category as the 'expert (undefined)' and the 'lunatic (trade not stated)'. A rather pleasing coincidence perhaps, but one which serves to remind us that in the 'five social classes' of the Census the owners of capital are lost to sight, as are the self-employed[3]. Although therefore we may note that other systems of *grading* or *ranking* are possible, the essential fact is that the Census categories of 'social class' rest on a concept of class as status[4].

The dimensions of social class in sociology

In sociology, as in the Census, much work on social class is concerned in one way or another with status[5]. Two broad tendencies can be distinguished. The one relates to the granting of status in the sense of *esteem*. Apt to figure here are those interviewer's probes that seek to elicit the interviewee's own estimation of his or her class membership and that of other 'classes'. Never far away is that out-and-out psychologism, according to which classes do not exist if people do not say they do. The other way in which status enters in is evidence by attempts to categorise by *status group*; that is, by actual style of life. A recent work on class differences in Britain (Reid, 1977) is probably sufficient introduction to both of these concepts of class as status. It contains information on what class people think they belong to; it is bedecked with tables akin to *Table 3* above, and while 'prestige' appears in the index, 'property' does not. The ownership of television sets is documented, but not ownership of the means of production of televisions or of anything else. Any account of class struggle as a structural dynamic is entirely absent. The nearest we get to this is a reported survey finding that 60 per cent of interviewees 'thought there was a class struggle'.

More sophisticated sociologists resist the assimilation of class and status; indeed Weber's work (Gerth and Mills, 1948, ch. 7) made much of the distinction between them[6]. Even so, their theoretical work tends to reduce class to one factor among others in a multi-dimensional view of social stratification. Thus, in the case of C. Wright Mills (1953) a distinction is made between class (economic), occupation, status and power; and in the case of Goldthorpe and Lockwood (1963) reference is made to the economic, the normative and the relational dimensions of class stratification.

Occasionally, the multi-dimensional approach takes on a different form. In this version (Lenski, 1966) each dimension itself becomes the basis for one of a number of *different* 'class systems', yielding, for example, an educational class system, a religious class system, a racial class system, an age-related class system and so on. But apart from such absurdities the multi-dimensional approach is generally adequate to its purpose. For to sum stratified positions and clusters of social attributes into 'social class' and then, as is often the case in empirical research, to treat occupation as an indicator of this, can illuminate many features of social life—infant mortality, electoral support for political parties, differential performance at school, or, as in *Table 4*, inequality of educational opportunity.

Nonetheless, as at least one sociologist (Dahrendorf, 1959, p. 76) has made a point of telling us, *class* should always be a category for purposes of the analysis of the dynamics of social change and its structural roots, and *stratum* a category for describing hierarchical systems at a given point in time. And from this standpoint much sociology must be said to be concerned with social stratification rather than with class.

Marxists criticise sociology because, among other things, they hold that it conflates class and status, that it is descriptive rather than explanatory, and that it concerns itself over-much with the origins and the social mobility of agents. In short, as we noted earlier, it is held to concern itself too much with effects and too little with causes of a fundamental kind. The most weightily expressed criticism, however, is the one which claims that to analyse class relations it is necessary to have a prior understanding of the labour theory of value and the processes of capital accumulation (see for example Stolzman and Gamberg, 1973). The question obviously arises therefore of what a contemporary marxist analysis, which does claim such an understanding, looks like. Is it really all that different?

In an attempt to shed some light on this we will take some of the arguments made in what has been one of the most influential recent books in this area, *Classes in Contemporary Capitalism* (Poulantzas, 1975; see also Poulantzas, 1973). From this we may, by way of contrast, learn something further about the approach to class in sociology. But we may also learn that problems remain in the analysis of class relations for marxists, problems that, for them as for others, cannot be reduced to merely technical, statistical, issues.

Table 4: **Percentages obtaining education of a grammar-school type among children of different classes born in the late 1930s**

Father's occupation	*at ages 11–13*	*at age 17*
Professional and managerial	62	41.5
Other non-manual	34	16
Skilled manual	17	5
Semi-skilled manual	12	3
Unskilled	7	1.5
All children	23	10.5

Source: Banks (1968) p. 55

The place and condition of social class in modern marxism

Observations about the large number of wage and salary earners employed outside manufacturing, together with ideas about increasing automation, a decline in wage and status differentials, and more recently the rise of white-collar unemployment and unionisation, have become standard ingredients for sociological and popular analyses of the class structure. Within marxism itself a major focus of debate about class also now centres on the relationship between different elements of wage-labour, leading to theories of a 'new working class' (the technicians of Mallet, 1975), to theories of a working-class expanded through deskilling (as reflected in the work of Braverman, 1974), to theories of one big working-class (including pretty well everyone except for a handful of capitalists)[7] and to yet other formulations which posit the rise of 'intermediate social strata' (the middle ranks of the state apparatus and management, self-employed professionals, lawyers, etc.).

This last concept of 'intermediate social strata', which suggests the existence of strata without class, is from a marxist point of view perhaps the most surprising. Yet the political strategy of the 'anti-monopoly alliance', which characterises the French Communist Party (the PCF), and also the British, is closely bound up with this.[8] And whereas Communist Party theorists may protest that they do not share the social democratic notion of a 'wage-earning class', their political conclusions do tend in this direction. Or so Poulantzas maintains. *Classes in Contemporary Capitalism* is therefore both an attempt to recover the ground he sees to have been lost by some modern marxists, in particular by the PCF, and a warning against what he sees to be the dangerous political conclusions to which they are led by such an analysis.

In what way, then, does Poulantzas break with much which claims to be marxism? To begin to answer this question it is necessary to grasp three things, the first two of which will be explained at greater length below. These are: *one*, that he grounds his class analysis on a labour theory of value; *two*, that he uses a concept of 'place' in the social division of labour which is theoretically prior to any consideration of what is referred to here as 'condition'[9]; *three*, that for Poulantzas the 'position in the conjuncture' of any particular stratum (say, managers fighting redundancy alongside shop-floor workers) is not evidence of class membership. Were this to be so, the managers in our example would of course shift into and out of the working class in accordance with their support for workers.

Poulantzas holds that in the capitalist mode of production, productive labour is labour that produces surplus-value while directly reproducing the material elements that serve as the substratum of the relation of exploitation. Moreover, and this is fundamental, the working-class is itself necessarily defined by productive labour. There can be no doubt, therefore, that a theory of surplus-value is crucial for Poulantzas.

This stress on the importance of productive labour has invited criticisms of Poulantzas for having an economistic concept of social class. This is something he disputes strongly[10]. For him, social class refers to the overall effect of the structure on the field of social relations and on the division of labour. Structured class determination therefore includes the place of a class in terms of the *political* and *ideological* relations of the social division of labour as a whole. Let us take two instances of this:

1. The wage labour of managers[11] and technicians. This labour is productive insofar as it performs the work of co-ordination. But Poulantzas argues that these managers and technicians occupy a controlling place in political relations, and that as 'mental labour' they occupy a dominant place vis-a-vis 'manual' productive labour in ideological relations (secrecy, monopolisation of knowledge and the mystique of qualifications being the constituents of their place in ideological relations, not ideology in the sense of the ideas that these people have in their heads). It is because of the place they occupy in ideological and political relations that Poulantzas excludes managers and technicians from the working class.

2. Wage labour that is not productive. For Poulantzas the performance of such labour *always* spells exclusion from the working class. Indeed, he argues that such wage labourers belong to a *new* petty bourgeoisie which, in turn, is aligned with the traditional petty bourgeoisie (artisans, small shopkeepers, etc.). This conclusion, like that arrived at in (1), is again justified on ideological and political grounds, and despite the fact that the traditional and new petty bourgeoisies have a different relationship to the means of production. In the event then, this hardly amounts to an economistic analysis. In practice, ideological and political relations do play an important part in Poulantzas's analysis. Or to put it in his terms: structured class determination includes the place of a class in terms of the ideological and political relations of the social division of labour as a whole.

It can be seen from (1) above that according to Poulantzas it is not necessary to perform unproductive labour to be excluded from the working class. But to perform such labour is always sufficient for exclusion. This has the following consequence: that those who perform unproductive labour are still excluded from the working-class even if the *condition* of their lives is substantially similar to that of those whom Poulantzas includes in this class. The cleaner at a bank or the woman on the cash register at Tesco, for example, may do work which is boring, insecure and badly paid as well, but they perform their labour in the spheres of circulation and commerce. Since only productive labour produces surplus-value, and since surplus-value is not produced in these spheres, they are not working class.

Now such a scheme of analysis is clearly informed by different principles to much other marxist writing. For example, Wright's recent work on class boundaries in effect defines the working-class as a class that is dispossessed (Wright, 1976). It is a class which lacks not only effective economic ownership but lacks *possession*, both in the sense of control over physical means of production, and in the sense of control over the labour power of others. Poulantzas's analysis cannot be reduced to this. As far as he is concerned an official in the state apparatus, say a lowly tax collector, must be designated petty-bourgeois by virtue of the unproductive labour that he performs and the place that he occupies in the social relations of the division of labour as a whole. Tax collectors and their ilk—no matter how wretched their condition—are bearers of social relations which mark their place as a petty-bourgeois one. And they remain petty-bourgeois even if they do lack control ('possession') over the labour power of workers within their own administrative departments. It is in this sense that Poulantzas's analysis of place is theoretically prior to an analysis of condition.

So far, though, we have not seen how Poulantzas takes account of the effects which Wright deals with so neatly in terms of his concept of possession; the effects which we have referred to as 'condition'. As a consequence of this it appears that Poulantzas includes bank managers within the new petty bourgeoisie as well as the bank cleaners instanced above, the supermarket middle manager as well as the woman on the cash register, and most types of state employees, and of course professors like himself. This is indeed the case, but Poulantzas argues that the new petty bourgeoisie contains within it certain fractions with a 'proletarian polarisation'. Amongst these fractions, which constitute the majority of the new petty bourgeoisie, are to be found those unproductive workers—like the cash register operative and the bank cleaner—whose *condition* approximates to that of his working class[12]. These, he argues, are prime candidates to be won over to the side of the working class—they have a 'proletarian polarisation'. But they are not *of* the working class; in fact they have to be *won*, and could be *lost*.

Theoretically, then, Poulantzas takes us a fair distance from the analysis of class in sociology, and in much modern marxism. And this is so, to go back to our introductory comments, because he grounds his analysis directly on a theory of surplus-value, and because, following through the ramifications of the fundamental relation of exploitation, he treats the social division of labour as a whole as the primary matrix into which he only then proceeds to situate the effects that the condition of labour broadly defined—the various work, status and market situations, if you like, of neo-Weberian sociology.

Class, theory and politics

At this point it is perhaps useful to put forward some comments of a summary kind. Of the Registrar General's 'social class' it may be said that it is a classification according to status. This itself is founded on a notion of hierarchy—of gradation rather than opposition—which, especially when taken in conjunction with ideas about social mobility (which are fostered by all the main political parties), is quite consonant with a dominant ideology of the 'national interest'. Of 'social class' in sociology, we may say that it operates primarily at the level of 'condition', and, as with the Registrar General's classification, insofar as it concerns itself with hierarchic notions of social stratification (something which, incidentally, ties in with the stress on social mobility and studies of the recruitment to elites)[13] it does not treat class relations as historical forces of explanatory power. Sociology gives us 'social class' in plenty, but along with political parties, race/ethnicity and various status rankings (for instance those based on educational qualification)—in fact it gives us many potential and actual bases of power, without the prior situation of these into class relations.

As for marxism? Marxism is a mixed bag. All marxists agree that class location is not a matter of capitalists consuming more goods than workers, but of the relationship to the means of production. Yet this—and at a fundamental level a two-class model—is the beginning of analysis only. Considerable room for dispute still exists among marxists, and it is most certainly an error to assume that they can rest content once they have labelled the sociologist's approach to class as 'neo-Weberian'. Consider the work of British marxists for example. Much of this has aimed to demonstrate the continued existence of inequalities in this society. It has attempted to expose the falsity of notions about the Welfare State, and about widespread educational opportunity and social mobility. It has stressed the continued existence and concentrated ownership of private property. It has also exposed the oddity of those stratificational analyses in which there is a 'middle class', with a 'working class' underneath, and—a sort of bald class structure this—nothing on top. But, as with sociology, much of this work (e.g. the trojan work of Westergaard and Resler, 1975) might well be claimed to be descriptive and to operate only at the level of 'condition'.

A case could be argued, of course, that analyses conducted at the level of 'condition' are to be valued precisely *because* they bear most closely on the level at which experience is given most directly to consciousness. Also that if marxists, no matter how 'theoretical', really are concerned with social change (of which more shortly), they should not be too eager to deny the possible relevance and propaganda value of such analyses. However, the main point which concerns us here is that some marxism looks remarkably like some sociology.[14] It is for this reason that special attention was paid above to the more explicitly theoretical, and different, work of Poulantzas.

Poulantzas' work itself is best seen as a significant contribution to the opening of a debate, the long term consequences of which remain to be seen[15]. Already it is apparent that he is far from having everything his own way. His work is not free from epistemological problems (see Hindess, 1977) or indeed empirical ones[16]. There are yet other rival theories, of the middle class for example, which like Poulantzas's also claim marxist credentials (see Carchedi, 1975). And, even the marxist origins of his concept of productive labour, which is so fundamental to his approach, is open to dispute[17].

Some marxists, like Wright (1976, p. 18), challenge the very relevance of the productive/unproductive distinction for the determination of classes. Furthermore, some marxists themselves are again now asking awkward questions about the labour theory of value,[18] the removal of which would put the skids under Poulantzas's entire, elaborate, theoretical structure.[19]

Yet it would be wrong to leave the discussion of the definition of class as if it were some arid, thoroughly aseptic, technical matter. As Glaberman (1975) reminds us about the working class, how this is defined relates to the problem of whether it is considered to be a viable instrument for social change. In fact, among marxists such definitions are likely to carry within them notions about what sort of social change, and what sort of socialism, *are* viable.

The questions of *who?* and *what?*—what sort of socialism, and essentially for whom—are never far away. At the turn of the century for instance, discussion of the rise of a 'new middle class'—and in some versions the theoretical addition of this to the working class—was one of several attempts to characterise classical 'revisionism' (see Bernstein, 1961; and for a commentary, Gay, 1952, p. 210). And then, as now, the 'anti-revisionists' insisted that what was at issue was the question 'reform or revolution?': a question that was 'basically, in another form but the question of the petty bourgeois or proletarian character of the labour movement' (Luxemburg, 1900,

p. ix). Of course, the 'character' of the labour movement encompasses much more than the matter of its social composition. But generally it might be said that the looser the definition of the working class (or more precisely, the more the interests of the working class are considered to be similar to those of the traditional petty bourgeoisie, the various agents of social control, and even small and medium capital) the less the qualitative shift that the promise of socialism is held to represent. And *vice versa*: the more constricted the definition, the greater the shift.

To take the more constricted definition of the working class first, it would seem that, *theoretically*, this tends to rest today on a 'politicisation' of social relations (Poulantzas's reasons for the strict exclusion of managers and technicians can be considered in this light: although wage labour, they are excluded because they perform the work of control). And *politically*, partly because it is often associated with a view of the state as an irredeemably bourgeois institution, it tends to be shared by those who eschew a 'parliamentary road to socialism', who emphasise the importance of crises and workers' direct struggle (and thereafter, in socialism, workers' self-management, from below). By contrast, if we look now to the looser concept of the working class, it would seem that, *theoretically*, this takes the form of a relative lack of 'politicisation' of social relations (grossly so in formulations of the kind: the working class=all wage/salaried labour). And this meshes well with a *politics* that promises an 'administrative socialism' (rational planning of more or less conventionally structured state enterprises, from above). All of which—even though these compressed remarks are far from a definitive statement—should alert us to the fact that it is quite insufficient to conclude that the pertinent difference between Poulantzas and the PCF is that they 'classify' segments of the population differently. For the brunt of Poulantzas's analysis of the working class/new middle class boundary is to emphasise a *political* point: that monopoly capital is not the only enemy, and that the European Communist Parties had therefore better be *very* careful in allying themselves with non-proletarian elements, and in their related preference for a parliamentarian strategy.[20]

Of course, the above might suggest that various marxist theorists first decide who they want to include in the working class, and then construct their 'theory' around this. The reality is that theory informs politics and politics theory, and that 'the definition of the working class' is all of a piece with this. In the case of marxism and class, this means that at the very heart of the matter are questions about who is on what side in the dominant relations of exploitation, what the consequences of this are and what they can be made to be. The constraints and possibilities are theorised—but the theorisation itself serves political ends.

Notes

1. See, for example, Armstrong (1972). Armstrong is useful on the development of the Census, as is Marsh (1958, Chapters 5 and 6). For a critique of the 1951 Census see Cole (1955, Chapter 6).

2. For further details of the above and other classifications of social class in official statistics see Reid (1977) and *Social Trends* (1975, pp. 10-32, especially the Appendix). *Tables 1-3* above are drawn from this source.

3. The Census occupational classification was completely revised in 1961 when the number of occupational unit groups was cut from about 600 to 200. As a consequence 'the capitalist' has now been purged entirely. Note, though, the political economy that informed the Census of 1861: there the 'unproductive classes'—'certain ladies (who) like the lilies of the field, neither toil nor spin', and as many 'gentlemen', along with 'children', the 'infirm', and 'gypsies' were contrasted to 'the greater part of humanity'—those who were employed 'during the whole of their days in making articles of exchangeable value . . . supplying *our* wants, executing *our* wishes, gratifying *our* tastes, edifying *us*, protecting *us*, from danger, preserving *our* property' (*1861 Census*, vol. 3, Appendix to Report, p. 225, my emphasis.)

4. For another system of grading see Hall and Jones (1950); for an example of the obvious point that some people rate the labour of, say, dustmen above that of advertising men—which of course raises the question of what it is that is being evaluated—see Young and Willmott (1956).

5. The present account does not of course claim to be comprehensive. In particular, we leave aside here the now largely discredited 'functional theory of stratification' (on which see Heller, 1969, Part VIII) and Dahrendorf's (1959) distinctive attempt to translate Marx's classes into authority groups.

6. A view which, incidentally, has its supporters in high places, including, so it appears, Garter Principal King of Arms: 'Social classes' he tells us, meaning status groups, 'and economic classes are not the same thing and, though at times they coincide, often do not.' (See his letter to *The Times*, 24 December 1976).

7. Seemingly a popular view with some currents of North American marxism. See for example Freedman (1975) and Loren (1977). For two classic texts that make clear Marx's analysis was not exhausted by the dyad bourgeoisie and proletariat, see *The Eighteenth Brumaire of Louis Bonaparte* and *The Civil War in France*.

8. For the British Communist Party see the collection *Class Structure* (CPGB, 1974). For an effective critique of the Party's old programme statement *The British Road to Socialism* (now being revised) see Warren (1970). See also Hunt (1977a) for a slight change of emphasis.

9. 'Condition' overlaps loosely with what Giddens (1973, p. 108) calls the 'proximate structuration of class relationships: the division of labour *within* the productive enterprise; the authority relations *within* the enterprise; and the influence of . . . "*distributive* groupings" ' i.e. common patterns of *consumption*. (Giddens distinguishes the 'proximate' from the 'mediate structuration of class relationships'—seemingly the distribution of mobility chances—but this is not the same as Poulantzas's 'place'). Italics mine.

10. See his contribution to Hunt (1977b).

11. Top managers are excluded here. Like Wright (see below), Poulantzas argues that these 'managers' have effective economic ownership and stand in the place of capital. Dahrendorf uses the split between juridicial ownership and effective economic ownership—the so-called 'separation of ownership and control'—as a key element in his attempted rebuttal of Marx. For a largely descriptive critique of this sort of managerialistic theory see Nichols (1969). For a concise theoretical statement, see De Vroey (1975).

12. In practice, these workers tend to be those wage/salary earners who lacl authority. But note that for statistics to bear on even a concept of the working class which, unlike Poulantzas's, *included* such workers, information would be necessary on 'possession' in both its aspects, and that the RG's social class classification does not give this. The SEG classification does of course have the advantage that it presents 'foremen' separately, and also the self-employed (but this conceals another problem since whereas workers on the lump constitute a separate juridical category, they are, in effect, wage labour). As for Poulantzas's concept of productive labour—to order official data on this would be an heroic, probably impossible, task.

13. For a guide to sociological treatments of elites and power in Britain see Crewe (1974); Stanworth and Giddens (1974); and Urry and Wakeford (1973).

14. The irony of this has not been lost on some sociologists: see Goldthorpe (1972).

15. For the opening shots see the exchange between Poulantzas and the British marxist Miliband in Blackburn (1972).

16. An extensive—and readable—critique of Poulantzas is provided by Wright (1976).

17. The argument, I think a correct one, is that Marx did not define productive labour exclusively in terms of material production. See *Capital*, vol. 1, (1976, p. 644). For 'what Marx really meant' see Gough (1972).

18. Note for example the unsettled tone of Anderson (1976, p. 115).

19. For the beginnings of a recent attempt to re-think Marx, *minus* the labour theory of value, see Hodgson (1976). Fine and Harris (1976) usefully situate Hodgson's position and provide a guide to other recent tendencies in modern marxist economic theory.

20. Although a recent interview with Poulantzas (1977) makes interesting reading in this context. One might suggest in the light of this that the implication of his theoretical 'politicisation' of class relations is not that an entire superincumbent strata of bourgeois society must be 'sprung into the air' but the very opposite—that the superincumbent strata now weigh so heavily on the working class that they *cannot* be 'sprung into the air', *have* to be worked with by the PCF and that it is just because of this that the PCF must be very careful. Be this as it may, this takes us a long way from any pretence that the analysis of class relations is merely a technical or statistical exercise.

Bibliography

Anderson, P., 1976, *Considerations on Western Marxism*, London, New Left Books.

Armstrong, W. A., 1972, 'The use of information about occupation', in E. A. Wrigley (ed.), *Nineteenth Century Society: Essays in the Use of Quantitative Methods for the Study of Social Data*, London, Cambridge University Press.

Banks, O., 1968, *The Sociology of Education*, London, Batsford.

Bernstein, E., 1961, *Evolutionary Socialism: A Criticism and Affirmation*, New York, Schocken Books (first published 1899).

Blackburn, R., (ed.), 1972, *Ideology in Social Science*, London, Fontana.

Booth, C., 1886, 'Occupation of the people of the U.K., 1801-81', *Journal of the Statistical Society*, XLIX.

Braverman, H., 1974, *Labor and Monopoly Capital: The Degradation of Work in the Twentieth Century*, New York and London, Monthly Review Press.

Carchedi, G., 1975, 'On the economic identification of the new middle class', *Economy and Society*, vol. 4, no. 1.

Clarke, S., 1977, 'Marxism, sociology and Poulantzas' theory of the state', *Capital and Class*, Summer 1977.

Classification of Occupations, 1951, London, HMSO.

Cole, G. D. H., 1955, *Studies in Class Structure*, London, Routledge & Kegan Paul.

Communist Party of Great Britain (CPGB), 1974, *Class Structure*, London, CPGB.

Communist Party of Great Britain, 1977, *The British Road to Socialism*, London, CPGB.

Crewe, I., (ed.), 1974, *The First British Political Sociology Yearbook*, London, Croom Helm.

Dahrendorf, R., 1959, *Class and Class Conflict in Industrial Society*, London, Routledge & Kegan Paul.

De Vroey, M., 1975, 'The separation of ownership and control in large corporations—the marxist view', *Review of Radical Political Economy*, vol. 7, no. 2.

Fine, B., and Harris, L., 1976, 'Controversial issues in marxist economics' in R. Miliband and J. Saville (eds.), *The Socialist Register 1976*, London, Merlin Press.

Freedman, F., 1975, 'The internal structure of the American proletariat: a marxist analysis', *Socialist Revolution*, vol. 5, no. 4.

Garter Principal King of Arms, letter to *The Times*, 24 December 1976.

Gay, P., 1952, *The Dilemma of Democratic Socialism: Eduard Bernstein's Challenge to Marx*, London, Collier Macmillan.

Gerth, H. H., and Mills, C. Wright, 1948, *From Max Weber: Essays in Sociology*, London, Routledge & Kegan Paul.

Giddens, A., 1973, *The Class Structure of Advanced Societies*, London, Hutchinson.

Glaberman, M., 1975, *The Working Class and Social Change: Four Essays on the Working Class*, Toronto, New Hogtown Press.

Goldthorpe, J. H., and Lockwood, D., 1963, 'Affluence and the British class structure', *The Sociological Review*, vol. 11, no. 2.

Goldthorpe, J. H., 1972, 'Class, status and party in modern Britain: some recent interpretations, marxist and marxisant', *European Journal of Sociology*, vol. 13.

Gough, I., 1972, 'Marx's theory of productive and unproductive labour', *New Left Review*, no. 76.

Hall, J., and Jones, D. C., 1950, 'Social grading of occupations', *British Journal of Sociology*, vol. 1, no. 1.

Heller, C. S. (ed.), 1969, *Structured Social Inequality*, London, Collier Macmillan.

Hindess, B., 1973, *The Use of Official Statistics in Sociology*, London, Macmillan.

Hindess, B., 1977, 'The concept of class in marxist theory and marxist politics', in J. Bloomfield (ed.), *Class, Hegemony and Party*, London, Lawrence & Wishart.

Hodgson, G., 1976, 'Exploitation and embodied labour time', *Bulletin of the Conference of Socialist Economists*, no. 13.

Hunt, A., 1977a, 'Class structure and political strategy', *Marxism Today*, July.

Hunt, A. (ed.), 1977b, *Class and Class Struggle*, London, Lawrence & Wishart.

Lenski, G. E., 1966, *Power and Privilege: A Theory of Social Stratification*, New York and London, McGraw Hill.

Loren, C., 1977, *Classes in the United States: Workers Against Capitalism*, California, Cardinal Publishers.

Luxemburg, R., *Social Reform or Revolution*, London, Merlin Press, n.d. (first published 1900).

Mallet, S., 1975, *The New Working Class*, Nottingham, Spokesman Books.

Marsh, D. C., 1958, *The Changing Social Structure of England and Wales*, London, Routledge & Kegan Paul.

Marx, K., 1976, *Capital*, vol. 1, London, New Left Review/Penguin.

Mills, C. Wright, 1953, *White Collar: The American Middle Classes*, New York, Oxford University Press.

Nichols, T., 1969, *Ownership, Control and Ideology*, London, Allen and Unwin.

Poulantzas, N., 1973, *Political Power and Social Class*, London, New Left Books.

Poulantzas, N., 1975, *Classes in Contemporary Capitalism*, London, New Left Books.

Poulantzas, N., 1977, 'The state and the transition to socialism', *International*, vol. 4, no.1, Autumn (an interview with H. Weber).

Reid, I., 1977, *Social Class Differences in Britain*, London, Open Books.

Social Trends, 1975, article on 'Social commentary: social class', London, HMSO.

Stanworth, P., and Giddens, A., (eds.), 1974, *Elites and Power in British Society*, London, Cambridge University Press.

Stevenson, T. H. C., 1928, 'The vital statistics of wealth and poverty', *Journal of the Royal Statistical Society*, vol. 61.

Stolzman, J. and Gamberg, H., 1973, 'Marxist class analysis versus stratification analysis as general approaches to social inequality', *Berkeley Journal of Sociology*, vol. 18.

Urry, J., and Wakeford, J. (eds.), 1973, *Power in Britain*, London, Heinemann.

Warren, B., 1970, 'The British road to socialism', *New Left Review*, no. 63.

Westergaard, J., and Resler, H., 1975, *Class in a Capitalist Society*, London, Heinemann.

Wright, E. O., 1976, 'Class boundaries in advanced capitalist societies', in *New Left Review*, no. 98.

Young, M., and Willmott, P., 1956, 'Social grading by manual workers', *British Journal of Sociology*, vol. 7.

12.

Ann Oakley and Robin Oakley

Sexism in Official Statistics

Sexism is a type of discrimination between people based on their social classification as female or male. Such discrimination may involve behaviour, emotions, conscious attitudes and values, or the domain of unconscious ideas and assumptions. The concept of sexism is commonly used to refer to discrimination against women, but it may also be used to refer to discrimination against men (or to discrimination *in favour of* one sex or the other). Any differentiation between the sexes amounts to sexist discrimination when sex is not a relevant characteristic. The notion of 'relevance' here is highly problematic (where one person may consider sex relevant, another may not). We would argue that a person's sex is only relevant where the (currently irreducible) biological sex differences of childbirth and lactation are themselves relevant. Otherwise differentiation between men and women is 'sexist'. We would add that we do not use this term in a pejorative but in a descriptive sense, and that even to those opposed to sexism certain sexist distinctions may well be necessary in order to generate particular kinds of information relevant to its eradication.

Most human cultures are, or have been, sexist in one way or another (Mead, 1962; Oakley, 1972). The *particular* ways in which industrialized capitalist society is sexist have begun to be documented over the last ten to fifteen years, as the growth of women's liberation movements has generated an increasing awareness of what it means socially to be female or male (see, for example, Mitchell, 1971). Since sexism is culturally thematic in this way, it follows that in discussing sexism in this chapter we are referring not to an isolated area of behaviour or attitudes or 'social facts' (such as whether women are paid as much as men, or how men and women appear in volumes of official statistics) but rather to an underlying characteristic of our society. The backdrop to any such discussion of sexism is the continuing oppression of women in modern industrialized society: their role as unpaid domestic producers and reproducers, their restriction to low paid and low status employment, their minimal involvement (compared with that of men) in professional occupations and in the exercise of political and economic power.

The extent to which sexism is present in official statistics raises all those generic problems (discussed in more detail elsewhere in this volume) to do with the status of official statistics as a particular kind of ideological representation. Kitsuse and Cicourel have drawn attention to the discrepancy between what they call 'the behaviour-producing process' and 'the rate-producing process' (Kitsuse and Cicourel, 1963). On the one hand are processes which generate units of behaviour, and on the other are those from which are derived 'official' notions of the incidence rates for particular kinds of behaviour. While it is conventionally assumed that the 'behaviour-producing' process explains the 'rate-producing' process, on the contrary, both should be seen as different sets of social facts requiring different types of explanation.

As Hindess observes:

> Like all products they [statistics] must be examined in terms of the conditions and instruments of their production ... we may distinguish between two sets of instruments—the 'technical' instruments of the social survey and 'conceptual' instruments, the system of concepts and categories governing the assignment of cases into classes. (Hindess, 1973, p. 12).

Elaborating this distinction between 'technical' and 'conceptual' instruments, it can be said that sexism may enter into the production of official statistics at the following levels:

1. in the *areas* chosen for statistical analysis (e.g. 'employment', 'fertility', 'household composition', etc.);

2. in the *concepts* employed to organize and present the statistics (e.g. 'family', 'head of household', 'chief economic provider');

3. in the *collection* of data (this would include, for example, the kind of interaction that takes place between the official person collecting Census data from households and her/his 'informant');

4. in the *processing* of the statistics (the tabulations and breakdowns chosen for analysis); and

5. in the *presentation* of the statistics (for example which sex category is consistently presented first).

Of these five levels, the *conceptual* level is the most fundamental. The conceptual scheme used in the production of official statistics embodies a particular (sexist) mode of thinking (although it also reflects institutional 'needs'). This conceptual scheme structures the areas chosen for analysis, the data that are collected and the way in which the statistics are both processed and presented. Thus, far from being a superstructure imposed on raw unbiased data, the conceptual scheme employed constitutes *the* structure of the data. The statistics themselves can only be 'made sense of'—that is, understood in their relation to social reality— when the structure of the conceptual categories is first exposed. In underlining the importance of the conceptual dimension we are *not* implying that official statistics are sexist because government statisticians are evil people (usually men) plotting to oppress women. The conceptual armoury of sexism is, in a sexist society, ubiquitous, and government statisticians are not likely to be more or less implicated than most other social groups. (We are also fully aware that government statisticians have little control themselves over this aspect of their work.)

In the rest of this chapter we aim first to describe the differential visibility of the sexes in official national statistics, and, second, to look at sexism in three particular areas. (These areas are chosen because they appear to us to be some of those in which the presence of sexism is most clearly shown.)

The visibility of the sexes in official statistics

The notion of 'visibility' has been previously used by one of us in an analysis of sexism within the discipline of sociology. (Oakley, 1974b, Ch. I). Considering the lack of attention paid to women historically by social scientists, three different criteria of visibility were suggested. The first relates to the *actual representation* of women in the various sub-fields of sociology; the second refers to the 'match' between this and the part played by women in social life; the third focuses on the *conceptual* issue of how far the subject-classifications and conceptual-systems within sociology 'make sense' from the perspective of women's particular situation. The same criteria of visibility are relevant to the present discussion (and of course apply to the analysis of men's visibility as well).

The equivalent, so far as official statistics are concerned, of the first criterion of visibility could be taken to be the extent to which women as a category appear in official statistical publications. Neither the CSO's *Guide to Official Statistics*, nor any other government publication so far as we are aware, offers any justification for, or explanation of, the differential use of sex as a variable in the collection, processing and presentation of statistical material.[1] But many kinds of statistics are broken down by sex. Taking the simple index of whether or not the figures for any particular area are broken down by sex, there are four possibilities:

1. no sex breakdown of figures covering a two-sex population;
2. a sex breakdown of figures covering a two-sex population;
3. no sex breakdown: figures cover females only;
4. no sex breakdown: figures cover males only.

Official statistics contain miscellaneous instances of 1; for example, neither the electoral statistics, the publications on tourism, nor the statistics on industrial accidents are subdivided by sex. Analyses by sex (case 2 above) are, however, commonly found in official statistical publications; *Table I* lists the major areas in which official statistics contain some breakdown by sex.

For certain topics, figures for women only (case 3 above) are presented. The most obvious example is fertility, where *Fertility Tables* analyse childbirths in relation to the married female population, including such variables as duration of marriage, place of residence and employment.

Fertility Tables for England and Wales, but not those for Scotland, also include data on the husband's social class: with this exception men do not appear in fertility data. Women are also singled out for special treatment in specific sub-topics such as part-time employment. For example, the *New Earnings Survey* presents data covering part-time employment among women, but not among men. There is also a separate *Survey of Women's Employment* (Hunt, 1968) from which such data are obtainable (but no equivalent for men), and the Department of Employment has published several 'manpower' papers on the subject of women and work.[2]

An additional mode of discrimination between men and women (which in a way *increases* women's visibility) is marital status. This is frequently offered as a subdivision for the figures on women in a particular area (such as employment) but not for men. Similarly, the variable of responsibility for children appears much more often in relation to women than it does in relation to men. An instance of this is the *General Household Survey*, which contains a breakdown of the percentage of women who have children of their own living with them; the figures are analysed by maternal age and by the age-group of the children. A parallel analysis is not available for men. This focus on women in the household composition tables and allied data is accompanied by a concentration on them as the appropriate predictors of future family size: the *Family Intentions Survey* is based on information obtained from women only with regard to intended family size.

Table 1: **Areas within British official statistics in which sex breakdown is given**

Major field	Major topics	Major sources
1 Population characteristics	Age, marital condition, birthplace, usual residence	Census
Population processes	Migration, marriage, mortality, fertility (women only)	Census; OPCS annual reports, and *Population Trends*
2 Household composition	Household composition	Census; *General Household Survey*
3 Economic activity	Economic activity, occupation, industry, socio-economic status and social class	Census; *Department of Employment Gazette* (monthly); *British Labour Statistics*
4 Income/Expenditure	Earnings, income/wealth (couples only, if married)	*New Earnings Survey*; *Department of Employment Gazette*; *Inland Revenue Statistics*
5 Education	School data (including universities etc.), educational attainment	*Statistics of Education*; Qualified Manpower Tables (Census)
6 Health, Welfare, Social Security	Disease and health care, welfare services data, social security	OPCS reports; *On The State of the Public Health*; *Personal Social Services Statistics*; *Health and Personal Social Services Statistics*; *Social Security Statistics*
7 Crime	Crime, punishment, imprisonment	*Criminal Statistics*; *Report on the Work of the Prison Dept.*

As to analyses in which men only appear (case 4 above) the mechanism here seems to be a rather more complex one of selective presentation. For instance, a large number of sub-topics under the heading of 'employment data' offer figures for men only. Whereas figures for the registered unemployed are given for both females and males, only *male* unemployment is analysed by region; working days lost through sickness and industrial injuries are also given for males only. This selective presentation is common to many official statistical publications, and leads to the over-representation of males.

Case-studies of sexism in official statistics:

1. *'head of household'*

The concept of 'head of household' is not inherently sexist, although it certainly appeals to a notion of inequality—an asymmetrical family structure—which is a feature of patriarchy. The equation between the role of the head of a household and the masculine gender role is not explicitly stated anywhere in official statistical publications.

The 'head of a household' according to the 1971 Census Summary Tables, is the person *reported* by an informant to be head of that household, but a 'head of household' must be over 15, usually resident at that address and not a domestic servant. (Households consisting exclusively of domestic servants interestingly are deemed to have no head.) However, the 'head of family' is taken to be 'the husband in a married couple'. Question B5 on the Census form contains the following instruction: 'Write "Head" for the head of the household and relationship to the head for each of the other persons: for example "wife", "son", "daughter-in-law".' (*Census 1971, Summary Tables*, pp. xix–xx). The *General Household Survey, Introductory Report*, contains the further qualification that the 'head of household' is (in order of precedence) either the husband of the person, or the person, who owns or is responsible for the rent of the accommodation. (*General Household Survey, Introductory Report*, p. 58). A link between the concept of 'head of household' and property relationships is thereby established.

Since it is nowhere explicitly stated that a head of household must be male, the possibility is theoretically allowed for that households consisting of, for instance, married couples, could properly report a female head. Indeed, it appears that this has been done and has not been challenged by the Census enumerator (cited by Mary Stott in the *Guardian*).

However, in yet another instance, on receiving the information that a household had a female head, the Census enumerator (in an encounter with the authors of this chapter) denied that this was possible within the terms of his brief. A certain ambiguity exists within the instructions interviewers are given, of course, since 'husband' conventionally indicates a male, but this is not explicitly stated.

Somewhat naïvely, the *General Household Survey* comments that 'The way in which head of household is defined was bound to result in a preponderance of male heads of household'. Their tabulation shows that nearly four-fifths are men, and 'Of the female heads of household, three in five lived alone and were therefore head of household by virtue of being the only household member.' (*General Household Survey, Introductory Report*, p. 59).

This shows that the concept of 'head of household' is a *normative* one, although it allows for cases of deviation (i.e. those situations in which a household contains no adult male who can thus be labelled). Given such a conceptual scheme, the coding process applied to the material is based on the relationship members of households have to their (predominantly male) heads;[3] the statistical picture that is subsequently constructed of the household composition of the country has the concept of male headship at its centre.

Given data obtained and processed in this way, one can neither subtract the dominant sexist model and examine the total ('real') picture nor draw out the probable internal contradictions within the data. This is clearly illustrated in the *1971 Census, Summary Tables* definition of a concept allied to that of 'head of household'—the concept of 'chief economic provider'. Certain household data are analysed by characteristics of the chief economic provider, a personage defined as either the head of the household or someone related to the head of the household who is aged over 15. Certain rules are applied in the selection of the chief economic provider:

1. those in full-time employment or not employed at all take precedence over part-time or retired workers;

2. married men or 'widowed or divorced persons in families' are preferred over other members of families or 'persons not in families';

3. males are preferred over females;

4. older persons are selected before younger. (*Census 1971, Summary Tables*, p. xxii).

In other words, the criterion of who is chief economic provider is *not* principally that of being the person in a household who contributes most income to it. The rules are geared towards the selection of males as chief economic providers; hence presumably the curious specification that those in full-time employment or 'out of employment' take precedence over those in part-time work. Only thus can the unemployed married man be included in the category of chief economic provider (rule 3 ensuring the exclusion of the unemployed married woman).

The result is that the statistical picture is so skewed in the direction of male-centred household composition that very little, if anything, can be concluded about the division of economic roles between females and males. For example, all those married couple households which depend chiefly on the economic contribution of the woman will, following the rules, be coded as possessing a male 'chief economic provider'.

The concept of 'head of household' is also crucial to the official statistical picture of stratification. Here the *unit* of stratification is not the individual but the family or the household, and it is the occupational status of the 'head of household' (again, assumed to be a masculine role) that is taken as the key to a family's social class. Official statistical practice thus implies that women have a derived, second-class position; that their actual life-experiences are some-

Table 2: **Married couples with both partners economically active, by social class of husband and wife**

Husband's social class	Wives whose social class is different from husband's
	per cent
I	93.8
II	66.2
III non-manual	48.7
III manual	87.8
IV	63.5
V	77.6

Source: Adapted from *Census 1971, Summary Tables*, Great Britain, *Table 36*

how derived from, related to, or reflexive of, the position occupied by their husbands or fathers in the capitalist market place. Women's own occupational identities and qualifications are deemed irrelevant (except in the deviant case in which there is no male to whose occupation a woman's social position can legitimately be linked).

Table 2 is adapted from a table in the 1971 Census and gives an indication of the *extent* of the discrepancy between the 'social class' (thus conceived) of husbands and wives resulting from this inadequate methodology. (Such a tabulation appears for the first time in 1971, and presumably indicates some awareness of the problem on the part of official statisticians.)

For four of the five socio-economic groups, the percentage of women whose economic classification differs from that of their husbands exceeds the percentage for whom it is the same. The one exception is Class III non-manual, where only 48.7 per cent of cases are discrepant; this is presumably due to the overall concentration of women in Class III non-manual occupations. (See Theo Nichols' chapter in this volume for a general discussion of official statistics and social class.)

Case-studies of sexism in official statistics:

2. *work*

So far as the production of statistics on work is concerned, sexism is evident on a number of levels. In the first place, through the definition of 'work' as meaning 'paid employment' and through the further concept of an 'economically active' or 'economically inactive' individual, the important domain of unpaid domestic work is omitted. Information on the unpaid domestic work force of the country is simply not officially available. (In part this is, of course, because the state would have no use for such data.) Yet independent studies indicate the following:

1. that women contribute a substantially greater amount of domestic labour than men to the maintenance of households and the physical welfare of household members;

2. that about 85 per cent of all British women aged 16–64 years are 'housewives' in the sense of being responsible for the running of a household;

3. that 'housewives' who do not have a paid job in addition to their household work put in an (officially invisible) working week which is roughly twice the average industrial working week;

4. that those who perform the two kinds of work, housework and paid employment work, carry a double burden of which by

definition only half appears in the official statistics relating to work. (See Oakley, 1974b, for references).

According to the *1971 Census, Economic Activity Tables, General Explanatory Notes*, a job means 'any work for payment or profit'. The following categories are included:

1. work 'on a person's own account';
2. part-time work, 'even if only for a few hours, such as jobbing gardening or *paid* domestic work' (emphasis added);
3. casual or temporary work (e.g. vacation work by students).

'Economically inactive' persons are those who are either:

1. retired i.e. formerly in employment but no longer seeking it: 'housewives and persons engaged on home duties are classified as "retired" or "housewife"';
2. students;
3. those permanently sick;
4. 'others economically inactive i.e. those persons never in employment or not seeking it. This group includes persons of independent means, housewives and others engaged on unpaid domestic duties, and, by convention, trainees in Government training centres and au pair girls'. (*Census 1971, Economic Activity Tables*, pp. xv–xvi). These definitions indicate a certain difficulty with the equation between 'work' and the concept of 'a job for payment or profit'. In part, this reflects the ideological tension within capitalist society itself, since the formula requires that individuals who do not meet the pay or profit criterion in an orthodox manner be assigned to a 'non-economic' category (whatever the actual nature of their 'work').

The current social and economic situation of women has of course intimate connections with the advent of industrial capitalism. The reorganisation of production which took place in the eighteenth and nineteenth centuries involved a split between work and home, with women increasingly assigned the role of homekeepers and child-rearers, a role in which the labour expended is concealed by an ideological appeal to the supposed biological fit between femininity and domesticity. (Oakley, 1974a). Thus the essential *cultural* artifact is ignored. Accordingly, the Census has trouble not only with the category 'housewife' but also with the allocation of employment status to 'family workers', and with the category of 'self-employed'. We are told that

> Self-employed persons are those working on their own account with or without employees . . . Self-employed without employees includes parochial clergy even if they employ curates. It also includes outworkers i.e. people who work at home but give the name of an

> employer other than themselves. *Domestic servants and family workers do not count as employees when determining whether or not a self-employed person has employees.* (emphasis added)

And further on it is explained that:

> Family workers are persons employed by and living in the same household as a relative. Family workers who are managers, foremen, and apprentices are coded as such, and not as family workers. *The status of family workers can only be given to persons who are enumerated in the same household as their employer, and are shown as a relative.* (emphasis added) (*Census 1971, Economic Activity Tables*, pp. xv–xvi.)

The object of this contorted logic is clearly the exclusion of family-based unpaid domestic work from the employment statistics.

While it is clear that official statistics relating to work render women relatively invisible with regard to their actual social role and men over-visible (through the inflation of the importance of one kind of work over others), it is also very obviously the case that the extent of under- and over-visibility cannot be measured from the statistics themselves. We cannot tell, for example, what proportion of men perform the kind of domestic work role that is indicated by the word 'housewife'. This term 'housewife' is nowhere in the Census notes defined as applying to the female sex only, but in a strange paragraph of the *General Household Survey, Introductory Report*, the relevant ideological formula is outlined. A tabulation of economically inactive persons aged 15 or over by major activity and by sex presents the conclusion that two out of three kept house, but 99.4 per cent of these were women. What of the remaining 0.6 per cent? A note explains that men who 'keep house' do not (normally) merit the title housewife:

> Persons shown here as 'kept house' will not necessarily be the same as those classified as 'the housewife' in the general classification of the household . . . 'Kept house' describes an activity during a reference week but is not applied to any person who, during that week, was also covered by one of the other activities which came higher in the priority order than 'kept house'. ['Priority order' defines the coding categories: 'paid no income' first, followed by 'unemployed', followed by various categories such as 'inactive', 'kept house'.] Housewife is a term describing the person in a household responsible for most of the domestic duties: therefore there has to be one and only one housewife in every household but there can be none, one or more than one person whose major activity is described as 'kept house'. (*General Household Survey*, p. 215.)

Just as every household must have a head, every household must have a housewife.

Within the statistics on employment and economic activity themselves, it appears that the full breakdown by sex contained in them gives 'complete and objective' visibility to sex differences in employment. Yet the application of the sexist model underlying the processes of data collection, processing and presentation, makes this doubtful. For example, as we commented earlier, women's employment is analysed in relation to responsibility for children, but that of men is not.[4] Because the self-categorisation of 'housewife' exists, many women who are actually employed in part-time jobs probably return themselves as 'housewife'; hence over half a million fewer women were recorded as active in the 1961 Census as were reported in the labour force by the Ministry of Labour in the same year. (Halsey, 1972, p. 100). In part the under-representation of women follows here from their more limited entitlement to unemployment benefit: this results in a lesser motivation to register as 'unemployed'. The 'official' statistics on unemployment therefore present a view of 'unemployment', which is inextricably bound up with the selectivity and inherent sexism of the data source.

Case-studies of sexism in official statistics:

3. crime

In a recent study of *Women, Crime and Criminology* Carol Smart observes that 'Official statistics represent a limited and problematical basis from which to commence an analysis of female criminality and delinquency'. (Smart, 1977, p. 23). Leaving aside for the purpose of this chapter the more fundamental question of what crime 'is', we note to begin with that the picture presented in the official criminal statistics is highly sex-differentiated, showing 'an overwhelming preponderance of men over women'. (*Social Trends*, 1974, p. 22). *Table 3* gives some indication of the degree and direction of this sex differentiation.

Men seem to specialise in 'violent' crime and crimes that involve other aggressive acts i.e. against property. Women, on the other hand, are relatively 'passive': the most typical female crimes are prostitution and shoplifting. Thus, in 1973, females made up 81.5 per cent of all those found guilty of prostitution and related offences, and 50.2 per cent of all those indicted for shoplifting. (Smart, 1977, p. 10.) This pattern reflects the different kinds of socialization to which the sexes are exposed and the different social roles which they play as adults. (Oakley, 1972, Ch. 2.) But the crime statistics constitute a particularly clear demonstration of how

Table 3: **Persons found guilty of indictable offences in England and Wales in 1973, by offence group**

	Males	*Females*
	per cent	*per cent*
Violence	10.6	4.9
Sexual offences	2.5	0.1
Burglary	18.0	3.8
Robbery	1.0	0.4
Theft and handling stolen goods	49.9	77.4
Criminal damage	10.8	3.9
Fraud	4.4	7.1
Other indictable offences	2.8	2.4
Total number (100%)	292,287	45,159

Source: *Criminal Statistics*. Cited in *Social Trends* no. 5, 1974, p. 22.

sexism enters into the process of statistic-production at all the various levels or stages (thus reinforcing and exaggerating the effect of socially-rooted sex differentiation).

The criminal law is held to be applicable to both sexes equally regardless of the type of offence involved. In official language:

> The criminal law applies equally to women as to men and provides in general the same range of penalties for the same offences irrespective of the sex and marital status of the offender and affords the same protections to the accused. (Quoted in Smart, 1977, p. 112).

In fact, both sex and marital status may affect the legal definition of an offence, the assessment of culpability and the treatment of accused and victim. For example, infanticide is a female crime only: its definition relates to the biological act of birth. Rape is defined as a male crime, although a woman may be accused of aiding and abetting in rape cases. A special defence plea is allowed for married women who commit an offence in the presence of their husband;

here the law considers the possibility that women defer to the superior authority of their husbands and do what they are told. (Murder and treason are excluded, however.) More well-known as an instance of sexism is the case of the Street Offences Act (1959) which discriminates against women who are prostitutes while exonerating their male 'clients'.

Where considerations of sexual status are built into the structure of legal/criminal definitions in this manner, the resulting statistics are bound to reflect a parallel sexism. And crime statistics also mirror in other ways women's disadvantaged position in society. Thus the visibility of women in statistics relating to social security abuses follows from the state's attempt to maintain women's economically dependent position via, for instance, the 'cohabitation' ruling. But official statistics on crime are subject to a substantial degree of sexist bias at the level of data-collection, since the processes whereby a person 'becomes' a criminal statistic are peculiarly vulnerable to the influence of sexist attitudes. One example of this is the use of the 'official caution' procedure; this is an option open to the police when they 'know' that someone has committed an offence but decide not to bring charges. A senior police officer delivers a caution, no further action is taken, and the statistic is recorded but is not normally released by the Home Office. For sentences of imprisonment the ratio of male to female offenders is 30:1; but for probation it is about 3:1 and for 'cautioning' it is between 3 and 4 to 1. (*Social Trends*, 1974, p. 22). Figures released by the Home Office in 1973 showed that three times as many girls are cautioned for an offence of violence as are actually convicted and that there is a more pronounced tendency to caution female offenders involved in violent crimes than those involved in other types of crime. (*Sunday Times*, 22 July 1973).

Since social scientists and others concerned with the meaning behind the official picture of crime have been on the whole remarkably blind to the influence of sexism (see Heidensohn,1968) research into *how* and *why* sexism operates in the creation of crime statistics is only in its infancy. Interestingly, sociological and other theories aimed at explaining deviant behaviour in females and males have commonly *assumed* the applicability of a sexist model— rather than looking at the possibility that the reasons for deviant behaviour may be essentially the same for both sexes (though concealed behind their different social roles). Studies continually reveal the existence of a double standard. For example, sexual misdemeanours amongst females are more heavily sanctioned; thus, girls committing sexual misdemeanours are more likely to be placed in institutions than either girls committing non-sexual offences or boys committing any type of offence. This double standard emanates from the sentencing policy of the juvenile courts, but it is also significantly to be found in the judgements of probation officers. (Smart, 1977, pp. 132–3; see also Smith, 1978).

In view of this kind of distortion behind the official statistics on crime, it is impossible to judge the status of the statistics themselves. What kind of correspondence with social reality (if any) exists? Studies of 'self-admission' rates for criminal behaviour go some way towards answering this question (although such inquiries are also methodologically problematic in their own right); these indicate that the male to female ratio for admitted crimes might be as close as 1 or 2 to 1 in contradiction to the 'official' ratio of about 8:1 (Campbell, 1977). The fact that official statistics show a rise in female crime relative to male crime in recent years (particularly for the category of violent crime) seems to suggest that these figures are measuring a 'real' phenomenon, the intervening explanation usually being that they must reflect the general changes in sex roles accompanying women's 'emancipation'. However, since one of the features of this so-called emancipation has been an increased sensitivity to sex status as a variable, a second and equally plausible explanation is that there has simply been a rise in the charge and conviction rate among women.

Conclusion

The three areas discussed above are specific instances where sexism can be shown to exist in official statistics; there are many others. Much of this sexism is 'first order', i.e. it is a reflection of a fundamentally sexist social reality. This point is differently applicable to different areas. For example, we noted earlier that some unemployment among women is officially invisible because the social security system renders a greater proportion of women than men ineligible for unemployment benefit: this is clearly a case where official statistics must record sexist practice. The practice itself will only change with a radical revision of the social security system which in turn would mean, or follow from, change in the social and economic division of labour between the sexes.

Stratification statistics present a rather different case. Here the argument cannot be that the official model of stratification is simply a duplicate of the model that 'exists' in the real world—that women are discriminated against in the official model because they are discriminated against in society. The data on which models of stratification are built consist of the household/living patterns of individuals, the relationships between these individuals, and their position in the occupational system. We know from empirical evidence that the interconnections between these variables do not constitute a uniform pattern, and there is hence a lack of conformity with the official model of stratification—a model according to which every household is made up of a nuclear family whose lifestyle is determined by the occupation of its male 'head'. According to 1966 Census data (to take just one example of this evidence, in this case obtainable from elsewhere in the official statistics), 58 per cent of all British households are not of the nuclear family type, one in twenty of households is a single-parent family, and about one in twelve of the population do not live in families at all (*Sample Census 1966, Household Composition Tables*, Table I). In the case of stratification then, sexist bias in official statistics must be identified as 'second order', as it consists in large measure of the imposition of a sexist model on the data.

Ultimately, much of the sexism discussed in this chapter relates to an ideological differentiation between the sexes: to a conceptual framework which conceives of femininity and masculinity as opposed and contradictory (although at times 'complementary').

This ideological element in sexism is, as we said at the beginning, thematic not only to the official statistical treatment of the sexes, but to the nature of our culture. Moreover, the ideological differentiation takes the particular form of perceiving women as a 'minority group' not in the statistical sense but in the same sense as ethnic subcultures are allocated minority group status within the dominant culture. (Hacker, 1951). Hence, insofar as official statistics represent the concerns of government and government represents those of the majority group, the dominant culture, women are bound to receive special (different) treatment.

It is for this reason that 'sexism', here and in other contexts, more often means discrimination against women than discrimination against men. In society generally, women are the oppressed sex and men represent the standard against which women are compared. It is always the case that in relation to men women are said to be in receipt of less than their 'fair share' of justice, opportunities, or whatever resource is in question.

It has not been our concern in this chapter to tie in any changes there have been in official statistical representations of the sexes with changes in the social position of men and women. This would be a valuable exercise; from it one might learn more about the function of official statistics as an ideological instrument. Nor have we discussed what official statistics 'ought' to become, i.e. how the generation of official statistics could be transformed into a nonsexist product; the answers to this question in most cases are obvious (though of course problematical e.g. in disturbing time-series of data). To the question of *why* official statistics *should* be non-sexist we have not provided an answer either. The argument here has to do with basic values about the rights and responsibilities of men and women as people. It also has to do with the uses to which official statistics can be put. Sexism limits their usefulness, as we have seen throughout this chapter, since it is impossible to subtract the influence of sexism from the data offered, and it is often difficult for social scientists, activists and others to establish just what the position of women (or men) is from the official statistical data. But here we are back to the function of official statistics as officially defined, and their function is not, as we noted earlier, that of providing material for social scientists, but that of satisfying the 'needs' of government departments and thus indirectly those of government itself. Since these 'needs' are intimately bound up with the preservation of a sexist social order, the presence of sexism in official statistics has an ideological function which will help ensure its longevity.

Notes

1. In *Social Trends*, no. 5, 1974, there is however an article entitled 'Social commentary: men and women' which shows some awareness of the 'problem' of sex differences.
2. For example, no. 9, *Women and Work: A Statistical Survey*; no. 10, *Women and Work: Sex Differences and Society*; no. 11, *Women and Work: A Review*; and no. 12, *Women and Work: Overseas Practice* (Department of Employment, 1974a, 1974b, 1975a and 1975b).
3. In the Census each person in a household is given a two-digit code; the first digit indicates the relationship to the head of the household either of that person or of the head of that person's family. (*Census 1971, Summary Tables*, p. 20).
4. See Peter Moss, 'The current situation', in *Mothers in Employment*, edited by Nickie Fonda and Peter Moss, Brunel University (1976) for a discussion of available data on the employment of women and responsibility for children.

Bibliography

Barker, D. L., and Allen, S. (eds.), 1976a, *Sexual Divisions and Society: Process and Change*, London, Tavistock.
Barker, D. L., and Allen, S. (eds.), 1976b, *Dependence and Exploitation in Work and Marriage*, London, Longman.
Brownmiller, S., 1975, *Against Our Will*, London, Secker and Warburg.

Campbell, A., 1977, 'What makes a girl turn to crime?', *New Society*, 27 January 1977.

Department of Employment, 1974a, *Women and Work: a Statistical Survey*, London, HMSO.

Department of Employment, 1974b, *Women and Work: Sex Differences and Society*, London, HMSO.

Department of Employment, 1975a, *Women and Work: a Review*, London, HMSO.

Department of Employment, 1975b, *Women and Work: Overseas Practice*, London, HMSO.

Fransella, F., and Frost, K., 1977, *On Being a Woman*, London, Tavistock.

Hacker, H., 1951, 'Women as a minority group', *Social Forces*, pp. 60–69.

Halsey, A. H. (ed.), 1972, *Trends in British Society since 1900*, London, Macmillan.

Heidensohn, F., 1968, 'The deviance of women', *British Journal of Sociology*, June, vol. 19, no. 2.

Hindess, B., 1973, *The Use of Official Statistics in Sociology*, London, Macmillan.

Hunt, A., 1968, *A Survey of Women's Employment*, London, HMSO.

Kitsuse, J. I., and Cicourel, A. V., 1963, 'A note on the uses of official statistics', *Social Problems*, vol. 11.

Land, H., 1976, 'Women: supporters or supported?' in Barker and Allen, (1976a), above.

Mackie, L., and Pattullo, P., 1977, *Women at Work*, London, Tavistock.

Mead, M., 1962, *Male and Female*, Harmondsworth, Penguin.

Mitchell, J., 1971, *Woman's Estate*, Harmondsworth, Penguin.

Moss, P., 1976, 'The current situation', in N. Fonda and P. Moss (eds.), *Mothers in Employment*, Brunel University.

Oakley, A., 1972, *Sex Gender and Society*, London, Temple Smith.

Oakley, A., 1974a, *The Sociology of Housework*, London, Martin Robertson.

Oakley, A., 1974b, *Housewife*, London, Allen Lane.

Rowbotham, S., 1973, *Hidden From History*, London, Pluto Press.

Seccombe, W., 1974, 'The housewife and her labour under capitalism', *New Left Review*, no. 83.

Smart, C., 1977, *Women, Crime and Criminology: A Feminist Critique*, London, Routledge & Kegan Paul.

Smith, L. S., 1978, 'Sexist assumptions and female delinquency: an empirical investigation', in C. Smart and B. Smart (eds.), *Women, Sexuality and Social Control*, London, Routledge & Kegan Paul.

Toner, B., 1977, *The Facts of Rape*, London, Arrow Books.

Wilson, E., 1977, *Women and the Welfare State*, London, Tavistock.

13.

Christopher Hird and John Irvine

The Poverty of Wealth Statistics

Official statistics on the distribution of wealth play a central part in the long-standing debate over how unequal people are in Britain, and even whether it is still basically a capitalist society. One major problem in resolving this debate is that these statistics can, apparently, be simultaneously used to point out that massive inequalities still exist in Britain (for example, that the richest 1 per cent of the population own as much as the poorest 80 per cent), and to argue that a definite equalisation in the distribution of wealth has taken place over time (for example, that while in 1912 the richest 1 per cent of the population owned 70 per cent of the wealth, their share had by 1960 been cut down to 42 per cent). Given the crude treatment of these statistics in political debate and the newspapers, interpretations of the data often diverge even further. The official statistics on wealth are clearly of crucial importance in both radical analysis and politics: to use them critically we need to be aware of how and why they are produced.

Statistical sources

The most systematic and detailed presentation and analyses of British wealth statistics are those provided by the Royal Commission on the Distribution of Income and Wealth (commonly referred to as the 'Diamond Commission' after its Chairman, Lord Diamond).[1] This Commission was set up by the 1974 Labour Government, following widespread discussion of the distribution of wealth and power in Britain and the success of the Labour left-wing in inserting a proposal for a wealth tax in their election manifesto. The terms of reference of this committee were:

> to help to secure a fairer distribution of income and wealth in the community . . . The Government . . . ask the Commission to undertake an analysis of the current distribution of personal income and wealth and of available information on past trends in that distribution . . . (*Diamond Report*, no. 1, 1975, p. v).

The main, regular source of information on the distribution of wealth is the annual HMSO publication, *Inland Revenue Statistics.* The data provided by the Inland Revenue (IR) are, however, the processed by-products of tax-returns, and in both their scope and orientation reflect the information requirements of administering the tax system rather than any direct concern with assessing the distribution of wealth. It is only since 1961 that the IR has gone to the trouble of providing such analyses—resulting in an official 'series' that commences only with the 1960 figures. The 1958 *Radcliffe Report* had first recommended that the IR use death duty returns to estimate the distribution of wealth. This was not 'to secure a fairer distribution of wealth', however, but for purposes of state financial management: Radcliffe hoped that an analysis of wealth holdings would help explain the wide fluctuations in patterns of saving, and thus facilitate forecasting and planning the operations of the monetary system.

Inland Revenue figures still provide the basis for most estimates of the distribution of wealth—including those recently made by the Diamond Commission. It was because of the lack of alternative data sources (even within the massive range of official statistics) that Diamond decided to re-use the Inland Revenue figures, making adjustments where possible in order to compensate for some of the more glaring deficiencies. Alternative methods for developing such estimates have been considered, notably a sample survey of British households in which questions would be asked relating to the extent of wealth holdings. Both Radcliffe and Diamond argued that this approach could be of only marginal importance—the rich are not only more difficult to locate and sample accurately given their greater geographical mobility and seclusion, but also might, not unexpectedly, be reluctant to disclose the full extent of their wealth.[2] A further approach considered by Diamond, before deciding to concentrate on reworking and improving the IR figures, was that of the 'Investment Income' method. Here personal tax returns are analysed in regard to the likely capital investment that is necessary to produce the invest-ment incomes declared to the Inland Revenue. Projecting wealth holdings in this way on the basis of declared income and estimated yields is again subject to many shortcomings: it covers only the people who have (or declare) such investments, excludes certain forms of wealth not producing regular incomes, and is subject to inaccuracies (resulting from problems in differentiating earned from investment income in cases where high levels of interest payments are deductable from tax).[3]

Table 1: **Inland Revenue estimates of personal wealth based on estate multiplier method, United Kingdom, 1975**
Numbers of identified wealth owners and amounts of net wealth, by range of net wealth (series A)

Range of net wealth	Total		Males		Females	
£	Number thousands	Amount £ thousand million	Number thousands	Amount £ thousand million	Number thousands	Amount £ thousand million
0–999	3,463	1.9	1,767	0.9	1,695	1.0
1,000–2,999	4,849	8.9	2,719	5.2	2,129	3.7
3,000–4,999	2,514	10.0	1,429	5.7	1,085	4.3
5,000–9,999	4,707	34.6	3,050	22.5	1,657	12.1
10,000–14,999	2,688	33.0	1,762	21.7	926	11.3
15,000–19,999	1,038	18.4	605	10.5	433	7.9
20,000–24,999	603	13.8	350	8.0	253	5.8
25,000–49,999	809	28.1	462	16.9	347	11.2

50,000–99,999	252	18.2	131	10.6	120	7.5
100,000–199,999	69	11.1	40	6.6	29	4.5
200,000 and above	29	12.2	18	7.3	12	5.0
Under 10,000	15,533	55.4	8,965	34.3	6,566	21.1
10,000 and above	5,488	134.8	3,368	81.6	2,120	53.2
Total	21,020	190.3	12,333	115.9	8,687	74.3

Source: *Diamond Report*, no. 5, 1977, p. 69. (Figures do not add up to totals because of rounding)

The Diamond Commission was thus left very little choice in having to conclude that:

> any study of the distribution of wealth must choose between different methods of estimation, all of which are imperfect in certain respects; our judgement is that, for the moment, reliance must be placed primarily on the estate multiplier method. (*Diamond Report*, no. 1, p. 78).

The estate multiplier approach to wealth statistics

The way in which the Inland Revenue makes its estimates of the distribution of wealth is quite straightforward. It is based on information collected for taxation purposes on the estates of those people who die each year.[4] In processing this data the estate multiplier method

> operates by taking the wealth of the dead as a sample of that of the living . . . Thus for example, if an individual dies leaving £1,000 and the death rate of the group to which he belongs is one in twenty, the wealth of the group as a whole will be estimated at £20,000. When the appropriate mortality multipliers (i.e. death rates) are applied to all estates this yields estimates of total wealth and the number of wealth holders . . . The multipliers used by the Inland Revenue are calculated from the number of deaths each year by age and sex . . . The death rates used also differ according to country of residence (i.e. England and Wales combined, or Scotland) and by social class . . . (*Diamond Report*, no. 5, 1977, p. 230).[5]

It is thus assumed that the estates of those people who have died during the previous year are typical of those of the living. Given that the average mortality rate of each group is known, the IR simply 'blows up' the figures from the estates of those who have died in accordance with the mortality tables. This then gives a 'picture' of the population and how it holds its wealth. *Table 1* depicts a recent IR estimate made in this way.

There are several problems with this system, but three 'serious deficiencies' were singled out for mention by Diamond:

> the exclusion of large numbers of people with relatively small amounts of wealth, the exclusion of certain kinds of property where no estate duty was payable, and the bases on which certain assets, such as life assurance policies, are valued. (*Diamond Report*, no. 1, 1975, p. 129).

That many people are missing from the IR estimates of personal wealth is evident in *Table 1*. Out of Britain's total population of 39.2 million adults, only 21.0 million seem to be classified as wealth owners. This is because many people escape the inspection of the Inland Revenue when they die—most often because their estate is worth less than the taxable limit of £15,000, or because of a 'surviving spouse settlement' allowable up to £30,000 without taxation. In addition, the estates of people who have avoided paying some tax, either by holding assets in a form which is exempt from taxation on death (such as forestry) or by transferring the assets to someone else whilst they are alive, are likewise under-represented.[6] In the main, though, it is the large masses of those who die poor who are excluded from this table. If they were included, the distribution of wealth holders would become more skewed to the bottom end—with the range £0–1000 being the slot occupied by the majority.[7] Also skewing the distribution in that direction are the estates of those who, while not managing to evade the 'tax net', had their liabilities drastically limited, often with the help of accountants skilled in investing their assets in exempt property and annuities to ensure better provision for their bene-ficiaries (usually their family) on death.

A whole range of rather more difficult technical problems arises in the valuation of assets at death, particularly in relation to insurance policies which are worth much more on the death of the insured than when they are alive. For example, yearly premiums may be paid on a policy which will pay a given sum on death; a 'whole-life' policy is worth nothing to the insured when alive; and an 'endowment' policy will generally have a lower cash-in value than its eventual redemption value or value at death. Since the IR figures are based on the value of life policies at *death*—that is, for the total amount assured, plus any accrued bonuses—the extrapolation of their figures to estimate the wealth of living individuals will overstate the value of this kind of asset. This assumption in valuation has implications both for estimates of the total amount of wealth in society, and for its *distribution*. It means that wealth appears to be more equally distributed than otherwise, since life-policies are an asset more equally spread than most—accounting for over a fifth of personal wealth in the IR estimates.

Problems of valuation arise even in relation to seemingly easily-valued items such as consumer goods. Again, the issue is one of the bases on which valuation should be made—replacement cost, current market value or historic cost. For clothing, as for many durables, a valuation at second-hand market prices may well result in rather lower levels of wealth holding than might be expected. In the case of pension rights that cease to exist at death, which the IR treats as worthless, there have been complaints from conservatives about this form of valuation since they are anxious to see the income accruing from such rights to the living treated as wealth—with the right to a pension now a matter of course, an enormous apparent equalisation in the distribution of wealth would result from the IR taking up this suggestion.

Overshadowing all these difficulties is the fact that the value of certain assets can be very volatile indeed, while that of many others is moderately so in times of inflation. The volatile nature of share-prices has been especially striking in recent years. In 1974, for instance, the *Financial Times* Index—which measures the changing level of share prices—fell to 150. Less than three years later it had risen again to over 500, greatly increasing the wealth of those one and a half million or so people who own shares.[8] (Despite the growth of pension funds and insurance companies, about two-fifths of shares in quoted companies are still held by individuals.)

This raises the more general question of valuing shares in public companies—a task with potentially large margins for error, for while shares represent only about 6 per cent of the private wealth of individuals in the United Kingdom, they account for almost 27 per cent of the wealth of those with over £200,000 worth of assets (*Diamond Report*, no. 5, Table 29). The problem is that the stock market value of a company's shares is generally below the value of its assets as shown in its balance sheet. It has been demonstrated that up to one-fifth of the total wealth in Britain may be represented by this difference (Revell, 1967; and Revell and Roe in *Diamond Report*, no. 4).

These technical problems of valuation are, however, not the end of the story; still other critical points can and need to be made.

> In addition (continued Diamond), the statistics . . . present little information on the regional distribution of wealth, and *none on the relationships between inherited wealth and lifetime accumulation.* They also do not allow the wealth of husbands and wives to be aggregated . . . (*Diamond Report*, no. 1, 1975, pp. 129–30, emphases added).

Such 'additions' to the three 'serious deficiencies' are not as insignificant or minor as one might imagine. Particularly serious is the absence of data on inheritance and accumulation—which would be useful in assessing the way social classes reproduce themselves. In not being able fully to piece together and analyse such data, the Diamond Commission was forced into a descriptive rather than an analytical approach to their brief.

These problems repeatedly arise because the IR statistics are produced as a by-product of the taxation system, and the statistical categories employed and range of data considered all reflect these administrative practices. The state has had little real interest in developing statistics that are directly relevant to assessing the distribution of wealth in Britain, and has made little effort to do so.

This is why the Diamond Commission was forced to conclude that:

> the gaps in the official statistics which it will be necessary to fill before we can describe the distribution of income and wealth adequately are numerous, and some are major . . . In the case of wealth there are important questions about its distribution which can only be answered on the basis of new sources of information, although techniques for adjusting estate multiplier data can fill some of the gaps for the time being. In the case of income, it is more a matter of a large number of gaps none of which itself is crippling but which, taken together, severely limit our analysis. (*Diamond Report*, no. 1, p. 120).

The existence of income tax explains the relative superiority of statistics on income.

Diamond's technical adjustments of the statistics on wealth

The limitations inherent in the data available on wealth did not prevent Diamond from producing an enormous amount of detailed and useful material. A major focus of this work was the adjustment of the crude IR figures to take into account the wealth of the excluded part of the population, the undervaluation and exclusion of certain assets, and the inclusion of occupational and state pension rights. This work went much further than that carried out by earlier researchers (such as Atkinson, 1972).

Diamond did not, however, attempt to produce *one* best set of figures claiming to represent *the* most accurate estimate of the distribution of wealth. Even if this had been technically feasible, it would not have been possible, given the debate over what constitutes wealth and the political implications of defining it in a particular way; as a Royal Commission, Diamond et. al. were constrained within relatively rigid political guidelines. They realised this right from the beginning of their work:

> the definition of personal wealth was necessarily left open and we received many different views on the conceptual issues involved. Our study of the evidence presented to us on this matter led us, like many others, to conclude that no single definition was ideal in all circumstances. The concept of personal wealth cannot be reduced to a single definitive statement. (*Diamond Report*, no. 1, p. 9).

Moreover, they made clear that how one defined wealth was not just an abstract academic matter:

> . . . different definitions will be appropriate for different purposes. For those concerned with the distribution of immediate command over resources, personal wealth may best be defined in terms of the ownership of marketable assets only; while for those concerned with the distribution of economic welfare in a more general sense, the definition may be extended to cover the value of a greater or lesser range of non-marketable assets as well. (*Diamond Report*, no. 1, p. 11).

Different definitions may also be appropriate for different political purposes too, but this question was side-stepped by Diamond presenting a range of separate assessments of wealth distribution using different sets of assumptions. These are summarised in *Table 2*. Quite marked differences are evident between these estimates, which deserve discussion.

The Series B and Series C figures are attempts to adjust the IR (Series A) data to take account of the exclusion of part of the population and the under-valuation and exclusion of certain assets. Because the Series B figures include the whole adult population in its estimates, yet assess the wealth of those excluded from the Series A figures as nil, the result is a marked concentration of wealth holdings at all levels except in the poorest 80 per cent, whose share of total wealth is estimated at only 18.2 per cent of the total. The Series C figures, in contrast, include not only the missing population but an estimate of its wealth—which was judged to be £1,156 per person for 1975. They also take into account the value of certain types of assets excluded from the IR figures, such as those represented in exempt trusts, surviving spouse settlements, etc. Since these excluded assets are largely those of the rich, the result of adjusting the figures in this way appears as an increased concentration of wealth at the very top of the scale. This is counterbalanced, of course, by an increase at the bottom end through inclusion of the estimated wealth of those people excluded from the IR figures— who are typically the poorest.[9] This calculation, which is probably the best estimate of the distribution of wealth, shows that the richest 1 per cent own just over 24 per cent of the wealth and the poorest 80 per cent own just under 24 per cent.

The upward revision of estimates for the wealth of the top 1 per cent—from 17.2 per cent in Series A to 24.3 per cent in Series C—is drastically reversed in Series D and Series E. Adjustment is made for the value of occupational pensions in Series D[10] and for state pensions in Series E. As something like 12 million people are currently entitled to occupational pensions, their inclusion in-

Table 2: **Comparison of estimates of the distribution of wealth on the basis of different concepts of wealth, 1975**
Percentage shares of personal wealth owned by given quantile groups of the total population aged 18 and over, 1975

	Series A	Series B	Series C	Series D	Series E
	Unadjusted IR statistics	Inclusion of excluded population. (Wealth assumed as nil)	Inclusion of wealth of excluded population and value of excluded assets	Inclusion of value of occupational pensions	Inclusion of value of state pension rights
Top 1%	17.2	23.2	24.3	21.0	13.9
2–5%	17.8	23.3	21.8	20.3	14.9
6–10%	12.3	15.9	13.9	13.7	10.7
11–20%	16.0	19.4	16.2	16.9	14.3
21–100%	36.7	18.2	23.8	28.1	46.2
Cumulative basis					
Top 1%	17.2	23.2	24.3	21.0	13.9
Top 5%	35.0	46.5	46.1	41.3	28.8
Top 10%	47.3	62.4	60.0	55.0	39.5
Top 20%	63.3	81.8	76.2	71.9	53.8

Source: *Diamond Report*, no. 5 (1977). Series A and Series B are derived from *Table 28*, p. 70; Series C from *Table 38*, p. 86; Series D from *Table 41*, p. 89; and Series E from *Table 43*, p. 90. Note also that the estimates in Series D and Series E exclude Northern Ireland, but since the adjustments that would be necessary are relatively minor, comparability can still be made with the other series.

creases the apparent sharing-out of wealth. If entitlement to state pensions—which everyone gets—is included, wealth appears to be spread even more equally. Including occupational pension rights has the effect of reducing the share of wealth held by the richest 1 per cent to 21 per cent; taking in state pension rights as well knocks it down further to 13.9 per cent. The share of wealth of the top 20 per cent is reduced by these means to 71.9 per cent and 53.8 per cent respectively.

The argument often advanced for including the right to a pension in the distribution of wealth statistics is that such entitlements provide a secure source of future income in essentially the same way as do the interest on a loan or dividends from shareholdings. It has even been argued that the same principle should be applied to other entitlements such as the right to a cheap council house, free coal for miners, cars for company directors, and so on (see Polanyi and Wood, 1974). But to do so would be to introduce a rather different conception of wealth. At least, the three series A–C, while providing different sets of estimates, fit in with Diamond's broad conception of wealth as a 'stock, representing the capitalised value of resource claims at a given point in time', (*Diamond Report*, no. 5, p. 6). They do not confuse it with the conception of income as a 'flow'.

The occupational and state pension rights included in Series D and Series E relate to the definition of wealth as a 'stock' in only a marginal way. First, as Diamond points out, there is a difference between marketable assets (such as the goods one owns), and nonmarketable assets, which provide only an entitlement to an income (which in general vanishes on the death of the holder). Second, Diamond estimated the total value of occupational pension entitlements at around £42 billion (*Diamond Report*, no. 5, *Table 40*)—far more than the value of the assets in the pension funds that will provide this income. This is partly because some pensions are paid on a 'pay as you go' basis, with the money collected from members handed immediately across to pensioners. It also partly—though less importantly—results from some funds being in deficit and unable to meet all their obligations at any particular time. Moreover, within the terms set by Diamond's definition, state pensions seem to have an even more tenuous basis for being included in the distribution of wealth statistics, despite their making a particularly large contribution to reducing the apparent level of inequality. Run on a 'pay as you go basis', there are no established resources to guarantee future payment of pensions; instead, it is a political task to set appropriate national insurance contribution levels.

It is when one compares Diamond's broad-based definition of wealth with the usual meaning of wealth as the '*ownership* of valuable assets' (*Diamond Report*, no. 1, p. 9, our emphasis) that the contorted logic which justifies presenting the Series D and Series E estimates becomes most apparent. Such a definition is clearly useful for 'purposes' of conservative politics: the adjustment of wealth statistics by taking account of pensions means the inclusion of a form of 'wealth' much more widely distributed among poorer people than other forms of wealth. The inclusion of these vast amounts of 'wealth', which pensioners neither own nor possess legal rights over (apart from the promise of a future income), results in an apparently more egalitarian distribution of wealth than do the other series. It is small wonder, then, that Diamond 'received many different views on the conceptual issues involved' in defining wealth (*Diamond Report*, no. 1, p. 9). Diamond's pluralist parliamentary context resulted in different sets of estimates, each based on different technical assumptions and embodying different conceptions of wealth, being produced. That Diamond does not recommend any one as the most accurate, means that a 'political' choice can be made about which to use, which is just what happens.

While choosing may be a simple matter for the person wishing to announce the arrival of the classless society, this is not necessarily the case for the radical critic. Even the estimates which show the highest degree of inequality of wealth do not give an adequate picture for critical analysis. The overall conclusions Diamond reaches are doubtful, to say the least—it is suggested that while distribution of wealth is still extremely one-sided, 'the continuation of the long-term trend towards a more even distribution of wealth in 1975 is noteworthy' (*Diamond Report*, no. 5, p. 100). It can be argued that Diamond focuses on the wrong dimensions of wealth if the hope is to even begin 'to secure a fairer distribution of income and wealth in the community', and, that an inadequate conceptual orientation has inevitably led to the Commission's reaching the sort of conclusion presented above. While data presented in Diamond can be used by radicals to make this argument, the alternative it suggests is by no means another case of making a few technical adjustments.

Capital and the concept of wealth

The major problem with the work of the Diamond Commission has been its focus upon the largely technical problems of measuring the *distribution* of wealth in different ways. The result has been that crucial questions relating to understanding the control of the *production* of wealth have by-and-large not been raised.

The first step here is to look at the position of capital in wealth. It is almost a precondition for producing wealth in our society that one own and control capital. This is also perhaps the main factor determining the distribution of wealth: workers can generally fight for higher wages only while owners and managers make the investment decisions which determine what will be produced, how and where. Capital is thus different from other forms of wealth: shares in an industrial company, for example, will typically grow in value over time, produce a regular dividend, confer legal ownership over part of the company's material assets, and are, moreover, easily marketable when necessary. Other forms of wealth are quite different: consumer goods generally depreciate and have a low second-hand value; the value of houses may in the main appreciate, but they are often difficult to sell, and the owner generally needs to buy another as replacement; pensions provide an entitlement to a future income only for as long as the pensioner lives, are not transferable, and often depreciate in value; and cash, although it confers immediate economic power through its purchasing power, generally depreciates. It is changes in the ownership and control of the means of production that need to be treated as the central criterion in assessing the distribution of wealth, for changes in other forms of wealth are intimately related to these.

Diamond touched on many of these points in discussing different concepts of wealth and their measurement—distinguishing, for example, between whether assets are marketable or non-marketable, liquid or non-liquid, to be valued in terms of current market prices or as a going concern, and so on. But these characteristics do not provide a means of demarcating capital from other assets. Even when forms of capital are prominent in a particular analysis, capital itself remains in Diamond's presentation and interpretation as only one among many forms of asset. Assessing the distribution of wealth is for Diamond really only a question of assessing the distribution of the money values of assets at a particular time. And treating capital in this way tends to focus attention away from the overwhelming concentration of ownership of the means of production in the hands of the very rich.[11]

It is when one considers estimates of the distribution of private ownership of the means of production that Diamond's figures of overall distribution of wealth—themselves indicating substantial inequalities—are really put into perspective[12]. *Table 3* presents a breakdown of the estimated distribution of personal assets for 1975 in terms which allow us to see the importance of selected specific categories of asset and the importance of capital as a whole. The information reproduced here is remarkable. 0.1 per cent of the population are shown to own well over a quarter of capital assets; moreover, the top 8.3 per cent own 94.6 per cent of listed ordinary shares and 90.9 per cent of all land (as well as 80.5 per cent of listed UK Government securities)[13]. At the other end of the scale, the wealth of the poor is held mainly as household goods, cash, national savings and life policies; in the middle ranges, the main feature of importance seems to be the large holdings of wealth as dwellings and building society deposits. Thus the very rich not only own an inordinate amount of wealth, but they hold it in those forms of assets that carry economic power. By failing to evaluate this central feature in wealth holdings, Diamond's statistical analyses become extremely misleading: the reader might never grasp that the production, reproduction and distribution of wealth are all controlled by a small section of the population. But for critical social scientists, it must be the ownership of capital, not consumer goods, houses, or the right to a pension that forms the central element in assessing the patterns of social inequality.

Indeed, it is highly probable that *effective* control of wealth is even more concentrated than this picture suggests. Take, for example, pension entitlements which Diamond sought to include in the estimation of personal wealth. The assets in pension funds— something in excess of £20 billion, mainly consisting of shares, property and government bonds (*Financial Statistics*, no. 185, *Tables 8* and *15*)—are controlled by the investment managers of these funds. Thus while Diamond's figures take into account the financial value of the benefits that derive from such holdings for employees and pensioners, they fail to consider the question of who actually *controls* these assets. It is the fund managers who have the power to influence what goes on in industry and to dictate terms to the government if it wants to borrow money; and their decisions reflect the logic of the capitalist system which spawns them.

Precise information on the concentration of assets in the pension industry and its sister insurance industry is, however, very sparse. The only guide of any use at all is the (relatively old) Department of Trade survey of insurance companies, *Insurance Business Statistics*, 1969–70, published in 1974. Its *Table 22*, part 2, shows that the thirty insurance companies with assets of over £100 million control 85 per cent of the £15,286 million assets in the hands of insurance companies. The five largest companies control 38 per cent of the assets. Since 1970 the value of assets in the hands of insurance companies has increased to over £31,000 million (*Financial Statistics*, no. 185, *Table 8.13*) and the level of concentration has probably also increased.

This growth of insurance funds is encouraged by the tax system, which allows tax relief on insurance premiums, and taxes

Table 3: **Distribution by range of wealth of selected personal assets, 1975**
United Kingdom (Series A)

Asset	Range of net wealth (lower limit) in percentages							Total
	£0–£4,999	£5,000–£9,999	£10,000–£19,999	£20,000–£49,999	£50,000–£99,999	£100,000–£199,999	£200,000–and above	
Capital								
Company securities	1.2	1.8	2.3	20.2	23.2	20.9	30.3	100
Listed ordinary shares[1]	2.4	2.7	6.6	21.4	21.0	16.7	29.3	100
Land	0.8	2.2	6.0	20.4	23.7	19.4	27.4	100
Monetary assets								
Cash and Bank deposits	17.4	15.7	19.4	19.8	11.5	7.5	8.7	100
Building Society deposits	14.4	17.3	26.1	28.0	9.4	3.4	1.4	100
National Savings	35.2	22.8	23.5	13.0	3.1	1.4	1.1	100

Other

Dwellings	5.2	23.4	37.0	22.8	6.8	3.1	1.8	100
Household goods	17.0	20.5	25.7	16.9	7.5	5.0	7.4	100
Life policies	17.2	23.0	31.3	21.7	4.6	1.5	0.7	100
Net wealth	10.9	18.2	27.0	22.0	9.6	5.8	6.4	100
Number of people in range as percentage of estimated total number of wealth owners	51.5	22.4	17.7	6.7	1.2	0.3	0.1	

[1] Includes Unit Trusts

Source: Derived from *Diamond Report*, no. 5, *Table 30*, p. 72

income from insurance policies at a lower rate than dividends received directly. As a result, the personal sector is increasingly switching from holding shares to holding insurance policies, with the result that the names of individuals disappear from the share registers, and the power to exercise corporate voting goes to the fund managers. The figures above suggest that a relatively small number of people—perhaps a couple of hundred—control virtually all the assets of insurance companies.

The pattern is repeated with pension funds. At the last count there were around 64,000 pension schemes in Britain (*Occupational Pension Schemes*, 1971), but 74 per cent of them had less than 50 members. The nationalised industry pension funds—there are six large ones—have assets of £6,000 million (*Financial Statistics*, no. 185, September 1977, *Table 8.15*). The private sector pension funds have, in comparison, assets of £9,354 million. The management of these is likely to be even more concentrated than that of the companies which pay into the funds. Some large funds—such as Esso, ICI and Barclays Bank—have their own managers, but many small funds are managed by professional investment companies and merchant banks. No precise information exists on the concentration of this activity, but around a dozen specialised investment concerns handle most of the business. It has been estimated in work being carried out for the Wilson Committee—which is reviewing the operation of financial institutions—that the largest 34 pension funds account for 60 per cent of total pension fund assets. Frequently, too, the directors of merchant banks are advisors to state industry's pension funds—thus helping to cement the power linkages between the financial institutions.

Moreover, the occupational pension industry is currently being dramatically expanded as new government legislation has made it compulsory for all employees to be either a member of a company-run pension scheme or to join the state's alternative. As a result, new schemes are being established, often under the aegis of one or other of the big insurance companies. Since contributions to the pension funds are a form of enforced saving, it seems likely that the growth of pension schemes will divert funds into the hands of merchant banks and insurance companies from other forms of saving—from building society deposits in particular. Not only is this likely to increase the concentration of control over the nation's wealth, but it is also likely to result in quite major changes in the statistics on the distribution of wealth.

The changing structure of British industry points to a further dimension missing from Diamond's picture of wealth. Over the last forty years it has, like industry elsewhere in the world, become increasingly concentrated. Fifty groups alone account for a third of Britain's output. On average, less than five companies account for two-thirds of the output in any one particular trade. As a result, industrial power also rests in fewer and fewer hands. The financial institutions which have massive shareholdings in industrial companies are not necessarily able to exercise control over them. Their opportunities for intervention are limited: shares entitle them to vote at annual meetings and to receive dividends, but not automatically to have a direct say in decisions over how money should be spent. Company directors like to be independent of day-to-day control by governments, shareholders and workers. Even though the directors may not own the businesses, they directly control their assets; they have considerable independence and power so long as they keep the company profitable and provide investors with adequate dividends.

This partial separation between ownership and control clearly poses important questions for assessing wealth. The control and privilege accorded to certain forms of senior management need to be taken into account in evaluating, for example, the degree to which the contributions to pension schemes that are invested by insurance companies in industry should really be regarded as 'wealth'. Although directors may not always own a big share in the companies they manage, their life is made tolerable by high salaries, chauffeur-driven cars, cheap housing loans, expense accounts, and so on (see particularly the Review Body on Top Salaries, 1978). The concentration of industrial and financial power is cemented by cross-directorships between companies, merchant banks and financial institutions. While little significant and comprehensive work has been carried out on this since the 1950s, it has been shown that over half the 90 largest companies had one director in common with one other such company. And in 1966 there was a merchant banker on the board of four in every ten of the 150 largest companies in Britain.[14] Many of these people are numbered among the 0.1 per cent of the population which owns almost 30 per cent of the listed ordinary shares in the UK.

The owners and controllers of the major means of production constitute an enormous missing area in Diamond's view of changing economic power and wealth in society. Their increasingly powerful position as controllers of capital, which is crucially different from other forms of wealth, places in their hands key decisions concerning the production, reproduction, and distribution of wealth in our society.

Trends in the distribution of wealth

Diamond's evidence, and the popular wisdom it supports, seem at variance with the argument that economic power is becoming increasingly concentrated in society. This is clearly due in part to the definitions of wealth used. Certainly, the growth in owner-occupied housing and life insurance schemes have contributed to the underlying trend towards more equal distribution of some assets. And if it becomes more acceptable to include pension rights as wealth, then the apparent trend towards greater equality in wealth in Britain may even accelerate.

However, while it is easy to account for changes in the distribution of wealth at the lower levels, doing so at the higher is rather more difficult. With relatively high levels of estate duty, tax avoidance and tax evasion become increasingly attractive (see, e.g. Whalley, 1974). We would need to understand the role of the family in the reproduction and transfer of wealth—a role whose significance may be gauged from the estimate that around 25 per cent of all wealth is inherited, with a much higher proportion among the very rich (*Diamond Report*, no. 5). Big estates may often be broken into smaller ones—but the components are frequently being distributed within the same family, as the rich minimise their liability to taxation at death. The IR statistics must be affected by such practices – they even classify as non-holders of wealth those children who are yet to inherit the fortunes waiting for them in trust. Again, technical adjustments are less than adequate to deal with what is basically an issue of the economic power relationships which lie at the heart of class differences.

Official data on wealth—including Diamond's reanalyses and innovations—can be invaluable in critical analyses of inequality and class relations. But they are statistics that have been developed in the administration of death duties and capital gains tax, and thus fail to address the role of capital in our society—as a form of wealth which while only minimally taxed (as compared to taxes on wages and consumption), is yet a central determinant of economic power. Changes in the distribution of other forms of wealth—from pension rights to washing machines—should be seen in the light of the increasing concentration of economic power, that is control of the production of wealth, in Britain. In that light the claim that classlessness and equality are growing in our society stands revealed in all its hollowness.

Notes

1. Since we wrote this article, Atkinson and Harrison (1978) have produced a detailed, in parts technical, critique of wealth statistics. Taking issue with Diamond over several points concerning the constituents of wealth, and how its distribution should best be measured, they present some important new 'adjustments' of the data. For a comprehensive review of the statistical sources on the distribution of wealth, see Atkinson and Harrison (1977).

2. For discussion of some of the problems and pitfalls in this approach, see *Diamond Report*, no. 1, pp. 76–78.

3. See *Diamond Report*, no. 1, pp. 75–76 for further discussion of this method and its associated problems. Although problematic, analyses of this sort have been made: Diamond cites Atkinson and Harrison (1974) as a recent case.

4. Until recently this was a by-product of the system of levying death duties. Although death duties have now been replaced by capital transfer tax, which is levied when gifts are made between the living, as well as at death, this is unlikely to alter the IR statistics or its calculations to any significant extent.

5. This method is explained in detail in *Diamond Report*, no. 1, pp. 223–236; a shorter summary is given in the same Report on pp. 74–75.

6. Minimising tax liabilities in this way is often termed 'tax avoidance'. This is, of course, done within the bounds of the law, although often at its extremities, and contrasts with the use of illegal methods in 'tax evasion'.

7. The precise criteria used by the IR are summarised in *Diamond Report*, no. 5, 1977, pp. 231–234.

8. Technical adjustments can, of course, be made here to take this change into account. Any such estimates would, however, be crucially dependent on their underlying assumptions. Whereas the *Diamond Report*, no. 5, suggested that the first year of rapidly rising share prices (1974–75) had little impact on the distribution of wealth because of the parallel growth of other forms of wealth, Atkinson and Harrison (1978), in contrast, consider the volatility of share prices to be important. In conversation with one of us, Atkinson criticized Diamond's adjustments as too crude, and argued that a 50 per cent rise in share prices could increase the share of wealth held by the richest 1 per cent, half of whose assets are held in shares, by around 4 per cent.

9. The Series C revision involved a great deal of detailed technical work by both Diamond and the CSO. The essential input by the CSO was a specially produced 'audit' of the entire personal sector wealth holdings in the UK (see *Diamond Report*, no. 5, *Table 36*, p. 82). This 'balance sheet' therefore included estimates of both the wealth of the excluded population, as well as asset items not taken into account by the IR. The latter alone was estimated at £8,500 million for 1975. What Diamond then did was to compare total wealth estimated by this balance sheet approach with that estimated by the IR estate multiplier approach—this produced a figure of £238,927 million for 1975 compared with the IR's estimate of £190,290 million. Further analysis by Diamond, attempting to adjust for problems caused by differing methods of valuation in these approaches, gave the Series C estimate—which is perhaps now regarded by social scientists as the most acceptable assessment of the distribution of wealth. (For further discussion as to how these adjustments were made, see *Diamond Report*, no. 5, pp. 81-87, and for the technical details see *Diamond Report*, no. 1, appendix I, pp. 219–222).

10. Occupational pensions are those provided by employers (including State employers)—or pension funds under their control—to people who have worked for them. They are separate from the state pension.

11. Even when Diamond went beyond the scope of previous analyses and evaluated the importance to the distribution of wealth of holdings of different forms of assets, the result is to occlude the importance of capital. In *Diamond Report*, no. 5, an attempt is made to assess wealth distribution in terms of 'realisation values' (rather than as 'going concern values' as is the case in Series C) with the aim of providing data on holdings of liquid wealth—the resultant distribution of wealth broken down into cash, liquid and marketable assets. Most importantly, these figures are then used to provide a basis for estimating the distribution of *financial* resources, for 'it is often thought that physical assets, such as dwellings and household goods are relatively evenly distributed, the implication being that the overall distribution of wealth must be attributed to a much greater degree of inequality in the ownership of financial assets . . .' (p. 97). Because the category of financial assets includes such items as life insurance policies and cash which are widely distributed among the poorer sections, their conclusion that 'in practice the distribution of financial assets is not greatly dissimilar from the distribution of wealth as a whole' (p. 97) comes as little surprise. (For further discussion, see *Diamond Report*, no. 5, pp. 91-98).

12. Also providing an important basis for comparison are alternative estimates of the overall distribution of wealth. Atkinson and Harrison (1978) have estimated that for 1972, the top 1 per cent owned between 30 per cent and 33 per cent of the wealth; the top 5 per cent between 53 per cent and 57 per cent; and the top 10 per cent between 66 per cent and 69 per cent. Diamond's readjusted (Series C) figures, which for 1972 are 24.3 per cent, 46.1 per cent and 60.0 per cent respectively, clearly need to be regarded with some scepticism.

13. We need to remember that these figures are still an underestimate of the wealth holdings of the rich. As we saw before, the IR estate multiplier method, on which this table is based, does not take into account certain forms of assets owned by the very rich.

14. These studies are discussed in Westergaard and Resler (1976) in the context of a wider debate about the ownership and control of capital. See especially Part 2, chapter 7 and Part 3, chapters 1 and 2.

Bibliography

Atkinson, A. B., *Unequal Shares*, London, Allen Lane.

Atkinson, A. B., and Harrison, A. J., 1974, 'Wealth distribution and investment income in Britain', *Review of Income and Wealth*, series 20, no. 2, pp. 125-142.

Atkinson, A. B., and Harrison, A. J., 1977, 'The distribution of personal wealth', in W. F. Maunder (ed.), *Sources and Nature of the Statistics of the UK*, London, Heinemann.

Atkinson, A. B., and Harrison, A. J., 1978, *Distribution of Personal Wealth in Britain*, Cambridge, Cambridge University Press.

Board of Inland Revenue, *Inland Revenue Statistics*, 1976, London, HMSO.

CSO, 1974, *Insurance Business Statistics, 1969-70*, London, HMSO.

CSO, 1977, *Financial Statistics*, no. 185, September 1977, London, HMSO.

Diamond Reports: Royal Commission on the Distribution of Income and Wealth (Chairman, Lord Diamond)
  (a) *Initial Report on the Standing Reference*, 1975, (Report no.1), Cmnd. 6171, London, HMSO.
  (b) *Second Report on the Standing Reference*, 1976, (Report no. 4), Cmnd. 6626, London, HMSO.
  (c) *Third Report on the Standing Reference*, 1977, (Report no. 5), Cmnd.6999, London, HMSO.

Occupational Pension Schemes 1971, 1975, London, HMSO.

Polanyi, G., and Wood, J. B., 1974, *How Much Inequality?* (IEA Research Monograph 31), London, Institute of Economic Affairs.

Report of the Committee on the Working of the Monetary System, 1958 (The Radcliffe Report), Cmnd. 827, London, HMSO.

Revell, J., 1967, *The Wealth of the Nation*, Cambridge, Cambridge University Press.

Review Body on Top Salaries, 1978, *Report No. 10*, London, HMSO.

Westergaard, J., and Resler, H., 1976, *Class in a Capitalist Society*, Harmondsworth, Penguin.

Whalley, J., 1974, 'Estate duty as a "voluntary" tax: evidence from stamp duty statistics', *Economic Journal*, vol. 84, no. 335, pp. 638–644.

14.

Jim Kincaid

Poverty in the Welfare State

In Britain today the richest 8 per cent of the adult population owns 91 per cent of all land and 88 per cent of all the company shares held by individuals. The less wealthy *half* of the population owns, in comparison, less than $\frac{1}{2}$ per cent of the land and slightly over 1 per cent of shares[1]. As judged by the maldistribution of basic forms of property such as land and the productive resources of private industry, capitalism thus remains a profoundly unequal system.

If general public acceptance of the legitimacy of these economic inequalities is to be maintained, the welfare role of the modern state is clearly crucial. On the face of it, the state is anything but neutral, since it tolerates a fantastic concentration of key economic resources in the hands of a small minority. But those concerned to defend the fairness of existing institutions can argue that the essential benevolence and democratic responsiveness of the state is proved by an elaborate system of welfare services and benefits directed towards economically and socially vulnerable sections of the population.[2] We may not all be equal, but at least poverty and deprivation on any large scale have been abolished. So runs the argument—coupled often, in its more confident versions, with the assertion that the state is too generous, permitting a widespread abuse of welfare benefits and weakening work incentives by failing to concentrate welfare services on those in real need.

Social role of the welfare state

There are many counter-arguments: for example, that a large proportion of welfare expenditure is directed toward the more affluent middle classes. It is their children who dominate the higher education sector, where per capita costs are particularly heavy[3]. It is the middle classes who have the skills, the contacts and the leisure to make exceptional demands on health care resources (see Townsend, 1974) and whose mortgages, life insurance and generous superannuation schemes are heavily subsidised by tax relief.[4]

Another counter-argument points to the multiplicity of complex social security schemes, many of which involve an intrusive and stigmatising means-test, and which result in large numbers of the most deprived missing out on benefits to which in theory they are entitled. For example, it has been officially estimated that 600,000 pensioners failed to claim supplementary benefit for which they were qualified in 1975. The total benefit lost was £65 million. A further £175 million was unclaimed by 300,000 people under pension age[5]. In 1975, this unclaimed £240 million equalled 22 per cent of the total cost of supplementary benefit.

A third counter-argument focuses on the system of taxation. The welfare state is financed by a tax system which is progressive only to a very limited extent. This is because a large proportion of state revenue is raised by forms of taxation (expenditure taxes, rates) which bear more heavily on lower than higher income groups[6]. Social security fiddling occurs on a trivial scale compared with tax evasion, especially as practiced by the wealthy[7].

The welfare state is not concerned primarily, or essentially, with the alleviation of poverty. Rather, its major economic role is to help train, maintain and motivate the labour force.[8] In practice, welfare resources tend to be concentrated on present and future workers. The poor are relegated to the margin because in terms of the capitalist economy their productive capacity is limited or non-existent. They cannot work because of old age, handicap, single parenthood, unemployment, sickness. However, although neglected, the poor are by no means ignored. Holman (1975) has argued cogently that:

> the poor help to preserve the existing division of society and thereby the disproportionate distribution of resources . . . the use of the poor as a reference group persuades those sectors of society (which are neither wealthy nor poor) that their lot in terms of status, resources and power is acceptable. Consequently the possibility that they will strive to change the position of the elite is reduced. Further the poor act as a warning. They demonstrate the fate of those who do not conform to prevailing work and social standards. Their plight is needed to reinforce the will of others to work for low returns in unpleasant and even degrading conditions from which the economic output gives a disproportionate financial reward to a minority of existing resource holders. Not least, those in poverty act as scape-goats, a vulnerable group on whom the blame for social problems can be placed, so diverting attention away from that minority which has some control over social affairs. (Holman, 1975, p. 411).

There is, of course, an apparent conflict between Holman's line of argument and propaganda claims that the development of a welfare state has virtually abolished poverty. This contradiction is resolved in practice by the creation and maintenance of an impression that the poor consist mainly of work-shy scroungers. The existence of poverty on a large scale is not only legitimised, but put to use as a warning to whole sections of underpaid workers, when dependence on welfare benefits is presented by the mass media as a financially rewarding, but socially contemptible, way of life. Scrounger mythology, based on the vast publicity given to occasional court cases, is thus a pivotal element in the ideological justification of the modern welfare system. (See Deacon, 1977).

The official picture of poverty

Centrally involved in these political arguments are questions of fact and of definition. What are the numbers, the social composition and the living standards of the low income population? How is the nature and incidence of poverty affected by changes in the economic situation and in Government policies? Although at first sight answering these questions seems easy, this is not the case. While each year the Government produces large and expensively generated bodies of data on the various sources of household income, most of this material throws little light on questions of poverty.[9]

Official, as well as unofficial, estimates of the level and incidence of poverty nationally, rely heavily on two inter-related bodies of data produced by Government departments—the annual *Family Expenditure Survey* (FES) and the monthly *Retail Price Index* (RPI).

Politically, these are among the most crucial of official statistics. The *Index* is the sole and widely publicised measure of the impact of inflation on both the living standards of wage earners and those dependent on social security benefits. It is extensively used in wage and salary negotiations and by the government to determine the level of welfare benefit increases.[10]

Despite all its limitations, the FES is the least unsatisfactory source of information in the estimation of poverty levels within the population. However, the calculations and assumptions involved are in many respects arbitrary and questionable, partly because the FES is carried out for administrative purposes other than the measurement of poverty. Its main objective is in fact to establish household spending patterns over a broad sector of the population —this information being required in order to construct the RPI. These limitations are made glaringly obvious in a recent attempt to estimate poverty levels from FES data (Fiegehan et al., 1977), which concludes that, depending on the technical assumptions made during the calculation, between 4.9 per cent and 8.5 per cent of the population were in poverty in 1971. Between the upper and lower estimate lie some 2 million people.

In this inquiry, as in virtually all post war studies, the criterion used to define poverty is an income below the level laid down in Supplementary Benefit regulations.[11] Yet this is a peculiar procedure to adopt and is rather like measuring distances with a rubber ruler. If the government allows SB scales to lag behind average wages (thus increasing the incidence of poverty) the effect is to lower the numbers *estimated* to be in poverty.

Estimating poverty realistically

The alternative to this procedure would be to make assessments about what households in varying circumstances *need* to have as a standard of living if they are not to be considered in poverty, and then to estimate the amounts of cash required. Yet since the classic studies of Seebohm Rowntree,[12] no British research has attempted to draw conclusions about basic needs in any comprehensive way, or to cost the extra requirements for income arising because of physical or mental handicap, extreme old age, sickness, or being a single parent etc. This was only a beginning, however, and many of the assumptions and methods of Rowntree have rightly been discredited. His definition of poverty was based largely on physiological criteria of efficiency, and was expressed in terms of a fixed standard of living little altered over time by increases in the average level of real wages. Furthermore, the minimum standard of living could only be achieved by those on the threshold of the poverty level of income if household spending patterns were exactly as prescribed by Rowntree. No account was taken of actual working class spending customs which differed from the largely middle-class patterns of expenditure he used as a base-level. This form of distortion, as we shall see, still continues in current government practice.

In more recent research, the idea of defining poverty in terms of a detailed standard of living has still not been taken up. The argument has been that the judgements involved are inherently political and unscientific. However, by adopting a Supplementary Benefit criterion of poverty researchers have not achieved their supposed stance of 'neutrality'. They have merely avoided taking independent responsibility for their assumptions and conclusions.[13] In effect, judgements made by the state about what constitutes a reasonable minimum income have been adopted as the premise on which much of this research is based.

Yet such evasion has its limits and limitations. Inconveniently, the Supplementary Benefits Commission does not have a single unambiguous scale of so much money a week for households of varying size and composition. For instance, the investigator of poverty has to decide whether to use the long-term or the short-term SB rate. All old-age pensioners are on a long-term rate, which in 1978, for example, involved an additional £2.40 a week for a single person, and £4.80 a week for a married couple.[14] Households under pensionable age move to the long-term rate after they have been on social security continuously for more than two years. A special exception, however, is made for the unemployed, who are never given the long-term rate. Only adults get the long-term rate; all children are assessed on the short-term rate. The official justification for the higher long-term rate is the necessity of meeting certain expenses (replacement of household equipment etc.) which accumulate over time. It would appear then, that the elderly have long-term needs which must be met immediately; for the sick and single parent families, these needs will begin to appear after two years, while the unemployed are not considered to have any long-term needs at all. Such official procedures place a great strain on academic neutrality, so obvious are the political evaluations which underlie them— the ostentatious extra help given to the elderly, the grudging payment to families with children, the punitive exclusion of the unemployed.

Other equally political choices must be made in assessing poverty. Households on SB are allowed small amounts of income without having their SB entitlement reduced: for a single parent this involved, in 1978, earnings of up to £6 a week, and for someone unemployed, up to £2 a week. The interest on savings up to a certain level is disregarded.[15] The SB can also make occasional discretionary lump sum payments: for heating or hire purchase bills, removal, redecoration or funeral expenses, etc. The question is: should all of these be included when poverty is defined? This is difficult when the choices made in order to arrive at poverty criteria so obviously affect estimates of the numbers in poverty. For example, Abel-Smith and Townsend (1965) reported that 3.8 per cent of the population in 1960 had incomes below the basic national assistance scale (rent included). Yet setting the poverty line at 40 per cent higher, to allow for additional allowances paid by national assistance, raised the poverty estimate to 14.2 per cent of the population. Political choices are again clearly inherent in accepting or rejecting officially defined poverty levels.

Distortions in official poverty estimates

For these and similar estimates, the most widely used source of information on incomes is the FES. Each year a supposedly 'representative' national sample of households, in 1978 about 11,000, is asked to provide an account of its income, together with a detailed breakdown of expenditure, based on keeping a diary of all spending over a two-week period. An interview supplements the diary, with information collected about spending patterns occuring at less frequent intervals; e.g. on rates, season tickets, holidays and fuel bills.

Given the effort involved by respondents, and the small payments made (each member of the household over 16 gets £2 a completed diary), a response rate of about 70 per cent is creditable. However, refusals to co-operate are high among the elderly and the self-employed, two groups with a much greater than average chance of being in poverty.[16] Since the survey is concerned only with households, the homeless are excluded, as are people living in hotels, hostels and hospitals, and students living away from home. A third limitation is that the Survey asks respondents to report their *normal* earnings. People who have a lower income than usual because of illness, short-time working or unemployment are asked to state their income during the most recent period of 'normal' earnings. On the basis of such data, total incomes are necessarily overestimated.

Another problem in measuring poverty is that income totals are not calculated for individuals but for the household as a whole. The underlying assumption is that household income is completely pooled. Yet some 20 per cent of British households are of a non-nuclear sort. In such cases, the Survey procedure will miss poverty arising because some members of the household, e.g. sons and daughters with their own income, do not in fact pool that income.

Many of the limitations of the FES in estimating poverty levels arise because the Survey is not carried out specifically for this purpose, but rather to establish the proportion of their income which households spend on various goods and services. These weightings are required in the construction of the monthly RPI.

Although official acknowledgement is made of the limitations of the RPI it has become an extremely important statistic in politics and everyday media debate. We therefore have to be clear about the reasons why the present RPI underestimates the extent to which inflation undermines the standard of living of people in poverty.

First, the expenditure pattern on which the Index is based is that of a typical household. Low income households spend a higher proportion of their budget on basic necessities such as fuel, food and housing.[17] Since 1968, a separate price index has been published for pensioners. This tends to rise faster than the general retail price index and in any case, is subject to its own forms of distortion. Rent and other housing costs are excluded, although in most years these have outpaced other items in the index. Also, the pensioner index is based on the expenditure patterns of all pensioners, thus including the quite large numbers of middle class pensioners with substantial retirement incomes. There is no separate index either, for the three million pensioner households which live below, or very little above, the supplementary benefit standard of living. Nor are separate price indices published for the unemployed, the handicapped, the long-term sick, workers with low wages, single parent families, or other groups whose incomes, like those of pensioners, are highly vulnerable to exceptional increases in the prices of basic necessities.

A second weakness of the general RPI is that it makes no allowance for the actual purchasing customs of households. Having established the proportion of income which the average household spends on various goods, Department of Employment officials are sent out each month in a sample of areas to check on the prices of these goods in a sample of shops. The assumption is that all households buy retail goods and services at the national average price calculated from this inquiry.

Yet there are sizeable geographical differences in the prices of food, fuel, housing, public transport and other important items. Nevertheless, apart from an index for London, no separate regional price indices are published for other big cities, for rural areas or for particular regions.

More seriously still, groups in poverty are not in a position to budget and spend in the most economical way. They lack cars to reach supermarkets and hypermarkets. Their mobility is limited by old age, handicap or children to look after. They are obliged to buy in small quantities—the Price Commission found in one study that the smallest can of processed peas cost proportionately 79 per cent more than the most popular size. Most importantly, fuel costs more because of discrimination in fuel pricing. Thus, a study by the National Consumer Council (1977) reported that a low-income family using electric fires might pay up to £44 for warmth that would cost a family in a well-insulated home with gas central heating only £6. Furthermore, interest rates are exceptionally high for small-scale borrowing with legal and collection charges often swelling the size of over-due bills.

To sum up, the FES gives a low estimate of both the numbers on low incomes and the extent of their poverty. Because price-index calculations are based on expenditure patterns derived from this survey, its underestimates are transmitted in turn into the official RPI. Further distortions arise because of the methods used to calculate the impact of price increases on household budgets and no account is taken of the many ways by which, in comparison with the average household, goods and services purchased by low-income groups tend to cost more and to rise more rapidly in price.

The consequence is that official statistics represent both the nature and extent of poverty in a considerably more complacent way than would be possible if a serious effort were made by the state to define and assess it.[18] This, as we have seen, is not likely in a society in which the welfare role of the state is oriented largely towards maintaining an adequate work force for capitalist production and towards legitimising the inherent inequalities of this system. Measuring and monitoring the 'real' level of welfare would entail an entirely different set of state practices—oriented towards abolishing poverty rather than merely limiting the human damage caused by capitalism.

Notes

1. The figures are drawn from Table 30 in the Royal Commission on the Distribution of Income and Wealth (1977). See also Hird and Irvine, this volume, for a general discussion of wealth statistics.
2. Saville (1975, p. 62) documents the historical emergence of the welfare state partly in terms of, 'the recognition by property owners of the price that has to be paid for political security'.
3. This is documented in detail in Westergaard and Resler (1976, Part 4).
4. In 1975-76 tax relief cost the Exchequer £1 billion for mortgage interest, £240 million for life insurance and £2 billion for superannuation schemes. The cost of these three subsidies was equivalent to about 10 per cent of the total expenditure of Central Government in that year.
5. Full details are provided in Supplementary Benefits Commission (1977, chapter 10). The 75 per cent take-up rate for supplementary benefit is a good deal higher than for most other means tested benefits. E.g. for Family Income Supplement and Rates Rebate, only 50 per cent of those eligible actually get the benefit. See Lister (1974) for details.
6. For further details, see Kincaid (1977, chapter 6) or Field et al. (1977).
7. The state estimates (Hansard, 24 May 1976, Col. 79) that in 1974-75 there were overpayments of £8.7 million out of a total social security expenditure of £8,900 million. Only £2 million of those arose from fraud by claimants and £6.7 million because of errors by officials. By comparison, the Inland Revenue Staff Federation estimates the cost of tax evasion at over £1,000 million annually. (Field, 1977, p. 154). Yet, in the Tory press it is not tax evasion by the rich, but social security fraud by the not so rich which is given massive publicity.

8. This point is developed at length in Gough (1976) and O'Connor (1973).

9. The *New Earnings Survey* (annual), Dept. of Employment, provides detailed information about wages, but nothing about the family composition and other income of wage earners.

Social Security Statistics (annual), Dept. of Health and Social Security, contains data on the numbers of benefit payments of various sorts made each year, but nothing about the size and income levels of recipient households.

Inland Revenue Statistics (annual), while providing a multitude of data on taxpayers, contains virtually nothing about people with incomes below the threshold at which income tax starts to operate.

Income distribution figures are provided in the *National Income and Expenditure Bluebook*. These are commented on in detail in the Reports of the Diamond Commission, 1975–78. The accuracy of such data is, however, questionable; while in 1973–74, for example, total personal income was estimated at £63.5 billion, the Bluebook income distribution figures add up to only £52.3 billion. The biggest part of the missing £11.2 billion appears to be investment income unreported to the Inland Revenue. Until something is known about the social distribution of this gigantic sum, no accurate conclusions can be drawn about the level of income inequality in Britain, and still less about its trend over time. (See also Hird and Irvine, this volume).

10. The government generally claims to be committed to increasing pensions and other benefits in line with prices or wages (whichever is the higher). Not too seriously, though. In the 1976 uprating of benefits, the government changed the time period over which inflation is calculated. Previously, benefits had been increased to take account of inflation in the 12 month period up to the spring Budget. In the 1976 uprating, only the six month period up to the Budget was counted, and a forecast was made—in very optimistic terms—about the trend of inflation over the six months following the Budget. This change in time period allowed the government to leave out of account six months during which prices rose by 15.8 per cent and earnings by 14.4 per cent. The effect was that pensioners and other social security claimants were deprived of £500 million which they would otherwise have received in the year following. This loss was projected into future years because the base line from which benefit upratings were to be calculated was permanently reduced.

11. Or, for the period up to 1966, the National Assistance scales.

12. Rowntree's studies are well summarised in Atkinson (1975, chapter 10).

13. In one way, however, the use of SB scales adds to the political impact of poverty research. It has been a general state commitment that no one should have to exist on an income below SB levels. To establish that a significant proportion of the population are in this position is, in a direct way, to measure the failure of policy to achieve its stated objective.

14. I.e. for a single person this was 17 per cent above the short-term rate and for a married couple, 20 per cent higher.

15. Claimants (at the time of writing in 1978) may have up to £1,250 of capital without reduction in SB entitlement. For larger sums, benefit is reduced on a sliding scale.

16. An official report (Ministry of Social Security, 1967) found that the incidence of poverty was four times higher among the self-employed. For further, more detailed criticisms of FES procedures, see Townsend (1970) and Townsend (1976, chapter 18). An article in the official *Statistical News*, no. 39, November 1977, calculated that the under-representation of older age groups in the FES leads to an exaggeration of average income levels in the poorer sections of the population. E.g., the income of the second lowest decile in the 1971 FES income distribution was found to be overstated by 6.3 per cent.

17. A modest effort is made to reduce the bias against lower income spending patterns. Households above a certain income limit (£140 per week in 1976) are excluded when the standard weighting of expenditure in the RPI is calculated. But the spending pattern of the poor deviates considerably from that of households with around average income. The exclusion of the high income groups scarcely reduces the gap between average and low income spending patterns.

18. Valuable sources of critical comment on official statistics are provided by *Poverty*, journal of the Child Poverty Action Group, and by the reports of the Low Pay Unit. Useful, though limited, data on poverty are also provided by the periodic surveys they carry out.

Bibliography

Abel-Smith, B., and Townsend, P., 1965, *The Poor and the Poorest*, London, London School of Economics.

Atkinson, A. B., 1975, *The Economics of Inequality*, Oxford, Oxford University Press.

Butterworth, E., and Holman, R. (eds.), 1975, *Social Welfare in Modern Britain*, Fontana, London.

Deacon, A., 1977, 'Scrounger bashing', *New Society*, 17 November.

Fiegehan, G. C., et. al., 1977, *Poverty and Progress in Britain, 1953–73*, Cambridge, Cambridge University Press.

Field, F., et. al., 1977, *To Him Who Hath*, Harmondsworth, Penguin.

Gough, I., 1976, 'State expenditure in advanced capitalism', *New Left Review*, no. 92.

Holman, R., 1975, 'Poverty: consensus and alternatives', in Butterworth and Holman, 1975, above.

Kincaid, J. C., 1977, *Poverty and Equality in Britain*, Harmondsworth, Penguin.

Lister, R., 1974, *The Take Up of Means Tested Benefits*, London, Child Poverty Action Group.

Ministry of Social Security, 1967, *Circumstances of Families*, London, HMSO.

National Consumer Council, 1977, *Why the Poor Pay More*, London, Macmillan.

O'Connor, J., 1973, *The Fiscal Crisis of the State*, London, St Martin's Press.

Royal Commission on the Distribution of Income and Wealth (Chairman, Lord Diamond), *5th Report. Third Report on the Standing Reference*, Cmnd. 6999, London, HMSO.

Saville, J., 1975, 'The welfare state: an historical approach', in Butterworth and Holman, above.

Supplementary Benefits Commission, 1977, *Report for 1976*, Cmnd.6910, London, HMSO.

Townsend, P., 1970, *The Concept of Poverty*, London, Heinemann.

Townsend, P., 1974, 'Inequality and the health service', *The Lancet*, 15 June.

Townsend, P., 1976, *Sociology and Social Policy*, Harmondsworth, Penguin.

Westergaard, J., and Resler, H., 1976, *Class in a Capitalist Society*, Harmondsworth, Penguin.

15.

Richard Hyman and Bob Price

Labour Statistics

Labour statistics were first compiled officially in the late nineteenth century, when trade unionism was relatively weak and the most influential capitalists therefore felt little need for direct and systematic state intervention in industrial relations. Early official interest in labour matters probably owed more to pressure from 'progressive' politicians with a concern for social welfare than to distinctively capitalist priorities. For this very reason, the first few decades of compilation were marked by limited resources and amateurish methods, and the value of the resulting statistics is questionable.

Collection and publication of labour statistics was agreed by the House of Commons in 1886, on the proposal of the radical MP Bradlaugh; the initiative coincided with the vogue for reform-oriented social investigation in the 1880s. Burnett, the General Secretary of the Amalgamated Society of Engineers, was appointed to take charge of the new service. In 1893, the initial token facilities were expanded with the establishment within the Board of Trade of a Labour Department (a proposal raised by several members of the Royal Commission on Labour, then in session). Llewelyn Smith, who had previously played an important role in Booth's researches, was appointed to the new post of Labour Commissioner. In addition to an enlarged central staff, some thirty local correspondents (mainly trade union officials paid a small retainer) provided information for the new Department, and the monthly *Labour Gazette* was launched as a means of dissemination.

In its first issue (May 1893) the *Gazette* was described as 'a journal for the use of workmen, and of all others interested in obtaining prompt and accurate information on matters specially affecting labour.' This indicates clearly that the management and control of labour was not, as yet, a primary motive for the compilation of statistical information. Thus, it is not altogether surprising that within a few years *The Times*—then as now a mouthpiece of the capitalist establishment—could dismiss the Department as 'a body whose chief function seems to be to provide posts for trade union officials, and to publish inadequate reports and dreary statistics, of little or no practical utility' (16 January 1902).

In the present century, 'practical utility' has become increasingly central to the compilation of official labour statistics: one of the many consequences of the changing relationship between capital, trade unions and the state. In part, this reflects the general shift from laissez-faire to an increasingly interventionist governmental role in economic life (which, at different points in time, has involved the organisation of wartime mobilisation, the development of national policies of 'manpower planning', and—most recently—a succession of attempts to control wage increases). In part, it is a manifestation of the introduction and elaboration of state 'welfare' provision. In part, also, it indicates an assumption that the extension of trade union organisation has transformed labour into a 'problem' which can be controlled only on the basis of sophisticated methods of intelligence.

Enhanced governmental intervention in labour affairs was symbolised by the creation of the Ministry of Labour in 1917, and by its various metamorphoses into the present Department of Employment (D.E.). The importance attributed to the collection and analysis of labour force data is indicated by the immense expansion in resources devoted to this function, in comparison with the early beginnings: today some 30 professional statisticians are employed in the Statistics Division of the DE, in addition to some 300 clerical and administrative staff at the Department's headquarters and other specialists in the regions.

This stage has been reached, not by a smooth progression but in three main phases. The first occurred roughly in the second decade of the century. One impetus was the outbreak of war in 1914, generating governmental efforts to allocate men and women to arms production and the military; to monitor movements in prices and wages; and to suppress industrial unrest. Another was the programme of 'reform' legislation initiated by the pre-war Liberal government: the formation of Trade Boards (precursors of the modern Wages Councils), the introduction of state unemployment insurance, and the opening of a network of local labour exchanges. These initiatives, extended further by the Unemployment Insurance Act of 1920, provided both the motive and the mechanism for a considerable elaboration in statistical provision.

Between the wars (in a period of government cut-backs, and

when a trade union movement weakened by mass unemployment no longer appeared to threaten capitalist stability), there were no further developments of significance. But the 1939–45 war, and the further extension of the 'welfare state' by the post-war Labour government (though largely along lines projected by the Conservative-dominated wartime coalition), brought a second extension in the range and detail of official statistics. A third phase may be discerned in the period since 1960, when the growing difficulties of British capitalism, and the increasing interdependence of the state and monopoly capital, have generated urgent demands for statistics as a means of planning and control. Relevance to the requirements of capital has become increasingly evident as the main influence on the form and content of official labour statistics.

This chequered history has thus involved regular but unsystematic extensions in the coverage and volume of official data. Not surprisingly, there are significant gaps which confront the non-official user, and these are considered briefly at the end of this chapter. But first, the data which *are* available are examined under the headings employed in the *British Labour Statistics Year Book (BLSYB):* wage rates and normal hours; earnings and hours worked; retail prices; employment; unemployment; vacancies and placing; family expenditure; membership of trade unions; industrial disputes; industrial accidents; labour costs; costs per unit of output; and output per person employed.

Wage rates and normal hours

This was one of the earliest series produced, covering minimum wage rates of manual workers analysed by industry group and by sex (until the implementation of the Equal Pay Act, which made formally differentiated male and female rates illegal). Annual and monthly changes are recorded, and an index of wage rates compiled. Data are derived from collective agreements, and from the decisions of such statutory bodies as Wages Councils. The basic inadequacy of this series is that the minimum rates prescribed for manual workers covered by some forms of collective regulation need bear no definable relation to the actual level and structure of earnings within the labour force. In most large-scale manufacturing industry, for example, nationally agreed rates are often substantially supplemented by piecework and overtime bonuses, and by other increases negotiated at plant level; even in more weakly unionised sectors of employment, it is common for a minority to earn significantly above the minimum.

Earnings and hours worked

The compilation of this series reflects official recognition of the inadequacy of statistics of wage rates and standard hours. A national earnings survey was conducted at the beginning of the century. This was a one-off exercise in response to a widespread campaign against the evils of sweated labour, designed to identify the extent of this problem. The practice was resumed in 1968, and has continued annually since 1970. (The main motive was almost certainly the interest of governments in restraining increases in earnings; the inadequacy of earnings information was strongly criticised by the Prices and Incomes Board.) The *New Earnings Survey (NES)* was initially published as a single volume, but since 1974 has been published in six parts. Data are presented in detail and are organised under various headings: male and female, manual and non-manual[1] workers, industry and occupation, region and county, and age group.

The information is derived from employers in respect of a 1 per cent random sample of employees recorded for PAYE tax purposes. It would appear that returns are completed for roughly 80 per cent of full-time employees in the survey; the accuracy of the information provided by employers is, however, impossible to assess.[2] The survey is officially recognised as an inadequate guide to earnings of part-time employees, many of whom earn below the tax threshold; while the self-employed (including 'lump' labour) are not covered at all.

As a source of data on the structure of earnings for full-time employees, and of changes in this structure, the official statistics are of considerable value. But it is important to bear in mind that their main purpose is to assist government control of wages and salaries, rather than to indicate the dimensions of economic inequality in contemporary Britain. The main *NES* analysis excludes part-time employees, juveniles, and those whose earnings are affected by absence; thus, the full dimensions of low pay—let alone the more general problem of poverty—are not documented. At the other extreme, the published distribution tables do not adequately indicate the pattern of top salaries, or of fringe benefits (which, as the Royal Commission on the Distribution of Income and Wealth has shown, are of particular importance at the highest earnings levels). And *unearned* incomes—which are a key factor in the extremes of economic inequality—are necessarily excluded from the *NES*. Some sources which can help provide information on these issues are noted at the end of this chapter.

Retail prices

The retail price index (RPI) is (as Kincaid argues, this volume) one of the great mystifying devices of the century. Currently it is based on the weighted averages of the prices of some 350 commodities and services in various parts of the country. Suspicion of the index has been traditional and well-justified; in the 1939–45 war, for example, the government subsidised certain of the items in the index (which contained far fewer items, and reflected long outdated consumption patterns) in order to conceal the extent of price rises (see Hancock and Gowing, 1949, pp. 333–37). In recent years, a number of changes have been made in response to criticism. The weights of the various items, for example, are now revised annually on the basis of the *Family Expenditure Survey* (FES) (see below). The General Index excludes high-income households (in 1974, those in which the 'head of the household' earned over £100 per week), and also those in which at least three-quarters of total income derives from National Insurance, or similar pensions. Separate indices are published for pensioner households.

The main deficiency of the RPI today lies less in its technical derivation than in the uses to which it is conventionally put. Officially, the DE insists that it 'measures prices only: it is not a cost-of-living index' (for, as Kincaid shows, (this volume) the cost of living varies according to the purchasing and consumption patterns of each household). This distinction is rarely sustained in press or political comment; and, to this extent, it is used to support conclusions which it cannot properly bear.

Family expenditure

The annual FES was initiated in the 1950s to permit revision of the weights in the RPI. The survey is currently based on a sample of 10,400 addresses drawn from electoral registers; the response rate is roughly 70 per cent. Detailed results are published annually in the *Family Expenditure Survey Report*, expenditure patterns being broken down by range and source of income, region, and type and size of household.

The reliability of the survey is necessarily weakened by the relatively low response rate: in particular, there is evidence that both the highest and the lowest income groups are under-represented. It is also recognised that, for example, the survey substantially understates expenditure on alcohol and tobacco. Such weaknesses in turn affect the adequacy of the RPI.

Employment

The two principal sources of employment statistics are the *Census of Population* and the *Department of Employment Gazette*. Of these, the former is undoubtedly the most comprehensive, but it is undertaken only once every ten years—and then appears in published form some three to five years later. For most practical purposes, therefore, the annual, quarterly and monthly data published by the DE are much more useful.

The *Census of Population* is based on the self-enumeration principle, and includes in its estimate of employment those persons who declare themselves to be *in work in the week before the Census date*, or to be temporarily absent for reasons such as sickness, holidays, etc. Those in employment are divided on a status basis between the self-employed, managers and four other occupational groups. The Census method undoubtedly results in considerable underestimation of the numbers of part-time workers, seasonal workers, those who work at irregular intervals and unpaid family workers, since many do not qualify, or fail to record themselves, as in employment. Nevertheless the Census does provide the only comprehensive assessment of *occupational* employment, and is thus of particular importance to anyone who wishes to focus on changes in the social structure of the country. It also gives a very detailed breakdown of employment structure by industry, occupation, and local government regions and districts, thus providing a mine of useful information for social scientists, workers and trade unionists about local employment conditions.

The DE uses four separate measures of employment:

1. Employees—all employees insured under the National Insurance Acts;

2. Employees in employment—employees minus the registered unemployed;

3. Civil employment—employees in employment plus employers and the self-employed;

4. Working population—civil employment plus the unemployed plus the armed forces.

Each of these may be useful in different circumstances, and care must be exercised in ensuring that groups such as employers and the armed forces are included or excluded according to the specific needs of the user.

Since 1971, the DE has carried out an annual *Census of Employment*, which is based on returns from employers concerning their employees. It is based on a similar principle to the *Census of*

Population, and hence similarly understates the numbers of employees falling into the categories mentioned above. It includes only employees in paid employment at the Census date, together with employees temporarily absent because of sickness, holidays, strikes, etc., and those who worked in some other day in the Census week. It is particularly prone to understate the number of women workers who work casually or irregularly, and since it is based on PAYE pay points it fails to record those who do not pay tax.

Vacancies and placings

The DE collects statistics monthly on the number of unfilled vacancies notified to local Employment Offices and Careers Offices, and publishes them on an industrial basis. Additionally, the Department publishes a quarterly series of unfilled vacancies notified to Employment Offices on an occupational basis only. The number of successful placings by Employment Offices and Careers Offices is published monthly. However, DE data record only vacancies and placings notified to, and effected by, the Employment Services Agency; vacancies and placings through private employment agencies, small ads, trade journals etc., which account for the majority of job placements, are simply not included. Hence, the official series merely provide a general indication of the trends of supply and demand in the job market.

Unemployment

The numbers of unemployed workers by geographical area and industry are published monthly in the *Department of Employment Gazette*, and an occupational analysis of the unemployed appears quarterly in the same publication. In January and July each year, the *Gazette* also publishes an analysis of the age groups of unemployed persons registered in those months. Of particular interest in relation to the social consequences of unemployment, are the monthly data, also published in the *Gazette*, showing the duration of unemployment amongst different groups of workers.

The principal defect underlying all the DE statistics on unemployment is that they cover only those people actually *registered* as unemployed at the local offices of the Employment Services Agency, and the Careers Offices of local education authorities, on the day of the monthly count, and who are fit and available for work. However, experience over the last decade, in which unemployment rates have been rising, has indicated that many workers fail to register with the ESA, either because they are not entitled to unemployment *benefit* or because they do not wish to claim it, and hence are omitted from the official statistics. This most obviously affects married women who opt not to pay insurance contributions. They may be able to obtain work relatively easily when the economy is buoyant, but may experience long periods of unemployment in slumps and depressions; however, despite the fact that they require work, they fail to register with the DE in very large numbers, and, consequently, the existence of a very substantial pool of unemployment amongst such workers is hidden by the official data. In late 1977 the DE estimated that the undercount of unemployed women was between 150,000 and 200,000. Other categories of unemployed workers who frequently fail to register are young people who do not have the minimum number of stamps to qualify for benefit, retired people who still wish to work, those who have had a claim for benefit disallowed and those whose right to benefit has been exhausted. Some idea of the size of the total underestimation in the official unemployment series can be gained from the contrast between the number of unemployed persons recorded by the 1971 Census (1.4 million), and the official unemployment figure for the month of the Census of 0.8 million.

Young people looking for their first job, and unemployed adult students, have traditionally been recorded separately in the statistics, but the latter group has now been excluded completely from the official series in order to reduce politically embarrassing increases in the unemployment rate during vacation periods. The published figures also exclude workers who are temporarily stopped but who are registered for benefits, since it is assumed that they still have a job to which they will return.

Since 1970, the DE has attempted to provide information on unemployment and unemployment rates amongst 'New Commonwealth' immigrants. This has revealed a consistently worse pattern of unemployment amongst black workers, clearly reflecting the extent of racial discrimination exercised by employers. However, the published figures undoubtedly *underestimate* the extent of black unemployment, since the problems of non-registration discussed above are particularly serious amongst immigrant groups; furthermore, the notion of an unemployment 'rate', when the size of the black labour-force can only be guessed at, is particularly questionable.

Trade union membership

British trade union membership statistics have been collected and published by official agencies since 1892. Historical series covering the number of trade unions, and aggregate membership divided by male and female groups, are to be found in *British Labour Statistics 1892–1963*. Current data are published annually in the *Department of Employment Gazette*, usually in the November edition. The DE data cover 'all organisations of employees which are known to include in their objects that of negotiating with employers with a view to regulating the wages and working conditions of their members'. The application of this qualifying definition is left to the discretion of the DE in conjunction, in recent years, with the Registrar of Trade Unions under the 1971 Industrial Relations Act, and the Certification Officer under the 1974 Trade Union and Labour Relations Act. This has resulted, historically, in two distinct sources of bias in the statistics: on the one hand, the DE and its predecessors have failed to include 'professional' collective organisations such as the British Medical Association, the Royal College of Nursing, the Royal College of Midwives and the Law Society, whose middle-class ethos has led them to eschew the trade union label; on the other hand, a large number of organisations have been included whose commitment to the principles of trade unionism was questionable (such as the staff associations in banking and insurance), or whose negotiating and 'regulatory' activities were very limited (such as the National League for the Blind and Disabled or the Association of Town Clerks). Since the 1971 Industrial Relations Act, the first of these problems has largely disappeared, since many 'professional' bodies saw such advantages in registration under that Act that they overcame their reluctance to be identified with other trade unions and registered as such; this led to their automatic inclusion in the DE series.

The second source of bias has, however, been accentuated in recent years, since the 1971 Act encouraged the establishment and growth of anti-TUC staff associations, staff unions and other non-TUC bodies. The vast majority of such bodies have been included in the DE series, and while the total membership of these organisations remains extremely small relative to aggregate union membership, the *number* of trade unions—always a subject of critical comment in the mass media—is substantially inflated by their inclusion. The DE also publishes a *Directory* which lists all the trade unions included in its series, but provides no information at all on the membership of individual unions—a serious inadequacy where the relative growth of particular organisations is being studied.

An alternative and, in many ways, more satisfactory source of trade union membership data is the *TUC Annual Report*; this provides information on membership for each individual affiliated union, and thus complements the aggregate series provided by the DE. Non-TUC organisations are, of course, excluded, although this may not always be a disadvantage.

Both the DE and the TUC obtain their membership information from the unions themselves, either directly or indirectly, via the Registrar or Certification Officer. This allows considerable scope for variation in the definition of membership adopted by each union. Some include retired and honorary members; some exclude them. Some include members in arrears of up to a year; some strike off members after 16 weeks. Finally, it is worth noting that since power and influence at the TUC are significantly related to membership strength, there is a general tendency to adopt a favourable definition of membership, particularly where strong rivalry exists between organisations.

Industrial disputes

Only seven pages in the *BLSYB* are assigned to industrial disputes, but, of all the official labour statistics, it is probably these which attract the greatest public attention. Information is derived primarily from DE local office managers, supplemented by examination of the press and by reports from employers (in particular, nationalised industries). An analysis of each year's disputes is contained in the January and June issues of the *Gazette* in the following year. The main information published covers the number of disputes, workers 'directly' and 'indirectly' involved at affected establishments, and 'working days lost'. Breakdowns are provided by industry, region, and 'causes' (the classification of which was revised in 1973), size and duration.

The official statistics are incomplete in at least three respects. Some stoppages are simply not reported (the parties involved are under no obligation to do so) and fail to attract official attention. Disputes lasting less than a whole day, or involving less than ten workers, are excluded, unless the total of 'working days lost' exceeds 100. And only disputes relating to 'terms and conditions of employment' are included; thus, a number of important stoppages in recent years (such as the protests against the Industrial Relations Act) do not appear in the statistics.

There are, furthermore, several conceptual problems associated with the statistics. It is not always easy to determine whether or not a particular episode should count as a strike (or lock-out: the official data do not differentiate). The number of workers involved is often a matter of guesswork; while the precise time of beginning and ending of a dispute is not always clear. All these problems are compounded in the formulation of the figure of 'working days lost': a term which is itself seriously misleading, since workers involved in a stoppage might in many cases otherwise be laid off because of production problems or shortages of orders. (Indeed, employers often engineer stoppages in precisely such a situation.) The analysis of 'causes' is likewise unsatisfactory, since the issues involved in a dispute are typically complex and multiple; the published data are merely based on the demands articulated by the official representatives of the workers involved.

Industrial accidents

An indication of the priorities which underlie the compilation of official statistics is the derisory attention devoted to industrial accidents and diseases, in contrast to those topics which primarily concern governments and employers. The subject achieves a single page in the *BLSYB*, whereas wages and earnings take up 100 pages, and employment, unemployment and vacancies receive 180. It is clear that this reflects a general paucity of statistical information on accidents, and an even more serious lack of data on industrial diseases.

Traditionally, the principal source has been the *Annual Reports* of the Chief Inspector of Factories. The Inspectorate is now part of the new Health and Safety Executive, which issues separate reports on Industries and Services (including Railways and Explosives) and Mines and Quarries. The published data are unreliable for two main reasons. First, they cover only *notifiable* accidents: i.e. those involving fatalities, or injuries causing more than three days' loss of earnings. Second, notification is the employer's responsibility, and employers who fear prosecution for maintaining unsafe working conditions have every incentive to avoid reporting notifiable accidents; while the Inspectorate is far too inadequately staffed to police effectively the requirement to notify. Indeed, the Robens Report on *Safety and Health at Work* itself described the official statistics as 'intrinsically unreliable as measures of safety performance'; it quoted DHSS statistics to show that in 1970 there were 822,000 new claims for industrial injury benefit (almost all resulting from reportable accidents), whereas only 470,000 accidents were reported to the Inspectorate.

Labour costs; costs per unit of output; output per person employed

The term 'labour costs' is used in official sources to describe the total costs incurred by employers in the employment transaction. In addition to standard wages and salaries, which are identified as the 'basic' cost element, the following categories are identified as contributing to 'total labour cost': 'non-productive' wages and salaries paid for holidays, sickness, injury and other time off with pay; National Insurance contributions; redundancy payments contributions; employers' liability insurance; superannuation and welfare funds; and training and subsidised services. Recent surveys of labour costs in manufacturing industry were carried out in 1968 and 1973 with information coming uniquely from employer sources. Such statistics fail to make any allowances for the benefits accruing to employers as a consequence of expenditure over and above the 'basic' cost element in the shape, for example, of a healthier, less accident-prone and better trained labour force. They consequently help to build and sustain the pervasive illusion that such costs are unproductive impositions upon employers. They can, however, be seen also as a helpful quantification of some elements of the 'social wage' and are thus of value to shop stewards and negotiators.

'Costs per unit of output' are published by the DE on three different bases. The first is the *index of total domestic incomes per unit of output*, which shows the relationship between the growth of total incomes and the growth of total output. 'Growth' in this context is understood as either positive or negative; and 'total incomes' in this context includes gross profits, rent, income from self-employment and employee incomes, but these items are unfortunately not identified separately, and thus cannot be used to examine the proportions of total costs attributable to capital and labour. The second basis is the *index of labour costs per unit of output*, which shows the relationship between 'total labour cost', as defined above, and total output. The third basis is the *index of wages and salaries per unit of output* which shows the relationship between the growth of employees' earnings and total output.

Notes

1. The differentiation between 'manual' and 'non-manual' employees is extensively applied in the official analyses. This administrative dichotomy is not helpful for an understanding of the labour process: the 'non-manual' category lumps together groups with totally different work situations, authority, income and other advantages, from the managing director to the filing clerk.
2. C. Pond and S. Winyard (p. 21) comment that employers 'are unlikely to be enthusiastic about submitting information which shows them to be paying low (and in some cases illegal) rates of pay'. Conversely, they may also understate top salaries and emoluments.

Sources of Labour Statistics: Official and Unofficial

The most important general source remains the *Department of Employment Gazette*, which has appeared continuously (under various titles) since 1893. Since 1969, the *British Labour Statistics Year Book* has been published annually, roughly eighteen months after the end of the year covered. Data from earlier statistical series are summarised in *British Labour Statistics 1892–1968*. Each *Year Book* contains a brief introductory guide to more specialised sources of official statistics. Also valuable in this respect is the *Guide to Official Statistics*; sources on labour are discussed in ch. 5 of the 1976 edition. An article on 'Recent and forthcoming developments in labour statistics' (*DE Gazette*, April 1973) is also informative. Finally, concerning general sources, it may be noted that some of the series on labour are included in the *Monthly Digest* and *Annual Abstract of Statistics*, and in *Economic Trends*.

International comparisons of labour statistics are extremely hazardous because of variations in methods of collection and categorisation. Sources include: the International Labour Office *Yearbook of Labour Statistics* and the Organisation for Economic Co-operation and Development *Labour Force Statistics*.

There exists no detailed study of the historical development of official labour statistics in Britain. Some information can be found in V. L. Allen (1960). A reasonably full account of the first two decades of compilation is provided by R. Davidson (1972).

Some of the problems of the *NES* as a source on earnings have been discussed in the text above. Additional official sources are the various *Reports* of the National Board for Prices and Incomes, the Office of Manpower Economics and the Review Body on Top Salaries. The Royal Commission on the Distribution of Income and Wealth has produced the most comprehensive recent survey of the dimensions of economic inequality; its first five *Reports* (1975–78) comprise two on the Commission's general terms of reference, one on income from companies and its distribution, one on higher incomes from employment and one on low pay. Useful *unofficial* sources include the various publications of the Labour Research Department; Transport and General Workers' Union (1976); and F. Field (n.d.). A detailed discussion of employment data can be found in N. K. Buxton and D. I. Mackay (1977).

Official strike statistics are critically discussed in R. Hyman (1977), and in M. Silver (1973). Analyses of official data by DE statisticians have appeared in the *Gazette* in February and November 1976, February 1977 and January 1978. A more comprehensive treatment is provided in C. Smith, et. al. (1978).

The 'Robens Committee on Safety and Health at Work' commissioned a study of official accident statistics, and its *Report* includes a chapter containing a number of criticisms. For a far more trenchant analysis, see P. Kinnersly (1973).

One area of information which, somewhat surprisingly, is barely covered in the official statistics is the use of the machinery of labour legislation established in the past few years: covering such matters as redundancy, unfair dismissal, equal pay, sex and race discrimination. A somewhat dated official study of the operation of the Redundancy Payments Act is S. R. Parker et al. (1971); for a critique see R. H. Fryer (1973). The *Annual Reports* of the Advisory, Conciliation and Arbitration Service and the Central Arbitration Committee contain some data; while each June the *Gazette* surveys tribunal hearings on unfair dismissal. Each Tribunal case is recorded at the Central Office of Industrial Tribunals, but no statistical analyses are published by the official agencies. Regular surveys are, however, included in such publications as *Incomes Data Report* and *Industrial Relations Review and Report*. J. Coussins (1976) provides an important discussion of cases affecting women's rights. The Reports of the Equal Opportunities Commission and the Commission for Racial Equality may come to represent a useful source in their respective areas.

A less surprising but far more substantial gap in official provision is the almost total neglect of the *labour process*: the researcher who wishes to document developments in the rate of exploitation, or the intensification of labour, for example, will find little satisfaction from the official statistics. Among more helpful publications are those of the Conference of Socialist Economists (including the journal *Capital and Class*), Counter Information Services and the Labour Research Department.

Bibliography

Allen, V. L., 1960, *Trade Unions and the Government*, London, Longmans.
Buxton, N. K., and Mackay, D. I., 1977, *British Employment Statistics*, Oxford, Blackwell.
Coussins, J., 1976, *The Equality Report*, London, NCCL.
Davidson, R., 1972, 'Llewellyn Smith, the Labour Department and government growth 1886–1909', in G. Sutherland, *Studies in the Growth of Nineteenth Century Government*, London, Routledge & Kegan Paul.
Field, F. (ed.), n.d., *Are Low Wages Inevitable?*, Nottingham, Spokesman Books.
Fryer, R. H., 1973, 'Redundancy, values and public policy', *Industrial Relations Journal*.
Hancock, W. K., and Gowing, M. M., 1949, *British War Economy*, London, HMSO/Longmans.
Hyman, R., 1977, *Strikes*, London, Fontana.
International Labour Office, *Yearbook of Labour Statistics*.
Kinnersly, P., 1973, *The Hazards of Work*, London, Pluto Press.
Organisation for Economic Co-operation and Development, *Labour Force Statistics*.
Parker, S. R., et. al., 1971, *Effects of the Redundancy Payments Act*, London, HMSO.
Pond, C., and Winyard, S., n.d., 'A profile of the low paid', in F. Field, n.d., above.
Report of the Committee on Safety and Health at Work, (Chairman, Lord Robens), 1972, London, HMSO.
Royal Commission on the Distribution of Income and Wealth (Chairman, Lord Diamond) 1975–8, *Reports*, London, HMSO.
Silver, M., 1973, 'Recent British strike trends', *British Journal of Industrial Relations*.
Smith, C. et. al., 1978, *Strikes in Britain*, London, HMSO.
Transport and General Workers' Union, 1976, *Inequality*, Nottingham, Spokesman Books.

Official Statistics:

Advisory, Conciliation and Arbitration Service (ACAS), *Annual Reports*.
Annual Abstract of Statistics and *Monthly Digest of Statistics*.
British Labour Statistics, 1892–1968.
British Labour Statistics Yearbook.
Central Arbitration Committee, *Annual Reports*.
Department of Employment Gazette (monthly).

Economic Trends.
Guide to Official Statistics.
Incomes Data Report.
Industrial Relations Review and Report.
National Board for Prices and Incomes, *Reports.*
National Earnings Survey.
Office of Manpower Economics, *Reports.*
Review Body on Top Salaries, *Reports.*

16.   *Lesley Doyal*

A Matter of Life and Death: Medicine, Health and Statistics

1. The medical model

When we think about sickness and health, we tend to assume that they are not difficult to define—that we are either healthy or we have unpleasant symptoms and are therefore sick. If we are sick, we tend to assume that it is a chance occurrence rather than something produced by the society in which we live. Finally, we assume that if we do become sick, medical science is always the answer to our problems.

These issues, however, are much more complicated than such assumptions allow for. In different societies there are very different conceptions of health and illness, and very different ways of dealing with sickness.[1] Our own views of health, as well as any relevant data we may examine, have been constructed within the terms of a particular medical tradition (Kelman, 1975). In the developed world, the tradition which dominates both the theory and practice of health care is that of western scientific medicine (Wightman, 1971; Foucault, 1973; Sigerist, 1970). The historical development of this approach is important in understanding both the nature of contemporary medicine, and also the nature and content of statistics relating to health, illness and medical care.

What we know as western scientific medicine has its origins in the empirical science which developed during and after the Renaissance. Science was no longer to be concerned with understanding the *essence* of the natural world, but rather with understanding regular and recurring sequences of events in a quantitative and generalisable way. It was believed that this would make possible the control of nature by making accurate predictions geared to these generalisations. In other words, the new science increasingly equated an understanding of the natural world with the capacity to control it. However, the development of this new science did not take place in a social or economic vacuum. We have to understand the general development of science, as well as the specific development of medicine, as both shaping and also being

238 *Demystifying Social Statistics*

shaped by the emergence and development of capitalist society (Easlea, 1973; and Young in this volume). In the area of medicine, the 'new science' began for the first time to map out in detail the internal workings of the human body, and this formed the basis for the (much) later development of modern technological medicine. However, these early attempts at understanding the human body were founded upon a particular view of the nature of human beings, and of their sickness and health.

The most fundamental characteristic of this scientific medical model lies in its mechanistic approach to human beings. In its historical origins, medicine followed the more general pattern of Renaissance science in analysing phenomena as a set of mechanically related parts rather than as an organically integrated whole. This has continued to form the basis for medical thought and practice, so that the patient is viewed as a machine, with the role of the doctor being to mend the machine, thereby restoring the patient to 'normal' functioning (McKeown, 1971). It is important to realise that this model implies that individual malfunctions can be treated separately from the rest of the system and, in particular, separately from the physical and social environment of which the sick individual is a part. An extension of the mechanistic model is the assumption that it is possible to separate mind and body. In medicine this had the consequence that although physical and psychological illnesses were to be treated as separate entities, ultimately psychological illnesses would be assumed to be comprehensible within the same terms as physical ones. This helps to explain the longstanding search for an organic basis for psychiatric illness. Even where a non-organic basis *is* accepted, psychiatric problems are always treated primarily as *illness* rather than as a (possibly) reasonable response to a particular individual's own life situation (P. Brown, 1973). In addition, mechanistic definitions of both physical and psychological illness and health involve an emphasis on supposedly 'objective' rather than 'subjective' criteria for illness. Hence doctors are reluctant to regard as 'really' ill someone who just 'feels' ill. Such feelings need to be corroborated by the presence of observable or testable symptoms which will then enable the *doctor* to pronounce upon the patient's problem. Basically, then, within the western medical paradigm, disease is regarded as a clearly observable pathological abnormality of function, while 'health' is usually defined simply in terms of the *absence* of such pathology.[2] As a consequence, statistics on 'health' are really statistics on 'ill-health'. We can use them to find out how many people are *ill* (in a medical sense) but they cannot tell us how many people are in a state of 'well-being' in any more positive sense. There is a close relationship between this functional definition of health, and the atomised individualistic world-view which accompanied the rise of a capitalist mode of production (Kelman, 1975).

The medicine which is practised on the basis of this mechanistic model has emphasised the importance of cure at the expense of prevention.[3] Thus the essence of medical activity is assumed to be the intervention of doctors to cure an illness once it has developed, rather than the prevention of disease before it occurs. After the identification of germs in the late nineteenth century, medical practice concentrated increasingly on cure on an individualised basis. Public health measures, along with a generally improved standard of living, had drastically reduced mortality rates from infectious diseases, and this left medicine apparently free to concentrate on ever smaller and more specialised aspects of the functioning of the human body. Built into this increasing fragmentation and specialisation was an implicit acceptance that the causes of disease were to be found either in natural enemies in the environment, such as germs or viruses, or more often in defects in the individual's biological mechanism, as is often argued in the case of diabetes, cancer or schizophrenia. During the twentieth century, then, medicine has become less and less concerned with the environmental determinants of health and well-being, and has concentrated instead on high technology curative techniques.[4] It is not, of course, being suggested that specialisation has not had important positive consequences. The adoption of a mechanistic paradigm made possible those aspects of medicine which have been genuinely successful in preventing or curing disease (e.g. vaccination, antisepsis, anaesthesia and antibiotics), as well as making possible the relief of symptoms where the disease is incurable, and providing new means of controlling fertility. At the same time, however, the adoption of such a research programme strictly limited the nature and boundaries of the medical task. It is this limitation which we see reflected in medical statistics.

2. The state and health

A major factor in the development of modern medicine has been the tremendous expansion of the role of the state in organising health care in most advanced capitalist countries. In Britain, this process of state intervention culminated in the creation of the National Health Service (NHS), which came into operation in 1948. The introduction of 'socialised medicine' is often defined simply as a gain achieved through working-class struggle. Clearly it was a gain, and its progressive elements must be defended. However, we must also recognise the implications of sickness and health for the wider functioning of the capitalist system. The labour power which the worker sells is an essential input into the capitalist production process, and hence it becomes a matter of concern for capital as a whole to maintain the physical health of the labour force at a satisfactory level. As a consequence, it is workers and potential workers who receive rather better standards of health care than do, for example, the old or the chronically sick. However, as well as being maintained at a reasonable level of physical efficiency, it is also important that the current labour force should reproduce itself by providing the next generation of workers (but not too many of them!). To the extent, therefore, that medicine has now developed areas of effective reproductive technology (obstetrics, contraception, abortion) it has become an increasingly important agent in the effective physical reproduction of labour power. Finally, and probably most importantly, it is vital for capitalism that the labour force should be reproduced not just at the level of physical fitness and in adequate numbers, but also at an ideological level. This involves, on the one hand, socialisation processes whereby individuals are prepared in a variety of ways for the part they will play in the social division of labour, and for the rewards they will receive for so doing. On the other hand, it involves the legitimation of the existing mode of social and economic organisation, so that it appears in general terms to be the only right and possible way in which society *could* be organised. In the context of monopoly capitalism, one of the most important of these agencies of legitimation and socialisation is the 'welfare state' which, of course, includes the provision of socialised medicine. Medical statistics will therefore inevitably reflect this aspect of state activity to a greater or lesser extent.[6]

3. Statistics on medicine and health

It would be extremely interesting to look in more detail here at the *history* of medical statistics. For example, it would be especially useful to look at the development of 'political arithmetic' in the seventeenth and eighteenth centuries, or at the role of private insurance companies in ensuring the production of accurate mortality statistics and life tables during the nineteenth and early twentieth centuries (Cullen, 1975; Flinn, 1965; Gilbert, 1966). Here, however, we shall concentrate on those statistics generated either within the National Health Service itself, or as part of the wider system of production of official statistics. The major sources of such information are the annual *Health and Personal Social Service Statistics for England* (HPSSS-E), the *Health and Personal Social Service Statistics for Wales* (HPSSS—W) and the *Scottish Health Statistics* (SHS). Other relevant material is spread very broadly throughout other sources of official statistics and can most easily be found by using the *Guide to Official Statistics* (no. 2, 1978), produced by the Central Statistical Office (CSO). Finally, much of this material on medicine and health is summarised in an accessible form in the annual report *On the State of the Public Health*, and in the section on health in the annual publication *Social Trends* (CSO).

When we examine these statistics we are not seeing an objective representation of the physical and psychological well-being of the population, or even of their pattern of health care. What we see is a set of data which has been produced within the terms of the western scientific medical model and which reflects the particular concerns of the state as the major provider of health care. However, we need to examine these sources in more detail in order to decide what we *can* learn from them, as well as deciding what their limitations are as information useful in developing a broad understanding of the nature of health, illness and medical care in Britain.

4. Data on health and illness

The first point to be made here is the quite outstanding *lack* of available information on health and illness. We know very little indeed about the health problems of the British people. Although a survey of sickness was carried out from 1944 to 1952, this was discontinued, so that no continuous national survey of health and illness is now available.[7] This makes it very difficult either to assess historical trends in health and illness, or to obtain any reliable assessment of contemporary problems of ill-health. This lack of statistics on general well-being or illness reflects the narrow orientation of existing health statistics. We can only *infer* levels of health and illness from statistics produced for other purposes. These fall into four major categories: 1. mortality statistics; 2. statistics on the utilisation of the NHS; 3.sickness absence statistics; and 4. information collected from the *General Household Survey*. Let us examine each of these in turn.

Mortality statistics are regarded as an essential element in any set of national statistics and are therefore produced on a regular and reliable basis.[8] It is often useful to compare life expectancy data,[9] infant mortality rates,[10] or major *causes* of death[11] between classes,[12] both over time and between countries.[13] Such comparisons may be extremely important in indicating differences in social and economic conditions. Infant mortality rates in particular are regarded as being among the most sensitive indicators of the material conditions of a given population. However, mortality statistics are obviously only crude indicators of the state of health of those people who remain alive. Although there are diseases where high levels of morbidity are always associated with high levels of mortality, there are many other diseases where chronic and debilitating symptoms are not associated with high levels of mortality.

In the case of *statistics on the use of health facilities*, we are really dealing with two sets of data. First, there are *ad hoc* studies of the use of particular facilities (e.g. General Practitioner morbidity studies)[14] and, second, there are various sets of statistics generated within the NHS bureaucracy (e.g. Hospital In-Patient Enquiry—HIPE).[15] But such sources suffer from the basic problem that they only deal with the people who come into contact with the medical care system, which obviously limits their use as indicators of general patterns of morbidity. From these statistics we will know that certain people seek medical care for certain *specific* medical conditions, but we will know nothing about those cases of ill health which were not brought to the attention of a doctor and were therefore not officially recorded.[16]

In addition, of course, we cannot assess the relationship between the patient's *actual* condition, and the way in which the doctor has labelled it. Doctors have to find some definition within the bounds of scientific medicine to categorise the condition of the patient in front of them. Obviously the problem is less significant in the case of a broken leg, for example. But as we move away from straightforward physical disabilities, it becomes increasingly difficult to express in a simple diagnostic category the complex interaction between mind, body and environment which constitutes most illnesses. This definitional problem is at its most acute when we arrive at the end of the 'illness' spectrum labelled 'mental illness'. It is not possible to enter here into the complex discussion about the precise nature and causes of mental illness, and whether or not it even exists as a meaningful phenomenon. However, what *is* clear is that it is extremely difficult to make sense of the 'reality' behind the data on mental disorders, as they appear under the *International Classification of Diseases* (ICD).[17] Much critical work exists on the problem of psychiatric classification and diagnosis, documenting at its most simple level the extreme variability in diagnosis between different psychiatrists confronted with the same patients. Such work throws into doubt the utility of statistics, generated in terms of standard psychiatric diagnostic categories, for telling us very much about the patients concerned (P. Brown, 1973; Clare, 1976; Broverman et al., 1972). What the statistics *do* show, however, is the ever-increasing number of people receiving psychiatric treatment, and in particular, the numbers actually entering hospital, and how long they stay.[18]

Both the mortality statistics, and statistics on the utilisation of the NHS, suffer from additional disadvantages when one is attempting to make sense of the *distribution* of standards of health and illness in the population. Such statistics are usually presented only in terms of a very limited number of categories, and these are primarily of a bureaucratic rather than analytical significance. The major classifications are into age, sex and diagnostic categories, and—in the case of the HIPE and the *Mental Health Enquiry*—the hospital or health region. The categories which are most conspicuously absent are those of social class and any socio-economic classification of particular geographical areas. The earliest morbidity study of General Practice (1955–56) carried out under the NHS *did* include a social class breakdown of reasons for visits to the GP, and this provided some extremely useful information on class patterns of morbidity. However, the second morbidity study, published in 1974, did not include such a breakdown, ostensibly because of a parliamentary intervention in 1970 by Enoch Powell (Powell, 1970), who claimed that this would violate personal rights! Neither the HIPE nor the *Psychiatric Inpatient Study* are broken down according to class or race, so that we know very little indeed about the social class patterns of particular diseases, or of health and illness in general. One of the only regular sources of such information comes from the *Registrar General's Decennial Supplement* which gives a social class breakdown of the causes of death.[19] Information from this source demonstrates that disease processes are not randomly distributed. Both the 1961 and 1971 Supplements show that the differences in death rates *between* social classes have not decreased since the early 1930s, and that the most common health problems which contribute to these differential death rates include bronchitis, accidents (vehicles and outside of home), TB, pneumonia, cancer of the stomach, and influenza (Preston, 1974). This continuing differential in life expectancy rates and causes of death between social classes indicates strongly the involvement of socio-economic factors in producing particular patterns of disease. However, the limitations of the statistics make further investigation of the precise mechanisms involved extremely difficult.[20]

A third source of data on the health status of the population comes from the *statistics on sickness absence from work* produced by the DHSS.[21] These concern the payment of sickness benefit and are regularly produced since they are of obvious bureaucratic value. However, as a source of information on the health of the general population, they are again very limited. First, while they cover almost all men of working age (but, *not*, of course, the unemployed) they exclude all women not involved in full-time paid employment, as well as the majority of working women who until the Social Security Act of 1975 were able to opt out of the social security system by paying a 'married woman's stamp'.[22] In addition, they of course exclude by definition all those above and below working age. Furthermore, sickness absence statistics do not cover any periods of sickness absence which last less than three days, since such short absences do not entitle the patient to sickness benefit.

The picture becomes even more bleak when it is realised that any attempt to make sense of sickness absence statistics faces more fundamental problems than that of limited coverage. In Britain (as elsewhere in both Western and Eastern Europe) rates of sickness absence have been rising continually from the 1960s onwards. This is difficult to explain since the rates of certain diseases (such as TB, kidney infections and gastric and duodenal ulcers) which previously caused a large volume of sickness absence have now declined. However, others such as 'sprains and strains' and 'nervous debility and headache' have increased. Thus the 'harder', more objectively discernible causes of sickness absence have been replaced by more subjective ones. It is the presence of these new 'illnesses' which needs to be explained (Whitehead, 1971; Taylor, 1974). However, the data available to make such an explanation are very limited. The most important question which cannot be answered using these data concerns the relationship between changes in the nature of work and the recorded rise in sickness absence. It can be argued that these new illnesses are 'excuses' which the worker consciously uses to avoid an unpleasant work situation. This provides substance to the familiar argument that increases in such behaviour are causally related to the social security system providing sickness benefit. On the other hand, it can be suggested that work has now become for many not only physically, but also psychologically, a dangerous place to be. In this case, the increasing demands of boring, repetitive work produced at higher and higher speeds, and on unnatural shift systems, would be viewed as responsible for an increasing number of stress symptoms (Navarro, 1976b).

It is quite possible that both these explanations are correct. However, the subjective feelings of the individual can only be expressed in terms of the quantitative summation of the diagnostic categories in which they have been placed by the doctor. In order not to attend work temporarily, and still receive sickness benefit, it is necessary to 'be ill', and ill in a form certified by a doctor. Hence, the only data on this trend towards staying away from work are expressed in medical terms on 'sick notes'. So the significance in real terms of what is an important trend, is difficult to assess.

Another problem arises, however, when we try to use sickness absence statistics to compare the days lost through illness by different social classes. Obviously, different occupational groups will have different pressures acting on them when they decide whether or not to report sick. In particular, middle-class workers will tend to have more generous arrangements during illness, so that they would be more likely to take time off. They may also be less willing to 'tolerate' physical and psychological discomfort. This would structure the statistics in such a way as to represent a *higher* level of sickness for middle-class respondents than for working-class ones. However, it may also be the case that working class patients will be *more* likely to report sick because of the objectively less desirable—and possibly more physically demanding—nature of their work situation. We know that those in unskilled and semi-skilled jobs are much more likely to be absent from work through illness than those in professional and managerial jobs. Precisely how closely this reflects levels of morbidity in the general population is, again, very difficult to assess.

The final source from which we can infer levels of health and illness in the population is the *General Household Survey* (GHS), undertaken continuously for the DHSS by the Office of Population Censuses and Surveys (Mapes and Dajda, 1976). The GHS asks several questions relating to morbidity, including questions concerning acute sickness, long-standing illness and days off work. Long-standing illness is established by asking respondents whether or not they suffer from any illness which limits their activities compared with people of their own age. Alternatively, acute sickness is defined as sickness or injury which results in restrictions on normal activity at any time during the two weeks before interview. Data obtained from such a survey have the limitations of any survey data. In particular, they underestimate problems such as cancer or mental illness.[23] However, assessing morbidity levels on the basis of the GHS data clearly avoids the more serious problems encountered in the use of health utilisation and sickness absence statistics—in that respondents are themselves asked about their health. For this reason, it can probably be regarded as the least unsatisfactory estimate of the state of health of the population. The utility of the GHS data is enhanced by the fact that it is broken down into socio-economic groups. In broad terms the GHS data conforms with the general pattern of data provided by other sources of information, in that people in the lower socio-economic groups are more likely to die at an early age and are much more likely to suffer from acute or long-standing illness. However, the GHS, like other sources, gives us very little help indeed in trying to understand precisely *how* this is brought about.

5. Data on health care

Some of the data on the utilisation of the Health Service has been examined above in an attempt to assess its value as a source of data on general morbidity in the population. Here it will be examined in its own terms in order to see how effective it is as a direct source of information on the operation of the NHS. Again, the first point which must be emphasised is how very limited the data is. In particular, very little routine information is produced on general practice or other aspects of primary medical care. This is most significant when it is realised that approximately 90 per cent of medical encounters take place in this setting.

The main statistics available on the hospital sector are the HIPE and the *Psychiatric Inpatient Enquiry*. To be sure, these statistics are of bureaucratic interest to the NHS, giving information, for example, on mean and median duration of stay, estimated total number of discharges, and so on.[24] However, we have already seen that they are of limited value in assessing morbidity in the population. In addition, they add nothing to the very important debate about the differential use made of the NHS by working-class and middle-class patients (or indeed by different ethnic groups). This is a debate with a long history, which has had to be conducted in the absence of any national and continuous set of statistics on the utilisation of health care broken down by social class (Tudor Hart, 1975; Townsend, 1974; Cartwright and O'Brien, 1976). The nearest equivalent category employed by the DHSS in the presentation of data is the region. We know that there are regional differences in resource allocation and utilisation, but we know very little about how these differences relate to rates of allocation and utilisation in areas of different socio-economic composition. One particular problem is that the health regions are so large that statistics presented by region will conceal very large intra-regional differences.[25]

Recent independent studies have shown that these inter-area differences in medical resources are closely related to the social class composition of the areas. NHS facilities (both hospital and community based) are positively correlated with the proportion of Social Classes I and II in the area (Noyce, Snaith and Trickey, 1974). But this cannot be shown when data are presented on a purely regional basis. Hence, as Townsend has commented, 'the discussion of inequalities between regions and areas is too often sealed off from discussion of the underlying inequalities of class, income and housing and living conditions.' (Townsend, 1974.)

So far as the actual medical care provided by the NHS is concerned, statistics are available which, as we have seen, provide an 'accounting' of how many items of work are performed.[26] However, this provides little data about the patients on whom the work is done (see above); about the health workers who perform the work; or, very importantly, about the quality or therapeutic effectiveness of the work done. If we look first at the information available on health workers, we find that the different grades of worker are treated very differently in the production of statistics.[27] There is, relatively speaking, a large amount of information on doctors. The HPSSS—E includes 16 tables on doctors, providing an analysis according to factors such as grade, specialism, country of birth, type of contract, age and sex, and for GPs, the size and type of practice. However, as one moves down the NHS staff hierarchy, less and less information becomes available, with manual workers at the bottom being the most invisible. For instance, it has recently become a matter of concern to evaluate the situation of immigrant workers within the NHS. While we know the numbers of immigrant doctors, we know almost nothing about the obviously large number of immigrants among NHS manual workers—not even how many there are. All ancillary workers (of whom there are approximately 225,000 in NHS hospitals, compared with 25,000 doctors) are given only *one* table in the Health and Personal Social Services Statistics, and the data are presented only in terms of numbers in each occupation, with no class, sex or racial breakdown.[28]

So far as medical practice itself is concerned, the myth of 'clinical freedom' and the mystification of medical knowledge, have been influential in creating a situation where the NHS has taken almost no responsibility either for the quality of work of individual doctors, or for the monitoring of particular clinical processes. Doctors have always demanded the right to police their own practice, with the consequence that few doctors have their medical (as opposed to their sexual) activities examined at all. In the case of medical techniques and procedures, the jealous guarding by doctors of their medical knowledge, as well as the hierarchical organisation of the profession, have ensured that the monitoring and critical feedback of medical practice have again been left to doctors themselves. This lack of outside accountability means that we have no easily accessible data on the quality of medicine within the NHS or on the efficacy of specific (possibly very expensive) medical techniques. This issue has assumed greater significance in recent years, with the rapid expansion of high technology medicine. The NHS spends a very high proportion of its budget on acute, technological medicine, compared to its expenditure on the primary care sector.[29] It is only recently that a few doctors (and others) have begun to submit certain taken-for-granted techniques to critical analysis (Powles, 1973; Illich, 1975). These critiques have apparently stemmed from two sources—the financial crisis in the NHS, and more general disillusionment with the efficacy of high technology curative medicine. Two examples of techniques which have come under critical scrutiny have been 'intensive care' in cases of coronary heart disease (Cochrane, 1972), and the 'active management' of women in labour, in particular induced births (Richards, 1975; Chard and Richards, 1977).

The failure of the NHS to evaluate the content of medical practice (statistically or otherwise) is a necessary condition for the interests of both consultants and pharmaceutical and medical equipment manufacturers to continue to have greater priority than the general health of patients. Clearly the practice of the NHS is dominated in the final analysis by capitalist interests, since it is part of a capitalist social formation.[30] This influence is often indirect, but with the pharmaceutical and medical equipment industry and the private health sector, the influence is rather more direct and requires detailed examination. Not surprisingly, the official NHS statistics provide very little data on these activities.[31]

6. Conclusion

We have seen then that in Britain the information available on both health and illness, as well as medical care, is extremely limited. It reflects the functional orientation of western scientific medicine, which is concerned not with the physical and mental well-being of the whole person in any qualitative and holistic sense, but rather with mending broken people so that they can return to their tasks, in many instances simply to be broken again. In addition, the way the statistics are constructed means that it becomes extremely difficult to assess the social, economic and environmental causes of ill health.[32] Medicine deals with disease which has already occurred, and prevention is more or less limited to scientific techniques such as vaccination.[33] However, evidence is accumulating that a vast amount of the current burden of disease in advanced capitalist societies is a direct or indirect consequence of their mode of social and economic organisation. It is evidence on this, above all, which must be produced if statistics on health and illness are to play a part in developing that critical awareness of the nature of capitalism, from which a radically transformed and 'healthier' society can be created.

Notes

1. The anthropology of medicine is a fast-developing area of study. For a recent collection of readings in this field see: Loudon (ed.), (1976).
2. The World Health Organisation employs a *positive* definition of health which is often cited with approval. It defines health as: 'a state of complete physical, mental and social well-being, and not merely the absence of disease or infirmity'. (WHO Constitution Basic Documents, 1965). However, in the context of most Western medical practice such a definition is purely rhetorical.
3. This emphasis on cure rather than prevention is not simply inherent in a particular medical model, but reflects the structural limitations which exist in capitalist society on any attempt at truly preventive medicine.
4. For a critique of these developments see Powles (1973).
5. For a useful discussion of the relationship between theories of the state and the state take-over of health-care, see V. Navarro (1976).
6. See Note 7 on *choice* of data for publication. Clearly this section in particular deals with very complex questions in an extremely over-simplified way. For a more detailed exposition, see: V. Navarro (1977); L. Doyal (forthcoming).
7. Continuous statistics *are* available on *specific* health problems, namely cancer, congenital abnormalities and infectious diseases. Information on all of these is available in the HPSSS—E, HPSSS—W and also in the SHS. For more details on additional sources see the relevant sections in the *Guide to Official Statistics*. Statistics are also available on abortion, the most detailed source being the Registrar General's *Statistical Review of England and Wales, Supplement on Abortion*.

It is perhaps important here to distinguish between data which are *collected* and data which are *published*. Many more data are collected than are made available, and some of this additional material can be obtained on request from the DHSS. It is interesting to consider not only the question of which criteria guide the collection of data, but also which criteria guide the choice of data for *publication*.
8. Mortality statistics have been provided for each calendar year in the Registrar General's *Statistical Review of England and Wales* (two years in arrears). However, since 1975 this series has been discontinued and two smaller volumes now provide basic mortality data—*Mortality Statistics (Series DH1)* and *Mortality Statistics: area (Series DH5)*, both from OPCS. For more detailed information on sources, see the *Guide to Official Statistics*.

Mortality statistics are subject to particular technical problems in their collection and analysis, especially regarding *causes* of death. For a useful discussion of these problems see M. Alderson (1974). Also of interest is the *Report of the Work of the Committee on Death Certification and Coroners*, 1971.

At periodic intervals, what is often an illuminating report on the causes of maternal mortality is published. The most recent of these is the DHSS Report on Health and Social Subjects no. 11, 1975.

9. From 1838 up to 1975, yearly lifetables were produced in Part Two of the *Statistical Review for England and Wales*, showing the expectation of life at birth and age 15 years, 45 years and 65 years. These statistics have been available *since* 1975 in the annual OPCS *Mortality Statistics* (Series DH1). Relevant statistics are also to be found in HPSSS—E, HPSSS—W, and SHS. The *Registrar General's Decennial Supplement for England and Wales: Life Tables* is the most detailed (though obviously infrequent) source of such information.

10. Infant mortality statistics were published up to 1975 in the *Registrar General's Statistical Reviews for England and Wales* and for *Scotland*. It is worth noting that while the Statistical Review for England and Wales does *not* present this data on a class basis, the Scottish Statistical Review does do so. See also: *Infant Mortality in Scotland* (Scottish Health Service Studies no. 16) 1971. Since 1975, infant mortality data have been available in the OPCS annual volume *Mortality Statistics: Children (Series DH3)*.

A recent OPCS volume analyses the *causes* of children's deaths by social class: OPCS Studies on Medical and Population Subjects No. 31, by A. M. Adelstein and G. C. White (HMSO 1976).

11. Deaths by cause are analysed according to the *International Statistical Classification of Diseases (ICD)*. Until 1975 these statistics were available in the *Registrar General's Statistical Review for England and Wales*. They are now to be found in the annual OPCS publications *Mortality Statistics: Causes (Series DH2)* and *Mortality Statistics: Accidents and Violence (Series DH4)*.

12. At several points in this chapter the idea of class differences in health or in health care is introduced. The concept of 'class' is being used here not in a strictly marxist sense, but in a sociological/descriptive sense. Clearly there is no adequate theoretical basis to the Registrar General's Classification, *but* comparison of indices such as mortality rates, or psychiatric in-patient rates between socio-economic groups, gives us *extremely* important insights into certain aspects of how capitalism operates. See Theo Nichols' article in this volume, for a discussion of 'class' in official statistics.

13. Comparing health indices between countries is notoriously difficult. However, the main data sources for such comparisons are the various publications of the World Health Organisation. Their annual publication, *World Health Statistics*, is available in three volumes, of which vol. I, *Vital Statistics and Causes of Death*, is perhaps the most generally useful.

Clearly it is comparisons between developed and underdeveloped countries which are the most vivid but also the most difficult methodologically: see Doyal and Pennell (1976). International comparisons of various vital statistics are given in *On the State of the Public Health* and also in *Social Trends*.

14. 1955–56 Study: General Register Office Studies on Medical and Population Subjects no. 14, *Morbidity Statistics from General Practice* (vols I and II), HMSO, 1958, and 1960.

1970–1971 Study: OPCS Studies on Medical and Population Subjects no. 26, *Morbidity Statistics from General Practice, Second. National Study, 1970–1971*, HMSO, 1974. For a comparison of these two studies see: Crombie, Pinsent, Lambert and Birch (1975).

15. For details of all these sources see Alderson (1974) and also *Guide to Official*

Statistics. See especially HPSSS—E, HPSSS—W and SHS. Data on non-psychiatric hospital in-patients are contained in the HIPE and also in the *Scottish Hospital Statistics.*

16. In fact, we have evidence to show that the volume of illness brought to doctors' attention is an extremely small proportion of the actual volume of illness in a given population. For a discussion of this so-called 'iceberg effect', see R. G. S. Brown (1973), and Israel and Teeling-Smith (1967).

17. For example, using this I.C.D. the *Second General Practice Morbidity Study* presents data on the psychiatric part of GP caseloads, broken down into 24 diagnostic categories including anxiety neurosis, hysterical neurosis, phobic neurosis, obsessive-compulsive neurosis, depressive neurosis, *plus* 'other and unspecified neuroses'.

18. Statistics on psychiatric in-patients are available in HPSSS—E, HPSSS—W and SHS, as well as in the regular publications which are based on the Mental Health Enquiry. These are *Psychiatric Hospitals in England and Wales* and *Facilities and Services of Psychiatric Hospitals in England and Wales.* For useful occasional sources, see: *Guide to Official Statistics.*

19. Registrar General's *Decennial Supplement for England and Wales: Occupational Mortality Tables* (HMSO). The first publication in this series appeared in 1855, and since then tables have appeared at roughly ten-yearly intervals (except for a gap during the Second World War). It is therefore useful as a basis for comparing causes of death in different occupational groups over an historical period. The most recent volume appeared in 1977.

20. The organisation of the statistics makes it particularly difficult to deal with the class differences in disease patterns in *women*, since married women are generally classified by their husband's occupation. For an interesting attempt to explain *one* of the reasons for this class differential, see Wilkinson (1976).

21. Data on recipients of sickness benefit are given in HPSSS—E, the *Scottish Abstract of Statistics* and the *Digest of Welsh Statistics.* They are also to be found in more detail in the annual *Social Security Statistics.*

22. From April 1977, women who were *already* paying the smaller contribution were able to continue to do so. But women who married or entered the labour force after April 1977 had to pay the same amount as men.

23. As we have seen, sickness absence from work will also be influenced by class-related factors (see previous paragraph).

24. The essentially bureaucratic nature of the statistics is stunningly demonstrated by the fact that 'deaths and discharges' appear as a single category. Obviously, it matters little to the system which category they are in, but it is a matter of major concern to the patient! Also, these statistics are concerned only with in-patients, so that it is difficult to obtain adequate information on out-patient treatment.

25. In England there are 14 Health Regions and 90 Area Health Authorities. See Buxton and Klein (1975).

26. The most detailed information available is on work done by those workers who are paid for each item they perform—e.g. pharmacists, dentists—since such information is *required* for bureaucratic purposes.

27. Information on health workers is mainly contained in the HPSS—E, HPSS—W and SHS. For *occasional* sources see *Guide to Official Statistics.*

28. Although no *regular* data are available, there is one source of information (though out of date)—*Pay and Conditions of Service of Ancillary Workers in the NHS,* N.B.P.I. Report no. 166, April 1971, Cmnd. 4644. For a compilation of the existing data on the position of immigrant workers in the NHS see Department of Employment (1976).

29. Useful data are available in the *Annual Abstract of Statistics* and in . *National Income*

252   *Demystifying Social Statistics*

and Expenditure which make it possible to compare health expenditure with other components of public spending.

Information on the relative proportions of NHS expenditure going to different sectors of the NHS can be obtained from HPSSS—E, HPSSS—W and SHS, as well as information on how the NHS is financed.

Data on priorities in medical research can be obtained from the *Annual Report of the Medical Research Council*.

30. Again this point is rather oversimplified. See Navarro (1977) and Doyal (forthcoming).

31. For expenditure on pharmaceuticals within the NHS see HPSSS—E, HPSSS—W and SHS. The most detailed official examination of the activities of the drug industry is *The Report of the Committee of Enquiry into the Relationship of the Pharmaceutical Industry with the NHS in 1965-67*, London, HMSO, 1967.

For data on private practice within the NHS see: *The Fourth Report of the House of Commons Expenditure Committee on NHS Facilities for Private Patients*, London, HMSO, 1972. Also, see Lee Donaldson Associates, *UK Private Medical Care (Provident Schemes/Statistics)*, (Annual report prepared for DHSS).

32. The lack of adequate data on industrial accidents and industrial disease is obviously a particularly salient example, but this is a much wider problem than just the limitations of data on the workplace. It reflects the narrow focus of epidemiology, which is itself governed by broader economic and social considerations.

For official data on industrial accidents and disease see: *Department of Employment Gazette, British Labour Statistics: Year Book, Digest of Pneumoconiosis Statistics, Social Security Statistics* and *On the State of the Public Health*. See also Kinnersly (1973); and Hyman and Price, in this volume.

33. Although there has recently been an apparent swing towards prevention, this has concentrated on *persuading* people to change their life styles—in particular to stop smoking and drinking, and to take more exercise. This trend also needs to be understood as part of the campaign to legitimate expenditure cuts and falling standards in the NHS, as well as a means of obscuring the social and economic causes of ill-health. See: DHSS *Prevention and Health, Everybody's Business: a Reassessment of Personal and Public Health*, London, HMSO, 1976, and also DHSS *Prevention and Health* (1977).

Bibliography

Alderson, M., 1974, 'Central government routine health statistics', in W. F. Maunder (ed.), *Reviews of UK Statistical Sources Vol. II*, London, Heinemann and RSS/SSRC.

Braxter, M., 1976, 'Social class and health inequalities', in C. O. Carter and J. Peel (eds.), *Equalities and Inequalities in Health*, London, Academic Press.

Brotherston, J., 1976, 'The Galton Lecture, 1975. Inequality: is it inevitable?', in C. O. Carter and J. Peel (eds.), *Equalities and Inequalities in Health*, London, Academic Press.

Broverman, I., et. al., 1972, 'Sex role stereotypes and clinical judgements in mental health', in J. Bardwick (ed.), *Readings on the Psychology of Women*, New York, Harper and Row.

Brown, P., 1973, *Radical Psychology*, New York, Harper and Row.

Brown, R. G. S., 1973, *The Changing National Health Service*, London, Routledge & Kegan Paul.

Buxton, M. J., and Klein, R., 1975, 'Distribution of hospital provision: policy themes and resource variations', *British Medical Journal*, 8 February.

Cartwright, A., and O'Brien, M., 1976, 'Social class variations in health care', in M. Stacey (ed.), *The Sociology of the National Health Service*, Sociological Review Monograph no. 22, University of Keele.

Chalmers, B., et. al., 1976, 'Obstetric practice and outcome of pregnancy in Cardiff residents 1965–73', *British Medical Journal*, i, pp. 735–38.

Chard, T., and Richards, M. (eds.), 1977, *Benefits and Hazards of the New Obstetrics*, London, Heinemann.

Clare, A., 1976, *Psychiatry in Dissent*, London, Tavistock.

Cochrane, A., 1972, *Effectiveness and Efficiency: Random Reflections on Health Services*, Nuffield Provincial Hospitals Trust.

CSO, 1978, *Guide to Official Statistics*, no. 2, London, HMSO.

Crombie, D. C., Pinsent, R. J. F. H., Lambert, P. M., and Birch, D., 1975, 'Comparison of the first and second national morbidity surveys', *Journal of the Royal College of General Practitioners*, vol. 25, pp. 874–78.

Cullen, M. J., 1975, *The Statistical Movement in Early Victorian Britain, The Foundations of Empirical Research*, Sussex, Harvester Press.

Department of Employment, 1976, *The Role of Immigrants in the Labour Market: a Project Report by the Unit for Manpower Studies*, London, HMSO.

D.H.S.S., 1975, *Report on Confidential Enquiries into Maternal Deaths in England and Wales 1970–72*, Report on Health and Social Subjects no. 11, London, HMSO.

D.H.S.S., 1976, *Prevention and Health, Everybody's Business: a Reassessment of Personal and Public Health*, London, HMSO.

D.H.S.S., 1977, *Prevention and Health*, London, HMSO.

Doyal, L., and Pennell, I., 1976, 'Pox Britannica: medicine, health and under-development', in *Race and Class*, vol. 17, no. 2.

Doyal, L. (forthcoming 1979), *The Political Economy of Health*, London, Pluto Press.

Easlea, B., 1973, *Liberation and the Aims of Science: an Essay on the Obstacles to the Building of a Beautiful World*, London, Chatto and Windus.

Flinn, M. W., 1965, 'Introduction' to Edwin Chadwick, *Sanitary Report on the Condition of the Labouring Population of Great Britain*, Edinburgh, Edinburgh University Press.

Foucault, M., 1973, *The Birth of the Clinic*, London, Tavistock.

Fourth Report of the House of Commons Expenditure Committee on NHS Facilities for Private Patients, 1972, London, HMSO.

General Register Office Studies on Medical and Population Subjects No. 14, 1958 and 1960, *Morbidity Statistics from General Practice*, vols. I and II, London, HMSO.

Gilbert, B. B., 1966, *The Evolution of National Insurance in Great Britain: the Origins of the Welfare State*, London, Michael Joseph.

Illich, I., 1975, *Medical Nemesis: The Expropriation of Health*, London, Calder and Boyars.

Israel, S., and Teeling-Smith, G., 1967, 'The submerged iceberg of sickness in society', *Social and Economic Administration*, vol. 1, no. 1.

Kelman, S., 1975, 'The social nature of the definition problem in health', *International Journal of Health Services*, vol. 5, no. 4.

Kinnersly, P., 1973, *The Hazards of Work*, London, Pluto Press.

Loudon, J. B., (ed.), 1976, *Social Anthropology and Medicine. Proceedings of the Annual Conference of the Association of Social Anthropologists of the Commonwealth* (held at the University of Kent, 1972), London, Academic Press.

Mapes, R., and Dajda, R., 1976, 'Children and the GP: the General Household Survey as a source of information', in M. Stacey (ed.), *The Sociology of the*

National Health Service, Sociological Review Monograph no. 22, University of Keele.

McKeown, T., 1971, 'A historical appraisal of the medical task', in G. McLachlan and T. McKeown (eds.), *Medical History and Medical Care*, Oxford, Oxford University Press, pp. 27–55.

Navarro, V., 1976a, 'Social class, political power and the state', *Social Science and Medicine*, vol. 10, no. 9/10, September/October.

Navarro, V., 1976b, 'The underdevelopment of health of working America: causes, consequences and possible solutions', *American Journal of Public Health*, vol. 66, no. 6, June.

Navarro, V., 1977, *Medicine under Capitalism*, London, Croom Helm.

N.B.P.I., 1971, Report no. 166, *Pay and Conditions of Service of Ancillary Workers in the NHS*, April, Cmnd. 4644, London, HMSO.

Noyce, J., Snaith, A. H., and Trickey, A. J., 1974, 'Regional variations in the allocation of financial resources to the community health services', *The Lancet*, 30 March.

OPCS Studies on Medical and Population Subjects No. 26., 1974, *Morbidity Statistics from General Practice, Second National Study 1970-71*, London, HMSO.

Powell E., 1970, *Hansard*, 16 December, London, HMSO.

Powles, J., 1973, 'On the limitations of modern medicine', *Science, Medicine and Man*, vol. 1, no. 1, pp. 1–30.

Preston, B., 1974, 'Statistics of inequality', *Sociological Review*, vol. 22, no. 1, February.

Rein, M., 1969, 'Social class and the health service', *New Society*, vol. 14, 20 November.

Report of the Committee of Enquiry into the Relationship of the Pharmaceutical Industry with the NHS in 1965-67, 1967, London, HMSO.

Report of the Work of the Committee on Death Certification and Coroners, 1971, Cmnd. 4810, London, HMSO.

Richards, M. P. M., 1975, 'Innovation in medical practice: obstetricians and the induction of labour in Britain', *Social Science and Medicine*, vol. 9, nos. 11/12, pp. 595–602.

Rossdale, M., 1965, 'Health in a sick society', *New Left Review*, no. 36, pp. 82–90.

Sigerist, H. E., 1970, *Civilisation and Disease*, Chicago, University of Chicago Press.

Taylor, P., 1974, 'Sickness absence; facts and misconceptions', *Journal of the Royal College of Physicians*, vol. 8, no. 4, July, pp. 315–333.

Townsend, P., 1974, 'Inequality and the health service', *The Lancet*, 15 June.

Tudor Hart, J., 1975, 'The inverse care law', in C. Cox and A. Mead (eds.), *A Sociology of Medical Practice*, London, Collier Macmillan.

Whitehead, F. E., 1971, 'Trends in certificated sickness absence', in *Social Trends* (CSO), no. 2, London, HMSO.

Wightman, W. P. D., 1971, *The Emergence of Scientific Medicine*, Edinburgh, Oliver & Boyd.

Wilkinson, R., 1976, 'Dear David Ennals', *New Society*, 16 December.

Section Four:
Statistics in Action

The previous sections of this book have challenged the idea that numbers are themselves neutral; we now consider more specific practices that rely heavily upon statistical *techniques*. An understanding of both the technical and ideological assumptions underlying their use is a necessary precondition for challenging and changing them.

In the first chapter of this section, Mick McLean dispels much of the aura surrounding one of the most important symbols of advanced science and technology—the computer. In social research, computers are increasingly used to process large quantities of information and to produce impressive volumes of 'results'. McLean asks whether the massive use of the computer in this way really makes social research any more scientific, and argues that the quality of social research may actually be debased by the specialisation of tasks and automated procedures built around computerised social research. Computers, McLean argues, provide no automatic mechanism for producing the sophisticated social *science* that has long been the vision of positivist and empiricist researchers.

Opinion polling predates the electronic computer, but its scale and utility have been affected by the development of data-processing devices. Catherine Marsh's chapter examines the way in which opinion polls are used to structure 'public opinion', and their role in the contol and manipulation—rather than simply the measurement and transmission—of attitudes and ideologies. While specifically addressed to opinion polling much of her analysis here is also relevant to a more general critique of survey research.

The rapid development of operational research in recent decades is testimony to the increasing reliance on all-purpose scientific and technical solutions in dealing with the acute social and economic problems faced by modern capitalism. Operational research (OR) involves the use of a battery of mathematical techniques to determine so-called 'optimal' solutions to such problems—usually on the basis of quantified data. Jonathan

Rosenhead and Colin Thunhurst provide a general outline of these techniques and offer a critical appraisal of the 'scientific' character of OR. In so doing, they raise important questions about the consequences of the use of OR for scientists, technologists and other people involved in—or affected by—the decisions that it structures.

In the next article, Ian Miles and John Irvine show that behind the claim to be providing an objective account of reality, quantitative social science often plays an important role in maintaining and legitimating the dominant social order. Here it is the methods and techniques of social forecasting that come under critical scrutiny. Miles and Irvine demonstrate that forecasts of the future are invariably more concerned with attempts to secure *a particular type* of future than they are with a disinterested, neutral study of trends and counter-trends.

Finally, Bill Ridgers discusses one way in which statistics can be put into action for radical purposes. He discusses the advantages and problems attached to the use of statistical information in the work of Counter Information Services, outlining methods both of obtaining and of re-using statistics to further radical politics. Fundamental to the success of these methods, Ridgers points out, is an awareness of how, by whom, and for whom the statistical data are to be employed.

17.

Mick McLean

The Computerisation of Social Research

Introduction

> Computerised methods have increased the volume of quanti-
> tative social research by about 1,000 times since 1945; on the
> other hand they have only increased the amount of sound and
> useful work by 10 times.

This remark, which was made to the author by a (necessarily
anonymous) statistician and computer programmer with over 10
years experience of computerising the social sciences, summarises
and anticipates the main conclusion of this brief chapter. In
contrast to the view expressed above, most introductions to the
technology or economics of computing start with an array of
superlatives, outlining how the extent of computer usage, the
ubiquity of their use, and the increase in power of the individual
computer have grown exponentially since the development of the
first electronic computer in the 1940s. This rapid technical change,
with its far-reaching economic and social implications, has lent to
computers a mystique not shared by other techniques. This aura of
mystery has been reinforced both by the anthropomorphic nature
of much computer terminology (even apparent in the titles of
serious books like Ashby's *Design for a Brain*, 1952), and by the
widespread promotion of computing as an unprecedented force for
social progress and economic improvement.

The technology of computing is actually rather mundane;
computers are simply large pocket calculators with the ability to
store and retrieve information in electronic form. The most
important feature of a computer is its ability to store, retrieve and
act upon a set of instructions (a program), which enables it to carry
out complex instructions based upon a sequence of simple arithmetic and logical steps.[1]

Although the idea of constructing a programmable mechanical calculator had been conceived and explored by Babbage as
early as the 1850s, today's computer technology derives from the
wave of scientific and technical change which occurred in Britain

and the United States during the second world war. First used to produce navigational and artillery firing tables, and in deciphering coded messages, electronic computers were soon applied to the vast amounts of calculation made necessary by the Manhattan Project and the post-war development of the hydrogen bomb. In the United States, computer development was from the beginning a joint venture between government and industrial corporations; and the latter, personified by Thomas Watson of IBM, quickly realised the commercial potential of the new devices. Computing technology is still virtually monopolised by the USA, with IBM well on the way to becoming the world's largest multinational corporation.

Close links have been maintained between computing research in natural science and engineering. For some time to come physical science research establishments are likely to represent a significant proportion of the market for computers. Physical scientists and engineers were first to exploit computers for their work, and many of these early users of computers made big contributions to their design and manufacture. These early computers—such as those now exhibited in the Smithsonian Institute and the Science Museum, London—were put to a wide variety of tasks; the first elementary computer engineering textbook (Ledley, 1960) describes two of these, which give the flavour of the early days of computing. The first was the calculation of the trajectories of variously charged atomic particles in the field of a large dipole magnet. (The computers' calculations were confirmed in September 1958, by the explosion of a small atomic bomb by the US Air Force, 300 miles above the Pacific Ocean, spreading a thin layer of radiation completely around the globe.) The second used computers to design high-resolution lens systems for accurate high-altitude photography. (The success of this approach was illustrated by the 1962 Cuban missile crisis, where such photography detected the presence of Russian missiles in Cuba.)

Thus science and engineering departments of universities have long been well-endowed with people skilled in every aspect of computer usage. The most critical of these skills is *programming* – the preparation of the detailed instructions which enable a computer to perform specific tasks. In the 1950s and early '60s, programming was an esoteric art, requiring at least a rudimentary knowledge of binary arithmetic and computer engineering. Since then, the development of 'high-level languages' which enable the computer to be programmed in a language more closely approximating to English, has made computing more easily accessible to a wider group. Even so, most high-level languages have been constructed with particular problems in mind: FORTRAN and ALGOL for largely numerical applications, and COBOL for business purposes.

The development of high-level programming languages means that computer use requires fewer specialised skills. There has also recently been an extremely rapid decrease in the cost of computer equipment. These trends relate to the ever-increasing application of computers in scientific, military, business and administrative organisations. Taken together, these developments suggest that the full impact of computers on society has not yet been experienced or widely appreciated.

The likely social and economic consequences of the increased diffusion of computing technology cannot be dealt with adequately here. We should point out that recent research (e.g. Freeman, 1977; McLean and Rush, 1978) has indicated that such consequences may not be as desirable as were thought by the more optimistic commentators of the 1950s and 1960s. In particular, the incorporation of computing technology into the products and processes of a wide range of manufacturing and service industries may lead to significant changes in the nature and extent of employment in those industries.

As the computer industry approaches maturity, it seems likely that fears of structural unemployment due to technical change, long dismissed as unfounded, may prove to be fully justified. Furthermore, there is considerable evidence that the nature of work in many industrial sectors has already been drastically altered by the diffusion of micro-electronic computing technology. For example, overall skill requirements in the manufacture and maintenance of telephone equipment have declined tremendously since the adoption of computer-controlled exchanges (Robinson, 1977). In the computer industry itself, the job satisfaction and skill requirements of programmers have been lowered by the adoption of increasingly structured high-level languages; the status and rewards of computer programmers have likewise declined (Greenbaum, 1976).

The process of deskilling work is, of course, just one aspect of the principle of the division of labour, and its historical development predates the computer by several hundred years. (See Braverman, 1974; Griffiths, Irvine and Miles, this volume). Nevertheless, computer technology has created new opportunities for the division of labour in the fields of 'white-collar' and intellectual work not previously affected. (Jenkins and Sherman, 1977, discuss this and other impacts of computing). The social sciences as a form of intellectual 'work' have not escaped the deskilling process and this forms the principal theme of the final section of this chapter.

Computers have made considerable positive contributions to the social sciences; their future *potential* contribution is tremendous. These positive aspects can be gleaned from any of the recent standard texts on statistical analysis; this chapter will, in contrast, point to certain *negative* aspects of the computerisation of social research. The computerisation of social research is a poorly researched area—an interesting omission, given the extravagant claims for, and use of, the technology by social scientists—and this means that the conclusions reached in this chapter are not only not commonly accepted, but also lack the thorough documentation they deserve.

The computer and social science

The punched-card, for many still the most visible manifestation of the computer, was developed by Hollerith in order to speed up the analysis of the data gathered by the US Census of 1890. There is little evidence, however, that such technology had much general impact on the practice of academic social science; although it is likely that during the 1920s and '30s commercial polling operations in the US utilised the punched card equipment which IBM (the firm which Hollerith founded) was aggressively marketing at that time.

An early use of computers by social scientists came in the immediate post-war period, in the field of psychometrics. The US and British armed forces had been heavy users of intelligence testing; during the second world war testing was particularly important for selection purposes. Military organisations thus sponsored much of the research in this field. Factor analysis, a technique fashionable in psychometric research, had been possible only by using an army of clerks equipped with desk calculators. The availability of computers to the military enabled the early computerisation of factor analyses and led to a rapid development of factor analytic methods. The majority of social scientists remained somewhat on the periphery of computer developments, however, only encountering computers when they were installed in universities for the benefit of natural scientists.

Once a computer is purchased and installed for one department, its marginal use by others incurs little further costs. Thus, in the late '50s a few intrepid social scientists began to explore the possibilities of the machines which the 'imperatives' of nuclear physics had placed on their doorsteps. These early university pioneers wrote their own personal computer programs, typically to produce cross-tabulations and other statistical analyses from survey data. In the meantime, statistics departments were showing fresh interest in technically sophisticated methods which, like factor analysis, could now readily be implemented using computers.

Groups of researchers were formed at various universities in the US and Britain sharing a common interest in the use of computers in social research. These groups started to produce 'packages' of computer programs, first for their own use, later for teaching, and these brought together techniques for entering data into the computer, simple error-checking, and the production of cross-tabulations and statistical analyses. Such packages, of which BMD, ASCOP, SPSS, and GLIM are amongst the most well known, transformed quantitative research. Potential users now required little knowledge of computer programming or, indeed of statistics, in order to produce masses of highly complex and extremely impressive computer print-out.

This development of specialised program packages which can be used on the general-purpose computers acquired for, and still used mainly by, natural scientists and engineers, reflected and reinforced the increased reliance of the social sciences on large-scale surveys and mathematical statistics. This is apparently easy to explain: computers dramatically lower the cost of storing and processing data, and greatly reduce the time and resources required for complex statistical analyses. To researchers already committed to carrying out difficult calculations involving a mass of numbers, the use of a computer, if available at little cost, seems natural and inevitable. Thus, by 1973, about 85 per cent of all university social science departments in Britain made some use of computers, the main use being the statistical analysis of survey data (see Utting and Hall, 1973).

Computers have enabled drastic changes to be made in the practice of quantitative social research. No longer need researchers even possess a clear understanding of its principles to produce highly credible 'results'. Some skill may still be required to select, produce and justify the more complex analyses but a superficial knowledge of statistical packages often substitutes for any deep understanding. As an early review of computer usage by social scientists states:

> Acquaintance with technique does not necessarily lead to an understanding of the underlying idea of analysis. The computer is frequently called upon to do massive arithmetic; but the user who has little or no idea of what is to be done with the

> results is merely transforming his data from one form to another, equally, if not more complex than the original. (Hailstone, 1969, p. 9).

The most significant feature here is the division of labour between the writers of statistical packages and the users of those packages. This can be seen as a parallel to the more general process of 'deskilling' through computerisation. The consequences of such a pattern of development are, however, somewhat different for the social scientist than for the shop-floor worker. Let us examine them in more detail.

Computers and the research process

We have already noted the division of labour between computer programmers and expert statisticians, on the one hand, and the users of their computer programs on the other. In the course of evaluating the impact of computerisation on each successive stage of the research process we shall meet other examples of such specialisation.

It is generally argued in standard texts on the methodology of social research that some process of conceptualisation, hypothesis formulation, or theory development should precede any attempt to gather and interpret empirical evidence. But it has been observed that in practice: 'Pre-data hypotheses are commonly imprecise or even non-existent, and often one of the principal motives for undertaking a survey is to provide material from which some rather precise hypothesis may be dredged'. (Selvin and Stuart, 1966.) These authors go on to outline the many conceptual and technical drawbacks to various methods of 'dredging' for hypotheses; and they note that the use of computer programs greatly facilitates these somewhat dubious procedures.

A further stage in the computerisation process is to provide the data from which hypotheses of models can be dredged in the form of 'archives' of survey information stored magnetically and accessible only by computers. These archives (such as that of the Social Science Research Council at the University of Essex) make it possible to reduce the task of the social scientist to the computerised manipulation of computerised data produced by other people. Archives inevitably give the impression that the data they contain are 'objective' source material for further research, since the description of the methods and assumptions used in data production are rarely as amenable to computer storage (or as attractive to retrieve) as the data themselves.

Another recent development has been the production of such

computer programs as 'General Inquirer' for the automatic content analysis of novels and editorials, of discussion group transcripts, of field and clinical interviews—thus making such sources available for the dredging of hypotheses and subsequent computerised statistical analysis. (See Ellis and Favat, 1970).

The next stage in the social research process is generally identified as 'data-collection'. Even here social scientists have found a role for computers. Social psychologists, for example, now often use computer terminals programmed to type out questions to which the subject can respond directly by typing in the appropriate replies. A more worrying development in the area of data collection is the massive growth in the amount of information collected and stored in computers by governments and other organisations on individuals and political groups. (The political dimensions of the use of such data banks are well covered in the final section of Ackroyd et al., 1977). In future, some of the more routine sources could prove increasingly important to social researchers, who, having gained access to such deep swamps of data, could dredge away for many research lifetimes.

The phase of the research process upon which computers have, to date, had the most visible impact involves the statistical analysis of data. Some users of computerised statistical packages perform every conceivable statistical analysis on all of the available data. This is particularly ironic, given that statistics was first developed as a convenient means of simplifying and structuring empirical information; a vast mass of numbers could be reduced to a few simple statistics. But now it is not unusual for the data drawn from a small survey of about 20 individuals to yield 40 or 50 pages of computer-produced analysis! Every variable is cross-tabulated with every other; where perhaps only a few simple regressions are needed, factor analysis, path analysis, obscure scaling techniques and even a high order analysis of variance are used.[2] Rather than being tools whose adequacy and appropriateness are open to challenge and criticism, these statistical procedures have become ends in themselves. The designers of computer packages have certainly not discouraged this development; the most popular, SPSS, contains the tempting instruction 'STATISTICS ALL', which causes all conceivable statistics related to a particular statistical method to be printed out. (One of the originators of this package recently remarked that when he sees the line-printer ouputting SPSS runs, he is haunted by the image of disappearing Alaskan trees; see Coxon, 1977.)

Perhaps one of the most dramatic problems with the division

of labour between the writers and users of packages is that many of the computational procedures in some of the more widely used statistical packages simply do not work! This was pointed out by astute statisticians as long ago as 1967, but little has been done to remedy the situation.[3] As one such critic (Wampler, 1969) remarked of least-squares programs: 'In a number of programs the coefficients reported . . . were sometimes completely erroneous, containing not even one correct significant digit.'[4]

The most common fault found in statistical packages is that the methods used will not reliably calculate the correct statistic from every set of input information. This problem is well known to 'professional' statisticians and numerical programmers who can usually spot when a computer program has gone wrong. The average user of a statistical package, however, probably will not notice any such mistake; the computer package will give no indication that anything is amiss. This situation largely stems from the way in which computer packages were produced: the experts who wrote the packages did not make allowance for the naïve user. And while the obvious errors in such packages have been corrected, new features are being added faster than the old mistakes can be deleted. This problem is exacerbated by the policy of social science funding agencies who are unwilling to pay for the necessary maintenance; as a prominent member of the SSRC's Computing Committee has remarked:

> If a package survives and continues to be used, its continued maintenance, updating and servicing then becomes a problem, for it is not strictly 'research' in the Research Council's terms, and this problem remains a difficult one. (Banbury, 1977, p. 3).

The next stage of the research process is conventionally identified as 'interpretation'—a function which cannot legitimately be performed by computer. Nevertheless, compared to the tough intellectual labour of producing, evaluating and testing social theory, the production of computer print-outs is a relatively easy task; thus there exists a grave temptation to delimit or omit this stage altogether. In the early days of computerised social science, many Ph.D. theses consisted of little more than photo-reduced print-outs. Despite the ease with which computerised analyses can now be produced, a considerable mystique still clings to the impressively numerical output of statistical packages. This is shown in the relative lack of criticism of computerised social science from the users of packages. Any such attack might weaken the general interest, and it remains worthwhile for all to admire the emperor's new suit of print-out. Of course, there have been dozens, if not hundreds, of critical attacks by specialist statisticians on specific statistical methods incorporated in program packages, but these have rarely been appreciated or supported by the user of packages.

The mystique of the computer is also convenient for those social scientists who wish to impress sponsors and conceal assumptions and biases behind a numerical smokescreen. A fine example of this is to be found in the work of Jensen (1970), who in connection with Shields' (1962) data on the intelligence test scores of twins reared apart says: 'All the present analyses were calculated by computer, with figures carried to five decimals and not rounded until the final product.' Despite the impression of diligence and accuracy created here, Kamin (1977) has shown that Jensen has blindly reproduced several errors from Shields' own figures. No amount of computerised manipulation of data can eliminate errors of conception and measurement, or guarantee the meaningfulness and accuracy of results presented. Nor can vast quantities of data or analyses substitute for an intelligent and scholarly appraisal of empirical evidence. As long as the fragmentation of the tasks of archive keepers, computer programmers, statisticians and social researchers persists, the substitution of computation for rigorous conceptualisation cannot be excused as an occasional individual abuse subject to elimination through professional diligence. Rather, it must be recognised as stemming directly from the structure of the research process. Social scientists should be the first to recognise that the professional behaviour of individual social researchers is not independent of the social and economic framework within which such research takes place.

Of course, there are many obvious advantages to the various divisions of labour outlined above; computerised analysis, access to data archives, and the provision of standardised, easily accessible statistical packages, can all be of great value to social research. And the division of labour has economic advantages; as the Chairman of the SSRC Computing Committee has remarked: 'It is straight-forwardly not cost-effective to have every researcher generating his own programs for particular analytical facilities, when he may well be largely duplicating work already done by others.' (Banbury, 1977, p. 3). But there are less obvious *drawbacks* to such a procedure, as we have seen.

Practically every stage of the research process is now amenable to computerisation; the day of the completely automated social research programme is perhaps not far off. Starting from the computerised dredging of hypotheses and statistics from previous studies and data archives, with the appropriate statistical analyses produced automatically, a suitable computer program could draw its mechanical conclusions, write, typeset and print the final report—complete with graphs and an impressive set of references drawn from a key-word analysis of a computerised set of abstracts. The role of the researcher could be reduced to pushing the start button of the machine and admiring the resultant bound volume.

The division of labour may be eminently suited for the profitable manufacture of pins. However, although encouraged by the computerisation of social research, it may be less than desirable for the future development of the social sciences, where even a decade ago it could be remarked that:

> The number of research workers . . . is rapidly rising. Their training and command of their disciplines, including their ability to use . . . sophisticated statistical methods, are far above the levels attained by their predecessors of even one generation ago . . . And yet all this high-powered intellectual activity has yielded few important new or fresh insights into the way our society works and where it is headed . . . social science has become more and more compartmentalised, with its practitioners turning into ever narrower specialists— superbly trained experts in their own 'fields' but knowing, and indeed able to understand, less and less about the specialities of others. (Baran and Sweezy, 1968, pp. 15-16).

Notes

1. The technology of pocket calculators is directly derived from the computer components industry and the most recent 'programmable' calculators are effectively small computers as defined above. There exists a vast number of books purporting to explain just how computers work and what they can do; one of the best is that by Hollingdale and Tootill (1975).
2. The use of statistics in sociology is here criticised along similar lines to those in an article by Labovitz (1972).
3. The American Statistical Association has recently convened a committee to look into such problems, but it is unlikely that a lasting improvement in the situation will be achieved for reasons developed below.
4. See Longley (1967), and Francis (1973) for evaluations of the effectiveness of various types of statistical computation.

Bibliography

Ackroyd, C., Margolis, K., Rosenhead, J., and Shallice, T., 1977, *The Technology of Political Control*, Harmondsworth, Penguin.
Ashby, W. R., 1952, *Design for a Brain*, New York, John Wiley.

Banbury, J., 1977, 'Perspectives of the SSRC's Computing Committee', *SSRC Newsletter*, no. 33, March 1977.

Baran, P. A., and Sweezy, P. M., 1968, *Monopoly Capital*, Harmondsworth, Penguin.

Braverman, H., 1974, *Labor and Monopoly Capital*, New York, Monthly Review Press.

Coxon, A. P. M., 1977, 'Recent developments in social science software,' *SSRC Newsletter*, no. 33, March 1977, pp. 6–9.

Ellis, A. B., and Favat, F. A., 1970, 'From computer to criticism: an application of automatic content analysis to the study of literature', in E. M. Jennings (ed.), *Science and Literature*, New York, Doubleday.

Francis, I., 1973, 'A comparison of several ANOVA programs', *Journal of the American Statistical Association*, vol. 68, pp. 860–65.

Freeman, C., 1977, 'Unemployment and the Direction of Technical Change', paper prepared for OECD expert group meeting, Science Policy Research Unit, University of Sussex.

Greenbaum, J., 1976, 'Division of labour in the computer field', *Monthly Review*, vol. 28, pp. 40–55.

Hailstone, J. E., 1969, 'The effects of computers on scientific research', *SSRC Newsletter*, 6 June 1969, pp. 9–10.

Hollingdale, S. H., and Tootill, G. C., 1975, *Electronic Computers*, Harmondsworth, Penguin.

Jenkins, C., and Sherman, B., 1977, *Computers and the Unions*, London, Longmans.

Jensen, A. R., 1970, 'I.Q.s of identical twins reared apart', *Behaviour Genetics*, no. 1, p. 135.

Kamin, L. J., 1977, *The Science and Politics of I.Q.*, Harmondsworth, Penguin.

Labovitz, S., 1972, 'Statistical usage in sociology: sacred cows and ritual', *Sociological Methods and Research*, vol. 1, no. 1, pp. 3–37.

Ledley, R. S., 1960, *Digital Computer and Control Engineering*, New York, McGraw-Hill.

Longley, J. W., 1967, 'An appraisal of least-squares programs from the users' point of view', *Journal of the American Statistical Association*, vol. 62, pp. 819–41.

Mc Lean, J. M., and Rush, H. J., 1978, 'The impact of microelectronics on the U.K. economy', working paper, Science Policy Research Unit, University of Sussex.

Robinson, A. L., 1977, 'Impact of electronics on employment: productivity and displacement effects', *Science*, vol. 195, no. 4283, pp. 1179–86.

Selvin, H. C., and Stuart, A., 1966, 'Data-dredging procedures in survey analysis', *Journal of the American Statistical Association*, vol. 54, pp. 30–34, reprinted in D. P. Forcese and S. Richer, 1970, *Stages of Social Research*, Englewood Cliffs, N.J., Prentice-Hall.

Shields, J., 1962, *Monozygotic Twins Brought Up Apart and Brought Up Together*, London, Oxford University Press.

Utting, J., and Hall, J., 1973, *The Use of Computers in University Social Science Departments*, London, SSRC.

Wampler, R. H., 1969, 'An evaluation of linear least squares computer programs', *Journal of Research of the National Bureau of Standards*, vol. 73, pp. 59–90.

18.

Catherine Marsh

Opinion Polls—Social Science or Political Manoeuvre?

> I am monarch of all I survey,
> My right there is none to dispute;
> William Cowper

Introduction

The history of polling opinion in elections goes back a long way; almost as soon as candidates began to be elected by popular vote, newspapers and politicians attempted to develop ways of assessing the candidates' chances of getting elected (Webb and Wybrow, 1974, mention a straw poll of public opinion taken in Harrisburg, Pennsylvania in 1824). Opinion polling really took off when modern sampling techniques were developed earlier this century, for it proved possible to estimate the characteristics of a very large number of people from a very small sample *so long as it was selected at random.* (Cochran, Mosteller and Tukey, 1954).

But it was not just election polling that expanded quickly this century. There was also a growing demand for market research. Companies were set up providing field-forces of interviewers, armies of coders and a general staff of research personnel—all geared to systematic enquiry into public attitudes on anything from capital punishment to soap powders.[1]

The spectacular growth of this activity was reflected in the mushrooming number of organisations offering these facilities during elections. In Britain, Gallup was alone in polling the 1945 election. Since then, they have been joined by the Daily Express Poll (now defunct), Research Services, Opinion Research Centre, Lou Harris, Marplan, Business Decisions, National Opinion Polls, and Market & Opinion Research International—with most newspapers sponsoring polls at some time or another. Gallup is still the largest organisation, however, publishing as many polls as all the others put together.

Whilst most published polls are financed from two main sources—the political parties and the media - the balance between these two has changed considerably over the past few years, and I would estimate that the political parties currently spend more than the media.[2] The squeeze on newspapers in the last few years has led to a decline in the amount that they can afford to spend. There is also quite a substantial private sponsorship as we shall see below.

What is public opinion?

The very term 'public opinion' presupposes that there is a general social will which is open to empirical discovery; pollsters claim that it can be measured legitimately by putting the same question to a representative cross-section of individuals, and summing the individual opinions thus produced. And it is very tempting to believe that the 'will of the people' can be expressed so easily.

But the concept 'public opinion' is not without its critics. Individual opinions, one argument runs, should not be simply aggregated to produce public opinion, for in reality individuals do not contribute equally to its formation, some being more powerful than others (Blumer, 1948). This argument is relevant if one is trying to predict what will happen in society, but it ignores the fact that concepts like public opinion carry important political implications. If one were to treat this argument prescriptively, and suggest that in decision-making the opinions of some individuals *should* carry more weight than others, the result would be dangerously elitist.

Another criticism goes further and argues that public opinion is not any sum of individuated opinions but an objective spirit of society (Pollock, 1976); and, in a tradition stemming from Rousseau and Hegel, the argument goes that we should be looking for *volonté générale*, not *volonté de tous*. It makes the important suggestion that the general social will has the effect of creating individual opinions rather than being created by them.

But there are difficulties in accepting the idea of one social will in societies fundamentally divided by class. Moreover, to argue about what the expression of this social will *really* is, would be to ignore that public opinion polling has become a very real, thriving industry whose existence is daily attested by the media. Public opinion has come to be what public opinion pollsters produce, and we must begin our critique of it by addressing ourselves to the activities of this industry, to the techniques employed by the pollsters, and thence to the claims of legitimacy, and even democracy, that are made for these activities.

It is important to start this examination with the concept of 'opinion' which underlies the methods used in opinion polling. The notion is an extremely individualistic one; any of the usual activities undertaken in arriving at a view on an issue, such as discussing it with others, are forbidden in the interview situation, as the interviewer is supposed to elicit those views that the respondent holds as an individual. Fundamental to this approach is the idea that everybody holds an opinion about everything. Further, it is held that these opinions are fixed and latent, with the potential to cause actions or verbal behaviour; responses to questionnaire items can therefore be treated as indicators of underlying attitudes.

But this is a perversion of the way in which people have ideas, interact with one another and change their views. It may be the case that at one point in time, as a result of such individual questioning, one might discover that 60 per cent of people are for capital punishment and 40 per cent against. Yet if these same individuals had a decision to make about whether to hang someone and were given the opportunity to talk the issue through, the minority might persuade the majority (or at least some of them) to change their views. The clearest way to demonstrate the importance of this criticism of a fixed, individuated notion of opinion is to contrast it with behaviour—which is generally social and constrained by context rather than being performed in isolation. The failure of such individual responses to tally with the behaviour of some of the same individuals has been observed frequently. The classic illustration of this is a study by LaPiere of how people would behave towards ethnic minorities; many hotel proprietors, when questioned, claimed they would not accommodate a Chinese couple, but when such a couple arrived at their doorstep, only a few actually refused to serve them. (LaPiere, 1934). Of course, we should not expect complete consistency between verbal acts, such as the voicing of opinions or even stating behavioural intentions, and non-verbal acts. Verbal methods 'may be used to get at what people think, or at least at what they think they think, but not at what they actually express in social situations'. (Galtung, 1967, p. 112).

There are several useful discussions of this problem in the social psychology literature, and interested readers should pursue the debate there.[3] Opinion pollsters have themselves suggested several reasons for the persistent discrepancies, which range from blaming the respondent for the 'response error' to suspecting that there may be something wrong with the method of assessment. But whatever the reason, the discrepancy itself should alert us to the fact that individual opinion responses are not unproblematic, unchanging entities, waiting to be elicited by a pollster with a simple closed-ended question.[4] Blackburn reminds us that even the most methodical and rigorous of social surveys may produce very misleading results to questions about, for example, industrial conflict—one month after Goldthorpe had published the results of an attitude survey of car workers conducted at Vauxhall in Luton in 1963, and declared that the workers were generally compliant and had good relations with management, there was a strike provoked by what might be considered only a minor grievance (Goldthorpe, 1966). Blackburn criticises Goldthorpe for neglecting attitudes to profits in the survey, and correctly notes that in the car industry one never witnesses industrial peace, but only truce. (Blackburn, 1967). Issues such as labour relations are very complex, and as this example shows, even quite detailed questioning can fail to reveal this.

This is not necessarily to condemn opinion polls. On some issues most people in Britain are prepared to express very clear views, and simple questions may be sufficient to elicit them, as we shall see later. But all too often questions are asked which have the effect of creating public opinion rather than reflecting it, in that they are not topics the respondent has thought about, or at least talked about before;[5] moreover, the reporting of 'what everybody thinks about' has been shown to exert a strong pressure towards conformity in what people do think.

Questions which should routinely be asked about any poll

a. How important is the issue to the people interviewed?

Stanley Payne, in his classic work on question wording, reported a study in which a sample of Americans were asked how much they approved or disapproved of the 'Metallic Metals Act' of 1947; depite the fact that this Act was entirely fictitious, 70 per cent gave a clear verdict of approval or disapproval (Payne, 1951). It can be embarrassing to admit to some smartly dressed lady on your doorstep that you know nothing about legislation as impressive-sounding as the Metallic Metals Act. This finding highlights what is perhaps the most common fault of opinion polls: they give an opportunity for the people sampled to give what appear to be very definite and coherent opinions on topics about which, in reality, they have complex and contradictory opinions, or perhaps, no opinions at all.

This is not a blanket criticism of all attempts to investigate attitudes. Some of these difficulties have been overcome by looking at the *salience* of the issues to the respondent. Such techniques have been widely used in market research, for example, where opinions on products may be weighted by the salience of the item, or feature of the item, for each individual. But even though these techniques exist, they are rarely used in political opinion polling.

On some issues respondents have already developed clear-cut opinions, as can be seen from the *stability* of the responses to differently worded questions on the topic. It doesn't matter how much you rephrase a question on capital punishment or the closed shop issue; these are issues on which the vast majority of people in this country already have well-rehearsed opinions, and their responses will be relatively stable. However, responses to polls on such matters as foreign policy are very susceptible to minor changes of question wording. Very many of the early polls on the Common Market were certainly eliciting responses which those questioned would not have formulated clearly on their own.

Converse has shown that a given sample of Americans, whose opinion changes were monitored from 1956 to 1960, could be roughly divided into two groups; the attitudes of the first group of stable respondents did not change in this period, while the opinions of the second group fluctuated randomly. He concluded that the second group had not rehearsed or practised attitudes in the areas they were asked about, and rather than admit to having no opinion (which they had every opportunity to do) they responded at random (Converse, 1970).

An issue may be of low centrality to a respondent, either emotionally or cognitively, and it is important for attitude surveys to show this. In May 1968 NOP found that 67 per cent of people in this country said they approved of Enoch Powell's policies. However, when Social and Community Planning Research did a follow-up, they found that less than half could say what Powell's policies were (Jowell and Hoinville, 1969). Knowledge-questions of this kind are a great help in showing the existence of information on the topic in hand, and should be used in conjunction with more open-ended questions to establish the salience of issues for the people being interviewed.

Many of the methods currently used to test public opinion fail to establish an effective measure of neutrality or indifference towards the issue, which would allow certain respondents to abstain from giving their opinion. The social situation of an interview seems to make all respondents feel that they ought to have a personal opinion on every topic. Respondents may often drum up an opinion where there was none before; and such people are the most likely to be affected by the wording of a question, their perceptions of the interviewer's expectations and stereotyped responses. McKennell, in discussing ways of attempting to establish a neutral point, concludes:

> Although the problem would seem to be of great importance for obtaining, say, an unbiased measure of the weight of public opinion for or against an issue, little progress has been made on the operational definition of a neutral point on an attitude scale. (McKennell, 1977, p. 216).

b. How were the questions worded?

Text books on survey methods tend to portray different forms of question wording as more or less likely to reveal the 'true value' that lies waiting to be discovered by the interviewer (e.g. Moser and Kalton, 1971). The debate over whether particular forms of questions are biased or objective is misplaced; the truth of the matter is that minor changes in wording can often substantially alter the meaning of the question. For example, what conclusions would you draw about support for American Presidential policies and/or principles of question wording from the following examples? The first *does not invite* respondents to approve of the current situation:

> *Gallup, June 1969*
> President Nixon has ordered the withdrawal of 25,000 United States troops from Vietnam in the next three months. How do you feel about this? Do you think troops should be withdrawn at a faster or slower rate? ('Same as now' response not presented but accepted). Faster—42%. Same as now—29%. Slower—16%. No opinion—13%.

The second *explicitly suggests* that one alternative would be to endorse the current situation.

> *Harris, September–October 1969*
> In general do you feel the pace at which the President is withdrawing troops is too fast, too slow, or about right?
> Too slow—29%. About right—49%. Too fast—6%. No opinion—16%. (Cited in Schuman and Duncan, 1974).

The conclusion we may draw from this example is that some individuals who said 'faster' or 'slower' in the first version would have said 'about right' if they had been offered the second. (The three-month gap could not account for such a massive change in the numbers endorsing the current rate). So, no sense can be made of the idea of a true opinion lying waiting to be extracted. These appear to be two different questions and therefore elicit different responses, even though they are very similar in content. The resulting opinion does not exist independently of the question asked.[6]

But many of the problems of question wording are unique to each topic. For example, an opinion poll carried out by *Panorama* asked a sample of immigrants: 'Would you like to return to your country if you received financial help?'. Not surprisingly, this question received a high positive response: just put yourself in the shoes of an Asian, interviewed out of the blue on some street corner, being asked how he or she would feel about a trip 'home' if somebody else paid for it. No mention was made about not coming back, although it was perhaps supposed to be implied in the word 'return'. This survey stung two experienced survey researchers into a response in *New Society* in which they compared this question to asking married men: 'Would you like to return to bachelorhood if you received help with domestic chores?'. They concluded that such polls are not to be taken seriously (Jowell and Hoinville, 1969).

The questions asked may also be too simple to allow respondents to express complex attitudes. For example, when New Zealanders were asked the general question: 'Do you believe that the 1973 Springbok team should be allowed to come to New Zealand?', the results indicated 68 per cent in favour and 30 per cent against. Innes and Vaughan (1972) piloted other forms of question about the proposed tour: they found that by asking 'Should an all-white Springbok team come to New Zealand?' they could reverse the situation and get 36 per cent in favour and 59 per cent against. It could be that respondents took the first question to be about political interference in sport and the second to be about racism in sport, but it seems to me that the apparent change here is better explained by a differentiation between the two situations in what appeared to the respondent to be the socially desirable response (See Edwards, 1957).

McNemar recommended as long ago as 1946 that single questions to tap attitudes should be replaced by multiple questions, to form an attitude scale (McNemar, 1946). McKennell, discussing ways of testing whether these scales do indeed tap one dimension, wonders why such sound advice has not been taken up by pollsters, for the technical know-how has been in existence for a long time (McKennell, 1977).

However, it is usually possible to judge whether the wording has seriously restrained or prompted the expression of particular views. In this respect, consider the following question asked in a survey of attitudes to nuclear power reported in *New Society* (White, 1977), and subsequently widely reported in the national press:

Eventually, coal, oil and natural gas will run out. Which of these two alternatives do you think is the best way of tackling this problem:

1. start building more nuclear power stations now, to ensure future supplies of energy; 2. do everything possible to save coal, oil and gas, and continue looking for other sources of energy apart from nuclear power?

The seemingly factual quality of the first sentence is heavily dependent on how long 'eventually' is taken to be. Naturally, only a minority of the people interviewed opted for the second, head-in-the-sand policy, rather than the policy which *ensured* energy supplies.

A useful way to deal with these problems is to pilot all the questions in draft form with a set of respondents, and then to go back over each question with some of them. This allows the researcher to elicit, at much greater depth, what each respondent understood by each question and what they thought the researcher was driving at. The results of doing this for questions asked in the *National Readership Survey* show that even simple questions are often dramatically misinterpreted (see Belson, 1968). But note that this interesting research was done on a survey in which the accuracy of the information was important for the sponsors; firms use the results of this survey to make decisions about where to advertise.

c. How was the sample drawn?

The basic principle of selecting a representative group by random sampling is quite simple: if you have a large jar full of red and blue marbles in equal quantities, so long as you shake it well first, you need only a smallish sample, if selected at random, to work out reasonably accurately what proportion of each colour is in the jar.

But this principle was not widely accepted until early this century. The *Literary Digest* conducted a poll in 1936 to determine who would win the Roosevelt/Landon US Presidential election. They predicted incorrectly that Landon would win because their sample, although containing 2.5 million responses, was drawn from the telephone directory; this biased the sample against poorer respondents who were less likely to own a telephone but more likely to vote for Roosevelt. Gallup predicted correctly that Roosevelt would win on a random sample one fiftieth the size (see Webb and Wybrow, 1974).

There are two things to check about any sample: first, whether the list of the population from which the sample is drawn is the one that is relevant for the study; and second, whether the method of selecting cases from the population is truly random. For example, using the electoral roll as the list of the population ignores anyone not on that list; among non-electors, there is a higher proportion of the young, the geographically mobile, and the sick. This could be important in, for example, a poll of attitudes towards housing policy.

Many opinion polls do not make use of random samples at all but use what is known as *quota sampling*, where, within certain guidelines, the interviewers are allowed to choose whom they like to interview; they are told they must interview certain proportions of men and women, so many in different age groups, so many full-time and part-time workers and so on. (Moser and Kalton, 1971, chapters 4-8). Quota samples have the advantage of speed, but the error margins around the results are known to be a lot wider than with random sampling designs (Moser and Stuart, 1953). It is good practice to report the error margins with all results, but this is done infrequently.

The most common bias in sampling is in self-selected samples. Nobody regards the letters people write to MPs as a representative sample of views of electors, yet many opinion polls reported rely on similar 'volunteer' samples. (See below in connection with the nationalisation of banks). Note, too, that where the numbers of people who do not respond rises to a substantial proportion in a randomly selected sample, representativeness cannot be claimed.

d. *How carefully have the results been reported?*

Representatives of four regularly published opinion polls met in January 1974 and agreed a code of conduct for the reporting of the findings of opinion polls. (See the appendix to Harris, 1974). Among other things, they agreed that it was important to publish information about the sampling method used, the sample size, the dates of fieldwork, details of the number of people who were 'don't knows' in response to particular questions, and the original question(s) asked. Next time you see a poll reported in the press, look to see if this code is being followed: despite an informal agreement by Fleet Street to abide by this code of conduct, it is more frequently broken than kept. The failure to report the actual question asked is most common, and can lead to very misleading statements indeed. Apart from salving a few consciences in the polling organisations, it is in any case questionable what effect codes of this kind have.

In December 1976, Gallup undertook a survey of a variety of industrial/political attitudes for the TV programme *Man Alive*. One of the questions asked was: 'Which of these do you think has the most power and influence in the country today—Mrs Thatcher (Leader of the Opposition Party); Mr John Methven (Chairman of the Confederation of British Industry); Mr James Callaghan (The Prime Minister); Mr Jack Jones (General Secretary of the Transport and General Workers' Union)?' Of the 1,028 individuals interviewed in a quota sample, 53 per cent opted for Jack Jones, 25 per cent for Callaghan, 5 per cent of Mrs Thatcher, 3 per cent for John Methven, and 15 per cent said that they did not know, or could not answer. Press reports, however, failed to specify with whom the comparison was being made: the *Daily Mail* of Tuesday 4 January 1975, for example, casually referred in passing to 'Mr Jones—named the most powerful man in Britain in a public opinion poll . . .' There is no guarantee whatsoever that those would be the four individuals most often selected if an open-ended question had been asked, such as 'Who do you think is the most powerful and influential person in this country?' It is this choice, not only of the question, but also of the pre-designated answers, that gives the designer of the poll the ability to put opinions into people's mouths.

Remember, also, that these polls are conducted in order to be reported back to the public; they are meant to be read. Salty though the crocodile tears may be of the pollsters who claim that they are being misinterpreted and misreported, their claims must nevertheless be taken with an additional pinch of salt.

Many more polls are commissioned and conducted than are actually reported. We have been talking up to now almost exclusively about public opinion polls for public consumption, but there are a large number of private public opinion polls carried out with no intention of publishing the results, or where the results are made public only if they happen to fit with the desired outcome. Evidence for this activity is hard to find for obvious reasons. One of the companies to which I sent a questionnaire estimates that only some 35 per cent of its results ever get published—30 per cent in mass circulation newspapers and magazines, and 5 per cent in specialised journals. The other 65 per cent are not intended for publication. Later we discuss the large amount of private polling over the EEC referendum. In his book on ITT, Anthony Sampson mentions the commissioning of opinion polls by the CIA in Chile around the time of Allende's election to establish whether there was any need to intervene in the political situation. (Sampson, 1977, p. 243). In *Bad News*, the results of a confidential survey carried out by the BBC on public attitudes to television are quoted (Glasgow University, 1976). It was reported in the *International Herald Tribune* of 22 September 1977 that the United States Information Agency was commissioning polls of attitudes towards the United States in sixteen countries, including Britain, in order to advise the President on security and to help plan 'Voice of America' broadcasts. One suspects that these activities are the tip of an iceberg, but, like any iceberg, its actual extent is hard to estimate. The power to make information public or not gives those with the money to buy the information in the first place even more control over the creation and management of public opinion.

The analyses of results reported in the newspapers can rarely be checked unless the newspaper or polling organisation grants access to the data. Many will do this willingly, and indeed Gallup and NOP regularly deposit their social and political surveys at the SSRC Survey Archive at Essex University for the explicit purpose of secondary analysis. Other organisations are not so keen: ORC, for instance, does not let the Survey Archive have the results of the private polls it does for the Conservative Party, while MORI deposits private polls done for the Labour Party, but with a five-year embargo placed on them by the Labour Party.

e. *Who sponsored the poll and why?*

This is perhaps the most important question to ask. This is particularly so since opinion polls have been used in industrial life in a big way, and are frequently used in a way that serves to build up pressure against strikers. For example, the *Daily Mail* of 18 June 1975 reported the results of a poll done for them when there was the prospect of a rail strike. They asked a sample of railway workers: 'There is a threat of a national rail strike on June 23rd. Are you personally in favour or against the proposed strike?', and discovered that only 31 per cent were in favour and 59 per cent against. By talking of strikes as a 'threat', the question had already set the tone for the interview. The *Guardian* was critical of these results on the following day. Their reporters had had more lengthy discussions with about 25 railwaymen and came away convinced that the *Daily Mail* poll had not asked sufficiently searching questions to reveal the complex reasons behind support for this national strike; although most railway workers were against strikes, they insisted, reluctantly, that a walk-out was necessary—and one simple question had not elicited this more complex response. This interpretation of the railway workers' views would need to be established using a wider sample with more controlled forms of questioning, before we could accept it. The important point to remember is the kind of pressure put on strikers by this sort of journalism.

A referendum is, of course, something of a logical extension of opinion polling. It will be instructive, therefore, to look at public opinion during the referendum campaign on Britain's entry into the EEC. The future of Britain as a sovereign state was supposedly dependent on the results of an opinion poll type of question asked in this referendum.

The electorate of Britain has not always been so committed to the Common Market. In the early sixties public opinion was highly volatile; the referendum appears to have come at the high-tide of public favour towards the EEC in the last 10 years, as can be seen from *Table 1*.

Table 1: **Attitudes towards the EEC**

Balance of pro-EEC sentiment (obtained from subtracting % of 'antis' from % of 'pros'

	percentages
August 1961	+45
January 1963	0
July 1966	+44
November 1967	− 6
March 1970	−42
April 1972	− 1
1 January 1973 Britain entered EEC	
October 1973	−17
May 1974	−16
August 1974	−18
October 1974	−19[1]
March 1975	+ 8[1]
April 1975	+29
May 1975	+31

(*continued over page*)

5 June 1975 Polling Day	+34
January 1976	+26
March 1976	+22
July 1976	+ 9
September 1976	− 4
January 1977	− 6
June 1977	− 9

ᴸ But if the question had been prefaced by the condition of renegotiated terms (unspecified), +21 would have been obtained, in October 1974, and +37 in March 1975
Sources: Butler and Kitzinger, 1976; NOP and Gallup

The decision to remain in the EEC does not appear to be so popularly based if a longer period of time is considered. Of course, what this table shows only too clearly is the *effect* of the Labour government's decision to recommend staying in on renegotiated terms, and its vigorous campaign to support this. The high-tide of the EEC's electoral popularity coincided with the referendum, not with entry.

When the resources and expertise made available to the 'Britain Into Europe' lobby (the pro-EEC campaign) are considered, it is clear how carefully the polls were used and the public wooed in this crucial period. (Butler and Kitzinger, 1976). The executive of 'Britain into Europe' included Humphrey Taylor, an experienced pollster. Bob Worcester of Market & Opinion Research International also worked for the Referendum Steering Group. John Hanvey of Harris polls did much of the polling for BIE in a very revealing way—each survey he reported was immediately presented to a publicity committee which then did two things: it drafted a publicity directive and made suggestions for revising the questionnaire for the next survey. Bob Worcester commented thus on information gained from a private survey he did for the government which showed the growing lead of the BIE in the polls:

> This should have considerable impact on the strategy of the campaign. When you are ahead (as we are) you reassure people and encourage them to cast their vote. It is not the time to frighten them

with the spectre of communism, fear of the consequences of a No vote, or bogeymen. (Butler and Kitzinger, 1976, p. 246).

NOP did a survey in February 1975 in order to try out several forms of wording; the results are shown in *Table 2*.

It would be wrong to conclude from this that, come polling day, differences in wording could have produced differences of 23 per cent in replies, but there has been no research to substantiate the claim that in the final referendum the wording was irrelevant.

Table 2: **Wording effects in referendum**

	Majority 'Yes' over 'No' among intending voters *per cent*
Do you accept the government's recommendation that the United Kingdom should come out of the Common Market?	+ 0.2
Should the United Kingdom come out of the Common Market? IN OUT	 + 4.6 +10.8
Should the United Kingdom stay in the Common Market?	+13.2
Do you accept the government's recommendations that the United Kingdom should stay in the Common Market?	+18.2
The government recommends the acceptance of the renegotiated terms of British membership of the Common Market. Should the United Kingdom stay in the Common Market?	+11.2
Her Majesty's government belives that the nation's best interests would be served by accepting the favourably negotiated terms of our continued membership of the Common Market. Should the United Kingdom stay in the Common Market?	+16.2

Source: Butler and Kitzinger, 1976, p. 60

The embryo BIE executive was already operating in February 1975, and Humphrey Taylor spent an estimated £33,000 on surveys which explored in depth the knowledge of voters about the EEC and the way in which their anxieties about it were phrased (Butler and Kitzinger, 1976, pp. 257–58). The anti-Marketeers had neither the same resources nor equivalent expertise at their disposal, and it was not until they were assured of a government grant for their campaign that they were able to enter the field of polls. When they did, all they could afford were four quick polls, which merely confirmed their gloomy impression that they were going to be defeated.

Public opinion, according to polls of this type, has since been swinging away from the EEC. However, the Secretary of State for Prices and Consumer Protection commented in a Granada TV programme on 27 June, 1977, about a poll in the North West: 'It is clear that if we had another referendum campaign, which we won't, and if we expose the issues in the way the referendum campaign would expose them, then the North West would vote more or less as they voted last time, which is to stay in'. (Quoted in *The Times* the following day). The evidence provided in *Table 1* suggests that groups with access to resources and expertise do indeed have the power to influence the results, if not directly through the campaign propaganda then indirectly through controlling the direction of events, wording, timing, and so on.

So, to sum up the actions taken by the sponsors of this glorified opinion poll, the government:

1. chose when to call the referendum;

2. had access to research showing the effects of different wording;

3. conducted a vigorous campaign (strengthened by the support of an all-party committee and every single Fleet Street newspaper);

4. used the results to reconfirm the rightness of the decision every time fresh doubts were raised about the EEC.

f. The role of opinion polls in capitalist society

This chapter has tried to draw attention to the ways in which opinion polls do not conform to the criteria usually regarded as acceptable in social science. While technically superior methods exist for eliciting views from people, these are rarely used in opinion polling. (See Jowell and Spence, 1975, for an example of how quite complex opinions towards the EEC can be drawn out by a social survey).

Having briefly reviewed the ways in which public opinion polls are open to manipulation, we must now consider whether such polls could fulfil a democratic function even if all the questions we have asked so far were satisfactorily met. This is a rather different sort of question than previous ones, for this is to some extent a moral, philosophical question. Irving Crespi, one-time Vice-President of Gallup, termed opinion polls 'continuing elections'. They are often quoted with the voice of democratic authority by lobbyists trying to gain credence for their cause. But are they really an extension of democracy? If public opinion polling and referenda were increased on a dramatic scale, would the level of popular participation in public policy-making substantially rise?

Of course not! Debate and discussion, the basis of informed consideration and effective democracy, are entirely absent from this activity. The interviewer arrives unannounced to an individual in his or her home, with strict instructions to try to prevent discussion ensuing between the respondent and anyone else present, for it is the respondent's views alone that are sought; a lot of preformulated questions are put to this individual by an interviewer keen to get through her quota of interviews as quickly as possible; then all the individual replies .are merely added together to produce the resultant public opinion.

The sponsors take all the important decisions. They can choose what to have a poll about, how to word it, when to have it, whom to ask the questions of; and newspaper owners can control how and when and whether it is reported. And we have seen how each of these decisions can markedly affect the appearance of this public opinion. Something as open to manipulation as this can never be used to further democracy.

The conclusion could be that polls are therefore something to be brushed aside. Jowell and Hoinville, *op. cit.*, conclude their article in *New Society* by saying: '. . . as long as the public remains sophisticated enough to ignore their results, . . . the bulk of opinion polls will continue to be more entertaining than harmful'. But the public is not unaffected by polls of this kind. British evidence suggests that election polling affects the way people vote; in four successive General Elections (1966, 1970, February 1974, and October 1974) the party ahead at the polls did much worse than expected. In this case, knowledge of what other people are supposed to think seems to produce an anti-bandwagon effect, probably by depressing the turn-out of those who think the party they support is going to win. But this is the only case of this type. Evidence from social psychology strongly suggests that knowing what other people think has a strong tendency to force the respondent to voice similar views. (See Asch, 1951, and Allen, 1965). In the field of attitudes towards crime, Berkowitz and Walker showed that individuals' stated opinions towards specified crimes could be shifted quite strongly to conform with the answers that they were told their peers had given. (Berkowitz and Walker, 1967). Bearing this in mind, look at this illustration of an advertisement published in the Autumn of 1977 by the clearing banks as part of their campaign against nationalisation.

Polls are not social scientific; they are not democratic; they are often employed so as to reconfirm their own results; but most importantly they may be used to confer a kind of legitimacy to those people who can quote their results and 'scientifically prove' that they have majority backing. It is this appearance of ultra-democracy that gives them their power.

Margaret Thatcher, leader of the Conservative Party, seems to have realised this fully. On 18 September 1977, she told a television interviewer that she might seek a referendum to resolve a confrontation with a trade union if she were Prime Minister. This is only a slight extension of the present practice of conducting opinion polls during major industrial disputes to bring pressure on those involved. Sometimes such polls claim to 'reveal' that the workers involved do not 'really' support the dispute. But we should not be surprised that the democracy that operates within a trade union in the discussions that precede a decision to take industrial action arrives at different conclusions from the pseudo-democracy of an opinion poll on the sponsor's own terms.

Public opinion polls undoubtedly play a powerful part in social control, reminding individuals of what everybody else thinks about various issues. This is not to argue that they are infinitely manipulable, or that they are worthless or that they should be banned. The answers chosen by respondents to closed-choice questions, or what they are prepared to reveal to an interviewer in a fairly formal situation, are not without interest. But the relevance is severely circumscribed by the considerations discussed in this chapter, and so polls can, in the author's opinion, in no way be considered as a desirable input into a democratic decision-making process. Individuated closed-choice opinion questions mirror closely the type of closed-choice democracy that we have in Britain at the moment; perhaps both reflect individuated mass society in which community becomes eroded. To imagine that increased recourse to ballots of public opinion would increase the power of ordinary people to affect major decisions is as much of a pipedream as the very notion of a unified social will.

BANKS DEBATE. Broadsheet No.4

DID THE POLLS GET
YOU RIGHT?

Should Britain's four main clearing banks be nationalised?

The Prime Minister, most of the Cabinet and the majority of Labour supporters say no, but last year the Labour Party Conference voted in favour of nationalisation.

We (the banks named below) have been asking you, through these Banks Debate Broadsheets, what you think.

Every day the issue becomes more widely discussed, as we see from our postbag.

So far, over 28,000 have taken part in the Debate. And over 90% of them wrote to tell us

that, for many reasons, they are against bank nationalisation.

Independent polls.

Since the Debate was opened, there have also been two public opinion polls by independent organisations on this important issue. Both interviewed a complete cross section of the British public. One was conducted in July by Market & Opinion Research International (MORI) and the other in August by Gallup.

One of MORI's questions asked, "Do you think this industry (banking) should be

nationalised?" 74% said no; 14% said yes. The remainder were uncommitted.

Concerning the Banks Debate itself, 90% of people said that they liked being given the chance to express their views. So we're printing some of the actual questions from both polls here, with the results. You might like to tick the appropriate boxes and see whether your opinion matches up with the majority view.

If you'd like to send us the page when you've filled it in, we will be pleased to add it to the growing fund of information on the public's opinion about the future of its banks.

Banks and their customers.

1. "If the banks were nationalised, customers would get better service than they do now." PUBLIC OPINION 11% YOUR OPINION 70%

2. "If the banks were nationalised, bank charges would go up." 67% 16%

3. "If the banks were nationalised, there would be a wider choice of services than there is at present." 17% 53%

4. "If the banks were nationalised, the 17% 62% standard of management would rise."

Banks and Britain.

5. "If the banks were nationalised, do you think they would do a better or worse job for Britain?" 27% 55%

6. "If the banks were nationalised, it would be good for investment in Britain." 18% 54%

Banks and Investment.

7. "The Government would be likely to make better use of the banks' money than the banks do now." 27% 55%

8. "The Government would use some of banks' customers' money to support unsuccessful businesses." 50% 21%

9. "If the banks were nationalised, people would be less willing to save or invest their money in them." 60% 18%

What's your opinion?
We want to hear from everyone, whether they're for or against bank nationalisation. So please tick the boxes in this advertisement and send us the page or, if you would

prefer, write us a letter giving your views.
You can deliver it to any branch of any bank listed here, in an envelope marked "The Banks Debate". Or you can post it to us at the address on the right.

THE BANKS

Diagram 1

Notes

1. For a journalistic account of this information explosion, see Hopkins (1973). For a general discussion of opinion polling in Britain, see Teer and Spence (1973). For American material, see Roll and Cantril (1972), and Bogart (1972).

2. These trends emerged from a small questionnaire I sent to the top eight companies doing opinion research in Britain.

3. Some attitude psychologists have attempted to grapple with this problem by building models which take into account four separate factors: attitudes (in the sense of feelings), beliefs, intentions and behaviour (Fishbein and Azjen, 1975). Gross and Niman (1973), Smith (1971), and Festinger (1964), discuss this problem as it relates to opinion polling. The most sophisticated and up to date review is Schuman and Johnson (1976). See also Deutscher (1973) and Jones and Davis (1965). Lane and Sears (1964), discuss the process of formation of political opinions.

4. 'Closed-ended' questions require respondents to choose from a limited number of alternatives formulated by those conducting the survey; 'open-ended' questions, on the other hand, allow each respondent to formulate his or her own response.

5. See Converse (1970), for a discussion of the importance of respondents being practised in voicing attitudes.

6. There are some elementary rules for framing questions in questionnaires. See Payne (1951), Scott (1967), and Sudman and Bradburn (1974). The closed-choice questions must be carefully researched. One should not ask ambiguous or complicated questions, and especially not ask double-barrelled questions or questions with double negatives in them. It is important to either avoid or identify and correct for a tendency that many people have to say 'Yes' to anything they are asked. Scott, 1967, pp. 236–38, discusses different response patterns including such patterns of 'acquiescence'.

Bibliography

Allen, V. L., 1965, 'Situational factors in conformity', in L. Berkowitz (ed.), *Advances in Experimental Social Psychology*, vol. 2, New York, Academic Press, pp. 133–75.

Asch, S., 1951, 'Effects of group pressure upon modification and distortion of judgement', in H. Guetzkow (ed.), *Groups, Leadership and Men*, Pittsburgh, Carnegie Press, pp. 177–90.

Belson, W. A., 1968, 'Respondent understanding of survey questions', *Polls*, vol. 3, no. 4.

Berkowitz, L., and Walker, N., 1969, 'Law and moral judgements', *Sociometry*, vol. 30, no. 4, December.

Blackburn, R., 1967, 'The unequal society', in R. Blackburn and A. Cockburn (eds.), *The Incompatibles*, Harmondsworth, Penguin.

Blumer, H., 1948, 'Public opinion and public opinion polling', *American Sociological Review*, vol. 13, pp. 542-54.

Bogart, L., 1972, *Silent Politics: Polls and Awareness of Public Opinion*, New York, Wiley Interscience.

Butler, D., and Kitzinger, U., 1976, *The 1975 Referendum*, London, Macmillan (see especially ch. 10 on polls).

Cochran, W. G., Mosteller, F., and Tukey, J. W., 1954, 'Principles of sampling', *Journal of the American Statistical Association*, vol. 49, pp. 13–35; reprinted as pp.

168-86 in D. P. Forcese and S. Richer (eds.), *Stages of Social Research: Contemporary Perspectives*, Englewood Cliffs, N.J., Prentice-Hall 1970.

Converse, P. E., 1970, 'Attitudes and non-attitudes: continuation of a dialogue', pp. 168-89 in E. Tufte (ed.), *Quantitative Analysis of Social Problems*, Reading, Mass., Addison-Wesley.

Deutscher, I. (ed.), 1973, *What We Say/What We Do*, Glencoe, Ill., Scott, Foreman and Co.

Edwards, A. L., 1957, *The Social Desirability Variable in Personality Assessment and Research*, New York, Dryden Press.

Festinger, L., 1964, 'Behavioural support for opinion change', *Public Opinion Quarterly*, vol. 28, pp. 404-17.

Fishbein, M., and Azjen, I., 1975, *Belief, Attitude, Intention and Behaviour: An Introduction to Theory and Research*, Reading, Mass., Addison-Wesley.

Gallup Poll, 1971, *Gallup Political Index*, London.

Galtung, J., 1967, *Theory and Methods of Social Research*, London, Allen and Unwin.

Glasgow University Media Group, 1976, *Bad News*, vol. 1, London, Routledge & Kegan Paul.

Goldthorpe, J. H., 1966, 'Attitudes and behaviour of car-assembly workers', *British Journal of Sociology*, vol. 17.

Gross, S. J., and Niman, C. M., 1973, 'Attitude-behaviour consistency: a review', *Public Opinion Quarterly*, fall.

Habermas, J., 1971, *Towards a Rational Society: Student Protest, Science and Politics* (Translated by J. J. Shapiro), London, Heinemann.

'Harris and ORC Election Surveys; October 1974'. Research review produced by Louis Harris International Inc., London.

Hopkins, H., 1973, *The Numbers Game: The Bland Totalitarianism*, London, Secker and Warburg.

Innes, W., and Vaughan, G. M., 1972, 'The proposed 1973 Springbok rugby tour: testing public opinion', unpublished study, Psychology Department, Auckland University, New Zealand.

Jones, E. C., and Davis, K. E., 1965, 'From acts to dispositions', in L. Berkowitz (ed.), *Advances in Experimental Social Psychology*, vol 2, New York, Academic Press.

Jowell, R., and Hoinville, G., 1969, 'Opinion polls tested', *New Society*, 7 August.

Jowell, R., and Spence, J., 1975, *The Grudging Europeans*, London, Social and Community Planning Research.

Lapiere, R. T., 1934, 'Attitudes vs. actions', *Social Forces*, vol. 13, pp. 230-37.

Lane, R. E., and Sears, D. O., 1964, *Public Opinion*, Englewood Cliffs, N.J., Prentice-Hall.

McKennell, A. C., 1977, 'Attitude scale construction', in C. A. O'Muircheartaigh and C. Payne (eds.), *The Analysis of Survey Data*, vol. 1, London, Wiley.

McNemar, Q., 1946, 'Opinion attitude methodology', *Psychological Bulletin*, vol. 43, pp. 289-374.

Moser, C. A., and Kalton, G., 1971, *Survey Methods in Social Investigation*, 2nd edn., London, Heinemann Educational.

Moser, C. A., and Stuart, A., 1953, 'An experimental study of quota sampling', *Journal of the Royal Statistical Society*, series A, vol. 116, pp. 349-405.

NOP, *NOP (Political) Bulletin,* 1964, London; continued as *Political Social Economic Review* after 1975.

Payne, S. Le Baron, 1951, *The Art of Asking Questions*, (Studies in Public Opinion, 3), Princeton, N.J.

Pollock, F., 1976, 'Empirical research into public opinion', in P. Connerton (ed.), *Critical Sociology*, Harmondsworth, Penguin.

Roll, C. W., and Cantril, A. H., 1972, *Polls: Their Use and Misuse in Politics*, New York, Basic Books.

Sampson, A., 1977, *The Sovereign State: The Secret History of ITT*, London, Coronet Books (first published 1973).

Schuman, H. and Duncan, O. D., 1974, 'Questions about attitude survey questions', in H. L. Costner (ed.), *Sociological Methodology 1973-74*, San Francisco, Jossey-Bass.

Schuman, H., and Johnson, M. P., 1976, 'Attitudes and behaviour', *Annual Review of Sociology*, no. 2.

Scott, W. A., 1967, 'Attitude measurement', in G. Lindzey and E. Aronson (eds.), *The Handbook of Social Psychology*, vol II, (2nd edn.), London, Addison-Wesley.

Smith, M. B., 1971, 'A psychologist's perspective on public opinion theory', *Public Opinion Quarterly*, vol. 35, 1971-72, pp. 36-43.

Sudman, S., and Bradburn, N., 1974, 'Response effects in surveys: a review and synthesis', *National Opinion Research Centre Monographs in Social Research*, no. 16, Chicago, Aldine.

Teer, F., and Spence, J. D., 1973, *Political Opinion Polls*, London, Hutchinson.

Webb, N. L., and Wybrow, R. J., 1974, 'Polls in a changing world', *Journal of the Market Research Society*, vol. 16, no. 4, pp. 263-69.

White, D., 1977, 'Nuclear-power: a special *New Society* survey', *New Society*, 31 March.

19.

Jonathan Rosenhead and Colin Thunhurst

Operational Research and Cost Benefit Analysis: Whose Science?

Operational Research is a problem-solving activity carried out for the management of large enterprises by staff specialists, usually with a science- and particularly mathematically-based training.[1] From seemingly accidental beginnings in Britain in the late 1930s it has spread round the world, and has become part of the standard fixtures and fittings of virtually all substantial industrial, commercial and financial undertakings—and increasingly of local and national government too. Operational researchers have taken over from industrial statisticians the task of interpreting the often suspect and highly variable data on which managerial decisions must be based. There are masters degrees in and chairs of operational research at many British universities and polytechnics; journals offering the latest developments in theory and (sometimes) practice proliferate. There are probably now over ten thousand operational researchers in Britain. As a separate identifiable discipline it constitutes a comparatively new but significant planning and control element in the trajectory of advanced capitalism. But, as we shall show below, the roots of operational research can be traced to the very foundation of capitalism itself.

Because it is explicitly designed to control rather than to understand social phenomena, operational research (OR) should perhaps be regarded as social engineering rather than social science. Yet it is clearly relevant to social scientists—for a number of reasons. First, its deployment in industry is, as we shall show, part and parcel of the development of the whole range of management and behavioural sciences, many of them with a much more explicit social science orientation. Second, as it spreads through the public sector, OR is increasingly being applied to problem areas—for example, health and welfare services—where social scientists and social administrators have an established interest. Lastly, operational research is an especially clear example of a more general tendency in our society: the presentation of potentially divisive social and political issues as if they were purely technical matters, to be solved by the judicious application of science by experts. This technocratic drive needs to be more widely and deeply appreciated, by scientists and non-scientists alike, if it is to be challenged. That is one of the principal aims of this chapter—to aid in the demystification of the management uses of science.

The history of operational research

The 'authorised history' of OR locates its origins in the late 1930s, in the active British preparations for the second world war.[2] The development of radar led to a whole range of novel organisational problems—for example, how to reduce the time taken after picking up incoming bombers on radar before the fighters take off; and how to identify and eliminate distortion of radar readings caused by local topography. Interdisciplinary groups of scientists were put to work on these problems, using in part their technical knowledge, but also what could loosely be called 'the scientific method'. The results were striking, and these 'operational research' units were rapidly established in one branch of the armed forces after another.

One classic study can illustrate the approach. In the anti-submarine war, depth-charges dropped from aircraft were proving less effective than had been hoped. An OR study, using data from aircraft logs, developed a plausible hypothesis—that the only U-boat likely to be sunk was one caught unawares virtually on the surface. Their recommendation was that depth-charges should be set to explode at a minimal depth below the surface, whereas previous practice had been to set charges to catch U-boats which would already have dived. The result was an immediate increase of sinkings by a factor of about three. By manipulation of one control variable (depth of explosion), and at no extra expense of resources, 'inefficiency' was eliminated. The result had been achieved by applying the classical scientific method (define problem—collect data—formulate hypothesis—test hypothesis—adopt, adapt or reject) to a problem in 'the world of affairs'. This is the legend of OR. And it is a legend that some operational researchers still think they are living.

After the war it was increasingly realised that the problems of running a large industrial enterprise in peacetime had much in common with those of managing the various branches of the armed forces in wartime. In the newly nationalised industries, especially the National Coal Board (Tomlinson, 1971), and in heavy industry such as steel, OR groups were soon established. After all, if OR could apply the scientific method to maximise deaths, why not maximise the output of coal, or just good old profit?

OR had crossed the Atlantic during the war, and quickly flourished in the United States. Whereas in Britain it was used initially in the control and rationalisation of *production*, the state of US capitalism led to a different emphasis. OR was heavily used in *marketing* (devising media schedules, deciding advertising budgets, assessing the relative effectiveness of advertising, price, special offers, shelf-space, etc.) as firms set out to control their consumers—Galbraith's 'revised sequence' of advanced capitalism.[3] But on both sides of the Atlantic operational research spread from industry to industry and from function to function.

The typical uses of OR in the twenty years immediately after the war, whether by publicly owned or private industry, can be classed as *tactical*. The application of OR became routine in such tasks as stock control, equipment maintenance and replacement, vehicle routing, the scheduling of construction projects, and the siting of warehouses and retail outlets to reduce transport costs or increase sales, as well as in the direct planning and control of day-to-day production operations. Operational research provided the means by which management could squeeze out a few extra percentage points of production from the same labour and resources, or shave a few per cent off the costs.

Since the mid-1960s, operational research has increasingly been employed by commercial and industrial management on more *strategic* problems—that is, on those which affect the future structure or even viability of the enterprise. Computerised corporate planning models, for example, have been used to predict how future cash flows will be affected by major investment decisions. (OR is also being used directly in finance and banking, reflecting the increasing dominance of finance capital.) The other major new growth area for operational research, particularly in the 1970s in Britain, has been local and national government. We will discuss these trends in more detail below.

The growth and content of operational research

As OR grew up it shed its back-of-the-envelope origins. From the 1950s onwards, powerful new mathematical techniques were developed to solve recurrent problems with particular structures, often using the power of electronic computers. Profit seeking enterprises, existing in an often uncertain environment, were less concerned with adopting a general problem-solving approach than with employing practitioners who could offer 'tried and proven' techniques. There is now a wide range of such techniques—queueing theory, dynamic programming, graph theory . . . But three techniques have dominated all the others in terms of applications.

In particular there is *mathematical programming*, the most widely used of all. This is based on the assumption that one can formulate the objective of management as a simple mathematical combination (usually a linear weighted sum) of a number of control variables. For example, if the firm manufactures several different products, then the objective (profit) can be expressed as the number produced multiplied by the profit per unit, summed over the list of products. This mathematical expression is called an 'objective function'. There are always constraints which prevent an unlimited output—the firm has only a certain amount of the raw material used in several of the products; there is a limit on the throughput of particular machines; only a certain number of hours per week can be obtained from the workforce. The problem is to select the values of the 'control variables' (here, weekly output of each product) to maximise the objective function without violating any contraints. Mathematical programming offers an efficient, automatic search procedure for finding the solution which 'optimises' the objective function. Efficiency is essential, since the number of variables, or of constraints, can easily run into thousands when the 'problem' is the operation of, say, a complex oil refinery.

Critical path analysis is a technique devised for a much more limited class of problems—how to schedule a set of activities, some of which must be completed before others can start, so that the completion of an entire project is achieved as quickly as possible. Applied to the development of the Polaris missile system, it was credited with saving eighteen months. Now it is applied routinely to reducing the duration of construction projects. (Critics have claimed that the resultant speed-up has led to increased fatalities on construction sites; others have held that, when applied to the scheduling of urban development planning, critical path analysis has reinforced bureaucratic inflexibility by removing any slack and so increasing the time penalty of any delay.)

The third widely applied technique concerns the handling of *stock control* problems. A set of polices has been derived which, it is argued, will minimise the total stock management costs—costs of ordering, costs of holding stock, and costs of running out of stock. The importance of the technique, however, is not that it produces optimal solutions (some of the 'costs' are notional in the extreme), but that it produces rules which can be applied routinely on a computerised system. By this automation of 'programmable' lower management decisions, the firm can free some of its lower level management staff for more creative work—or free them to find jobs elsewhere.

Alongside these, mention must also be made of *computer simulation*, though it is not strictly a technique. Rather, it is a method of getting some answers when the world of the corporation refuses to be quite as simple as the available techniques require. (Since this happens rather often, simulation is very widely, and increasingly, used.) There is, then, no short cut method to 'optimal' solutions. However, it may be possible to programme the computer with the entire complex set of constraints, relationships and decision-rules of the situation under study. The computer can then be made to reproduce (symbolically) any required length of history of the system. By changing some of the relations in the computer model and re-simulating, it is possible to see what the effects of any changes in equipment or operating procedures might be.

These methods produced changes in the nature of OR. There were now heavy investments in computer packages for carrying out particular techniques, or in patent computer languages to facilitate the writing of simulations. There was less emphasis on the 'scientific method', and more on forcing the messy material of business life into the strait-jacket of an available technique. Operational research was becoming the latest victim of the spread of commodity relations through society. OR itself became a commodity to be bought and sold. And to be bought and sold it had to be standardised, packaged and presented in a recognisable form and to be of proven effectiveness.

It should be clear from this brief account that both in its history and in its current practice, OR is deeply rooted in wider social processes. Developments in OR can only be understood in terms of the development of capitalism as a whole. This is true of the very *existence* of operational research. The birth of the subject should not be seen as just a 'lucky' accident, nor as the result of penetrating intellect or inspirational leadership. OR, as such, happened because of some of these, but it didn't *just* happen. To understand why the times were ripe we must look rather further back than 1939, and rather more deeply into the 'laws of motion' of capitalist society.

The pre-history of operational research[4]

Operational research is sometimes known as management science, and management (as we know it today) developed only with the Industrial Revolution. Before capitalism such simple co-ordination and planning as were required in manufacture were performed as an integral part of the individual craftworker's cycle of production. In the early stages of capitalism production was carried out in the workers' homes, under the 'putting out' system. Long after the development of factories, much work was still carried out under variants of this system.[5] Even when the factory system was quite mature, the owners or delegates of capital had little management, as such, to do. The details of *how* work was done were decided much nearer to the point of production.

Capital was reaping only part of the benefit of the control potential which the factory offered. The factory could instil regular work habits into a wayward, recently agricultural, work-force. But it could also be used to 'rationalise' the way in which the work was to be done. A new and systematic division of labour could provide greater production from a given number of workers; and, by 'de-skilling' the work-force, management weakened the potential stranglehold of skilled workers over production. Simultaneously, by taking over the mental processes of work, management could claim legitimacy for its own controlling role (see Marglin, 1971).

It was in this context that Frederick Winslow Taylor developed 'Scientific Management', from the 1890s onwards. Taylor, by study of the activities of selected workers, divided up complex tasks into individual elements, and decided on the 'one best way' in which each should be performed. Workers who would not (or could not) work this way were sacked—no problem for the firm, since the higher production rates squeezed out meant that the workforce could be drastically reduced.

Taylorism, and its more sophisticated derivatives, is still an active force in capitalist society.[6] New areas of blue- and increasingly white-collar work are continually being redesigned in accordance with its principles—the dissociation of the labour process from the skills of the workers; the separation of conception of a task from its execution; and capitalist monopoly over knowledge for the control of each step of the labour process and its mode of execution.

But from the earliest days the organised work-force has resisted its encroachments in fierce and sometimes locally successful struggles.[7] The entire range of sciences on which management now relies for the design and control of the work process—time and motion study, production engineering, ergonomics (also called human engineering), as well as the various schools of organisation theory, industrial sociology and industrial psychology—can be seen as elements in a Taylorist offensive, or as managerial tactics to head off the workers' angry response.[8]

Operational research is one of these management sciences. And both these tendencies—to control the workplace and to control the response—are present within it. It is part of the forces of production, which under capitalism are the means by which the work-force is more efficiently exploited; and it is part of the ideological superstructure, the dominant system of ideas which dictate that the workers must accept the conditions of their exploitation.

Operational research as part of the forces of production

The development of the management sciences[9] occurred in a period characterised not only by an increasing division of labour but also by intensified economic concentration. In fact the management sciences have been concerned as much to maintain centralised control over these burgeoning enterprises as to devise methods of squeezing more surplus value out of the labour power of the workers.

In a small workshop the activities of a handful of apprentices and journeymen could be directly supervised by the master. But, in a massive modern corporation, employing perhaps hundreds of thousands, and with a dozen hierarchical levels separating top management from the shop-floor, control problems become crucial. The organizational hierarchy itself provides the control structure, operating as a bureaucracy. The division of labour into routine, repetitive jobs means that what any worker, or department, achieves can be easily measured. This information can then be passed up the hierarchy, and the degree to which performance targets are being met can be assessed. These, then, are the prerequisites for control at a distance: fragmentation, quantification and information. Scientific Management helped and helps to make them possible.

This much has been gain to management. But there have also been adverse effects. Once you have 'taken the workers' heads off' you cannot expect them to generate ideas about how the job might be done more effectively. And workers' ideas have often been a major source for technological innovation. Innovation in work methods now needs to be injected from outside the immediate workforce. Second, workers tend not to like acting merely as human cogs in a machine, and their attitudes and responses can threaten the organization. Third, massive bureaucratic structures respond very sluggishly to changes in their environment—an environment that is now very turbulent. The actions of other massive bureaucracies, plus the uncertainties of reliance on advanced technology, make the organization highly vulnerable. (The collapse of Rolls-Royce in 1971 is only one dramatic instance of a general problem.) Each of these problems has called for new management sciences. Operational research, in particular, has operated as a force for the resolution of all three.[10]

Tactical operational research serves to improve the exploitation of labour power. Techniques such as mathematical programming are used to extend the logic of time and motion study to plant level. With an emphasis on maximisation (profits, of course) or minimisation (costs), their aim is to squeeze the greatest possible return out of all input resources—'natural' resources, manufactured resources and labour power alike. This role for operational research takes on a particular significance when viewed against the development of the massive multinational, in place of the small entrepreneurial firm. As a result, many transactions which would formerly have been conducted by independent firms now take place entirely within a single corporation. The tactical coordination which previously took place through the market has had to be replaced by new control mechanisms which operate within the corporation. Operational research provides them (see Hales, 1974).

Strategic operational research helps the firm adapt to a turbulent environment. It does this in two ways. First, it can assess the effects on the organisation's performance of many combinations of external circumstances and internal decisions. For example, a multinational corporation may decide on whether to invest in a Third World country by estimating the 'subjective' probabilities of different types of political development—socialist revolution, army coup, etc.—and the likely ranges of policies towards foreign investment which might then materialise. OR provides the framework for this analysis (see Byrnes and Chesterton, 1973). Second, it can assist management in its attempts to pacify the environment, by horizontal or vertical integration, by control of the market or of raw material sources. Thus operational research can assist in studies of possible mergers or takeover bids—examining the compatibility of product lines, scope for economies of scale and 'rationalisation', strategies open to the opposition, etc. The combination of complexity and uncertainty can be at least apparently 'tamed' by the application of OR's formal, rationalist method. A variety of approaches—computer simulation, decision analysis, game theory, policy analysis—offer this strategic potential. Even the tactical, optimising, techniques can be pressed into service in a 'what if . . .?' mode—that is, by computing the various optima that might occur in a number of possible future environments, making it possible (however inefficiently) simply to explore the possible consequences of any selected set of decisions.

So far, in this and the previous section, our discussion has been conducted in terms of the individual capitalist enterprise, whether industrial, commercial or financial. But paralleling the massive growth of state planning and economic intervention (as well as of state enterprise), operational research has increasingly been applied in the public sector.

Operational research in the service of the state

State intervention is multi-faceted.[11] It provides infrastructure (e.g. transport facilities, basic research, education and training) which no individual enterprise could afford; it attempts to stabilize the economy to produce predictable market conditions; if necessary, it provides the market, using taxpayers money; it attempts to harmonise potentially destabilizing conflicts between conflicting power blocs; it provides (on the cheap) the social welfare safety net which attempts to defuse the resentments of the under-privileged, and of the reserve army of the unemployed; and it runs the repressive apparatus which maintains 'order', and would attempt to restore it if 'things got out of hand'.[12] The trades unions, by inhibiting spontaneous or grass-roots organisation and action, have become a valuable element in the disciplining of the work-force, their top bureaucrats having been admitted into the ruling circles. But the dominant interest (whether under Tory or Labour governments) is towards the greater and greater accumulation of capital. The monolithic arrangement is sometimes called the Corporate State.

In most of these state activities operational research now has a role. In nationalised industries (British Steel, for example) OR is used in much the same way as it is in large-scale private industry —for production scheduling, for assessing alternative capital investments, for financial planning, and for making decisions about the location of new plants or the closing down of old ones. Much of the same approach transfers across to the other types of enterprise run directly by the national or local state, those concerned with 'welfare' or social control—for example, the National Health Service, the employment service, the police, the fire service. OR concerns itself with the scheduling of police patrols, economies of scale through 'rationalising' hospital supplies, stocks and services, the location of job shops or fire stations, and so on. The only real difference here is that since these enterprises do not produce 'profit', either surrogate measures of performance need to be invented, or the equivalent but inverse procedure is taken—of minimising cost. Which is convenient, particularly in the current economic climate, but scarcely what most people thought the National Health Service (say) was originally there for.

At the strategic level the approach must be different, particularly for state agencies whose main function is planning— that is, attempting to condition the decisions which will be taken by formally autonomous capitalist enterprises. Now the 'environment' can no longer be seen as a source of random extraneous disturbance, but is itself the object of planning.[13] In this context, the watchword is 'co-ordination', not 'optimisation'. And here the operational research contribution comes in the guise of systems analysis (or systems science). This approach to the study of complex systems has roots both in control engineering and in biology. Its general concern is to design systems which 'control' themselves, in the sense that they have built-in self-correcting mechanisms or 'negative feedback'. The underlying assumption is that stability is a self-evident objective; although the system must adapt to survive, it is important that the structural relationships of the status quo should be maintained. Also built into the very methodology of the approach are assumptions on the inevitability of both consensus and hierarchy.[14]

Though systems analysis does have its practical functions, its major usefulness to the preservation of the system lies elsewhere, in the realm of ideas. This leads us naturally on to OR's third major role, the amelioration of attitudes of the work-force. Though less immediately apparent than the others, it is at least as important.

Operational research as ideology

In any period of history the dominant ideas support the interests of the dominant class. This was as true of the doctrine of the church in the Middle Ages, as of the polemics of the Social Darwinists in the nineteenth century. Their ideas seem bizarre to us now, but they were the product of no conspiracy. They were *logically* necessary, since no organisation of society can persist in the long run with fundamental dissonance between its ideology and its practice. Ideas, being more malleable than material relationships, do most of the adjusting.

Capitalism consists of the appropriation by those who control capital or surplus value created by those who actually do the work. Since the latter at any point in time constitute a far larger group than the former, it might seem that only physical force employed by the state (on behalf of capital) could maintain the system. Indeed, force is the ultimate back-up, nowadays in a variety of more or less sophisticated forms (see Ackroyd et al., 1977). But such measures are for crises only, and can easily, if used prematurely or inappropriately, be counter-productive. It is far more effective if the working class can be persuaded, by one means or another, to accept its exploitation—or even, as in some recent developments, to manage its own exploitation. So capital needs to legitimate its domination over the process by which things are produced. Religious prescription, fear of starvation, inculcation of deferrence have all been used, but are not particularly suited to current circumstances. The 'will of God' is unsatisfactory as a justification for the status quo, when all known social relations are being visibly and purposefully changed in the pursuit of profit. Deference to the boss cannot survive his disappearance into some remote eyrie in a holding company or multinational. The gap is being filled by 'scientism', and operational research is one of its leading edges.

In essence, scientism consists of claims that the social and economic world, like the natural world, can only be understood by technicians trained in the correct application of science. Thus, scientism implies that decisions which might formerly have been considered exercises of power, and hence political, are not in fact political decisions at all but 'scientific' or 'rational' ones. The siting of an airport or a motorway, the running speed of a production line, the health hazards to which a production worker is exposed are all treated as if they were susceptible to the same mode of analysis as might be applied, say, to the composition of a chemical. They are not, therefore, issues to be negotiated or bargained over, but problems for which there is a single 'objective' answer (the 'optimum') which can, of course, be determined by 'our' experts.[15]

In fact, there is not just one answer because there is more than one question. The problems of management are not the problems of the workers—indeed many of the latter are the consequences of the solutions to the former. Operational research presents the problems of management as *the* problems; the fundamental conflict between management (as the representative of capital) and labour is assumed away (though OR is not the only means to achieve this). Thus, both the problems and their 'solutions' have as a concealed presumption the continuation of the existing relations of production, in which capital controls labour and disposes of the surplus. So the purposeful projection into the future of unequal relations is dressed up in the guise of technocracy—government by experts. Technocracy is claimed to be both adequate and necessary. Adequate, since with consensus on ends taken as self-evident, the only questions needing answers are technical ones about means. And necessary, because the technical apparatus (such as operational research) for answering these residual questions is so complex.

Cost benefit analysis—ideology rampant

This process can be seen at its most blatant in the technique, closely related to operational research, of cost benefit analysis (CBA).[16] CBA is a method for assessing not just the identifiable cash profit or loss of a public project, but also elements of 'intangible' social cost and benefit. In principle this might seem a progressive innovation since, in theory at least, effects of the environment, or even work-force, which formerly were neglected, can now be incorporated into the analysis. And to some extent they are, but in CBA all these apparently incommensurable dimensions (noise, time, grief) are compressed onto a single dimension—money.[17] Qualities which had previously been assumed as inalienable are now given a price tag. Even life itself. It has been pointed out that it is only logical, rational, to ask: '. . .and how much for your grandmother?' (see Adams, 1974). (Indeed, if life is valued at one's prospective contribution to Gross National Product, an average grandmother is worth a negative sum.)

The logic of CBA is that the value of something is what people are willing to pay for it. So, it may be that the effect of noise from a planned motorway is to be included in the CBA calculations. Easy—just see what current price differentials are between houses exposed to existing motorways, and similar houses not so afflicted. The difference is the amount that people are willing to pay to avoid noise. (Needless to say, the money is not normally given to those who suffer; the calculations are to demonstrate an optimal aggregate social benefit, not to redistribute real resources.) If, sadly, there is no market in, say, grief or picturesque landscapes, then the most tortuous arguments are developed in order to 'infer' from other behaviour what the price *would* be, if there were a market. For example, the value of a stretch of landscape might be inferred from the number of people who picnic there, and the distance they have travelled to reach it. Of course, there is endless room here for 'judiciously' adjusting the data to give the desired results. But the method will tend to give the answers expected of it even without direct assistance—for the distorted values of our society are already enshrined, as apparently given facts, in the prices which the market generates. Thus in transport planning, a salesman's car trip will be valued five times more highly than a bus journey of the same duration by a woman encumbered by two children and heavy shopping—because the job market rewards the businessman highly and home work scarcely at all.

So, although CBA provides operational researchers with their needed 'objective function' to optimize, it is by no means objective. But tricked out in its cosmetic disguise of 'science' it can *appear* objective to the unsuspecting. In so far as this disguise is successful, those who will suffer the adverse effects of planning may be persuaded that these are necessary, indeed natural, for some higher common good. To this extent social life is depoliticised, which benefits those who control the resources and the techniques. Both operational research and cost benefit analysis are elements in the thrust towards technocracy. Their elaborate technical apparatus proclaims the need for expertise, and so validates the exclusion of the passive human objects of planning from the decision-making process.

Conclusion

Capitalism is in crisis. Rampant inflation, long dole queues, cuts in public expenditure and social services, factory shut-downs and layoffs, shrinkage of capital investment and of profit margins, and the chaos of the last ten and especially five years in the arrangements for financing world trade, are all symptoms of different stages of the world-wide crisis. But the boom-slump mechanism is an integral part of the process by which capitalism periodically rejuvenates itself—bypassing, transcending or crushing obstacles to its further development.[18] Whether the current crisis will follow this pattern, or will threaten the very existence of capitalism, can still only be a matter of speculation. But the crisis is clearly of unusual length and severity, and is world-wide in scope. One result has been a progressive polarisation of attitudes. As the crisis has developed, members of the working class in advanced capitalist countries have increasingly confronted their day-to-day immiseration and exploitation directly. Symptoms of disaffection have multiplied in all areas of life, and especially at work. In Britain there is grass-roots agitation against the centrally directed reduction of real wage levels 'in the national interest'; and in virtually all western countries there is an increase in direct confrontation at the work place, in the form of sabotage or more open violence in industrial action. Alongside the economic crisis there is a crisis of legitimation.

Operational research can contribute useful, but secondary, services for capitalism in this situation. Current trends are for greater co-ordination, centralisation and standardisation in society, and an intensification of these tendencies is an element in almost any plausible solution to capitalism's current problems. With the increasing scale and complexity of operation, OR and systems analysis offer systematic methods for the increasingly difficult task of keeping capitalism manageable. In other words, OR, having already provided a replacement within large corporations for the market's co-ordinative mechanism, is now also substituting for the market between large corporations.

But at least as important is OR's role in legitimation. With the developing corporate state, the façade of liberal democracy becomes increasingly hollow. Operational research as a purveyor (although by no means the only one) of the twin messages of 'leave it to the expert' and 'we're all in the same boat, don't rock it', helps to justify the more and more effective exclusion of the mass of people from power.

So OR helps to maintain a regime of trivial, de-humanising work within the corporation, and ultimately contributes to perpetuating capitalism itself. This is an object lesson in the power of capitalism to co-opt and distort progressive potential in innovations which do not challenge it directly. For some OR-like activity will be necessary, even life-enhancing, in any feasible non-exploitative society. Socialism is not possible without relative abundance. Complexity and uncertainty will remain, and the ramifying consequences of particular decisions will need to be carefully assessed. Intuition will need to be educated and supplemented by formal analysis.

Notes

1. For an accessible introduction to operational research see Beer (1967); for an account of the underlying methodology see Ackoff (1962); for a comprehensive textbook see Wagner (1969) or Hillier and Lieberman (1967); for other radical critiques see Thunhurst (1973), Hales (1974), Chesterton et al. (1975), Rosenhead (1976), and Dando and Eden (1977).
2. See, for example, Crowther and Whiddington (1947).
3. The 'revised sequence' is a description of the way in which oligopolistic firms control their markets, not the reverse as classical economic theory would have it. See Galbraith (1967).
4. See Braverman (1974) for the argument on which this section is based, and for much more besides.
5. Even today, some of the most exploitative jobs, such as envelope addressing and dressmaking, are frequently 'put out'.
6. Indeed, not only in Western capitalist society. Lenin (1918) was to write immediately after the Russian Revolution: '. . .we must raise the question of applying what is scientific and progressive in the Taylor System . . . we must organise in Russia the study and teaching of the Taylor System.'

7. See Palmer (1975) and Brown (1977).

8. Some of these managerial activities may seem superficially benevolent. For example, ergonomics is used to design equipment controls which are easier for the worker to operate. However, this redesign is only implemented if the change can be justified through increased throughput. Profit considerations dominate, and any benefits to the workforce are by-products.

9. While management *science* is virtually synonymous with operational research, 'management sciences' denotes the broader group of science-related aids to management referred to above.

10. We should emphasize that this is by no means the total story of operational research. We shall not consider here the continuing military application of OR, though it remains significant. Nor, as we mentioned above, shall we discuss the Soviet Union's use of OR, which merits an extended comparative analysis.

11. See, for example, O'Connor (1972).

12. See Miliband (1973) for a fuller discussion.

13. See systems theorists Emery and Trist (1969) on how a turbulent environment can be held to necessitate shared policies and shared values—in general a more monolithic organisation.

14. For the general approach, see Churchman (1968); for the most ambitious attempt to apply it, see Beer (1974); for a critique see Hoos (1972); for a discussion of its applications in the social sciences, see Phillips (1976).

15. Even the adoption of a 'socially responsible' objective function, such as minimal resource usage, would not overcome the objections to optimisation. Optimisation and democracy are incompatible. Optimisation involves a complex technical process which assumes consensus as regards its objectives and thus derogates from the need for a political process. Popular democracy substitutes a richer political process for most of the technical sophistication, being built both on a recognition of people as active subjects, and upon an explicit acknowledgement of the diversity in objectives that optimisation assumes away.

16. For an introduction to cost benefit analysis see Layard (1972); for a critique see Self (1970) or Self (1975).

17. The *technical* explanation for this phenomenon is that it is impossible to optimise on more than one dimension at a time. And so, in order that an 'optimal' (hence unchallengeable) decision can be proclaimed, a uni-dimensional scale of measurement must be devised. Money is taken as the 'natural' mechanism through which people express their preferences and thus the natural scale of measurement to select. It does, of course, have certain other 'advantages'.

18. For a more extended treatment see Hobsbawm (1975) or Mandel (1975).

Bibliography

Ackoff, R. L., 1962, *Scientific Method: Optimizing Applied Research Decisions*, New York, Wiley.

Ackroyd, C., Margolis, K., Rosenhead, J., and Shallice, T., 1977, *The Technology of Political Control*, Harmondsworth, Penguin.

Adams, J. G. U., 1974, '. . . And how much for your grandmother?' *Environment and Planning*, A., vol. 6.

Beer, S., 1967, *Management Science: the Business Use of Operations Research*, London, Aldus.

Beer, S., 1974, *Designing Freedom*, London, Wiley.

Braverman, H., 1974, *Labor and Monopoly Capital: the Degradation of Work in the Twentieth Century*, New York, Monthly Review Press.

Brown, G., 1977, *Sabotage*, Nottingham, Spokesman Books.

Byrnes, W. G., and Chesterton, B. K., 1973, *Decisions, Strategies and New Ventures*, London, George Allen and Unwin.

Chesterton, K., Goodsman, R., Rosenhead, J., and Thunhurst, C., 1975, 'A comment on Ackoff's "The social responsibility of operational research"', *Operational Research Quarterly*, vol. 26, no. 1.

Churchman, C. W., 1968, *The Systems Approach*, New York, Delta.

Crowther, J. G., and Whiddington, R., 1947, *Science at War*, London, HMSO.

Dando, M., and Eden, C., 1977, 'Reflections on operational research. A report from the Euro II Congress', *Omega*, vol. 5, no. 3.

Emery, F. E., and Trist, E. L., 1969, 'The causal texture of organisational environments', in F. E. Emery (ed.), *Systems Thinking*, Harmondsworth, Penguin.

Galbraith, J. K., 1967, *The New Industrial State*, London, Hamish Hamilton.

Hales, M., 1974, 'Management science and the "second industrial revolution"', *Radical Science Journal*, no. 1.

Hillier, F. S., and Lieberman, C. J., 1967, *Introduction to Operations Research*, San Francisco, Holden-Day.

Hobsbawm, E., 1975, 'The crisis of capitalism in historical perspective', *Marxism Today*, October 1975.

Hoos, I. R., 1972, *Systems Analysis in Public Policy*, Berkeley, University of California Press.

Layard, P. R. G., 1972, *Cost Benefit Analysis: Selected Readings*, Harmondsworth, Penguin.

Lenin, V. I., 1918, 'The immediate tasks of the Soviet government', *Isvestiya*, April 1918 (in *Collected Works*, vol. 27).

Mandel, E., 1975, *Late Capitalism*, London, New Left Books.

Marglin, S., 1971, 'What do bosses do? The origins and function of hierarchy in capitalist production', unpublished mss., Harvard University, August 1971; an abridged version of the argument appeared in *Review of Radical Political Economy*, vol. 6, Summer 1974.

Miliband, R., 1973, *The State in Capitalist Society*, London, Quartet.

O'Connor, J., 1972, *The Fiscal Crisis of the State*, London, St James.

Palmer, B., 1975, 'Class, conception and conflict: The thrust for efficiency. Managerial views of labor and the working class rebellion, 1903–22', *Review of Radical Political Economy*, vol. 7, no. 2, Summer 1975.

Phillips, D. C., 1976, *Holistic Thought in Social Science*, Stanford, Stanford University Press.

Rosenhead, J., 1976, 'Some further comments on the social responsibility of operational research', *Operational Research Quarterly*, vol. 27, no. 1.

Self, P. J. O., 1970, 'Nonsense on stilts: CBA and the Roskill Commission', *Political Quarterly*, vol 41.

Self, P. J. O., 1975, *Econocrats and the Policy Process*, London, Macmillan.

Thunhurst, C., 1973, 'Who does operational research operate for?', mimeo.

Tomlinson, R. C., 1971 (ed.), *OR Comes of Age*, London, Tavistock.

Wagner, H. M., 1969, *Principles of Operations Research*, Englewood Cliffs, N.J., Prentice-Hall.

20.

Ian Miles and John Irvine

Social Forecasting: Predicting the Future or Making History?

For a good part of 1972 the mass media in the West speculated wildly about imminent world catastrophe. A new best-seller had been published: *The Limits to Growth* (Meadows et al., 1972). In a gripping and non-technical style, widely emulated in TV documentaries and magazine articles, this reported the startling results of a computerised simulation of the future development of the world economy. Its forecasts appeared to give credence to the worst fears about the consequences of economic growth and population growth, indicating that if they were not halted in the very near future, catastrophe would ensue. It warned that one or other of a number of 'collapses' would follow directly from uncontrolled growth—natural resource depletion, famine or unbearable levels of pollution.

By no means everyone accepted this forecast, however, even though the claims to 'scientific' impartiality and rigour were portrayed as beyond question by its authors. An intense controversy developed, and, indeed, still continues. At stake was the status of such forecasts: do sophisticated mathematical techniques and advanced computer technology guarantee neutral and value-free prediction? This question was of more than academic significance, for the ideas and arguments presented by *Limits* became fuel for the rapidly growing ecology movement as well as for drop-outs seeking justification for their belief that building a better world is impossible, managers needing to persuade workers to be satisfied with lower 'real' wages and politicians explaining why the problems of world poverty were insoluble.

For radical critics of society such social problems were to be seen as neither inevitable nor insoluble—no matter whether they were the outpourings of a conservative ideologue or the output of an electronic computer. The critique of scientific forecasting was political: reactionary assumptions put into a computer produce no less reactionary forecasts (Enzensberger, 1974). *Limits* brought home this point with a vengeance. The general questioning of the ideology and practice of science developed in other chapters of the present book is clearly relevant to forecasting, for here is another example of the supposed 'neutrality' of science being invoked to lend authority to decision-making. In the case of *Limits*, reactionary social policy could be portrayed as inevitable, even desirable.

Similar questions should also be asked of less sensational forecasts. Frequent, routine forecasts have become such a part of day-to-day life that they are generally unremarked items in news reports. Short-term economic forecasts (covering periods of up to two or three years) are, for example, produced on a regular basis in Britain by a number of expert groups, such as the National Institute for Economic and Social Research, the Henley Centre, and the Treasury itself. Although generally less controversial than *Limits*, they are no less politically important—for example, often being cited by the mass media in discussions concerning the 'Social Contract' in the mid-1970s. In what became rather a monotonous news feature, forecasts concerning economic conditions such as the inflation rate or unemployment level were presented in a kind of statistical logic: if wage rises were not limited, things would get worse; if wages were contained, the future would be brighter (or at least, less gloomy).

While these examples point to some of the ways in which forecasts may be used to further the interests of dominant groups and classes, it by no means follows that all, or even most, forecasts are simply cynical manipulations. In one sense any forecast is a fabrication—it is a statement about a state of affairs that does not (yet) exist—but this does not necessarily make it a deliberate attempt to deceive. Certainly, forecasts may be used to justify decisions, or to win support for a marketed product or political programme that promises future rewards. But this alone does not explain the extent to which forecasts are now funded and used. Forecasts are often directly 'policy-relevant' (as the forecasting literature has it); they are used as information resources by civil servants and company managers.

Forecasts play important roles in the management and planning of both state and corporate activities. To understand their uses here, as well as their political and ideological roles, we need to examine both the origins and techniques of forecasting. What will be shown is that such techniques are no more 'neutral' than their uses. Just as the future itself will be the product of human actions, so forecasts of the future are socially constructed.

Statistics for seers

Among the most basic and common forecasting techniques is

the *extrapolation* of a trend or supposed trend. The most elementary form of this is known as 'naïve extrapolation', the classic example of which can be found in Malthus' work. In his *Essay on Population* (1798), Malthus put forward a pessimistic view of the future which set the stage for *Limits to Growth* and a host of lesser studies. He simply assumed that, without such checks as war and natural disaster, human populations would tend to double in size every twenty-five years.[1] Then, arguing that food supplies could not be increased at anything like this rate in the long term, he concluded that famine would result from population growth if no other 'checks' operated on it.

Unlike more recent forecasters, Malthus did not set out to predict in detail the future awaiting Britain or the world. Indeed, he did not even attempt to forecast when Britain, in the absence of 'checks', would run up against what are now known as 'Malthusian limits'. This would have been a bold operation given the sketchy state of demographic statistics when he was first writing—the first British Census was not taken until 1801—but, in any case, his aim was different. He was not forecasting to help plan food production or anything similar. Rather, he was explicitly concerned with undermining the social philosophies of egalitarianism and social progress put forward by such influential thinkers as Condorcet, Godwin and Rousseau.

But, irrespective of Malthus' somewhat limited intentions, his arguments were soon put to wider use. In the wake of the French Revolution, disturbances such as the 1780 Gordon Riots, and risings in Ireland, they were mobilised against demands for social change. As Beales remarks:

> The *Essay* had not only the practical value of an insurance against Godwin's utopian dreams or Spence's nightmare plan to nationalise land . . . the quiet philosopher had laid down the missing half of the ideological foundations of economic liberalism (that is, social conservatism) . . . he had driven such proposals as that of Whitbread (1796) for a national minimum wage out of the arena of significant discussion; he had made impossible such safety-valve flirtation with sentimentalism as Pitt's Poor Law reform project (1796) (1953, p. 9).

According to Malthusians, improving the income and housing of the poor would simply encourage the rapid growth of population, and hasten the rate at which the demand for food overhauled food production.[2]

Even in Malthus' own time, doubt was cast upon the validity of his assumptions and the use of extrapolative methods in social analysis. Nevertheless, it is still fairly common to find extrapolations used with little more caution than Malthus exercised. Many forecasts are based merely on 'common-sense' analyses of possible trends, or simply on vague feelings that social change is proceeding in a particular direction. But those extrapolations which are presented as scientific forecasts are now often based on statistical data. Historical values of some variable are plotted against time: if they seem to show a fairly uniform trend, this is extended beyond the empirical record to give presumed future values of the variable.

Traffic forecasting in Britain, for example, has been based upon little more than naïve extrapolation (see Adams, 1974; and Gershuny, 1979). Since, historically, there has been a trend to increasing car ownership, so it is argued, decisions about building new roads can be based on the assumption that this trend will continue. The processes generating such a trend are here taken for granted—and so, when some of the processes are themselves the consequences of decisions or policies, the assumption that these remain unchanged is thus built into the forecast. Thus, various policies encouraging private car ownership are implicitly built into traffic forecasting. The forecast of an increasing number of cars on the road is then presented as support for the continuation of road-building programmes. The forecast itself becomes the future.

The calculated crystal ball

Extrapolation is often carried out by visually inspecting a trend and then extending it by hand, but mathematical methods for estimating future values of a variable are also available, and are increasingly widely employed. This increasing technical sophistication may be used to reinforce the frequent claim that 'forecasting is value-free: it is an attempt to arrive at an objective view of the future using given assumptions' (Wood and Fildes, 1976, p. 10).

These methods were originally developed for the purpose of *interpolation*; that is, estimating the values of a variable falling between the numbers of a series of observations. Bowley's *Elements of Statistics* (1901), reflects the attention paid by statisticians to the analysis of business cycles and other social changes in the last quarter of the nineteenth century—a time of relative stagnation and renewed political conflict in the industrial countries. Bowley devoted much discussion to interpolation and to issues associated with the smoothing of fluctuations in time-series data (so as to produce regular trends and precise accounts of cyclical variations, thus providing a better basis for estimating unknown values). Forecasting, and extrapolative techniques, received little attention however. The use of regression techniques in trend analysis was incorporated only into the later editions of Bowley's text. Such methods of fitting a trend to a set of observations are nowadays fairly routine for purposes of extrapolation.

In the period immediately after the first world war, business forecasting became fashionable in the United States: at that time, for example, some 35,000 individuals and firms subscribed to the briefings produced by five of the business forecasting agencies (Hansen, 1951). The increasing volume of official statistics and new methods of statistical analysis gave economic prediction a plausibility it previously lacked. The depressed nature of capitalist economies in this period was both stimulus and nemesis to business forecasting: the economic uncertainty provided it with a growing market, but the fallibility of the forecasts was dramatically revealed by their failure to predict the slump and Great Depression.

These business forecasts of the 1920s were concerned with rather more limited and short-term changes than, for instance, that of Malthus, and were derived with various degrees of statistical sophistication. Many were based upon trend analyses which were only made possible by the economic statistics first produced in the early twentieth century. Since the main focus of concern was on cyclical fluctuations, rather than on sustained rates of growth, many of these forecasts were based on the inspection of past trends. Sometimes there would be a search for regular patterns in these trends that could be projected forward (e.g. a cycle of boom and slump periodically repeating itself); and sometimes attention would be paid to deviations from trend lines (the idea being that a 'deviation' would return back to the trend, and perhaps overshoot it, as if a law of action and reaction was operating). Crude and rule-of-thumb as much of this work was, it provided a powerful stimulus to the development of what are now fairly standard statistical techniques, such as the 'correction' of statistical data to take account of seasonal variations.

Business forecasting in this period also made use of the analysis of leading and lagging indicators. Essentially, this method involves identifying variables that tend to change in a particular way rather sooner than those variables which one needs to forecast or monitor. In the United States, the National Bureau of Economic Research has since the 1920s produced sets of 'leading' economic indicators intended to be of use in anticipating economic upturns and downturns. Thus, for example, measures of orders for capital equipment and of job vacancies have often served as indicators for subsequent levels of production and employment. More recently, attitude survey data concerning people's expectations for the economy have been used in a similar way to predict consumer spending (Katona, 1960).

While statistical data have formalised and in some respects improved routine forecasting, they have their own limitations. The 'lead time' of such indicators is short, while their preparation takes some time, so that the forecast is often obtained only at the same time as a turning point in the business cycle; however, this does not necessarily render them useless commentaries on what is already known, for such turning points are themselves often not identified as such until some months have elapsed.[3]

Until the 1929 stock market crash, business forecasts had been widely thought of as useful (although their success in predicting cyclical fluctuations is now known to have been fairly low). But faced with glaring failure to anticipate qualitative changes in the economy, forecasting rather lost credibility. In the 1970s, too, business forecasters were caught on the hop by the onset of a generalised recession. According to *Business Week* (Anon., 1974) economists 'will remember 1974 as the year the forecasters blew it'. With markedly changed economic conditions, forecasters were unable to interpret their data with any confidence, and were 'scrambling to revise the projections they made so bravely'.

More sophisticated techniques did not, then—indeed cannot —overcome a general problem of forecasting: the limited reliability of any prediction based upon assumptions that the status quo will continue largely unchanged. In general, forecasters are not able, and do not attempt, to consider large-scale or qualitative changes. The political implications are obvious: forecasts will tend to reproduce conservative views of the world. Moreover, this constraint can be a positive virtue for those who stand to gain most from the status quo. For example, when the Confederation of British Industry uses managers' stated intentions on investment and production plans to develop its economic forecasts, a powerful intervention into the state's economic and political strategies is being made. Forecasts that a given policy will create economic havoc can be more powerful political weapons than mere expressions of dismay from big business.

Social forecasting and technological change

Increasingly sophisticated forms of extrapolation were applied to a wider range of social phenomena in the USA immediately before and during the Depression, much of this under the aegis of the sociologist William F. Ogburn. Ogburn fused two strands of conservative thought into a remarkable programme of social and technological forecasting—the first being the belief in a slow and lawlike unfolding of most social trends, the second the idea that technology in itself is a major determinant of human affairs. With minor modifications, these remain dominant features of much contemporary forecasting.

The deepening economic crisis of the interwar years had made evident massive social problems in the US, and in order to cope with these a number of social scientists and politicians seized upon the idea of 'social trends'. This led to an annual statistical series concerning social change (commencing with Ogburn, 1929), and the massive report *Recent Social Trends* (Ogburn, 1933). Ogburn argued that inspection of such trends shows that they typically change only slowly: thus one could reliably forecast the social future by extrapolating time-series data. As for why social change happens at all, he believed technological innovation to be the underlying motor force, and therefore portrayed society as the product of its determining influence. To him we owe the idea of 'cultural lags'—that social change trails some distance behind technological change—a vulgarised version of the marxist conception of 'base and superstructure'. On the basis of this account, he claimed that social changes can be predicted by monitoring current 'leading' technological developments.

With this deterministic view of social change, Ogburn was able to introduce a number of now-familiar forecasting techniques (ironically, these have overshadowed his contributions to developing systematic social statistics). For example, the exponential curve, with its rapid acceleration, was brought into play as an adequate model of technological innovation; while the S-shaped logistic curve would serve to describe the adoption of a technology by increasing proportions of a population.[4] Both of these curves are often used now, not only as convenient descriptions of statistical data, but also in order to forecast social changes.

To justify the use of such deterministic formulations as tools for forecasting, recourse is often made to analogies between social change, and biological growth processes such as the accelerating growth of unrestrained animal populations, or the S-shaped growth curve of an individual organism. For example, returning to the example of traffic forecasting, Hanlon (1975) cites an official witness at a planning inquiry as arguing that 'if growth in car-ownership behaves like other social and biological phenomena, it will lie on a logistic growth curve'.

Several points need to be made here. Not only are forecasters trying to capture something of the sense of rigour that accompanies the 'hard' sciences with their mathematical analyses; these approaches also reinforce the idea of human activities as being fundamentally governed by biological laws, laws which can be identified by statistical approaches (e.g. Lenz, 1968). Appeal is made to these 'laws' as atheoretical facts, existing in nature, to justify predictions and the policies based on them. Yet these extrapolations are profoundly theoretical. This is revealed particularly clearly in the case of the logistic curve, where the forecasts that may be derived from its use are crucially sensitive to assumptions about its 'ceiling', the level at which the trend ceases to increase.

Take, for example, the case of traffic forecasting again. Here the 'ceiling' represents the level at which car ownership will stabilise. As Hanlon (1975) shows, the procedures whereby such saturation levels are calculated do not rest purely on technical assumptions, and can actually be used to estimate a whole range of ceilings: for Britain, the estimates range from one car to every three people to 1.7 cars per person (and, for Scotland, there is literally no saturation level). Yet the rules-of-thumb by which a particular and apparently realistic estimate is in practice chosen acquire great significance in the justification of road planning by appeals to science. Hanlon (1977) remarks that a recent revision of the saturation level from .45 to .5 cars per person means revising upwards forecasts of cars on British roads in 1995 by one million. The logistic growth curve, far from being an expression of the future operation of a social law, merely reproduces the 'commonsense' theories of the forecaster; needless to say these are firmly wedded to the status quo.

Through their role in the policy making process, such forecasts of the future actually become part of the making of history. The history and future history of Britain's roads has thus been made on the basis of political judgements concealed behind statistical analysis. The logistic logic, so dismissive of railways and other forms of public transport, and so encouraging to the motor industry and its associated lobbies, is presented so that it is not apparent that it has been made into a self-fulfilling prophecy. For it is by no means improbable that state provision of an ever-increasing network of motorways—rather than, for example, the maintenance and improvement of rail transport—is one of the main factors contributing to a continuing expansion of car ownership. As in Ogburn's work, modern traffic forecasting, together with a host of other forecasts used in policy making, has been based upon a mechanical approach which takes technology to be *the* driving force in society.

While this often provides a convenient way of rationalising existing changes, and of predicting the sorts of accommodation which society must make if the dynamics of technological change under capitalism are left unchecked, it effectively restricts the range of social choices that are considered. By assuming the continuation of past patterns of development, the possibility of new dimensions for the design and use of technology is given no place in the future. Proponents of 'future studies' claim to transcend the narrow determinism of such forecasting studies; however, as we shall now see, their success is frequently limited too.

From forecasting to futurology

The most sophisticated attempts at forecasting derive from recent changes in the structure of capitalist society. With the development of new, 'science-based' industries, such as those involving electronics or pharmaceuticals, and the recruitment of large numbers of research and development (R & D) specialists by firms, modern capitalism has experienced the uncertainties associated with a whole series of technological revolutions. Attempts to predict future technological capabilities by extrapolating from the past performance of technologies became increasingly prominent after the second world war. In particular, they were taken up on a large scale by the US military and aerospace industry, as the Pentagon and sections of big business colluded in the continuous innovation of ever more expensive means of destruction.

Both military forecasting, and technological forecasting in industry more generally, tend to be associated with rather longer-term perspectives than those broached in business-cycle analysis. A characteristic of the huge monopoly organisations of 'late capitalism' is their high level of investment in R & D with a consequent acceleration of technological innovation (Mandel, 1975). While companies face increasing competitive pressures to develop expensive new technological projects, considerable time-lags are involved between the initial invention and marketing the process or product. In this context of uncertainty and the mounting costs of commercial failure, techniques of long-term corporate planning and technological and associated market forecasting have become increasingly necessary.[5]

Lengthened perspectives have similarly been forced upon capitalist states by their having to take responsibility for risky or unprofitable large-scale projects (especially those supplying such infrastructures as transport, energy and telecommunications), and for 'crisis management' (attempting to moderate business cycles and social problems through state intervention). It was these problems that set the stage for the development of 'futurology'.

The term 'futurology' was coined in the 1940s by Ossip Flechtheim, an Austrian consciously seeking to create a science which could provide desirable non-marxist images of the future (Arab-Ogly, 1975). However, widespread public interest in futurology developed only in the late 1960s, when popularised accounts of the work of a number of groups researching long-term social changes became available. Among the most influential of these studies was Kahn's and Weiner's *The Year 2000* (1967). As with much futurology, their work drew heavily upon the experiences of forecasting for military and associated purposes—Kahn had worked for the RAND Institution, a think-tank deeply involved in preparing forecasts for the US Airforce. The main forecasts in *The Year 2000* were based upon extrapolations of the national incomes of major nations, and rather vague, qualitative projections of a 'long-term multi-fold trend' in Western societies which they used to predict life-styles and social values. Around these main 'surprise free' trends, they developed a set of 'scenarios' (another forecasting device extensively developed for military purposes—see Wilson's *War Gaming*, 1970), in which the consequences of certain major changes were evaluated. Among the preoccupations informing these scenarios were the strength of communist movements, and the possible challenge of Europe and Japan to the US dominance of the world economy.

Even in the increasingly sophisticated arena of futurology the basic technique underlying very many long-term social forecasts is still extrapolation. *Limits*, for example, for all its enormously complicated computer paraphernalia, actually says little more than that accelerating trends (in population, consumption of raw materials, etc.) will inevitably be incompatible with other trends (for example, the supply of food and materials) that are only increasing arithmetically, at best. On the other hand, especially with the end of the post-war boom, and the growth of overt social conflict in industrial societies since the late 1960s, it was grudgingly recognised that even the more sophisticated extrapolations of past trends into the future were problematic. The development of scenarios by forecasters has been one attempt to cope with these problems—although, as in *The Year 2000*, such scenarios are often highly conditioned by an assumed underlying trend. Often, too, scenarios represent no more than contrasting extrapolations of long-term and more recent trends, the former described as representing a 'return to normality', the latter as a 'continued instability'.

Thus, again, scenario-analysis usually rests upon extrapolations based largely upon untheorised assumptions about the stability of whatever social relationships are held to be generating trends. Nor do many of the popular futurological alternatives to extrapolation achieve much more. Indeed, use of the 'Delphi' technique (again first developed in military and technological forecasting) may encourage even greater complacency. Delphi involves the polling of a group of 'experts' about what events they expect to happen in their field of interest, and when they estimate these will occur. The experts are subsequently circulated with information on the judgements emerging from the group, and are then asked to re-estimate the date of occurrence of a selection of the events (which may be technological breakthroughs, social changes, or, in one notable study, the feelings generated by a set of photographs!) In this iterative process, some degree of conformity typically ensues—with experts adjusting their estimates in the light of each others' responses. The circulation of questionnaires usually takes place just a few times before estimates converge—estimates which then provide the raw material for a forecast. The focus upon consensus, and the use of expert groups, often sharing similar assumptions and prejudices, make Delphi technique, as generally used, approximate a kind of intuitive extrapolation of elite views of the world.[6]

There are yet other forecasting techniques in the repertoire of modern futurology. The 'cross-impact matrix', for example, was developed out of the Delphi approach in an attempt to overcome one of its major drawbacks: it is apparent to anyone who has ever taken part in a Delphi study that the 'discrete' events whose future occurrence is being judged are more often than not highly interrelated. If one event occurs, it tends to make a second one more or less likely; for example, the development of a cheap and efficient electric car would have implications for the future of the internal combustion engine. In the conventional Delphi study, different events are fragmented and their possible relationships not subject to analysis. Despite this, it is likely that most judges, rather than treating each event separately, develop a mental 'scenario' of the future, in which they relate together answers to the different questions while making their judgements. In technological forecasting, where the development of a new product or production process is often dependent upon a whole sequence of events, such analysis of the 'cross-impacts' between events was thought to be important for planning as well as forecasting.

Like Delphi, the cross-impact matrix involves a set of expert judgements. In this case, they are experts' ratings of the perceived likelihoods of each of a set of events, given the prior occurrence or non-occurrence of each other event in the set. A table of probabilities is thus produced, often by computer. This approach has also been used for making rather broader social forecasts than those involved in technological forecasting—asking, for example, what effect the establishment or non-establishment of a new policy by OPEC might have on US attitudes on world trade. Military chiefs and planners of foreign policy would obviously be interested in assessing likely patterns of future events.

Attempts have been made to computerise the production of scenarios from such matrices, involving mathematical manipulations based on the set of probability estimates (see McLean, 1976, for a critical discussion). As with Delphi, these apparently precise and solid forecasts are founded upon no more than a set of largely unarticulated assumptions. Whether or not these are experts' assumptions, it is hard to believe that quantifying and processing opinions provides an adequate substitute for rigorous analysis of the processes and structures underlying the course of social change. These mathematicised scenarios are thus again little more than an elaborate codification of the attitudes of elite groups, but one which can, however, be used to reinforce these very attitudes.

The cross-impact matrix is, of course, not the only forecasting technique to use computer analysis. The large data processing capacity of computers is often the only way to cope with the complexity of social change: by producing complex simulation techniques and models of a complex world. Studies such as *Limits* represent a fairly sophisticated level of simulation forecasting—involving 'dynamic' models that consider non-economic as well as purely economic data. Early models tended to be concerned with economic factors only, and to be 'static'. Static models represent the 'system' in question by a number of equations concerning relationships between variables (derived by regression analyses of empirical data, for example, or from economic theory). Then, given information or assumptions about the levels of certain variables at a future time, the values of the remaining variables at that time may be calculated. Dynamic models, in contrast, attempt to portray the course of development of a system over a period of time, given initial values of the variables included in the model. The difference between the output of static and dynamic models is rather like that between, respectively, a snapshot of one moment in time, and a movie concerning a whole period.

Models were initially introduced for forecasting economic

trends and the possible consequences of economic policies. In Britain, for example, an interest in medium-term economic models in the late 1950s resulted from the poor performance of the economy (relative to European competitors) after a decade of reactive 'stop-go' policies, and from the need to co-ordinate programmes involving public expenditure spread over a number of years (Worswick and Blackaby, 1974). In the United States, computer simulation and other techniques of 'systems analysis' were quickly (and profitably) applied to urban policy making, often with farcical results (see Hoos, 1972). In urban and regional planning, simulation models are often based on a form of 'social physics' which treats social behaviour as if regulated by laws analogous to those attributed to nature—thus the 'gravity model', 'entropy model' etc. (Gough, 1976; and Sayer, 1976, 1978). In the gravity model, for example, it is assumed that the tendency of people to visit, say, a particular shopping centre is inversely related to the distance that they would have to travel to get there. (See Constable, 1973; and Turner and Cole, 1978, for a critical study of one such model and its uses).

World Dynamics (Forrester, 1971) was the first study to extend computer simulation techniques to the analysis of world futures, providing the basis for the more elaborate and much more heavily promoted *Limits*. Despite the mass of numbers produced in this study, the only documented statistical data employed in *World Dynamics* concern world population in 1900 and 1970: other variables and relationships were estimated on the basis of Forrester's judgement of their ability to mimic plausible world trends. *Limits*, in contrast, employed a great deal of empirical data but, unsurprisingly, it emerged with predictions of world disaster similar in most respects to Forrester's—for the structure of both computer models was determined by the same thoroughly Malthusian assumptions.

One advantage claimed for such world models, of which there have now been several (see Clark and Cole, 1975), is that they can simultaneously deal with a wide range of features of the world, unlike (supposedly) unaided human thought. Thus some world models are actually several hundred times larger than that of *Limits*.

Claims for 'holism' notwithstanding, simulation models tend to consist of little more than an electronic pasting-together of a set of sub-models, each of which rests upon the assumption that purported historical relationships will continue to hold true in the future. While such global future studies may be of less immediate 'practical' use than more specific long-term forecasts, they are nevertheless widely used, at least as background material in controlling or preparing for change in the business environment, national economy or military field. But, often, they also reveal more overt political interests. Cole and Miles (1978) assessed some sixteen world forecasts produced since the mid-1960s (mostly, that is, since the end of the postwar boom), concluding that the types of forecast produced, and the kinds of policies seen as necessary to ensure a positive future, closely reflect the interests of different national and regional groups in the world economy. Thus, for example, the images of fabulous wealth conjured by Herman Kahn (and by Soviet futurologists!) presuppose and justify a world order serving the needs of US economic imperialism (or Russian hegemony); the Malthusian scenarios of the Club of Rome have been related to the concern of European multinational corporations to ensure stable resource supplies and prices; while very few forecasts reflect a sympathy with interests in the Third World which are seeking to retain a greater share of the wealth produced in the 'periphery' of the world economy.[7]

The futurologists' promise to provide more holistic, less deterministic, assessments of the future than less technically sophisticated forecasters cannot be taken at face value, despite their scenario analyses, oracular Delphis, and computer simulations. Rarely are the theoretical underpinnings involved in creating such integrated packages spelt out, and even more rarely are these foundations more than one or other version of conservative scientism. For all the impressive gadgetry and pronouncements of the futurologists, they are still largely propounding only the renovated world view of a society whose contradictions endanger the very possibility of a long-term future for the human race.

The limits to forecasting

Forecasts and futurological studies are not objective, neutral assessments of the future, whether presented crudely as what *must* happen, or in a more sophisticated form as a range of options for what *might* happen. However technically sophisticated such studies are, their neutrality remains a myth; but, like organised religion, the mythology of science is an important social force.

Whatever dazzling changes they may predict, forecasts based on the simpler techniques, such as extrapolation and the use of expert judges, can usually be shown to rest squarely on the assumption that the future will, at root, be pretty much like the present. More complicated approaches such as computer simulation are generally used to erect a bewildering framework of technical procedures around a core of restrictive assumptions that the non-initiate may be hard pressed to locate.[8]

It is certainly possible to apply many existing forecasting techniques to uses other than those currently dominant. These alternative applications, however, demand different ways of using the techniques, and recognition of the dangers of carrying empiricist and other conservative assumptions over into analysis. One example of a forecast running counter to the dominant applications is a computer simulation study carried out by a group of Latin American scientists in response to the gloomy prognostications offered for the Third World by *Limits*. These researchers did not restrict themselves to an extrapolation of current trends and structures. Instead, the goal of a world society in which the physical needs of all were met was postulated; and they set out to show that such a future would be physically feasible in a matter of decades in a socialist world order (Herrera et al., 1976).

Adequate analysis of the conditions needed to establish a better future is part of the process of creating that future. Methods of assessing the contributions that alternative actions (changing political or technological organisation, for example) might make to realising social goals are necessary, and some of the existing forecasting techniques may well be applicable—if it were absolutely clear that the use of these methods was itself part of the process of making history. Forecasting practices which treat people as doing no more than reacting passively to changes beyond their control need to be replaced by people assuming responsibility for democratically formulating and planning social goals.[9]

In contrast, the vast bulk of contemporary forecasting is based on a view of the future as largely determined by factors such as 'technological imperatives' and 'market forces', supposedly outside human control. Insofar as forecasts are used to plan for and legitimate this alienated social order, they do not merely reflect it—they help, if only in a small way, to maintain it, both technically and ideologically. In this respect, as in others, forecasting may tell us more about the present than about the future.

Forecasters are, indeed, involved in determining the future; but not in the sense of using scientific tools to achieve an objective understanding of the future. Closely tied to a set of new disciplines oriented to planners and policymakers,[10] they are creating new roles for social science in the making of history. Far from being neutral, these roles and techniques are overwhelmingly conditioned by the dominant interests in our class-divided society. The elaboration of new disciplines and specialities, new layers of technical sophistication and new mountains of data, may help to disguise, but not to alter these foundations. Only radical challenges to the assumptions of forecasting—and of the society which spawns it—can do this.

Notes

1. In the first edition of his essay, this assertion was very poorly substantiated: he argued that populations grow at a geometric rate, doubling in successive periods of similar duration, from the flimsy 'theory' that 'passion between the sexes . . . will remain nearly in its present state'. The statistics used to justify a twenty-five year doubling period were, however, very weak. Later editions of his *Essay* became increasingly overweight with data Malthus used to support his views.

2. For an interesting commentary on the ideas and background of classical Malthusianism, see Glass (1953). Meek (1953) presents both his own dissection of Malthus, and the classic criticism made by Marx and Engels. Weissman (1971) has added an uninspired New Left foreword to a later edition of Meek's book. For relations between Malthusianism and contemporary scientific racism, see Chase (1977).

Though particularly famous, Malthus' forecast was by no means a unique act of the imagination. In 1761, Wallace had similarly argued that major social improvements were ruled out of question by demographic considerations—well-fed and secure people would rapidly overpopulate the earth, he reasoned. And, in 1865, Jevons' *The Coal Question* substituted fuel for food in the Malthusian equation: a stir was caused by the forecast that civilisation as we know it would be brought to a standstill by exhaustion of its coal supplies.

Demographic forecasting in the period before the second world war was largely preoccupied not by Malthusian issues, but by fears similar to those currently being resurrected by Conservative ideology, namely that Western populations were declining, and that the 'national intelligence level' was sinking due to the supposed tendency for people of lower intelligence (so-called) to have more children. See, respectively, Glass (1975) and Duncan (1969).

3. In the post-war period, with emphasis on state management of the economy, this approach has been often attacked by economists as 'measurement without theory' (see, for example, articles in American Economic Association (1966). For recent studies of the record of such forecasts, see Fels and Henshaw (1968) and O'Dea (1975). These and other business forecasting techniques are discussed in a large number of introductory texts; for example, Wolfe (1966); Wood and Fildes (1976). The identification of 'leading' technologies is often employed in technological forecasting: for example, developments in commercial aviation technology have often drawn upon advances previously made in military aircraft technology, and thus the changes in the latter may be used to predict those in the former. And, of course, some countries or social groups are often seen as foreshadowing the development of others—the United States and Sweden are, for example, often cited as possible models of Britain's future.

4. For a selection of Ogburn's work, see Duncan (1964). Ogburn's close collaborator, S. Colum Gilfillan also deserves mention. Gilfillan (1970) wrote a revealing autobiographical account of his interests in prediction, sociology and eugenics. In an interesting earlier article (Gilfillan, 1968), he attempted to assess the record of success and failure of past forecasts of technological change, and describes several notable forecasts made during the first half of the twentieth century.

5. This is closely related to the development of operational research; see Rosenhead and Thunhurst's article in this book. For introductions to technological forecasting, see Bright (1968), Bright (1972) and Jantsch (1968).

6. The technique may be employed in a variety of different ways, however; see, for example, Strauss and Ziegler (1975). One obvious appeal of Delphi is that it permits forecasts to be made of qualitative changes which by definition lie outside quantitative trend extrapolation. For a slamming attack on Delphi, see Sackman (1975).

7. See Cole (1978) and Cole and Miles (1978) for a comparative analysis of futures studies. On the work of Kahn, see Cole (1977). On the interests represented by the Club of Rome, see Atkinson and Kusch (1976) and Golub and Townsend (1977); on *World Dynamics* and *Limits*, see Cole et al. (1973); on other computer analyses of world futures, see Clark and Cole (1975). A 'Third World' computer forecast forms the substance of Herrera (1976), the only such study to declare itself to be concerned with the prospects for establishing a new world order rather than being disguised as an objective prediction of a necessary future or range of futures; Freeman (1974) provides a powerful critique of contemporary neo-Malthusianism.

8. For a cataloguing of ideologies in future studies—ethnocentrism, biological reductionism, technological determinism, and so on—see Miles (1978); a narrower review is presented by Miles (1975). For the critique of the post-industrial society notion—a prevalent image of the future of Western societies—see Goldthorpe (1971) and Kleinberg (1973). The classic exposition of forecasting techniques is Jantsch (1968); Encel, Marstrand and Page (1975) is comprehensive, more oriented towards social forecasting and rather more critical; Boucher (1977) provides an interesting collection of mostly well-informed articles on future studies and their techniques. For studies and applications of techniques, see also the journals *Futures* and *Technological Forecasting and Social Change*; more popular journals include *The Futurist*.

9. Forecasts are often produced by radicals, although the postulation and planning of revolutionary changes imply rather different 'forecasting techniques'. It is rare to find a serious attempt to specify precisely a radical alternative (i.e. post-revolutionary) future. On Marx's image of the future, see the exegesis by Ollman (1977); some other studies of interest are Bukharin and Preobrazhensky (1922), and Mandel (1968, final chapter). For an attempt to contrast 'conservative, reformist and radical' futures, see Freeman and Jahoda (1978).

10. Examples here are the new 'sub-disciplines' covered in such journals as *Policy Sciences*—programme evaluation, policy analysis, management science, social indicators research, etc. For a valuable discussion of relations between social science and state policy in the USA, see Horowitz and Katz (1975). To see what established social scientists think about forecasting in their own disciplines, see Freeman, Jahoda and Miles (1975).

Bibliography

Adams, J., 1974, 'Saturation planning', *Town and Country Planning*, December, pp. 550–54.
American Economic Association, 1966, *Readings in Business Cycles*, London, Allen and Unwin.
Anon., 1974, 'Theory deserts the forecasters', *Business Week*, no. 2337, pp. 50–59.
Arab-Ogly, E., 1975, *In the Forecasters' Maze*, Moscow, Progress.

Atkinson, P., and Kusch, J., 1976, 'Limits to growth or limits to capitalism?', *Science for People*, no. 33, pp. 12-14.

Beales, H. L., 1953, 'The historical context of the *Essay* on population', in D. V. Glass (ed.), 1953, below.

Boucher, W. (ed.), 1977, *The Study of the Future: An Agenda for Research*, Washington, National Science Foundation.

Bowley, A., 1901, *Elements of Statistics*, London, Staples.

Bright, J. (ed.), 1968, *Technological Forecasting for Industry and Government*, Englewood Cliffs, N.J., Prentice-Hall.

Bright, J., 1972, *A Brief Introduction to Technological Forecasting*, Austin, Texas, Pemaquid.

Bukharin, N. I., and Preobrazhensky, E. A., 1922, *The ABC of Communism*, reprinted Harmondsworth, Penguin, 1969.

Chase, A., 1977, *The Legacy of Malthus*, New York, Alfred Knopf.

Clark, J., and Cole, S., 1975, *Global Simulation Models*, London, Wiley.

Cole, H. S. D., Freeman, C., Jahoda, M., and Pavitt, K. (eds.), 1973, *Thinking About the Future*, London, Sussex University Press (in the US edition, *Models of Doom*, New York, Universe Books, a reply by Meadows is included).

Cole, S., 1977, 'The shape of things to Kahn', *Futures*, vol. 9, pp. 65-71.

Cole, S., 1978, 'The global futures debate 1965-1976', in Freeman and Jahoda (eds.), 1978, below.

Cole, S., and Miles, I., 1978, 'Assumptions and methods: population, economic development, modelling and technical change', in Freeman and Jahoda (eds.), 1978, below.

Constable, D., 1973, *Urban Growth Processes—A Critical Assessment of the Forrester Model*, Reading, Dept. of Geography, University of Reading.

Duncan, O. D. (ed.), 1964, *William F. Ogburn on Culture and Social Change*, Chicago, University of Chicago Press.

Duncan, O. D., 1969, 'Social forecasting—the state of the art', *The Public Interest*, vol. 17, pp. 88-118.

Encel, S., Marstrand, P., and Page, W. (eds.), 1975, *The Art of Anticipation*, London, Martin Robertson.

Enzensberger, H. M., 1974, 'A critique of political ecology', *New Left Review*, no. 84; reprinted in H. Rose and S. Rose (eds.), 1976, *The Political Economy of Science*, London, Macmillan; and in H. M. Enzensberger, 1976, *Raids and Reconstructions*, London, Pluto Press.

Fels, R., and Elton Henshaw, C., 1968, *Forecasting and Recognising Business Turning Points*, New York, Columbia University Press.

Forrester, J., 1971, *World Dynamics*, Cambridge, Mass., MIT Press.

Freeman, C., 1974, 'The luxury of despair,' *Futures*, vol. 6, no. 6., pp. 450-62.

Freeman, C., and Jahoda, M. (eds.), 1978, *World Futures: The Great Debate*, London, Martin Robertson.

Freeman, C., Jahoda, M., and Miles, I. (eds.), 1975, *Problems and Progress in Social Forecasting*, London, SSRC.

Gershuny, J., 1979, 'Fixing the future', in T. Whiston (ed.), *Uses and Abuses of Forecasting*, London, MacMillan.

Gilfillan, S. C., 1968, 'A sociologist looks at technical prediction', in Bright (ed.), 1972, above.

Gilfillan, S. C., 1970, 'An ugly duckling's swan song', *Sociological Abstracts*, February–April and May, I-XI.

Glass, D. V. (ed.), 1953, *Introduction to Malthus*, London, Watts.

Glass, D. V., 1975, 'The history of population forecasting', in Freeman, Jahoda and Miles (eds.), 1975, above.

Goldthorpe, J., 1971, 'Theories of industrial society', *Archives Européennes de Sociologie*, vol. 2, pp. 263–88.

Golub, B., and Townsend, J., 1977, 'Malthus, multinationals and the Club of Rome', *Social Studies of Science*, vol. 7, pp. 201–22.

Gordon, R. A., 1952, *Business Fluctuations*, New York, Harper.

Gough, A. H., 1976, 'Social physics and local authority planning', in Conference of Socialist Economists, *Housing and Class in Britain*, London, CSE.

Hanlon, J., 1975, 'Statisticians' motorway madness', *New Scientist*, vol. 68, (979), pp. 648–49.

Hanlon, J., 1977, 'Traffic figures in road planning', *New Scientist*, vol. 76 (1076), p. 269.

Hansen, A. H., 1951, *Business Cycles and National Income*, New York, W. W. Norton.

Herrera, A. (ed.), 1976, *Catastrophe or New Society*, Ottawa, IDRC.

Hoos, I. W., 1972, *Systems Analysis and Public Policy: A Critique*, Berkeley, University of California Press.

Horowitz, I., and Katz, E., 1975, *Social Science and Public Policy*, New York, P. Meyer.

Jantsch, E., 1968, *Technological Forecasting in Perspective*, Paris, OECD.

Kahn, H., and Wiener, A., 1967, *The Year 2000*, New York, Macmillan.

Katona, G., 1960, *The Powerful Consumer*, New York, McGraw-Hill.

Kleinberg, B., 1973, *American Society in the Post-industrial Age*, Columbus, Ohio, Charles E. Merril.

Lenz, R. C., 1968, 'Forecasts of exploding technologies by trend extrapolation', in J. Bright (ed.), 1968, above.

Malthus, T., 1798, *An Essay on the Principle of Population*, reprinted, 1970, Harmondsworth, Penguin.

Mandel, E., 1968, *Marxist Economic Theory*, London, Merlin (one volume edition).

Mandel, E., 1975, *Late Capitalism*, London, New Left Books.

McLean, J. M., 1976, 'Does cross-impact forecasting have a future?', *Futures*, vol. 8.

Meadows, D., et. al., 1972, *The Limits to Growth*, London, Earth Island.

Meek, R. L., 1953, *Marx and Engels on Malthus*, London, Lawrence & Wishart.

Meszaros, I., 1971, *The Necessity of Social Control*, London, Merlin.

Miles, I., 1975, *The Poverty of Prediction*, Farnborough, Saxon House.

Miles, I., 1978, 'Dangers of futures research', in J. Fowles (ed.), *Handbook of Futures Research*, Dorsey, Ill., Greenwood Press.

O'Dea, D. J., 1975, *Cyclical Indicators for the Post-war British Economy*, Cambridge, Cambridge University Press.

Ogburn, W. F., 1929, *Recent Sociological Changes in the United States*, Chicago, University of Chicago Press.

Ogburn, W. F. (ed.), 1933, President's Research Committee on Social Trends, *Recent Social Trends in the United States*, New York, McGraw-Hill.

Ollman, B., 1977, 'Marx's vision of communism: a reconstruction', *Critique*, no. 8, pp. 4–41.

Sackman, H., 1975, *Delphi Critique*, Lexington, Mass., Lexington Books.

Sayer, R. A., 1976, *A Critique of Urban Modelling*, London, Pergamon.

Sayer, R. A., 1978, 'Some comments on mathematical modelling in regional science and political economy', *Antipode* (forthcoming).

Strauss, H. J., and Siegler, L. H., 1975, 'Delphi, political philosophy and the future', *Futures*, vol. 7, pp. 184-96.

Turner, R., and Cole, S., 1979, 'Arbitrariness, social welfare and uncertainty: the case of urban shopping models' in T. Whiston (ed.), *Uses and Abuses of Forecasting*, London, Macmillan.

Weissman, S. (ed.), 1971, *Marx and Engels on the Population Bomb*, Berkeley, Cal., Ramparts.

Wilson, A., 1970, *War Gaming*, Harmondsworth, Penguin.

Wolfe, H. D., 1966, *Business Forecasting Methods*, New York, Holt, Rinehart and Winston.

Wood, D., and Fildes, R., 1976, *Forecasting for Business: Methods and Applications*, London, Longmans.

Worswick, G. D. W., and Blackaby, F. T., 1974, *Introduction to The Medium Term; Models of the British Economy*, London, Heinemann.

21.

Bill Ridgers

The Use of Statistics in Counter-Information

The information we are presented with about the society we live in is by no means the objective and balanced appraisal of events it is often claimed to be. The mass media present to the general public a highly *mediated* product, which plays an important role in legitimating the position and interests of the dominant groups in society. Members of these dominant groups own and control much of the media. In Britain, for example, just nine families or companies own and control all the high circulation and 'quality' newspapers, all the large circulation magazines, and have substantial shareholdings in independent radio and television. Key individuals from the world of industry and finance are directors of the central media institutions such as Beaverbrook Newspapers, the Mirror group and the Independent Television Authority.

As many recent studies have shown (e.g. Glasgow University Media Group, 1976; Emerson, 1975), news reporting tends to favour particular groups of individuals and institutions:

> This at its most damaging includes the laying of blame for society's industrial and economic problems at the door of the workforce. This is done in the face of contradictory evidence, which when it appears, is either ignored, smothered, or at worst is treated as if it supports the inferential frameworks utilised by the producers of news. (Glasgow University Media Group, p. 267).

Many important questions remain unaddressed in the media, and even in areas where statistics are freely available (on, for example, the ownership of land, companies and other forms of wealth, or on the links between state and industry) they are either not presented or presented in such a way as to have minimal impact. How often, for example, are events analysed in terms of class exploitation or oppression?

By effectively controlling the production, presentation and communication of information, the mass media and the information services of companies and the state mask much of the ugly face of the capitalist social system, while projecting a cosmetically touched-up image of society congenial to the dominant interests. Groups producing and disseminating counter-information seek to oppose this near monopoly on the use and supply of information and thus to provide material of use in developing alternative critical analyses of contemporary society. This chapter takes up some of the issues raised in producing counter-information by focussing on the work of one group involved in this activity—Counter Information Services (CIS). It deals in particular with the production and use of statistical counter-information.

CIS was set up by a group of journalists, trades unionists and others who were aware that the mass media, and the reports issued by companies and the state, presented information overwhelmingly in such a way as to obscure the experience and interests of substantial sections of the population. The production of counter-information needs, of course, inputs of both investigative journalist skills and financial resources. The first input was provided by a number of radical journalists with access to the information resources of the media organisations for which they worked; the second was provided by grants from organisations like the Transnational Institute and Joseph Rowntree Social Services Trust, supplemented increasingly by publication sales. Right from the beginning, the work of CIS has been directed primarily at those who are most directly exploited by the institutions we investigate. A clear idea of the needs of the users of counter-research must complement the particular features of the institution studied. The twin goals of CIS involve providing information resources for workers engaged in specific struggles, and exposing the nature of the social and economic system which is the cause and content of these struggles.

In particular, counter-information is needed by workers for day-to-day activity in their constant battle to maintain and improve pay and conditions. Information about the activities of their companies—on profits, for example—can be crucial here. Some Anti-Reports have been produced as a direct result of requests from workers' organisations. But, in nearly every case, the initial preparation of a report has involved the closest possible contact with the workforce. If necessary, this continues after its production; following the publication of the *GEC Anti-Report*, for example, CIS was involved in a company-wide gathering of workers, shop stewards and convenors. This led to the formation of a rank-and-file company-wide newspaper continuing the exposure of company operations on a regular basis: such newspapers are a vital means of disseminating counter-information among the workforce. This particular newspaper helped in overcoming the isolation of workers in the many different factories of the GEC group—an isolation that had enabled the company to implement large-scale redundancies. Dissemination of information is, therefore, clearly central to effective counter-information.

The Anti-Report

The information that companies are required to provide by law is minimal. It is there largely to protect the financial interests of the shareholders, rather than, for example, to inform workers about their employers' operations. Given that corporate interests are themselves often major shareholders, there is little pressure for further disclosure than is legally necessary. This secrecy makes it difficult to challenge the plans and activities of business and the state.

Companies, nevertheless, make public a certain amount of information through their annual Report and Accounts, which is sent to investors and shareholders along with the dividend. These 'glossies' contain a financial profit and loss account of the past year's trading—with success measured largely in terms of the levels of profitability achieved. Alongside this is other information held to be useful in assessing the firm's likely performance in the future, together with a typically self-adulatory report from its chairman and directors.

Thus many of the clues necessary for the formulation of counter-information are provided in the financial and operational data presented for entirely different purposes in company reports and City evaluations of their activities. This information is not just collected and republished, however, for we are not interested simply in the re-presentation of information. We are often able to situate this information within a critical commentary, to draw attention to overlooked or excluded relationships and factors. It is not by accident, then, that CIS calls its investigative publications Anti-Reports, or that the covers of the first few were almost perfect replicas of the reports of the companies investigated.

The reconceptualisation of information is, therefore, an important element in the production of Anti-Reports. Often, for example, a completely different 'profit and loss' account is provided from the one issued by the company under investigation—for, by going beyond the ideological structure of the business ethic, a completely different 'account' may be produced. The first Anti-Report on the Rio Tinto Zinc Corporation (RTZ) is a case in point. It contained a world round-up of RTZ's operations, and the profits made, as well as a survey of the human and environmental costs involved. The company's own report revealed that whereas only 7.7 per cent of the group's assets were located in South Africa—where they had extensive mining interests—42 per cent of the group's profits were created in that country. Using this and other information, CIS was able to show that the high profits and lucrative dividends arose directly from the low wages of the black workers employed in RTZ's mines. Living and working conditions of the company's workforce were similarly shown to be bad and served to underline this point: the Anti-Report described them as 'similar to the treatment of livestock by a moderately progressive farmer' (CIS, May 1972, p. 5). When RTZ's chairman, Sir Val Duncan, was questioned about the morality of operating in a political situation not dissimilar to Nazi Germany, he admitted: 'I could see that in any country that was unwise enough to have submitted to Adolf Hitler and the horrors he perpetrated on the Jewish community, we *might* have had difficulty in continuing operating there.' (CIS, May, 1972, p. 5, our italics).

It was made abundantly clear in the report that

> the basis of the company's action is profit maximisation, or in ordinary terms greed. RTZ is both a product and an accelerator of the economic system that it serves. Through this system the finite resources of the world are being exploited for the short-term benefit of a tiny minority. (CIS, May 1972, p. 2).

A key theme of CIS's work thus became the exposure of the profit drive of the corporate sector and the structures of exploitation based around this. The 'Anti-Report' on the textile giant Courtaulds demonstrated that the company's 'monopoly power and profitability had been achieved by exploiting the fears of both the workforce and the government over unemployment. It had consistently operated in areas of high unemployment where the workforce was most vulnerable' (CIS, November 1974, p. 39). Despite Courtauld's image of corporate responsibility—of supposedly being able to simultaneously operate profitably and in the 'national interest'—CIS found that its employees were among the lowest paid in the UK. Likewise, an investigation of the General Electric Company (GEC) revealed that this electrical colossus had, in the pursuit of profit, become the biggest *un*employer in the country—with thirty jobs lost every working day over the four years from 1967 to 1971 (CIS, September 1972, p. 33).

However, not all of CIS's work has been in the industrial sector. Indeed, in other areas of the economy exploitation is equally stark. In *The Recurrent Crisis of London*—an 'Anti-Report' on property development—CIS juxtaposed the deepening crisis of housing and homelessness, with the concentrated economic power of the property companies, relating the enduring nature of housing problems to the inhuman operation of the property market. 'Now as ever it is a question of power, both economic and political. The ten largest property companies control assets approaching the entire gold and dollar reserves of the UK. Nearly all these companies are *de facto* controlled by one or two men' (CIS, March 1973, p. 66). If housing provision (or, more accurately, lack of it) is to remain dominated by market forces, CIS argued, there will never be an end to slums, homelessness and the misery these bring.

What these Anti-Reports consistently show, then, is that we live in a society whose social priorities are determined by the workings of a profit-oriented economic system. They also demonstrate that it is possible to begin to counter the continual barrage of ideology emanating from industry and the state with thorough and well-researched information resources. Since the use and re-working of statistical sources has been an important element in CIS's reports, we now turn to a discussion of how this work is undertaken.

Producing counter-information: the radical re-use of statistics

There are, as we have seen, many types of counter-information. It may be produced directly by, for example, interview or observation; or it may be produced from existing records, such as official statistics or company reports. Whereas it is sometimes necessary to carry out original research (for example, the surveys on low pay by the *Low Pay Unit* or those on homelessness by *Shelter*), in other situations it may be possible to re-use already published data. CIS has tended to focus on this latter strategy of re-use.

The radical re-use of statistical information may take different forms:

1. Republishing statistics hidden away in obscure official and business publications, or in specialist literature. For example, in the report *Women Under Attack*, CIS used data from the *New England Journal of Medicine* (April 1974), which showed that 70 per cent of the users of anti-anxiety drugs in the UK were women, and that nearly all women over 15 used these drugs at one time or another (CIS, June 1976, p. 28). While these figures are startling enough in themselves, they become even more significant when integrated into a critical commentary on the social and economic condition of women. On another occasion, CIS republished figures on the

interest rates offered and profits made on 'gilts'—the bonds issued by the state when it borrows money in the city. For the bonds issued in 1976 alone, capital profits to the tenders amounted to almost £1 billion. These financial statistics—originally published to encourage the rich to invest in gilts—were in turn put to critical use by CIS to illustrate statistically the economic context in which savage cuts in state welfare spending were taking place (CIS, June 1977, p. 30). And, taking an example from our studies of companies, we were able, in the 'Anti-Report' on Ford, to establish from the company's statistics that their methods of accounting had been oriented to supporting their labour relations strategy—rather than to give a precise financial picture of how the company was operating. By exaggerating the profitability of Ford Werke, its West German operation, while simultaneously underrating that of Ford UK, the managers were able to threaten the UK workforce with its supposedly poor performance. This has been a crucial plank in Ford's strategy to counter the UK workers' rather more militant stand against the company than their German colleagues' (CIS, January 1978, p. 38).

Although these examples illustrate the utility of republishing information, this is not always possible—even with the most rigorous researching. To avoid embarrassment much official information is not merely obscure, but remains secret or unpublished. The work published by State Research in its *Bulletin* indicates the significance of secrecy in state activities: while a very useful role can be played by those who expose classified information as, for example, the Child Poverty Action Group did in the row about child benefits in 1977.

2. Presenting statistics in such a way as to highlight significant elements obscured in the original form. For example, CIS analysed the data on 'debt repayment' in relation to the statistics on overall state expenditure (*Public Expenditure*, Cmnd. 6393). Presenting this analysis in *Cutting the Welfare State: Who Profits?*, we were able to show that debt repayments had become the seventh most important item in public spending, and that the factors behind its growing size were important in understanding the cuts in welfare spending. More money remitted to the coffers of city financiers clearly means less is available for allocation to more socially necessary forms of expenditure (CIS, November 1975, p. 4).

There are many ways of reconceptualising data. CIS has regularly recalculated the profit figures presented in company reports: in contrast to the all-important figure to the shareholder of profit per unit of capital invested, we have represented this information in terms of profit per employee. Such information is clearly of interest to workers, particularly if it is shown over time and compared with, say, capital per employee, to indicate the extent of productivity increases extracted from the workforce. Similarly, in our report on the *Three Phase Trick* a crucial argument concerning the inequity of the wage-freeze was made by aggregating data derived from the Reports and Accounts of the largest companies in the UK. We compared the increases in average wages of the employees in these companies with the increase in profits per employee over the period of wage-restraint from 1971–74. Whereas wage increases (not adjusted to allow for inflation) had averaged around 10 per cent, profits per employee had risen by a staggering 32 per cent.

The re-use of data in this way can of course be much simpler. Making a crude comparison of the wages of employees with the salaries of executive directors (many of whom may be holding no more than honorary positions) can in itself be illuminating. For example, Henry Ford is *paid* in one year what it would take one of his employees more than two lifetimes to *earn*.

It is important, however, to be aware that the way data is marshalled and re-used is structured by the purposes of the Anti-Report in question. Counter-information is no neutral artifact: its form and content need to be tailored to the political task in question. Take for example, our work for Lucas Electrical Shop Stewards, who requested a report relevant to organising opposition to threatened redundancies. This demanded a number of approaches: first, to draw up a factual profile of Lucas operations world-wide. Second, to uncover the investment strategy of Lucas management as relevant to the workforce (investments were being increasingly directed *out* of the UK). Third, to establish the extent and rationale behind the proposed redundancy plans. Finally, we sought to make as many contacts as possible with the workforce: the report had to be accessible and useful to workers. Their experience and knowledge was an integral part of the generation and organisation of our data, and their active involvement in preparing the report also facilitated its distribution!

In contrast, our *Cutting the Welfare State: Who Profits* was produced at a more general level for a much wider audience. In this report we attempted to spell out the logic behind public expenditure cuts, in a way that would facilitate the defence of employment and welfare services by workers in all branches of the public sector and by people dependent on the welfare services, in their everyday lives. Here a wide variety of data was assembled and analysed: in addition to existing official statistics, Community Development Project studies of the local impact of the cuts, and information supplied by trades unionists and the research departments of unions were particularly useful. We were able to show that less than half of state expenditure went into housing, health, education and social security benefits. The use of terms like the 'social wage' to suggest that the state's expenditure on welfare services had outgrown our economic means obscured its massive expenditure on debt finance, the military and aid to industry. We were able to show that political commitments to welfare (which were at best already too low) were being abandoned in favour of maintaining profitability in the private sector; in fact, it was shown that by the end of 1975 a major reduction in the amount of money available for state expenditure was implied by the waiving of tax liability on corporations—a saving to business of nearly £2,000 millions. As the 1975 White Paper on Public Expenditure put it: 'the level of resources taken by the public sector will be cut and channelled into private hands to encourage investment'. We were also able to show that the reduction of tax liability meant that the government would have to borrow more to finance its expenditure and would thus involve itself in increasing debt repayments to private money lenders.

Thus counter-information may be used in a frontal attack on an ideological representation of social affairs, as well as for guiding political action. Whether this involves winkling out obscure data or re-using available information in a different way, it is vital to be aware of the sources of information relevant to a specific issue. It is to these sources that we now turn, for without knowledge of where to obtain data even the most sophisticated way of analysing and re-using statistics is of little real use.

Sources of information

Business and state institutions demand an ever increasing flow of information, most of which is readily available and may easily be critically re-used as counter-information. Despite the ethos of mutual confidentiality practised in Whitehall and the City, and barriers such as the Official Secrets Act, it is often possible to develop a relatively comprehensive overview of how these institutions operate.

Space permits us to outline only the major information sources: for further discussion concerning the production of counter-information, see Community Action's *The Investigators' Handbook* (1975; updating and supplements are published in *Community Action*). Research Organisations like *Counter Information Services* (9

Poland Street, London, W.1, 01-439 3764) and *Labour Research Department* (78 Blackfriars Road, London SE1, 01-928 3649), and academic researchers (especially left-wing ones) can prove helpful.

1. Libraries

As a central depository of information, a thorough library search for information is a necessary element in producing counter-information. The quality and holdings of libraries does, however, vary immensely. For CIS's work, the most useful library has been the *City Business Library* (55 Basinghall Street, London, EC2); a close second is the *Westminster Central Reference Library* (off Leicester Square). As with many of the larger libraries, requests for information may be made by phone. Particularly useful, also, are university and polytechnic libraries, most of which are open to the general public for reference purposes. Most large cities also have commercial or reference libraries; for specialised libraries, consult the *ASLIB Directory: Information Sources*. Many trades unions have helpful research departments, and the TUC and Labour Party have useful libraries (although permission to use them is needed). It can also be worth consulting both company libraries and those of government departments (the Office of Population Censuses and Surveys library at St. Catherine's House is particularly useful and is open to the public).

2. Newspapers and Periodicals

Newspapers are a key source of information. The procedure of 'dredging' for information is of course dependent on the area being researched. In order to dig out relevant material, CIS often begins with the *Research Index* (Business Surveys Ltd.) for references to articles on organisations and related topics. *McCarthy Information Services* produces 'cards' on most companies and major industries which are reproductions of relevant articles. The *Index* to articles in *The Times* and *New York Times* is also useful. The *Financial Times* regularly contains extremely useful economic and financial information, and has a telephone library service for the public on weekday afternoons (01-236-1341). Left-wing press papers like *Labour Weekly*, *Morning Star*, *Newsline*, *Socialist Challenge* and *Socialist Worker*, often contain useful material. The provincial newspapers also contain much information not covered in the nationals. A list of all newspapers can be found in *British Rate and Data (BRAD)* and *Willings Press Guide*. Many newspapers and companies keep files of cuttings on various topics to which you might be able to obtain access. Most libraries have back issues of newspapers, and the *British*

Museum at Colindale holds all the UK papers and many foreign ones, with a full range of back issues.

The information presented in specialist journals and periodicals is also worth keeping in mind. Those most used by CIS are *Economist, Fortune, Investors' Chronicle, Management Today, Economist Intelligence Unit Quarterly,* the *Banker* and *Business Week*. Each of the *Banks* and the *Bank of England* produce quarterly reviews. Most Government departments now have a journal, e.g. *Trade and Industry, Department of Employment Gazette*, etc. *New Society* has a weekly review of 'new' statistics.

3. Official Statistics

As the data source on an increasingly wide range of social and economic issues, as well as on state affairs, a knowledge of official statistics is crucial to the critical researcher. Since official statistics are dealt with in detail in Section Three of this book, we need say here only that the best source for the whole gamut of government statistics is *The Guide to Official Statistics* (2nd edition, 1978). This presents an index to official statistics and their main sources.

4. Information on Companies and Associated Individuals

Companies House, (55 City Road, London, EC1, and Cardiff) is the major source of information on companies. Their file on any company can be seen for 5p and contains a list of Directors, with their addresses and other directorships; a statement of the annual accounts; a list of shareholders; and sundry other information. Any public company with shares quoted on the Stock Exchange will publish a *Report and Accounts*, which is essentially as above minus the list of shareholders. The public can easily obtain a copy from the head office of the company concerned.

Extel Information Service provides concise financial summaries of companies, which are available in commercial libraries. *Who Owns Whom* lists companies, subsidiaries and associated companies. *The Stock Exchange Official Yearbook* provides useful summaries of public companies. *The Times 1000* lists Britain's top companies by size. The *Kompass Register of British Industry and Commerce* is an excellent source-book on some 30,000 companies. These are arranged geographically, with listings of address, directors, product groups, number of employees and parent company. A wide selection of *Trade Directories* on companies and products also may be consulted. Particularly important for critical work is Christopher Hird's *Your Employer's Profits* (Pluto, 1975) which gives useful advice for uncovering details of company operations. The direct approach is also often worthwhile: phone or visit the Public Relations Office of the institution you are interested in. Even the switchboard may be willing to help.

Information on the people who run big business and the state can be found in a number of sources: *Who's Who* (Britain and International), *The Directory of Directors*, *Burke's Peerage*, *Business Backgrounds of MPs*, *Who Was Who*, and *Current Biography*. These are available in most libraries.

5. Research Groups

It is always worth consulting groups or individuals who might have already done work on your area of interest from a radical or critical perspective. Among the many that might be cited are: *Social Audit* (which produces a journal bearing that name concerned with 'corporate social responsibility'); the *Low Pay Unit* (information on those workers often not included in labour statistics because they are involved in part-time and home-based work); the *British Society for Social Responsibility in Science* (produces *Hazards Bulletin* which contains information on workplace hazards, and *Science for People* which provides a useful general analysis of the social role of science and technology in capitalist society). State Research monitors the growth of the state apparatus and provides regular analyses in its *Bulletin*. All four organisations are based at 9 Poland Street, London, WC1.

Other London-based groups providing useful information include: the *Child Poverty Action Group*—which produces the quarterly journal *Poverty*, the monthly *Welfare Rights Bulletin*, and a number of guides and booklets which often contain detailed statistical analyses of welfare benefits and the operation of the welfare state. CPAG is based at 1 Macklin Street, WC2. *Shelter* (whose main publication is *Roof*) is based at 86 The Strand, WC2, and provides counter-information on housing conditions. *Anti-Apartheid* is at 89 Charlotte Street, W2; and the *Institute for Race Relations* is at 247 Pentonville Road, N1. In Nottingham there is *The Institute for Workers' Control*, at 45 Gamble Street.

There are also a number of information and action groups working at a local level. Among them are the *Coventry Workshop*, 40 Binley Road, Coventry, and the *South Wales Anti-Poverty Action Committee*, Merthyr Tydfil.

Organisations based outside the UK can often provide material useful in making international comparisons. Among the many helpful organisations researching in the area of international business, for example, are: *SOMO* in Holland (the Dutch counterpart of CIS), Paulus Potterstraat 20, Amsterdam 1007; *Corporate Data Exchange*, 198 Broadway, Room 707, New York 10038, USA; and international trade union organisations such as the *International Union of Food Workers* (IUF), Rampe de Pont Rouge 8, Petit Lancy, Geneva.

CIS Reports

Rio Tinto Zinc, May 1972
General Electric Company, September 1972
Consolidated Goldfields, November 1972
Recurrent Crisis of London (Property developers), March 1973
British Leyland: The Beginning of the End, June 1973
Three Phase Trick—a handbook on inflation and Phase III, October 1973
Your Money and Your Life (Insurance and Pensions), January 1974
The Unacceptable Face (Conservative Government, 1970–74), April 1974
The Oil Fix (The Oil Companies and Energy Crisis), May 1974
Business As Usual (Banking in South Africa), June 1974
Courtaulds: Inside Out (Textiles), November 1974
Unilever's World, April 1975
Where is Lucas Going?, September 1975
Cutting the Welfare State—Who Profits, November 1975
Who's Next for the Chop? (Unemployment), April 1976
Women Under Attack, June 1976
Racism: Who Profits? September 1976
Black South Africa Explodes, January 1977
Paying for the Crisis, May 1977
Highness—Jubilee Anti-Report, June 1977
Ford Motor Company, January 1978
Buying Time in South Africa, August 1978
The Nuclear Disaster, November 1978

Other References

Emerson, T., 1975, *Mass Media or Mass Deception*, Bristol, Falling Wall.
Glasgow University Media Group, 1976, *Bad News*, London, Routledge & Kegan Paul.

Section Five:
Conclusion

22.
Dot Griffiths, John Irvine and Ian Miles

Social Statistics: Towards a Radical Science

Where do we go from here?

Preceding chapters in this book have examined the historical development of statistical practices, the philosophy of quantification, the nature and role of official statistics. Taken together they constitute a cogent critique of the role of statistics in our society. This critique is much more than an academic exercise: it goes beyond posing issues of theory, to pose important implications for action. Critical social theory alone is insufficient: a critical practice is also necessary to challenge and change the practices with which we have taken issue. As Marx might have said: 'the statisticians have only quantified the world; what counts is our success in changing it'.

Critical statistical practice cannot be developed by pen, paper and calculator alone. While we should not understate the importance of theoretical work, critical practice is needed to sharpen, test, deepen and extend its analysis. Much of the form of such a practice can only be created through actually using statistics in political struggle. Here we can learn some useful lessons from the applications of statistics which have already been made in radical politics—as well as from the parallel experiences of scientists and technologists working in other fields of radical science.

In this chapter we attempt to formulate some guidelines for radical statistical practice. We shall first look at the development of critical responses to science and technology (S and T), for we can learn much from the successes and shortcomings of these responses that is relevant to the attempt to develop a radical statistics. We shall argue that radical approaches to S and T need to be related to the struggle for a structural transformation of society and to an understanding of how S and T are constituted within the existing structure of society. The fate of a radical statistics is intimately bound up with the development and use of forms of analysis effective for this struggle and the critical understanding that should accompany it. We shall then consider what elements are necessary for the theory and practice of radical statistics in capitalist society.[1]

1. Critical approaches to science and technology

a. Anti-science, anti-technology

An understandable first reaction to the problems people experience with statistics is to seek to discard them altogether. Statistical approaches may have limited use in the physical and biological sciences, it is argued, but their use in social analysis is anathema: quantification reifies social processes, inevitably turns people into objects to be manipulated and controlled, and is thus contrary to basic human values. This anti-statistics approach is perhaps most fully developed by 'humanistic' psychologists and 'interpretative' sociologists, but it is also a fairly common gut response among a wider public reacting against being 'reduced to numbers' in official statistics and social science (see Irvine and Miles, section 1, this volume).

This reaction to statistics shares much with a broader response to some of the social problems of contemporary science and technology, which achieved clearest expression in the anti-S and T approach promoted extensively in the late 1960s. This was a time of general questioning of the dominant values and cultural institutions of Western society, and for many young people this took the form of attempting to build, or declare the existence of, a 'counter-culture'. (See, for example, the work of Musgrove, 1974; Nuttall, 1970; and Roszak, 1968. For critical commentary, see Hall and Jefferson, 1976; and Silber, 1970). Based largely on middle-class youth, the counter-culture sought to establish an 'alternative society' of communes, digger shops, psychedelia and rock music. The focus was largely upon individuals and ideas: Charles Reich, for example, argued that a new consciousness—which he termed consciousness III—was in the making (Reich, 1970; for assessments of Reich, see Nobile, 1971). Leary, the 'high' priest of hippiedom, concentrated on the use of psychedelic drugs to create such a consciousness: according to him, each individual needs to

> realise that he (sic) is not a game-playing robot put on this planet to be given a Social Security number and to be spun on the assembly line of school, college, career, insurance, funeral, goodbye. (Leary, 1970, p. 131).

Particular criticism was directed by the 'counter-culture' at technology, or at least to what were seen as its archetypically Western versions. Modern *technology* was itself seen as directly

responsible for the uglier products of contemporary capitalism—
the ravages of the Vietnam War, contemporary patterns of illness
and disease, environmental pollution, impoverished personal relationships, and a host of other modern horrors (or modern versions of
ancient horrors). Science, on the other hand, was attacked more for
its approach than its products. The 'counter-culture' regarded the
scientific approach as inherently bearing an oppressive mode of
consciousness. Science was seen as leading on directly to the
perception and treatment of nature and human beings alike as mere
mechanical objects to be toyed with at the whim of unfeeling
scientists. Critical commentary on science abounded, and Bacon's
dictum of 'Knowledge is Power' was quoted ironically. The root of
modern horrors was identified, not as an oppressive mode of
production but as an oppressive organisation of knowledge. From
'Knowledge is Power' the 'counter-culture' drew the conclusion
'Science is Oppression'.

Commentators such as Theodore Roszak (1968, and 1973)
provided the intellectual foundations for this critique. (The work of
Marcuse (1964, 1969) was also often mined—and frequently
underestimated—in this context). Roszak argued that the amoral
and manipulative scientific consciousness has become the dominant
mode of understanding in advanced industrial societies. It under-
values or excludes experience and knowledge resistant to scientific
analysis, treating them as unreal or unacceptable. The 'counter-
culture' rejected this as an immensely restrictive vision of human
social development and of what counts as knowledge. Some of the
vitality needed restoring to our arid life: a liberated consciousness
should overthrow scientific rationality, opening up 'the province of
the dream, the myth, the visionary rapture, the sacramental sense of
reality, the transcendent symbol' (Roszak, 1973, p. 379). The
remedy, it seemed, lay in rejecting the whole methodological basis
of modern science. Statistics, moreover, was taken to be the most
extreme manifestation of the anti-human, repressive tendencies of
the scientific approach. For Roszak, 'this doctrinaire mathematisa-
tion of person and society, this statistical manipulation of human
beings as if they were so many atomic particles' (Roszak, 1973, p.
33) was the quintessence of technocratic rationality.

The rejection of Western science gave a new prominence to
subjectivism, mysticism, occultism and parascience. In many cases
the 'destruction' of an overripe ego, or the undermining of an
established outlook, left the individual with little more than a
cynical disdain for the possibility of change, or ready for recruitment by anyone from Charles Manson to Guru Maharaji. While

the 'counter culture' had raised awareness of alternative ways of life, it could do little to enable the mass of people to create and choose between such alternatives. It achieved no structural change in the society whose rationality it sought to question—the flamboyance of hippie lifestyles may even have reinforced the belief that every person in modern capitalist society is given a free choice as to how to organise their lives. Nor was it ever made exactly clear to the non-hip population how it could be that a rejection of Western S and T could be reconciled with extensive use of stereo-systems, light shows and credit cards.

The anti-S and T perspectives, like other innovations of the 'counter-culture', had important effects. The 'counter-culture' waned as a recognisable movement during the 1970s, but many of its attitudes, like the antipathy to statistics, are widely reproduced.

Despite the inheritance the counter-culture has left us with in the continuing tradition of anti-S and T^2, it has long lost its momentum—although ageing hippies, and occasional new recruits, may still be seen travelling to and from cults and gurus in search of cosmic consciousnss. Many of its adherents have returned to 'hip' (or not so 'hip') variations of orthodox careers. Some are still trying to recover from the collapse of their ideals. Others have sought new ways to advance these ideals.

The failures and defeats of many of its social experiments, and the rapid transformation of much of its style and ingenuity into commercial wares (many fashions were derived from the hippie lifestyle), led many of the counter-culture's most energetic proponents to a profound questioning of the viability, within technologically advanced societies, of strategies for social change which took as their starting point the transformation of individual consciousness. Often their conclusion was that reality cannot be magically changed just by thinking about it in new ways, and they have sought to realise their ideals through other social movements. The most important of these for the present discussion was the alternative technology (AT) movement.

b. Alternative science and technology

As is evident from the contributors, content and audience of magazines like *Undercurrents* and the *Journal of the New Alchemists*, the movement to develop alternative S and T has drawn upon members of the 'counter-culture' who have recognised the futility of a total rejection of S and T, as well as other people more concerned with specific problems they see to be linked with modern S and T—like ill-health, environmental pollution and resource depletion. Instead

of focusing only on changing consciousness and experience, the task
here has been presented as one of developing

> a *new* science and a *new* technology (which should) . . . operate on
> low amounts of energy; not irreversibly disperse non-renewable
> resources; use local and easily accessible materials; recycle materials
> locally; not produce waste products at a greater rate than they could
> be absorbed by the natural cycling processes; not liberate novel
> chemical compounds in more than trace amounts; fit in with existing
> culture patterns; satisfy those who operate it; lend itself to control by
> those who operate it; have safeguards against misuse. (Harper,
> 1973).

The diversity of the groups considering themselves to be part
of what is commonly referred to as the AT movement is reflected in
the varied forms taken by AT. These range from the search for
occult and paranormal phenomena (e.g. flying saucers and extra-
sensory perception) to the exploration of novel or non-Western
scientific systems (e.g. the medical alternatives of naturopathy and
acupuncture or the alternative psychology of group therapies and
'personal growth'). At the extremes, these approaches are often
oriented to suprasocial cosmic forces or to the asocial 'essence' of
individuals; in general they tend to offer no social programme other
than one of gradual conversion and personal commitment. Nevertheless, the more environmentally-oriented groupings, and particularly those concerned with the hardware of AT, have often been
explicit in their recognition of the need for broad social changes,
focusing on the threat of major environmental crises if this does not
take place.

In general the AT movement has taken a 'technological
determinist' view of social change. In other words, it is believed that
in S and T lie the motor forces of society, the roots of modern social
problems and the germs of change. S and T are largely treated in
isolation from their social determinants. It is believed that they can
be transformed simply by convincing people of the social, environmental and health hazards of such high technologies as supersonic
aircraft, nuclear reactors, factory farms and automated production
lines, and by providing them with alternatives. S and T must be
taken to the people; they must be small-scale and controlled by the
individual or community. With the diffusion and widespread
acceptance of AT, small communities would be able to grow their
own food, and produce ample energy, shelter and everyday
necessities (e.g. Bookchin, 1970). A changed S and T would in turn
change production patterns, consumption patterns and lifestyles: in
place of bureaucratised large-scale society with all its social

problems would be a simple life-style in harmony with nature. S and T, then, are seen as capable of being changed independently of other social conditions; the way to achieve an ecologically-sound world is through *technical* rather than social change.

Like the 'counter-culture', the AT movement has had some effects, especially in terms of introducing important issues into public debate. Some of the technological alternatives it has promoted—for example, solar energy devices—have proved sufficiently profitable to be incorporated into the mass market, although many others remain curiosities or toys for the rich. The associated political alternatives which have gone beyond mere information campaigns have largely centred around the 'Ecology' parties of several Western European countries, but these are rarely tied to any strategies of mass involvement (although they have made electoral gains which in some cases have alarmed traditional parties). More often, their inward-looking and anti-growth philosophies have meant that their success has been based upon alliances with unlikely, and often reactionary forces—particularly national capital against transnational interests.

Thus, although the AT movement has produced valuable assessments of the deleterious consequences of many modern technologies, these have rarely been carried through to an examination of their social roots (see Dickson, 1974, and Elliot and Elliot, 1976, for a more general, while sympathetic, critique of AT strategies). This is despite the links between some members of the AT movement and workers' struggles concerning the processes and results of capitalist production (e.g. the Lucas Aerospace workers' attempts to develop socially useful products, Elliott, et. al., 1977), and despite attempts to develop the concept of 'radical technology' (Boyle and Harper, 1976). Lacking an analysis of the social relations underlying contemporary systems of production and consumption, the AT movement has mainly been restricted to exhorting politicians, industrialists and the public to change their ways, coupled with threats (that often appear to be irresponsibly alarmist) about the likely consequences of failing to do so.

The limited appeal of, and response to, these formulae has led many AT proponents to decide that their own energies would best be spent improving their own lives and/or setting examples to others. They have, for example, attempted to develop environmentally-sound subsistence life-styles in farms, to find ways of conserving urban resources by recycling, and so on. But while this has involved changing their own patterns of consumption, the patterns of production they have retreated from remain dominant—in fact, they often depend upon them for scrap engines and copper wire for windmills, etc. Proponents of AT have thus often become resigned to creating only limited individual change; and their practical innovations have frequently been little more than free research and development for progressive firms.

These are major problems for the AT movement, but it would be both churlish and shortsighted to ignore its positive contributions to date, some of which have potential for considerable further development. First, as already pointed out, the AT movement has introduced new questions about S and T into public debate. In the case of nuclear power, in particular, both the direction and use of a major new technology are being questioned, bringing into play arguments covering such diverse issues as future requirements for energy (and thus the struggle over the provision of public, as opposed to reliance on private, transport) and the security of toxic radioactive material (thus illuminating the steady development of paramilitary police and security forces). Opposition to some forms of nuclear power has already been a focus for radical political initiatives, which raises the possibility of a more sustained conflict between elements of the AT movement and state power. Second, it would be incorrect to see all AT activities as relying on individual change or parliamentary pressure. The nuclear power issue has provoked mass demonstrations in some countries—and has led on occasions to violence and counter-violence. A different type of initiative has been displayed in the use of 'Green Bans', pioneered by Australian trades unions and now extended to other countries. 'Green Bans' entail a refusal by trades unionists, particularly in the construction industry, to work on socially or environmentally damaging projects.[3] The orientation of the campaigns of groups like the Lucas Aerospace workers around the right to *socially useful* work represents a more affirmative version of this strategy. Third, it is clear that contact with the AT movement has been a valuable stimulus to the efforts of radical scientists to develop an adequate critical approach to S and T (see, for example, Dickson, 1974; Elliott and Elliott, 1976). By raising awareness that the forms of S and T with which we are most familiar are not the only conceivable options for future society, the AT movement has contributed to our understanding of the social basis of S and T and of possible dimensions of social transformation.[4]

There are good grounds, then, for believing that the potential of the AT movement is not exhausted. An AT-type approach to statistics might well perform useful functions, if in a more limited sphere. But it would also have to contend with the problems engendered by any approach which tends to treat an area of science as if its theories and techniques can simply be replaced by alternatives, independent of any struggle to change the social structures which underpin the dominant forms and roles of S and T. Furthermore, the view of statistics as the hard core of positivistic science (see section 2, this volume), or as the ultimate in reification and dehumanisation, is likely to discourage any substantial attempt to promote an 'alternative statistics' in such terms.

Nevertheless, an 'alternative statistics' of sorts does exist, in the field of mathematical statistics rather than that of data production. This is Bayesian statistics, which has existed practically as an underground tradition for some two centuries. Some statisticians and social scientists have argued that this is an appropriate statistics for radicals to use, for it explicitly recognises that statistics has assumptions, and attempts to integrate these into the analysis (see, for example, Poirier, 1977, who also argues that the more familiar non-parametric statistics are more appropriate for radicals than conventional approaches). Certainly the Bayesian approach should be brought to the attention of critical social scientists, both as a possible tool for analysis and as a means of raising consciousness concerning the assumptions that are built into existing statistical practices. But as Atkins and Jarrett (this volume) point out, this approach is in itself no panacea. While it allows 'subjective' judgements to enter into the use of mathematical statistics, this may be used to justify relativism or a misguided search for consensus, without bringing into question the social sources of these judgements. Much interest in the Bayesian technique has actually stemmed from managers and technocrats seeking to incorporate their own presuppositions more directly into decision-making procedures. (For a general outline of Bayesian statistics for social scientists, see Phillips, 1973.)

There are also examples of AT-type strategies in data production in social research—particularly among psychologists, whose discipline is tied more firmly to quantitative methods than is sociology (in the UK at least). Humanistic psychologists, and clinical and social workers, have paid much attention to the use of 'personal construct' techniques (see Bannister and Fransella, 1971; Bannister and Mair, 1968, for overviews). The supposed advantages of these techniques is that, unlike conventional psychological tests, they allow the people whose perceptions are being researched to provide their own categories rather than forcing them to make judgements in terms of supplied categories. These techniques may facilitate communication in one-to-one situations, although there is a tendency for psychological researchers to apply them merely as more efficient means of extracting information from their 'subjects', so that the latter are simply presented with a more complicated version of the usual questionnaire.

Furthermore, while personal construct methods can, as their proponents argue, be used to move psychological research some way towards a more interactive project which avoids a crude categorisation of individuals into pre-ordained types, these methods may themselves be recuperated into the mainstream psychological programme. Thus a great deal of effort has been put into developing ways of processing the data produced by personal construct methods (by factor analysis, for example) so as to be able to grade the individuals involved along supposed personality dimensions such as 'cognitive complexity'). Social psychology has been remarkably quick to assimilate what at first appeared to be a subversive approach, and to divorce personal construct methods from the theory within which they were first developed. While the approach itself may have much to offer researchers and practitioners who recognise that human beings take a more constructive part in creating the social world than do most psychologists, the techniques it offers can, in and of themselves, effect no substantial change.

Attempts to develop new approaches to social statistics along AT lines may in principle contribute to the task of developing a radical statistics—not only by contributing to our understanding of the problems of existing statistical data and techniques, but also by suggesting some of the directions in which statistics could be transformed away from the practices presently dominant. But unless the development of new ideas and techniques is linked to more general attempts to bring about radical social change, they can carry little weight in a society whose S and T are likely only to change insofar as they can incorporate ideas and techniques useful to ruling class interests.

c. *Social responsibility in science and technology*

A rather more popular critical response to the problems with S and T among practicing scientists and engineers has been that of 'social responsibility' (SR). SR seeks to deal with the problems of modern society by calling for more and better S and T, rather than for abandoning them in pursuit of dubious alternatives. S and T are themselves seen as essentially rational activities: the problems arise only from their misuse. The role of radical scientists, and engineers, should be to work *within* S and T, and to make sure their work is used responsibly.

The notion of 'social responsibility' originated with the failure of a group of the scientists working on the initial development of the atomic bomb (the Manhattan Project) to dissuade the politicians and military from using it against Japanese civilian targets (Jungk, 1964), and their subsequent campaign to generate a wider public awareness of the consequences of nuclear warfare.

The events surrounding the use of the atomic bomb changed, forever, the relationship of many liberal scientists to science. Although the creators of the nuclear bomb had warned of its horrific power, it had still been used: the traditional separation between science and society could no longer be easily assumed. The awesome consequences of their work raised severe doubts in their minds about the control of S and T; doubts compounded by the growth of state planning of national research and development policies. As the 'pursuit of knowledge' became transformed into 'science in the national interest', the idea of the typical scientist working in splendid isolation from social pressures increasingly came under attack. Many liberal scientists saw social responsibility as the way to prevent their work being misused.

A second major impetus to the development of SR approaches to S and T came in the 1960s with the campaigns against nuclear weapons (e.g. the Campaign for Nuclear Disarmament (CND) in Britain), and, later, through the massive American involvement in Vietnam and the application, with gruesome results, of S and T to biological and chemical warfare. The concern of scientists about the napalming of innocent civilian populations and the defoliation and despoliation of vast areas was expressed in the formation of groups like 'Scientists and Engineers for Social and Political Action' (SESPA) in the USA, and the 'British Society for Social Responsibility in Science' (BSSRS) in Britain (see Rose and Rose, 1976).

The scientists and engineers who initially joined these groups covered a wide political spectrum; their differences were made relatively unimportant at first by the immediacy of the problems at hand. Both liberal and radical elements were able to unite under a common conception of S and T as ethically neutral, asocial, bodies of knowledge and technique: they could be used for good purposes or abused for bad ones. This conception of S and T—now commonly termed the 'use-abuse' model—takes problems, such as atomic warfare, as deriving from the abuse of S and T by elites for the inappropriate end of destroying life (whereas the scientists developing nuclear power were seen as intending it to enrich human life by providing cheap and unlimited sources of energy).

Thus it was not S and T *per se*, but their abuses, that came under attack.

The ways in which scientists and engineers should organise to press for socially responsible science and technology were, however, the subject of debate. Most saw SR as a matter for the conscience of the individual scientist; others argued that what was needed was a more informed (scientific) awareness on the part of state authorities of the need to develop more rational S and T policies; and a minority of radicals argued that SR was best fostered by scientists organising with other workers to press for rather broader-based institutional changes.

The main thrust of the SR movement was thus to argue that scientists have a duty to educate themselves about the adverse effects and likely abuses of their work. Only then would they be in a position to forewarn society of the potential hazards associated with particular directions of scientific research and development. Rather than questioning the bases for the social *production* of particular forms of S and T—other than condemning the levels of expenditure on military research and on the development of wasteful luxuries— the SR movement has restricted its criticism to abuses in the *consumption* of S and T. The main weapons in this campaign to prevent misuse of S and T have been information drives aimed at shaping the opinions of both the general public and the political elites, together with codes of practice to prevent irresponsible actions by deviant scientists and technologists. It was hoped that such criticism would enlighten the elites, and, if and when necessary, awaken public opinion through the mass media to such an extent that government and industry would be dissuaded from perpetuating these abuses.

An SR-type approach has been adopted by many statisticians and users of statistics, attempting to counter what they see as the widespread misuse of statistics. Critical commentaries on statistics —Reichmann's *Use and Abuse of Statistics* and Huff's *How to Lie with Statistics*, being perhaps the two best-known examples—tend to take a similar line. In these accounts, statistics is treated as a set of neutral technical procedures for processing data and assessing links be- tween different sets of data: the problems encountered in statistical usage are seen as arising from technical ineptitude or deliberate misrepresentation. Both problems can be solved relatively easily— the first by improving standards, through professionalising statis- tical practice and developing a higher level of public knowledge about basic statistical techniques and conventions; the second by SR in statistics. The socially responsible statistician would, typically, help develop and follow 'codes of practice', thus making public the bases and assumptions on which s/he has produced and assessed data. In this way, possible misuse of statistical work—especially misinterpretation of figures by politicians—would be thwarted and 'bias' and 'inaccuracy' removed. The socially responsible statistician would also have a duty to criticise offenders against this code publicly. Social scientists and others using statistics would need to guard in a similar fashion against political or journalistic 'distortion' of their analyses.

Such an approach has proved appealing to many scientists concerned about the problems associated with their work. Undeniably, SR has had its share of successes—its proponents have, for example, contributed to the demystification of specialised (or secret) knowledge and techniques, in respect of health and safety at work, for example. It has also been possible to effect, at least for a while, controls and/or changes in certain areas of scientific research—genetic engineering being a recent example. In some cases (e.g. environmentalism), dramatic appeals by individual scientists and technologists have helped stimulate major public debate over the effects of S and T. Mobilising the mass action necessary to reverse public policy is, however, generally beyond the scope of the SR approach, which relies on the willingness and ability of the mass media to stimulate awareness and structure action. Since the media will only rarely exert influence beyond the terrain staked out by party politics and the capitalist economy, effective action beyond these limits requires a degree and form of organisation that cannot be provided from above by scientific, engineering or journalistic elites or would-be elites.

More often than not these problems cannot even arise—for the most part, individual scientific workers are relatively powerless. A socially responsible conscience can in fact often turn out to be little more than an expensive liability, as was the case in a recent example of SR in which an engineer working for a large British electronics company wrote to the *Guardian* explaining his refusal to work on a contract to supply communications equipment to the South African Defence Department. The engineer in question was at first informed that, since he could not be trusted, his opportunities for promotion would be limited. The Company then suspended him from work; and while he was later reinstated, it would seem unlikely that he has a very rosy future with them—nor, for that matter, with any other electronics company.

Similar problems would surely be encountered if a few government statisticians decided to become 'socially responsible'.

In Britain, the Official Secrets Act could be hurled at them immediately: the statistician's role is to produce and process the data required by the state in an 'objective and dispassionate' manner, not to divulge them publicly as a matter of course, nor to interfere in political debate over interpretation of their significance. In the case of a serious breach, the offending statisticians could conceivably find themselves biding Her Majesty's pleasure in prison. If a significant number of statisticians were to organise themselves to take collective action this would have a far greater impact—but, for the reasons outlined by the Government Statistician's Collective (this volume), the hierarchical organisation, the fragmentation and the isolation of statistical work, make this seem extremely unlikely. Within groups like BSSRS, a recognition of problems with the SR approach was not slow in developing, and this critique of SR can help extend our analysis of statistics.

2. Towards an analysis of science and technology as social products

From its inception, there was an internal tension in BSSRS between liberal and radical elements. Among the liberals were the vast majority of BSSRS's more eminent members. They believed both in the neutrality of science and in the efficacy of SR in countering 'abuses'. The radicals, in contrast, argued increasingly that this notion of SR was insufficient. Environmental pollution, biological warfare and atomic bombs could be explained adequately neither in terms of accident nor ignorance. As the then chairman of BSSRS (sexual politics had not penetrated far in BSSRS by 1972) wrote in *New Scientist* on the organisation's third birthday:

> We have found ourselves driven to understand not just the particular abuse, but the social system which despite the benevolent potential of science somehow manages to produce abuse after abuse. (Rosenhead, 1972, p. 135).

The radicals saw scientific production as bound up with the class nature of capitalist society: a society oriented towards production for profit rather than need was bound also to produce continual abuses of science. The neutrality of science, with its beneficent potential, was seen to be systematically distorted under capitalism into a malevolent reality. Only with fundamental social and political change would this potential be realised.

Not surprisingly, such radical analyses did not appeal to the liberal membership who saw the radicals as arguing that S and T were *necessarily* warped in capitalist society, and began to define them as subversive opponents of the mixed economy and its pluralist polity. Having seen political controls undermining the autonomy of science in what they regarded as socialist states, many scientists and engineers were virulently anti-communist: problems with S and T were their responsibility, not those of politicians. They remembered the Lysenko affair in the Soviet Union all too well (see Lewontin and Levins, 1976; Young, 1978). The radicals, in turn, argued that the ethos of professionalism and individual SR were at best utterly impotent. The result was a predictable mass exodus of the liberals from BSSRS, with some subsequently regrouping in 1973 in the Council for Science and Society. This self-selected and openly elitist body (e.g. see J. Ziman, 1975), aided by thousands of pounds of Leverhulme Foundation money, continues to explore the social implications of certain areas of science in the way the BSSRS might have done in its early days. In line with the politics of SR, its deliberations are presented to the establishment in the form of expensive pamphlets (e.g. Council for Science and Society, 1976).

This exodus also had a profound effect upon BSSRS itself. From a pluralist pressure group arguing primarily for SR in S and T, it had become a radical group of scientists, engineers and others explicitly committed, in the main, to revolutionary social transformation. The recomposition of its membership meant that BSSRS's policies and strategies needed thoroughly rethinking. With its debate over the role of radical scientists and engineers in society concentrated in the revolutionary left, the critique of S and T under capitalism took on new dimensions.

Until the early 1970s the radical position on science and technology had been based, like that of SR, on the 'use-abuse' model. The questions for radical scientists and engineers were: how can we demonstrate that the problems with S and T lie in their misuse in a class-divided capitalist society? What form of societal organisation is needed to best realise the beneficent potential of S and T? In which organisations could radicals best bring about the political and social changes needed to provide the environment for their S and T to be better used?

Providing answers to these questions became increasingly difficult as, with the progress of the debate within BSSRS, emphasis was placed more and more on the *production* of S and T, as well as on their *consumption*. The debate drew in politicised elements from both the old counter-culture and the AT movement, who sought a critical examination of the *nature* of S and T in capitalist society. Was it not the case, they argued, that science was more than a set of methods and techniques; was it not also a system of concepts and social practices? Was it not the case that non-polluting and less alienating technologies, like solar energy, were not used—nor hardly dreamed of—in capitalist society because there was little or no incentive to actually adopt and produce them?

The crystallisation of the debate over S and T around overtly radical nuclei, enriched by the infusion of these other elements, finally resulted in the displacement of the 'use-abuse' model. S and T began to be seen in much broader social terms—as forms of *social* knowledge, *social* practices, and *social* applications developed within the framework of capitalist society. Scientific concepts were profoundly linked with other sets of concepts, which all reflected ideological elements. The hierarchical, elitist and sexist practices of science paralleled other social practices in capitalist society; the orientation and utility of S and T could not be divorced from the social and economic factors that conditioned their development. S and T as a whole needed to be seen in terms of their development, reproduction and roles within capitalist society.

This meant a major reorientation of the role of organisations like BSSRS (whose name was by now rather anachronistic). The development of the liberating potentials for S and T was thus more than just removing their mis-use through the purgative of a revolutionary social transformation. While certain forms of scientific knowledge and technique, and certain technologies, developed within capitalist society will surely be put to good use in a future socialist society, much might not. New sciences and technologies, a whole new concept of S and T, more appropriate to the needs of socialist society, may need to be created and developed. Just as society needs to be thoroughly transformed, so do the scientific and technological practices which are constituted in it. This analysis suggested that an important aspect of the work of organisations like BSSRS was to develop a critique of both the nature and practices of S and T, not as 'S and T under capitalism' but as 'capitalist S and T'.

Developments concerning statistics, similar to those in the radical science movement, have been occasioned by the more recently formed Radical Statistics Group (RSG) in Britain. As in the case of BSSRS, many of its founding members were drawn from an establishment professional organisation—in this case the Royal Statistical Society (RSS). Liberal members of this largely conservative society hoped to form a ginger group within it in order both to democratise it and to promote discussion on previously excluded issues such as politically motivated 'misuse' of statistics.

Indeed, largely as a result of pressure from RSG members, elections for the RSS council and presidency were held, for the first time in many years, in 1977. The establishment candidate, Sir Campbell Adamson, was embarrassingly beaten. (For details see various issues of *Radical Statistics Newsletter*, between 1975–77).[5]

Many RSG members saw their role as being mainly to develop a statistician's 'code of practice' which would ensure that the technical and theoretical assumptions in their work were made clear in the presentation of data—in short, statisticians should become socially responsible. Other areas of work seen as important have been in the area of 'misuse' of statistics—for example, in criticising the government's use of statistics in pruning the NHS[6]—and, to date less successfully, providing expert statistical help to community groups and others in struggles through what was dubbed a 'statistical fire-brigade'.

As with BSSRS, there has been an uneasy tension in the group between those who advocate a liberal SR strategy with a focus on the 'misuse' of statistics, and the radicals, more concerned with a critique of statistical practice in capitalist society. Even though the RSG's policy statement and its affiliation to BSSRS seem to indicate that its aims go beyond stopping abuse to a scrutiny of the class nature of contemporary statistics, these issues have not yet been confronted adequately.

As has also been the case for other areas of S and T, a general critique of the role of statistical practices in capitalist society is needed. Such a general critique has begun to be developed within the radical science movement, and is indispensible if scientists and engineers—and statisticians—are to work out how they can best facilitate social transformation. Strategies for the radical science movement can only be effective if based on such knowledge.

3. Science and technology in capitalist society

S and T can be seen as *integral* to both the maintenance and reproduction of modern capitalist society in two major ways. Scientific knowledge and techniques, as used to produce technological innovations, are vital to the search for profit and competitive advantage among business enterprises. And both S and T play a central role in facilitating social control: to suppress and repress threats to the existing social order, and to legitimate that order as humane and rational. S and T, then, are elements in a wider social system, whose operation needs to be evaluated in detail in developing perspectives on radical S and T.

a. Science and technology for profit within the capitalist enterprise

In capitalist production scientific research is the foundation on which both new products and new production processes are developed. Old products for new markets, new products for both old and new markets, and more efficient ways of producing them are the key to success in capitalist production. Both advertising and the elimination of existing alternatives help to create markets for new products, with profit rather than social need the watchword for their introduction. Completely new needs are created to serve an increasingly technologised production process—e.g. for deodorants, tranquillisers and goods purchased as status symbols as much as for other uses—often by playing on insecurities themselves engendered by capitalist society.

The nervous 'macho' of capitalist man is defined and reinforced by artefacts symbolising male dominance, the 'femininity' of capitalist woman by consumer goods—particularly cosmetics and fashion—reinforcing her role as mother, domestic labourer and sex object. Meanwhile, the basic needs of those people without sufficient resources to pay for commodities remain unfulfilled; for poverty goes completely unrecognised by market forces. The basic science needed, for example, to deal with many of the problems of age-related illness have just not been developed by the multinational pharmaceutical companies. Old people with meagre pensions just cannot generate demand for the expensive technological products the companies depend upon for their high profits. Similarly, the social and ecological consequences of capitalist production are ignored in the calculations made in deciding whether or not to develop and introduce new products, unless they are forced upon companies by political pressure. The psychological effects of assembly-line and shift work are problems to be dealt with only by paying marginally higher wages. Macho-man becomes an even more unthinking, uncaring and underdeveloped person; feminine woman as housewife retreats into pep-pills for the day, 'sleepers' for the night, doubly oppressed as both housewife and wage-labourer. Both are induced to become slaves to production at work, puppets to consumption at home. These stresses are made even worse by the pollution and disregard for health and safety which are similarly direct by-products of capitalist production.[7]

Statistics plays various roles in all of this, too. Market research, for example, attempts to quantify the extent of viable markets and the prices they will bear for different products—and sampling theory is particularly useful here. Many of the techniques of mathematical statistics were in fact initially developed for agricultural and industrial applications, notably to assess the relative efficiencies of different operations, (see Pearson, 1973; and Rosenhead and Thunhurst, this volume). Seen in wider historical terms, the development of the capitalist mode of production stimulated and structured a vast demand for quantification (see Shaw and Miles; and Young, this volume). The range and nature of statistical technique and practices with which we are now presented should be understood as intimately related to these social forces.

The wider application of S and T to the production process has not merely been a matter of increasing the efficiency (that is, profitability) of particular production methods; it has also involved facilitating and extending management control over labour.

Historically, the development of the factory system, and the consequent division of labour into a series of fragmented tasks, represented a major change in the organisation of production; one which had among its effects the shifting of control of the labour process away from craft workers. S and T both created the conditions for these changes and were stimulated in their development by them. Craft skills were first fragmented into constituent elements, each of which could be performed individually and more rapidly by different workers, and then machines were developed to take over specific simple tasks. Multi-function machines were introduced to take over whole groups of tasks; and it is now possible for an extensive production process to be automated—complete with fail-safe devices and cybernetic monitoring.

The skill, creativity and autonomy of craft workers were thus gradually and systematically eroded: workers were transformed first into machine appendages, then into machine monitors, and now, perhaps, into mere midwives and maintainers of machines. Skills which are passed on from one generation to another, and which take years for each worker to acquire, are made redundant overnight through their incorporation into machines; many skilled workers are replaced by the very machines they have helped to create.

The trivial, monotonous and stressful labour which characterises so many people's work experience, and is epitomised by the modern assembly line, is thus not a simple *abuse* of technical possibilities. The machines, the systems of production, have been designed and produced within the constraints of capitalist efficiency and control, not to provide rewarding jobs or useful products. Much of the monotony, toil and danger of modern industry would persist even if workers owned and controlled the machines in their existing workplaces. Monotony, toil and danger are consequences of the systematic development of technologies in a capitalist productive system where the criterion of profit overrides that of welfare, and where the initiatives and interests of workers are subordinated to those of an *efficient*, albeit alienated, labour process.[8] The scientific infrastructure servicing the demand for technological change is similarly no neutral end-product of the logic of scientific advance; nor are current scientific practices the only way of organising and carrying out scientific work.

One particularly significant facet to the process of deskilling involves the historical growth and subsequent change in the nature of scientific and technical work. Indeed, the displacement of labour by machines is often portrayed as if all workers were becoming more skilled, and, freed from the worst aspects of backbreaking labour, more able to develop and use their mental capacities at the workplace. Although this argument vastly overstates the extent to which a demand for trained, expert workers was created, the growth of sections of scientific and technical workers was important in the development of capitalist production. As the labour process was 'rationalised' by an elaborate division of labour, so design and technical work were separated from production, which was being reduced to repetitive, simplified jobs. Specialised and technical tasks of design and co-ordination were thus created, generating an expanding requirement for appropriate specialist workers. Research and development functions in firms were dramatically expanded, with increasing state support through the provision of scientific training in universities and colleges and the funding of basic scientific research.

The development of new scientific and technical workers' skills and knowledge was set in motion largely by and for capital, but these workers did, and often continue to, possess special status by virtue of their expertise. Often, they gain a greater measure of satisfaction and security from their work than shop-floor workers. Indeed, because of this, they often isolate themselves from the struggles of other workers, seeing themselves as professionals, and in some cases as a branch of management—even though their pay may now be little different from that of other workers.

In recent years, however, some industrial scientists and engineers (like many 'professionals' in service sector employment) have found that the processes of deskilling and redundancy have begun to threaten them too. Computer-aided design is a case in point: with it, standard components no longer have to be redrawn afresh on each design. Thus, the design staff are left to spend all their time drawing non-routine items. While this may release them from the drudgery of routine work, at the same time it takes the form of a speed-up; working continually on tasks requiring considerable concentration, the workers are now employed in more demanding and tiring work. And as the design process becomes increasingly rationalised, and more design items become either standardised or amenable to computerised treatment, so a smaller workforce is required. (See Cooley, 1976; and Gorz, 1976b).

This kind of experience has begun to undermine the 'professional' ideology of many scientific workers, for their work increasingly resembles that of shop-floor workers. Provided with less job satisfaction, they have clearly become little cogs in a big wheel whose movement they are in no position to control. Rather than being the autonomous and creative force they once thought themselves to be, scientists and engineers are now finding themselves subjected to the same threats of redundancy, speed-up and control as other workers.

As a result, scientific and technical work is acquiring a new political significance. The answer is not to opt out, or to become 'socially responsible': workers are finding it necessary to organise, to protect themselves from the growing 'rationalisation' of S and T for profit. Thus it comes as no surprise that the Association of Scientific, Technical and Management Staffs (ASTMS) is now Britain's fastest growing union—although like similarly fast growing unions of scientific and technical workers in other countries it still carries with it much of the baggage of 'professionalism'. Recruitment, significantly, has been particularly high in the computer field, one of the leading areas of recent deskilling.

b. Science and technology for social control: state and ideology

S and T have not only been central in the development and reproduction of the productive forces and relations of capitalist society. They have also been crucial to the development and reproduction of the everyday social practices which are necessary conditions for its existence, and which structure and maintain it. In liberal democratic capitalist states, educational and cultural institutions (often in the state apparatus) have proved remarkably effective in establishing and maintaining acquiescence—the 'consensus' of the 'silent majority'—to the established order, despite class divisions and exploitation. But there are contradictions within this complex balance of forces, which when exposed and politically acted upon can sometimes upset this apparently stable system. The development and use of S and T in social control—that is, to preserve the hegemony of capitalist social relations in cultural and social matters—is of vital importance. Statistical science plays a particularly, and increasingly, important role here.

Of course, physical coercion—let alone the potential for such coercion in the form of armies, etc.—is never completely absent, even in the most politically 'stable' state. In their military applications, S and T are instrumental in producing ever more sophisticated ways of killing, maiming and incapacitating the so-called 'enemies of the nation'. These means of destruction are not just developed and used in conflicts between nation states, but also in suppressing wars of liberation, and in controlling insurgent civilian populations. In Northern Ireland, for example, the British Army and police have in recent years introduced a variety of new techniques—CS gas, rubber bullets, sophisticated spying devices, and tortures such as sensory deprivation, designed to maim mentally while leaving no physical scars (see BSSRS, 1974; and Ackroyd et al., 1977). In addition, partly in order to facilitate the existing operations of the state repressive apparatus, and partly as insurance for future emergencies and as an investment in a 'strong state', techniques for the surveillance and monitoring of behaviour have been developed. Making use of recent developments in computer technology (and in turn developing them even more), the British police has recently established large, centralised data-banks which hold information on millions of people—on immigrant groups, trades unionists and political militants in addition to convicted criminals.[9] This is backed up by a sophisticated network which gathers the information to feed into the system, and involves various state agencies in Britain—notably MI5 and the Special Branch. Applied social research is busy, too, trying to place at the disposal of the political police a whole host of statistical techniques, often borrowed from the armed services but developed and improved upon in the course of civilian use. OR techniques, for example, are used to regulate and plan activities and operations (see Rosenhead and Thunhurst, this volume); techniques of quantitative social research have been developed and used to study and simulate civilian strife and insurgency so as to forecast and develop the best strategies to deal with them (e.g. see Horowitz, 1967. For a British example, see Noton et. al., 1974); and opinion-polling has been used to obtain information on such issues as levels of acceptable force in dealing with civilian strife or in planning strategy in publicly unpopular wars like that in Vietnam (where the USA turned to attitude surveys of the 'friendly' population and content analyses of interrogations of Vietcong prisoners). Again, these coercive uses of S and T—whether arbitrary or systematic—are no 'misuse'. They represent a body of scientific concepts, knowledge, techniques and practices, and technologies, in advanced capitalist society. They are the *products* of huge state investments in this area of S and T, and the horrors associated with them are nothing less than *necessary* by-products.

A less obvious, but also significant, role played by S and T in Western capitalist society is in the creation and reproduction of cultural meanings. As several chapters in this book have already shown, the contribution of statistics to maintaining the dominance of ruling class ideology is particularly important—in, for example, reinforcing elements of common sense which are both derived from and support the status quo (see, in particular, Irvine and Miles; Krige; Marsh; and Young, this volume). But scientific knowledge as a whole is presented as being free from political and ideological factors, as dealing with the realm of facts rather than that of values, and therefore as being free from the influence of particular narrow sets of interests. The sciences often seem inherently difficult and esoteric—especially when, as in statistics, mathematics is involved. Many people, mystified by science, defer to the allegedly disinterested opinions of scientific experts. Science thus simultaneously takes on the character of the most rational and reliable guide to decision-making—even in the social arena—and as something whose definition and practice should be left to experts. This deference reinforces the power of those in whose interests S and T have been developed and used—the class that owns and controls the means of producing S and T. Encouraging deference certainly pays dividends, as is indicated by the increasing application of the techniques of natural science (or at least their paraphernalia and terminology) to the analysis of social issues, in an attempt to render decision-making more 'rational'—and thus placing it above politics (Miles and Irvine section 4; and Rosenhead and Thunhurst, this volume; see also Blackburn, 1972; Mills, 1961; Pateman, 1972; and Shaw 1975, for related critiques of bourgeois social science).

Scientific authority is also invoked in support of the absence of decisive activity: for example, when science is used to provide arguments and evidence suggesting that inequalities of class, race and sex are essentially unalterable. The social division of labour between the sexes is explained in terms of innate biological differences in abilities and temperament between women and men (for example, see Eysenck, 1973; and Hutt, 1972. For a critique see Krige, this volume; Fairweather, 1976; and Griffiths and Saraga, 1979). Race and class divisions are similarly explained, respectively, in terms of the supposed innate intellectual superiority of whites over blacks, and of the ruling class over the working class—differences which are then used to justify the unequal distribution of reward and privilege in society (for a survey and critique of these ideas, see Kamin, 1977; and Rose, 1976).

Political challenge can be defused if these inequalities are seen to be founded upon fixed biological differences rather than as effects of the social structuring of peoples' education and opportunities, attitudes and aspirations. (See, especially, Science for the People, 1977). Statistically processed data are often used to provide the 'factual' evidence to back up such theories. Modern mathematical statistics was crucially shaped (as MacKenzie, this volume, demonstrates) by the attempt to provide rigorous quantitative formulations for the biological explanations of social inequalities.

This is not to say that the scientists and statisticians whose work is used in this way are all colluding in a gigantic capitalist plot to run (or ruin) society. But the body of more-or-less 'pure' scientists and academics that has developed along with the advance of capitalist industry did not develop as the spontaneous manifestation of an asocial, dispassionate thirst for knowledge. While individual scientists are sometimes motivated, in part at least, by the desire to produce knowledge for its own sake or because it might be useful for humanity, the choices which are available to them are limited in many respects. Scientists are part of a scientific community whose norms and sanctions influence their activities; they are constrained by pre-existing structures of scientific language, convention and practice; they cannot ignore the body of accepted scientific knowledge; moreover, the instruments and techniques available to them will delimit their endeavours. In addition, the concepts and practices of S and T are indirectly influenced by, and in turn influence, other social concepts and practices (see for example, Foucault, 1970; Sohn-Rethel, 1978).

This is to say nothing of such obvious factors as the constraints imposed by funding patterns—which, since they are largely controlled by industry and the state, reflect quite strongly the needs of capital rather than the needs of the mass of humanity.[10] Conflicts do arise, of course, between the professionalism of scientific researchers and these interests: for example, researchers often complain about the lack of investment in certain areas. But as we have seen, scientists are typically able to exercise little control over the nature and use of their product; social and economic factors structure their activities both directly and indirectly.

Analysing the ways S and T function for profit and for social control demonstrates the crucial importance of an assessment of S and T for understanding the powerlessness and deprivation in so many people's lives. And, as we have argued, statistics forms a particularly fine (precise) and tough (reliable) thread in the cloak of scientific neutrality behind which the basic structures of capitalist society operate. The power which statistics, as a means of creating, organising and assessing knowledge, brings to the capitalist production process is thus also invaluable in legitimating its class system.

Integral though statistics may be to the operation of capitalist society, its practices are not invulnerable to radical criticism nor totally resistant to change. Like other areas of S and T, statistics can to some extent be fashioned in opposition to the social and economic factors which shape the dominant sets of scientific practices. The concepts, techniques, instruments and practices of S and T are strongly *structured* but not completely *determined* by society; the social practices of scientists and engineers are not mechanical reflections of some more real all-powerful 'base'. There exists some room for the development and practice of a radical science—but to what degree and under what conditions is the vital issue. One of the conditions which can facilitate this practice is a critical understanding of the role of S and T, just as a failure to make a critical analysis can facilitate the dominant practices of S and T.

Armed with this understanding, radicals can both make interventions in the critique of capitalist society and begin to develop radical scientific practice. The development of a radical statistics, or for that matter any radical science, cannot wait for the fundamental social changes to take place that will provide structures for the development of an entirely new S and T—for the development of radical science practices may itself help effect, and can indeed form, a vital part of such changes. It is to these possibilities for developing a radical statistical practice, and the strategies needed to do so, that we now turn.

4. A radical statistics?

By stressing the political and economic roles of S and T in general, and statistics in particular, we can see how limited are the three common responses to their problems that were considered earlier. For a refusal to make use of quantitative data, or to counter statistical practices directly, is nothing less than disarming: a focus on developing 'alternative statistics' which does not confront the reasons for the dominant forms of statistical practice flourishing is unlikely to establish its own roots securely; and whilst a 'socially responsible statistics' might achieve some support, at best it could contain only the most overt of the continuing 'abuses' of statistics. Even the radical version of the 'use-abuse' approach is, as we have seen, severely limited insofar as it colludes with the view of S and T as neutral and latently beneficent—fighting for changes in the structures in which S and T are used, but not in the production of S and T themselves, can lead to extremely reactionary political positions and strategies.

It has only been through the development of an analysis of S and T as social products and practices that the radical science movement has really begun to formulate effective theory and practice. This experience can usefully be taken into account in looking at the possibilities and problems associated with the development of a radical statistics.

Radical scientists and engineers work in a great many political organisations, but in Britain two organisations in particular have shared S and T as their focal point: BSSRS and the Radical Science Journal Collective (RSJ).[11] While these groups have different working styles and objectives, they both seek to develop a better understanding of the production and use of S and T and to integrate this into political struggle. They have found it necessary to develop·their work on several different fronts. First, they have had to deepen the critique of S and T beyond the traditional stress on their uses, to embrace a wide range of concepts, techniques and practices. Second, they have had to work out ways of disseminating this knowledge, of making it available in particular to scientists and engineers, so as to help raise political consciousness and, in turn, to increase the effectiveness of political struggle. Third, they have had to formulate strategies for the use of S and T in furthering political struggle. Critical re-use of existing concepts and techniques, within existing practices, is sometimes extremely effective—as is shown by BSSRS' work in the field of occupational health and safety. Here, BSSRS has published a number of useful handbooks (on noise, oil and vibration as health hazards to workers) and produces *Hazards Bulletin*, a magazine which contains information on, and news of, workers' struggles over health and safety issues;[12] these publications draw together and reinterpret existing knowledge on health and safety. Fourth, on the basis of a critique of the limitations of 'radical re-use', they have sought to explore the prospects for developing a radical S and T—and to identify and facilitate the parts which scientific and technical workers may play here. (See Rose and Rose, 1976; and Werskey, 1975 and 1978, for differing assessments of the potential strategies for the radical science movement). They have thus had to take up, albeit at a fairly speculative level, the possible nature and role of S and T in a future socialist society as well as considering the forms and uses of S and T in non-Western societies.[13]

Radical approaches to statistics can learn from these objectives and strategies. Informed by, and working towards, a more incisive critique of the role of statistics in capitalist society, it should be possible to relate and further develop the interventions that may be made in the field of social statistics, and to assess the results that might be obtained by adopting different strategies in radical practice. We can make only a preliminary analysis of some possible interventions that may be considered. We examine, in turn, the critique of statistics, the possibilities for and limitations on its radical re-use, and, lastly, the potential for developing new forms of statistical data, techniques and practices.

a. *The critique of statistics*

It is to the critique of statistics that much of this book has necessarily been addressed—for without knowledge of the dimensions and roots of the problems with statistics, action to remedy the situation becomes pointless, and, by and large, doomed to failure. Attacking the notion that statistics is a surety for truth and objectivity in scientific knowledge of society, and a guarantor of rationality and freedom from bias in planning and policy-making, is an important political task. This position of privilege is rarely questioned: close inspection is normally forestalled by people who treat quantitative analysis as something for experts only, and/or as something which can safely be left to experts given the 'neutrality of numbers' and the impartiality of statisticians. Yet, as previous chapters have shown, such close inspection reveals that arguments for the objectivity and rationality of statistics cloak a social framework of control and exploitation, which itself conditions the development and application of statistical data and methods. Thus, for example, the section of this book which assessed official statistics demonstrated that these data are preconceptualised and produced according to both the ideology of the ruling class and its interests, articulated and co-ordinated through the state.

Other chapters showed that much can be learned about mathematical statistics through a study of their social origins (e.g. MacKenzie's account of the development of the correlation coefficient by eugenicists) and the conditions promoting their later development and expanded use (e.g. Atkins' and Jarret's account of the treatment of significance tests as guides to the discovery of 'social laws' and McLean's discussion of the use of computers as aids to 'objective' analysis). Other chapters attacked the increasing dependence upon technical experts using the latest statistical decision-making tools to provide supposedly scientific, rational solutions to social problems—thus limiting active, political discourse (e.g. Marsh on opinion-polling; Miles and Irvine on forecasting; and Rosenhead and Thunhurst on operations research).

But while it is certainly necessary to challenge the scientism and elitism inherent in the use of social statistics in these ways, it is important to extend this critique beyond exposing *abstractly* the foundations of statistics in the institutions and ideologies which articulate the dominant social interests. It must be linked to concrete political struggle. If not, the result may be merely to foster the 'anti-statistics' position which sees the problems with contemporary society as rooted not in capitalist exploitation and oppression, but in the scientific organisation of 'technological' society. Radicals might unwisely try to tap peoples' disaffection from the state bureaucracy, for example, by attacking quantification and statistics per se—there is some evidence that the degree of cooperation with national censuses and social research is declining. But such opposition can at most be limited, and may be countered by moves such as the annual 'Statistics Day' in Japan—with statistics competitions for schoolchildren and other paraphernalia —which have been instituted to overcome criticisms of the scale and burden of official statistical enquiries.

To change the forms and uses of statistics on any large scale means developing and presenting this critique in the light of the goal of achieving fundamental transformation in society. Political and social change on this scale can be produced only by the actions of a working class identifying its prime enemy as capitalism itself, rather than any particular group of 'bad' capitalists or politicians (both of whom 'misuse' statistics when it suits their ends), or any particular failure to rationalise the exploitative relations of capitalism (the 'rationality' of which is often demonstrated in statistical terms). Thus, the critique of statistics must be linked to the needs of the working class movement and the struggle of groups oppressed by imperialism, racism and sexism—moving beyond a critique of the inadequacy or oppressive use of statistics to demonstrating the class interests and assumptions underlying the claims made for objectivity of data and rationality of decisions.

Theoretical critique is not an end in itself: it should aim to facilitate radical social action. This involves showing not only that such claims for statistics further ruling class interests, but, crucially, that they oppose the long-term interests of other classes, and of women and other oppressed groups. A fair day's work for a fair day's pay may already be a powerful ideology supporting the systematic exploitation of workers (e.g. see Hyman and Brough, 1975; Mepham, 1972); when the level of fair pay is worked out using the latest statistical techniques and computers, the traditional fight between capitalist and workers over division of resources between profits and wages can be further depoliticised and seemingly reduced to a *technical* problem. Expert statisticians from management confront expert negotiators from union headquarters, and the rank-and-file workers see their interests reduced to one factor in a mathematical equation. Providing a theoretical critique of the scientism and elitism of such statistical practices is one thing; but their demystification—for example, by revealing the crucial assumptions of the methods to the people who are their targets—is also a practical activity.

b. Radical re-use

While there are many problems associated with existing statistical practices, there are nevertheless many occasions when radicals may need to use them—both in developing critical theory and analysis, and in political struggle. In this book, for example, Ridgers has demonstrated the utility of secondary analysis and the re-presentation of extant data for purposes of providing counter-information. The radical re-use of existing statistical data and techniques may be seen as taking three main forms: undermining the validity of dominant ideologies; developing radical theory; and applying these theories in political struggle.

In the first of these strategies, existing data are used to call into question theories or viewpoints that are used to promote conservative, or to oppose radical, theory and practice. Counteracting racist ideology is an important case in point. It is often argued by fascists in Britain that immigration is the prime cause of the current housing and unemployment crises; a component of much right-wing Tory propaganda, such arguments are fairly widely accepted. Yet statistics can be used to undermine these arguments on their own technical and ideological terms—by citing official data to show that unemployment is not correlated with immigration over time, and so on. The Anti-Nazi League has made particularly effective use of statistics in this way in their leaflets and other presentations. Obviously, a committed fascist is not going to be swayed by any amount of statistics, but many people who unreflectively accept racist politics on the basis of common-sense arguments about overcrowding, strains on welfare services, etc., may be receptive to such 'technical' criticism. This will apply to other political issues, too, especially where apathy and reactionary attitudes largely reflect the ability of the ideological apparatus of the mass media and the state to maintain a vacuum of ignorance and half-truth. It is particularly relevant as a strategy in circumstances where opportunities to develop and present a coherent alternative approach to the issue involved are restricted, and especially where the re-use of data may actually stimulate the interest and resources necessary to do so.

Thus, this strategy may be crucial in winning support in an immediate struggle, and may be an important first step to a more thoroughgoing ideological critique. But this is all: as a strategy it is limited. It criticises only the surface forms of bourgeois ideology because it almost always operates within the terms set by that ideology. While exposing the self-contradictions of an ideology can be useful, there are frequently enough variants of the ideology and opportunities for willing hands to elaborate them, that little is achieved beyond the receding memory of a debating point won. Where deeply entrenched views are confronted, the debate may easily become a mere technical argument which can be extended endlessly. The many strands of conservatism and liberalism are like the heads of the hydra: when chopped off, more are produced to return to the attack. So this use of data in 'technical' criticism, important though it is, is not enough. It certainly cannot substitute for an attack on the hydra's body, on the social roots of these ideologies.

This brings us to the second way in which statistics may be re-used—in the furtherance of radical analysis. Radicals should be able, in debates such as those discussed above on racism, to provide alternative theoretical explanations of the causes of unemployment and lack of housing, and to relate these to the statistics—drawing on data such as the numbers of unemployed construction workers and unoccupied houses. Like conservatives and liberals, they need data to support, and indeed to improve, their theories and arguments, which are otherwise liable to remain unconvincing, inadequate, or trapped at the level of pure abstraction.

The contribution statistics can make to this process of radical analysis is not restricted to the study of particular aspects of social conditions at a specific time—like the current levels of unemployment and homelessness; it can also be useful in making broad historical analyses that encompass and situate these more specific factors. In such an 'epochal' analysis of basic relations, or of social dynamics, over a long period of time—the prime example being Marx's attempt to understand the dynamics of the capitalist system set out in *Capital* and elsewhere—data have important uses in developing and illustrating theory. Thus the nature of crises within capitalism might be illustrated by historical data on levels of production, consumption and capital formation; or the long-term tendency of the rate of profit to fall might be related to statistics on the rate of return on industrial investment (see, for example, Mandel, 1975, who attempts to provide an account of 'late capitalism'; and Hussain, 1977, for a critique of his use of statistics).

A 'conjunctural' analysis, in contrast, involves attempting to understand a specific situation at a particular time and place. Many of Lenin's writings focusing on Russia in the late nineteenth and early twentieth centuries would fall into this category. Such analyses are also useful in providing a radical analysis of contemporary Britain; one might utilise them in seeking to understand the specific causes of unemployment in a town in Northern England. Whilst this could, without much difficulty, be seen in terms of the general recession currently hitting all the world's major capitalist economies, the specific nature of the situation would also need to be taken into account. For example, what is the industrial structure of the region, how does it relate to the national (and international) economy, why have particular local firms been hit (are they less competitive than other firms), etc.? Here, official statistics at both national and local levels would be used to illustrate and advance the analysis, which would of course also draw upon the more general forms of explanation referred to previously.[14]

The third way in which statistics can be re-used is in the application of radical theory. Effective political struggle cannot be carried out on an intuitive basis and the theoretical perspectives that must inform such action often call for relevant statistical data. Adequate information is important at the level of even the most basic of trade-union activities—negotiating wages and conditions. For 'if today's trade unionist is to bargain effectively, he [sic] must match management's statistical sources and techniques' (cover-blurb to Hedderwick, 1975). Both workers and their representatives need information on what firms could pay (i.e. what profits they are making), what similar firms are paying, what they are likely to be offered, how much their wages have been cut by inflation, and so on. Much of this information can be gained relatively easily from official statistics (see Hyman and Price, this volume) and is often available from trade-union research departments. For example, the Labour Research Department's monthly publication *Labour*

Research includes a digest of relevant statistics accompanied by critical commentary. Its tabulations of recent official statistics are particularly useful in this context.

The radical re-use of data is likewise often vital in developing and promoting effective single-issue political campaigns. Take, for example, the campaign to defend abortion rights in Britain co-ordinated by the National Abortion Campaign (NAC). Here, information was needed to support and promote the arguments put forward in public debate. By demonstrating the great need for abortions, using official statistics on operations performed, and by showing that in the absence of state provision, many women would risk a dangerous illegal operation, NAC was able to make more effective interventions. Again, this is not to say that all one has to do is to present the 'facts' and the argument is won—clearly the committed anti-abortionist, for example, is unlikely to be moved by NAC's arguments, however well presented—but well-researched and well-presented data was undoubtedly instrumental in winning support for NAC.

Some radicals may argue that the re-use of statistics is a strategy limited to reformist organisations like trade unions and issue-oriented groups which typically take their task as improving the lot of people *within* capitalism. Revolutionary political groups, however, also need relevant and reliable information to back up their political action dedicated to replacing capitalism with socialism.[15] As we have argued before, their success here ultimately depends upon helping broad sections of those people most able to accomplish this task (i.e. the working class, supported by and supporting oppressed groups of all kinds) to realise that the root source of their alienation and oppression lies in the capitalist social system, and that their interests would be best expressed and served in a socialist society. To do this, radicals need to understand how capitalism works and how it might be changed, and to be able to demonstrate that socialism is not a utopian dream but something that can be created through a sustainable political programme. (Indeed, if the human race is to survive in an age of high technology, the creation of a world socialist order is an urgent priority).

To understand what capital and the state are doing at any particular time, a wide range of social and economic data is needed. Radicals need this information to link and to extend often fragmented struggles across social boundaries such as those separating ethnic groups, factories, industries, regions and countries. If unemployment is rising, for example, they need to know why, where and by how much, in order to plan effective campaigns like that conducted by the 'Right to Work Campaign' (Ridgers, this volume, discusses sources of data for re-use in this way). An understanding of international movements of capital, too, is vital for assessing current and prospective changes in imperialism and imperialist policy.

Overcoming the problems with radical re-use is sometimes quite difficult. One of the most important and common tendencies is for many oppositional groups (whether issue-oriented or revolutionary) to reproduce a technical division of labour like that found in capitalist organisations—with consequent inclinations to lapse into elitism and reformism. Elitism follows from the all too frequent emergence of a rigid hierarchical structure; those at the top of this structure may become isolated from the broad mass of members and supporters—often seeking to dictate their actions through claims to 'correct' ideas and expert skills acquired as a result of their 'practice', their advantages of information. This tendency is especially marked in issue-oriented groups where—faced with immediate practicalities—the experts who provide information and advice may become little more than the unpaid (or even paid) versions of the expert advocates who appear in planning inquiries and on parliamentary committees. Furthermore, this situation too easily fosters the illusion that such inquiries are actually an occasion for democratic political debate, rather than for the exercise of class power. Diverting resources into such areas, while sometimes worthwhile, may thus come to be seen as a viable alternative to mass activities to challenge this power, similar to the way wage-bargaining has developed a system of co-opted experts at the reins of the trade-union movement, who sometimes actively combat rank-and-file militancy.

Certain steps can, however, be taken to prevent statistical expertise reinforcing the reformism and elitism that dog the radical left today. The technical skills that are needed in making useful analyses can, for example, be communicated—a 'statistics for the people' approach need not require presenting statistics as objective fact or neutral technique. Similarly, there should be more critical discussion of the often ridiculously naïve way in which radical groups use statistics in their arguments. So often in the socialist press either a 'conspiratorial plot' is 'exposed' in the presentation of data ('these damning facts are published in a drab official booklet to prevent workers from finding them out') or an alternative set of 'real' figures is proposed to 'prove' a particular argument. The critique of statistics must be accompanied by a minimum level of technical competence if radical arguments are to be more than tub-thumping—but this competence need not be confined to a few experts. Lessons might be drawn from the attempts of Claimants' Unions to spread the skills of analysing welfare legislation and the quantitative assessment of individuals' needs as a way of countering the reformist tendencies of issue-oriented groups.

However important the radical re-use strategy may be to radicals, and however hard we may try to overcome its limitations, there are problems that cannot, in general, be surmounted. In the case of statistical data, the first problem is the extremely selective nature of what is available. This, as analyses in this book have shown, is for two main reasons. First, official statistics reflect information needs, activities and priorities which often do not coincide with those of radical critics of society. Second, certain information is kept secret—supposedly in the 'national interest'. Thus, on the one hand there is little information available on poverty because its measurement and alleviation is not an important state activity; and, on the other, information on the size and budget of the political police is kept secret for reasons of 'national security'. Compounding this problem of the lack of data is the question of re-using data generated in one conceptual framework with another set of conceptual categories (see Hindess, 1973; and Triesman, 1974). The categories used to produce official statistics are frequently inappropriate to radical analysis—for example (as Hird and Irvine point out, this volume) the notion of wealth used in British official statistics does not lend itself to a direct analysis of the ownership of capital. Because of this, only relatively imprecise estimates can be made. Additionally, there often arise technical problems of disaggregating data—it is often difficult, for example, to obtain reliable spatial breakdowns of official data. Sometimes radicals can, through their involvement in 'academic' social research, extend the range and improve the conceptualisation of existing data; but often we simply have to make do with what is available.

The problems involved in re-using statistical techniques are of a rather different order. While descriptive or summary statistics are often of use to radicals, the contribution of sophisticated mathematical statistics and vast computer systems is more difficult to imagine at present; and complicated systems are particularly prone to the problems associated with expertise and the mystique of science (see above, and McLean, this volume). Apart from the restrictive and undialectical assumptions about causality underlying much of mathematical statistics, access to the use of such techniques is typically limited by their cost and the technical skills needed to produce or interpret analyses by such means.[16]

Sometimes, then, we may find that it is impossible to achieve satisfactory analyses and useful results on the basis of existing statistics. In order to provide statistical backing to a particular struggle, and to overcome the dominant social relations and practices of contemporary statistics, we may have to consider the use and production of new data and techniques.

c. 'Socialist' statistics

To accept the notions of 'radical' and 'socialist' statistics is to accept that contemporary statistical practices are to a great extent determined by capitalist social relations and interests, and that these are embedded as much in the concepts and techniques of statistics, as in its products and practices.

To make any significant changes in the nature and scope of official data will require a thorough transformation of the state; and the inspiration (not to mention the opportunity) to transform statistical techniques and practices will similarly require the commitment of a large number of people to a radical transformation of society. So, to develop a socialist statistics without changing the society of which the practice of statistics is a part is possible only to a very limited degree. Nevertheless, to accept that statistical practices are more than mere mechanical reflections of economic and ideological factors, is to accept that we can begin to fashion them into a tool to facilitate social transformation. We might more correctly term this *radical* statistics—that is, the critique, re-use and the limited transformation of statistical concepts, techniques, data and practices. We can, for example, go beyond the mere re-use of existing data and produce *new* statistics tailored explicitly to the needs of socialist politics.

In the case of poverty, for example, the Child Poverty Action Group has produced data on areas where official statistics are either sparse or non-existent. Similarly the Low Pay Unit has produced data on the earnings of workers below the tax threshold, who are not included in official statistics since they earn too little to pay income tax.[17] While the surveys used here are necessarily limited in scale, through lack of resources, they can be useful information sources for radicals as well as for more immediate reformist strategies. Radical journalists and academic social scientists have also often produced important new data through their work—on the composition of ruling groups, for example (e.g. studies such as those reported in Crewe, 1974; Stanworth and Giddens, 1974; and Urry and Wakeford, 1973).

While the potential for producing new data is significant, this strategy is limited by the enormous resources typically required for large-scale data production. One way of partially overcoming this problem involves striving to achieve certain changes in the data produced by and/or available from existing institutions. At one extreme, data may be 'leaked' by sympathetic civil servants or politicians; at the other, mass movements and pressure groups can press for the disclosure of information—parliamentary questions may be useful here. A longer term strategy is, of course, to struggle for more freedom of information and the removal of laws and sanctions limiting its availability (such as the Official Secrets Act in Britain).

We should also investigate the possibility of developing new statistical techniques for producing and procuring data. We referred earlier to the problems radicals encounter in adopting a traditional division of labour and reproducing the hierarchical expert-client relations when using the techniques of mathematical statistics. While the problems of overcoming such barriers are enormous—given the repugnance most people feel towards even simple statistical techniques—certain steps can be taken by stimulating changes in the wider research process (of which the use of statistics is one part). Attempts have been made to reconstruct investigative techniques such as the social survey, Carr-Hill (1973), for example, attempted to transcend the limitations of the conventional survey—which typically counterposes expert enquirers against isolated, passive informants. He developed in a totally 'biased' fashion a survey on education with the assistance of people in his town, employing it as much as a political consciousness-raising tool as a source of data for academic analysis. His interview situation was intended to stimulate respondents into questioning the relevance of their schooling to their current living patterns and appears to have achieved some success, as indicated both by the quality of the answers received, and the recruitment of some of the respondents into a discussion group on educational issues. Other groups have also modified survey techniques for radical purposes, similarly turning the survey into a much more interactive instrument, in which information flows between the survey designer and the respondent, and among groups of respondents. The prime example of this is probably the 'Workers' Inquiry into the Motor Industry' (IWC, 1977), in which background material on developments in the motor industry as a whole was provided to local union branches, along with questions designed to elicit their own experiences.[18]

While radical approaches to statistical technique may have much potential, they are typically limited in applicability. For reasons outlined elsewhere in this book, people rarely consider it worth their while, or even within their abilities, to attempt to comprehend statistical analysis, and it may take considerable effort to persuade them otherwise. Even 'radicalised' social surveys, which seek to reduce the distinction between researcher and subject, require that people see how their involvement in the study can be of benefit to them. Time and effort are required for such activities, and people are often rightly suspicious of the interests that lie behind social research. Even when they are convinced that statistical approaches are of practical use to a particular task, there is still the danger, without a political critique of statistics, that people may believe that 'highly technical' and 'value-free' devices are best left for sympathetic experts to worry about.

A different set of needs for statistics under socialism, and even in a heightened struggle for socialism, will generate different demands on statistical data and techniques, and different conditions for the development of new approaches. In the short term the development and application of new data and techniques can in principle contribute to the greater democratisation of skills and to undermining the mystique of statistics, thus helping raise levels of consciousness about the adequacy of radical statistical analyses. But these are likely to be significant tools of radical practice only to the extent that they can be based upon the growth of radical currents in society—those, for example, exerting pressure on the state to disclose information, or stimulating workers to consider the possibility of participating in the planning of their firm's future. Once again, we see that the practice of scientists is dependent to a large extent, in terms of both orientation and chances of success, upon wider social developments. Thus, any strategy of 'radical' statistics can hope for lasting achievements (other, perhaps, than the incorporation of alternative approaches into the dominant statistical tradition) only by being developed as part of a wider socialist practice; that is *within* and *for* an overall programme of social revolution. In the process, it will have been transformed into an explicitly 'socialist' statistics.

5. Beyond 'radical statistics'

Perhaps, a 'socialist statistics' can be developed only in a society undergoing urgent, active transformation to socialism. But perhaps, too, the notion of 'statistics' as a discrete, specialised realm of human knowledge would be increasingly problematic in a transitional society in which, with moves towards the abolition of class relations, the old division of labour would be under attack. Such speculation suggests not only that radical statisticians need to work *with* the socialist movement but that they need to work *within* it. In the same way as the battle against contemporary statistical practices should not remain the political preserve of statisticians only, so should statisticians involve themselves in other wider political struggles.

Of course, statisticians, like other scientists, have specific opportunities available to them to exercise pressures for change other than those more generally available—through both their expert knowledge and their place in the overall social and technical division of labour. There is certainly a role for scientists' and engineers' organisations in dealing directly and sensitively with S and T-related issues. These include trade unions as well as organisations such as BSSRS and the Radical Statistics Group.

While in issue-oriented groups it has often been difficult to overcome the fragmentation of political struggles, active work in trade unions provide radical scientists and engineers with the opportunity to press for the recognition and acceptance of their communality of interests with other workers. But they need to recognise the problems here—unions often treat their role as bargaining for marginal improvements and thus end up disavowing 'political action'. It is easy to become restricted to such reformist strategies, to do no more than press for higher wages for 'elite' scientific workers, as is largely the case in ASTMS. This is not to belittle the achievements of such organisations: it is often possible to win significant political gains without challenging directly the underlying framework of capitalist society, and these may themselves facilitate the development of socialist politics at a later time. However, the flexibility of capitalist society should not be over-estimated: concessions are far more readily granted in some periods than at others (the current 'cuts' and increased political repression being typical of the withdrawal of 'welfare rights' and 'civil liberties' in recessionary conditions); and these concessions are typically granted on terms which render them subservient to capital (e.g. as hard-won educational provisions are applied to training a docile workforce, so the right to form unions becomes a right to belong to a bureaucratised and largely incorporated organisation). Nevertheless, unions of scientific and technical workers are important both as agents of and sites for this struggle—to defend existing rights and to fight for their extension.

But many scientists and engineers have realised that it is not enough to attempt to reform S and T from within. They have learned from the limited achievements of the SR approach to S and T and its incorporation into the establishment worldview. More than this is necessary if the ever-more manifest scale and scope of science-backed threats to human existence is to be confronted; if the increasing role of scientism is to be challenged; and if the declining conditions and opportunities in scientific and technical work are to be halted. And often they have learned from the struggles of other workers, and from the themes and political perspectives forged and sharpened in these struggles. The student and counter-culture movements have played a role, if a brief one, in raising public debate about these issues. But what is most clear is that the connections with socialist currents must be strengthened and deepened—otherwise a 'radical science' or 'radical statistics' is likely to remain a dream or at best an arcane scholastic discipline. This might have been understandable when radicalisation seemed an impossible or far distant prospect in the early 1960s, but it is irresponsible to settle for dreams or scholasticism in the turbulence of the late 1970s.

In general, statisticians have hardly been at the forefront of the radical science movement—for reasons connected both with the nature of their subject and the sorts of employment they typically obtain. But with the increasing importance of statistics in capitalist society, statistical issues are likely to become more overtly political at the same time as the statisticians' work becomes less rewarding. In such circumstances, radical perspectives on statistics may well be developed and taken up more seriously. A significant contribution to the practical critique and transformation of statistics (and science) might then be made in an organised way by statisticians linking the specific issues with which they deal to the wider political and economic processes which determine, and are in turn shaped by, them. The prospects for a significant and lasting contribution to the creation of a new society being made in this way depend upon the integration of the work of radical statisticians—and social scientists using statistics—with that of the radical political organisations of the working class and oppressed groups. 'Radical statistics' is at best a way-station in this task: radical statisticians may succeed in quantifying the world in new ways, but what really counts is whether they succeed in helping to change it.

Notes

1. Our focus here will be on critical approaches and strategies as they have been developed within Western societies. Political struggles over S and T in 'Third World' countries, and the analyses that have been developed in these contexts, are important issues, but would inevitably demand lengthy separate treatment.

2. For a bibliography of anti-science, arcadian and other responses to industrial society, see Boyle and Harper (1976).

3. Information about Green Bans in Britain may be obtained from the Green Ban Action Committee, 77 School Road, Hall Green, Birmingham B28 8JG; developments on this front are also reported in the *Newsletter* of the Socialist Environment and Resources Association, who can be contacted c/o Tidys Cottage, School Lane, West Kingsdown, Kent; they are sometimes also covered in AT magazines like *Undercurrents*.

4. This aspect of AT is closely related to the development of interest in 'appropriate technology', a term used by development researchers in particular, to refer to the need to create products and production technologies for the 'Third World' which may be markedly different from those used in the West. The importation of techniques and products by multinational corporations has often merely exacerbated patterns of underdevelopment created in the ex-colonies. Instead of their capital-intensive technology, it is held that technologies consonant with the resource, skill and labour endowments of underdeveloped countries are needed—that is, lower-level and labour-intensive technologies (often called 'intermediate' technologies) are more appropriate to the 'Third World'. However, it is likely that, without socialism in these countries, 'appropriate technologies' will only be developed along the lines most profitable for local capital—and thus do little about local employment needs and environmental problems. Likewise, products which can meet the needs of the poverty-stricken masses are required, rather than luxuries which serve no purpose other than the consolidation of inequalities. Carr (n.d.) provides an annotated bibliography of the literature on appropriate technology; see also Boyle and Harper (1976), Dickson (1974), Disney (1976), Jéquier (1976).

5. Obtainable from: Radical Statistics Group, c/o BSSRS, 9 Poland Street, London W1V 3DG.

6. See, for example, the RSG Health Group's useful publications, *Whose Priorities?* (1976) and *In Defence of the NHS* (1977).

7. When these problems threaten the stability of capitalist society, the state is called in to mop up the worst of them. See Miles and Irvine, section 3 of this volume.

8. More comprehensive accounts of the development of industrial technology are provided by Braverman, 1974; Dickson, 1974; Gorz, 1976b; Marglin, 1974/75; (see also the articles by the Brighton Labour Process Group, 1977; Coombs, 1978); and, of course, by Marx, 1954, on which all these studies draw.

9. See Kitson, 1971, for the arguments of a 'counter-insurgency expert' as to why these developments are necessary to protect the liberal, democratic state; and, for informed critical discussion as to why there is more behind their development and use than a concern with protecting 'democratic' freedom, see Bunyan, 1976; Ackroyd et al., 1977; and various issues of *State Research Bulletin*—which is obtainable from State Research, 9 Poland Street, London W1V 3DG.

10. For more detailed treatments see Basalla, 1968; Bernal, 1939; Bukharin et al., 1971; Mendelsohn et al., 1977.

11. Both groups can be contacted at 9 Poland Street, London W1V 3DG. BSSRS publishes the quarterly journal *Science for People*, and the RSJ collective *Radical Science Journal*. In addition to these two *issue-oriented* groups, a number of the left political organisations are beginning to take S and T up as important problems. The

Socialist Workers Party has a science group, as does the Communist Party (which publishes the journal *Science Bulletin*). The International Marxist Group runs a monthly column on S and T by BSSRS in its weekly newspaper *Socialist Challenge*.
12. Available from BSSRS Work Hazards Group, 9 Poland Street, London W1V 3DG.
13. BSSRS, for example, held a conference in 1975 on the theme 'Is there a socialist science?'. Both they and RSJ have also held several series of seminars on the broad area of science and socialism. The American group 'Science for the People' sent a delegation in 1973 to study Chinese S and T. Their interesting report is presented in the book *China: Science Walks on Two Legs* (1974).
14. The Union for Radical Political Economics (URPE, 1978) has produced a reader which analyses in considerable detail the consequences of the current crisis for different groups of workers, for various economic sectors, for community issues and political organisations, in the United States. In Britain, the Community Development Project (CDP, 1977a, b, c) has produced valuable studies of industrial decline, housing problems and the land and property markets; various working groups associated with the Conference of Socialist Economists have been working on related issues (e.g. CSE, 1976). Economists and geographers have so far been at the forefront of these attempts to use quantitative data in radical analysis and action, and their journals—*Antipode, Capital and Class, Review of Radical Political Economics*—present material that is often of interest to all critical social scientists.
15. We here refer to those political groups attempting to create a socialist society which argue that this will entail fundamental changes being made in the political, social and economic structure of contemporary society, and that this will be achieved only through revolutionary struggle extending well beyond parliamentary processes, and will require establishing a new level of democracy as well as changing the ownership of the means of production. Examples of the voluminous recent literature here include Blackburn (1977), Miliband (1977). The classic Marxist positions were most notably developed by Marx, Engels, Lenin, Trotsky, Luxemburg and Gramsci.
16. There are exceptions. One is the use of the computerised analysis to demonstrate the viability of an egalitarian world society by Herrera et al. (1976), which might, even so, be seen as simply using the mystique of the computer against more reactionary analyses which had traded on this mystique. Another is Kidron's (1974) study of unproductive labour in the US—where the complexity of the material made computer analysis invaluable. As well as the contributions to this book, other discussions of the epistemological basis of mathematical techniques in social science may be found in Willer and Willer (1973), Zubaida (1974) and Sayer (in press).
17. Somewhere between the critique of statistics and the production of new statistics lies the sort of approach that has been used by Cowley Leyland workers in developing their own cost of living index, or in the French trade union price index (Plant, 1978). Here, workers' representatives have themselves monitored the effects of inflation, in order to strengthen arguments behind wage claims.
18. The Lucas Aerospace Workers' campaign, mentioned earlier, also involved extensive structured interaction between workers and coordinating shop stewards. In the Vickers Workers' campaign, similar production of 'data' from the shopfloor has been linked to more conventional analyses of the state of the industry (see Elliot et al., 1977; Beynon and Wainwright, 1979).

Bibliography

Ackroyd, C., Margolis, K., Rosenhead, J., and Shallice, T., 1977, *The Technology of Political Control*, Harmondsworth, Penguin.

Bannister, D., and Fransella, F., 1971, *Inquiring Man*, Harmondsworth, Penguin.

Bannister, D., and Mair, J. M. M., 1968, *The Evaluation of Personal Constructs*, London, Academic Press.

Basalla, G. (ed.), 1968, *The Rise of Modern Science: Internal or External Factors?*, Lexington, Mass., D.C. Heath.

Bernal, J. D., 1939, *The Social Function of Science*, London, Routledge.

Beynon, H., and Wainwright, H., 1979, *The Workers' Report on Vickers*, London, Pluto Press.

Blackburn, R. (ed.), 1972, *Ideology in Social Science*, London, Fontana.

Blackburn, R. (ed.), 1977, *Revolution and Class Struggle*, London, Fontana.

Bookchin, M., 1970, *Post-Scarcity Anarchism*, New York, Ramparts.

Boyle, G., and Harper, P., 1976, *Radical Technology*, London, Wildwood House.

Braverman, H., 1974, *Labour and Monopoly Capital*, New York, Monthly Review Press.

Brighton Labour Process Group, 1977, 'The capitalist labour process', *Capital and Class*, no. 1, pp. 3-26.

BSSRS, 1974, *The New Technology of Repression: Lessons from Northern Ireland*, London, BSSRS.

Bukharin, N. I., et. al., 1971, *Science at the Crossroads*, London, Frank Cass.

Bunyan, T., 1976, *The History and Practice of the Political Police in Britain*, London, Julian Friedmann.

Carr, M., n.d., *Economically Appropriate Technologies for Developing Countries*, London, Intermediate Technology Publications.

Carr-Hill, R. A., 1973, *Population and Educational Services: Preliminary Report on a Social Survey*, Geneva, UNESCO (reference PDEP/Ref. 7).

CDP, 1977a, *Profits Against Houses*, London, CDP.

CDP, 1977b, *The Costs of Industrial Change*, London, CDP.

CDP, 1977c, *Gilding the Ghetto*, London, CDP.

Cooley, M., 1976, 'Contradictions of science and technology in the productive process', in Rose and Rose (eds.), 1976a, below.

Coombs, R., 1978, 'Labour and monopoly capital', *New Left Review*, no. 107, pp. 75-96.

CSE, 1976, *Housing and Class in Britain*, London, CSE (55 Mount Pleasant, London, WC1.)

Crewe, I. (ed.), 1974, *The First British Political Sociology Yearbook*, London, Croom Helm.

Dickson, D., 1974, *Alternative Technology and the Politics of Technical Change*, London, Fontana.

Disney, R., 1976, 'Irrelevant technology' and 'Who does what in I.T.', *Undercurrents*, no. 18, pp. 8-9, 11.

The Ecologist (eds.), 1970, *A Blueprint for Survival*, Harmondsworth, Penguin.

Elliott, D., 1977, *The Lucas Aerospace Workers' Campaign*, Young Fabian pamphlet no. 46, London, Fabian Society.

Elliott, D., and Elliott, R., 1976, *The Control of Technology*, London, Wykeham.

Elliott, D., et. al., 1977, *Alternative Work for Military Industries*, London, Richardson Institute for Conflict and Peace Research.

Eysenck, H. J., 1973, *The Inequality of Man*, London, Temple Smith.

Fairweather, H., 1976, 'Sex differences in cognition', *Cognition*, vol. 4, pp. 231-280.

Foucault, M., 1970, *The Order of Things*, London, Tavistock.

Gorz, A., 1976a, 'On the class character of science and scientists', in Rose and Rose (eds.), 1976a, below.

Gorz, A., 1976b, *The Division of Labour*, Hassocks, Sussex, Harvester Press.

Griffiths, D., and Saraga, E., 1979, 'Sex differences in cognitive abilities: a sterile field of enquiry', in G. Boden, M. Fuller and O. Hartnett (eds.), *Sex Role Stereotyping*, London, Tavistock.

Hall, S., and Jefferson, T. (eds.), 1976, *Resistance Through Rituals*, London, Hutchinson.

Harper, P., 1973, 'Transfiguration among the windmills', *Undercurrents*, no. 5, pp. 3-4.

Hedderwick, K., 1975, *Statistics for Bargainers*, London, Arrow.

Herrera, A. (ed.), 1976, *Catastrophe or New Society?*, Canada, IDRC.

Hindess, B., 1973, *The Use of Official Statistics in Sociology*, London, Macmillan.

Horowitz, I., 1967, *The Rise and Fall of Project Camelot*, Cambridge, Mass., MIT Press.

Huff, D., 1973, *How to Lie with Statistics*, Harmondsworth, Penguin.

Hussain, A., 1977, 'Crises and tendencies of capitalism', *Economy and Society*, vol. 6, pp. 436-460.

Hutt, C., 1972, *Males and Females*, Harmondsworth, Penguin.

Hyman, R., and Brough, I., 1975, *Social Values and Industrial Relations*, Oxford, Basil Blackwell.

Institute for Workers' Control (IWC), 1977, 'Document: A workers' enquiry into the motor industry', *Capital and Class*, no. 2, pp. 102-118.

Jéquier, N., 1976, *Appropriate Technology: Problems and Promises*, Paris, OECD.

Jungk, R., 1964, *Brighter than a Thousand Suns*, Harmondsworth, Penguin.

Kamin, L. J., 1977, *The Science and Politics of IQ*, Harmondsworth, Penguin.

Kidron, M., 1974, 'Waste: US, 1970', in M. Kidron, *Capitalism and Theory*, London, Pluto Press.

Kitson, F., 1971, *Low Intensity Operations*, London, Faber.

Leary, T., 1970, *The Politics of Ecstasy*, London, Paladin.

Lewontin, R., and Levins, R., 1976, 'The problem of Lysenkoism', in Rose and Rose (eds.), 1976b, below.

Mandel, E., 1975, *Late Capitalism*, London, New Left Books.

Marcuse, H., 1964, *One-Dimensional Man*, Boston, Beacon Press.

Marcuse, H., 1969, *Eros and Civilisation*, London, Sphere.

Marglin, S., 1974/5, 'What do bosses do? The origins and functions of hierarchy in capitalist production', *Review of Radical Political Economics*, no. 6, pp. 60-110 and no. 7, pp. 30-55.

Marx, K., *Capital*, 3 vols.; English translations: London, Lawrence & Wishart 1954; 1957; 1960; also Harmondsworth, Penguin/New Left Books 1976, vol. 1.

Mendelsohn, E., Weingart, P., and Whitley, R. (eds.), 1977, *The Social Production of Scientific Knowledge*, Dodrecht, Holland, D. Reidel.

Mepham, J., 1972, 'The theory of ideology in *Capital*', *Radical Philosophy*, no. 2, pp. 12-19.

Miliband, R., 1977, *Marxism and Politics*, London, Oxford University Press.

Mills, C. W., 1961, *The Sociological Imagination*, Harmondsworth, Penguin.

Musgrove, F., 1974, *Ecstasy and Holiness*, London, Methuen.

Nobile, P., 1971, *The Con III Controversy*, New York, Pocket Books.

Noton, M., et al., 1974, 'The systems analysis of conflict', *Futures*, vol. 6, pp. 114-132.

Nuttall, J., 1970, *Bomb Culture*, London, Paladin.

Pateman, T. (ed.), 1972, *Counter-Course*, Harmondsworth, Penguin.

Pearson, E. S., 1973, 'Some historical reflections on the introduction of statistical methods in industry', The Statistician, vol. 22, pp. 165-179.

Phillips, L., 1973, *Bayesian Statistics for Social Scientists*, London, Nelson.

Plant, J. J., 1978, 'A workers' cost of living index', *Radical Statistics Newsletter*, no. 12, p. 3.

Poirier, D. J., 1977, 'Econometric methodology in radical economics', *American Economic Review*, vol. 67, pp. 393–399.

Radical Statistics Health Group, 1976, *Whose Priorities?*, London, RSG.

Radical Statistics Health Group, 1977, *In Defence of the NHS*, London, RSG.

Reich, C. A., 1970, *The Greening of America*, New York, Random House.

Reichmann, W. J., 1970, *Use and Abuse of Statistics*, Harmondsworth, Penguin.

Rose, H., and Rose, S. (eds.), 1976, (a) *The Political Economy of Science*, and (b) *The Radicalisation of Science*, London, Macmillan (jointly titled *Ideology of/ in the natural sciences*).

Rose, S., 1976, 'Scientific racism and ideology: the IQ racket from Galton to Jensen', in Rose and Rose (eds.), 1976a, above.

Rosenhead, J., 1972, 'The BSSRS: three years on', *New Scientist*, 20 April 1972, pp. 134–136.

Roszak, T., 1968, *The Making of a Counter-Culture*, London, Faber.

Roszak, T., 1973, *Where the Wasteland Ends*, New York, Anchor.

Sayer, R., A., in press, 'Some comments on mathematical modelling in regional science and political economy', *Antipode*.

Science for the People, 1974, *China: Science Walks on Two Legs*, New York, Avon.

Science for the People, 1977, *Biology as a Social Weapon*, Minneapolis, Burgess.

Shaw, M., 1975, *Marxism and Social Science*, London, Pluto Press.

Silber, I., 1970, *The Cultural Revolution: A Marxist Analysis*, New York, Times Change.

Sohn-Rethel, A., 1978, *Intellectual and Manual Labour*, London, Macmillan.

Stanworth, P., and Giddens, A. (eds.), 1974, *Elites and Power in British Society*, London, Cambridge University Press.

Triesman, D., 1974, 'The radical use of official data', in N. Armistead (ed.), *Reconstructing Social Psychology*, Harmondsworth, Penguin.

URPE, 1978, *US Capitalism in Crisis*, New York, URPE (Room 901, 41 Union Square West, New York).

Urry, J., and Wakeford, J. (eds.), 1973, *Power in Britain*, London, Heinemann.

Werskey, G., 1975, 'Making socialists of scientists: whose side is history on?', *Radical Science Journal* no. 2/3, pp. 13–50.

Werskey, G., 1978, *The Visible College*, London, Allen Lane.

Willer, D., and Willer, J., 1973, *Systematic Empiricism: Critique of a Pseudo-Science*, Englewood Cliffs, N.J., Prentice-Hall.

Young, B., 1978, 'Getting started on Lysenkoism', *Radical Science Journal*, no. 6/7, pp. 81–105.

Ziman, J., 'The Council for Science and Society', *Bulletin of the Atomic Scientists*, vol. 31, no. 2, pp. 18–20.

Zubaida, S., 1974, 'What is scientific sociology?', *Economy and Society*, vol. 4.

Index

SOCIAL SCIENCE LIBRARY

Manor Road Building
Manor Road
Oxford OX1 3UQ
Tel: (2)71093 (enquiries and renewals)
http://www.ssl.ox.ac.uk

This is a NORMAL LOAN item.

We will email you a reminder before this item is due.

Please see http://www.ssl.ox.ac.uk/lending.html
for details on:

- loan policies, these are also displayed on the notice boards and in our library guide.

- how to check when your books are due back.

- how to renew your books, including information on the maximum number of renewals. Items may be renewed if not reserved by another reader. Items must be renewed before the library closes on the due date.

- level of fines; fines are charged on overdue books.

Please note that this item may be recalled during Term.